The Black Baptist Experience in Canada

 **McMaster Divinity College Press**
McMaster General Studies Series, Volume 19
Canadian Baptist Historical Society Series 5

Other Volumes in the Canadian Baptist Historical Society Series:

- Heath, Gordon L., and Paul Wilson, eds. *Baptists and Public Life in Canada*. CBHS Series 1 (2012).

- Heath, Gordon L., and Michael A. G. Haykin, eds. *Baptists and War*. CBHS Series 2 (2014).

- Bowler, Sharon M., ed. *Canadian Baptist Women*. CBHS Series 3 (2016).

- Murray, Taylor, and Paul R. Wilson, eds. *Canadian Baptist Fundamentalism, 1878–1978*. CBHS Series 4 (2022).

The Black Baptist Experience in Canada

Edited by
GORDON L. HEATH *and*
DUDLEY A. BROWN

Foreword by George Elliott Clarke

◆PICKWICK *Publications* • Eugene, Oregon

THE BLACK BAPTIST EXPERIENCE IN CANADA

McMaster General Studies Series, Volume 19
McMaster Divinity College Press

Canadian Baptist Historical Society Series 5

Copyright © 2025 Wipf and Stock Publishers. All rights reserved. Except for brief quotations in critical publications or reviews, no part of this book may be reproduced in any manner without prior written permission from the publisher. Write: Permissions, Wipf and Stock Publishers, 199 W. 8th Ave., Suite 3, Eugene, OR 97401.

Pickwick Publications
An Imprint of Wipf and Stock Publishers
199 W. 8th Ave., Suite 3
Eugene, OR 97401

McMaster Divinity College Press
1280 Main Street West
Hamilton, ON, Canada L8S 4K1

www.wipfandstock.com

PAPERBACK ISBN: 978-1-6667-0433-4
HARDCOVER ISBN: 978-1-6667-0434-1
EBOOK ISBN: 978-1-6667-0435-8

Cataloguing-in-Publication data:

Names: Heath, Gordon L., editor. | Brown, Dudley, A., editor.

Title: The Black Baptist Experience in Canada / edited by Gordon L. Heath and Dudley A. Brown.

Description: Eugene, OR: Pickwick Publications, 2025 | Series: McMaster General Studies Series | Includes bibliographical references and index.

Identifiers: ISBN 978-1-6667-0433-4 (paperback) | ISBN 978-1-6667-0434-1 (hardcover) | ISBN 978-1-6667-0435-8 (ebook)

Subjects: LCSH: Church history | Canada—History | Canada—Church history

Classification: BR570 B53 2025 (print) | BR570 (ebook)

Contents

List of Contributors | vii

Foreword | ix

Chapter 1: Introduction | *Gordon L. Heath and Dudley A. Brown* | 1

Chapter 2: An Introduction to the Black Church in Canada, 1663–1867 | *Denise Gillard* | 21

Chapter 3: The Underground Railroad and its Intersection with the Black Baptist Church in Upper Canada | *Dudley A. Brown* | 49

Chapter 4: "Begging" Baptists: Central Canadian Regular Baptists and the British Fund-Raising Activism of Reverend William Troy and Reverend William M. Mitchell, 1850–1865 | *Paul R. Wilson* | 75

Chapter 5: Black Baptist Print Culture in Nineteenth-Century Canada West | *Nina Reid-Maroney* | 100

Chapter 6: Sojourners and Citizens: National Identity in the African Baptist Association, 1855–1914 | *Gordon L. Heath* | 118

Chapter 7: New Horizons Baptist Church: A History of Spirituality, Perseverance, and Social Justice | *Jennifer Riley* | 143

Chapter 8: Architecture and Experience at the First Baptist Church, Amherstburg | *Jennifer Cousineau* | 162

Chapter 9: Washington Christian (1776–1850) and the Founding of The First Coloured Calvinistic Baptist Church of Toronto | *Glenn Tomlinson* | 187

Chapter 10: "It Has Pleased God to Make Us of a Different Colour": Black Baptists in Victoria, British Columbia, 1876–1881 | *Taylor Murray* | 208

Chapter 11: AUBA Mothering and Maternal Activism in Education | *Késa Munroe-Anderson* | 222

Chapter 12: Revisiting the Reverend Jennie Johnson (1868–1967): Women's Ordination and Intellectual History in the Black Baptist Tradition | *Nina Reid-Maroney* | 245

Chapter 13: Revisiting Accounts of the Life of Mr. David George | *Hannah Lane* | 266

APPENDIX: Photos of First Baptist Church, Amherstburg (Chapter 8: Architecture and Experience at the First Baptist Church, Amherstburg | *Jennifer Cousineau*) | 297

Index of Persons | 303

Index of Subjects | 310

List of Contributors

Dudley A. Brown, McMaster Divinity College, Hamilton, ON.

Jennifer Cousineau, Historical Services Eastern Canada and the FHBRO, Gatineau, QC

Denise Gillard, WordWalk Global Ministries, Scarborough, ON.

Gordon L. Heath, McMaster Divinity College, Hamilton, ON.

Hannah Lane, Mount Allison University, Sackville, NB.

Késa Munroe-Anderson, Acadia University, Wolfville, NS.

Taylor Murray, Tyndale University, Toronto, ON.

Nina Reid-Maroney, Huron University College, London, ON.

Jennifer Riley, Hantsport Baptist Church, Hantsport, NS.

Glenn Tomlinson, Sovereign Grace Community Church, Sarnia, ON.

Paul R. Wilson, Canadian Baptist Historical Society, Cambridge, ON.

Foreword: On Witnessing African (Canadian) Baptism

George Elliott Clarke

THOSE NAMES—GOD, JESUS, ADAM, Eve, Moses, Peter, Solomon, Sheba, Mary, Mary Magdalen, etc.—compose a constellation, a cosmology, orbital touchstones that blaze in the mind and heart of the descendants of once-enslaved people, who heard the Bible preached by slaveholders' bishops, but who took to heart lessons opposite to what the slave masters' propagandists intended. What Caucasian clergy recited, chapter and verse, is not what the enslaved Negro peasantry *received*. Oral strictures got aurally transformed into freedom testaments. How true that was for the composers of the spirituals, who dramatize a "King Jesus" who crosses the Jordan River like Caesar crossing the Rubicon, who assures us, "No man's a-gonna hinder me"! And what about their "Mary" who doesn't need to "weep and moan," now that Pharaoh's army got "drown*eded*"—yes—*drowned* real good and dead? So, as a Haligonian youth in "Sweet Home" Nova Scotia, auditing the pulpiteers of Cornwallis Street (now New Horizons) United Baptist Church, I heard The Decalogue intoned, but I *understood* encoded liberation: That Moses will lead the Children of Israel out of bondage, that Jesus will whip the moneychangers out the temple, that God will chop down tyrants' heads right along with their crowns, and then table a feast for His servants— right before the mugs of their "enemies" (Psalm 23). Yet, I didn't only audit the tales of saints and dissidents, martyrs and apocalyptic prophets; I could also absorb a reference to William Hall of Hantsport, Nova Scotia, who singlehandedly put down the Lucknow Rebellion, thus keeping India "British" for practically another 100 years (which is a *sin*, really); or

I could attend to the voice of Portia White (my late great aunt), wowing the music critics of the *New York Times* in the 1940s. Once a teen, when I leafed African-American novelist James Baldwin's spirituals-titled books or plattered Mahalia Jackson thrilling audiences at Duke Ellington's "Sacred Concerts," or heard broadcast Martin Luther King, Jr.'s ornate orations, I felt at one with a border-crossing, Underground-Railway-crisscrossing continuum of Black Baptist song, sermonizing, and prayer. Next, when I *finally* did the right thing on Easter Sunday, April 9, 2023, and publicly confessed my sins and my welcoming of the eternal Lord Jesus Christ as my Redeemer and Saviour, before the congregation of the New Horizons United Baptist Church, and then let Pastor Britton and Deacon Thane, dip my entire body under the sloshing water of the baptismal pool, I knew that I was saved—salvaged—washed clean of my various offenses, but I also knew—in that wholly holy moment—that I was also answering the long-ago urging of the long-gone "Apostle to the African Race," namely, Rev. Richard Preston, D.Div. Who?

Aye: I regret that none of the scholars drawn to this volume attend to the singular figure that was Richard Preston (ca. 1799-1861)—an escaped once-slave in Virginia. Landed in Halifax in 1816, Preston found his mother—miraculously—on his very first day in colonial Canada; then, peeved by the segregationist practices of White-dominated Baptist churches, Preston slooped to London, argued for the support of Baptists and abolitionists, got ordained as a minister by Great Britain's Baptists, and sailed back to Nova Scotia with £800 to construct the "Mother Church" of the African Baptist Association. Over the next 20 years of constant church founding all about mainland Nova Scotia, Preston assembled a couple dozen congregations, consisting of mainly illiterate and impoverished Black Scotians *de souche*, and then had the temerity to proclaim the existence of the African Baptist Association of Nova Scotia, at Granville Mountain, in 1853. How righteously significant it is that my baptism into the Body of Christ—and specifically into the African United Baptist Association—occurred 170 years after Preston birthed its hand-clapping, tambourine-jangling insurgency! Clearly, the Afrocentric Christian Awakening that Preston inaugurated has never diminished; thus, the Christ-borne call that he issued in 1853 resonated all the way down to even myself in 2023. And it thunders still.

I praise God that I belong to a church that was literally raised up before the scowls of the oppressor and the howls of their hypocritical "thou-shalt-nots." To be an African Baptist—a Black Baptist—is to savour association with our Divine Lord whose sand-and-dust-soiled feet needed washing; who wept so fluently for our bedevilled humanity; who wandered, bare-headed as Lear, under starlight, moonlight, sunlight, and rain; who let the desperate touch Him and be healed; and who let the despotic abuse and assassinate Him so that He could quickly ascend and prepare the celestial chambers for His devout Believers. . . . To be a Black Nova Scotian Baptist is to situate the Jordan River as a tributary of Halifax Harbour, i.e., Bedford Basin as it shored up Africville; it is to relocate Bethlehem to Weymouth Falls—where an escaped, once-enslaved woman, wails at childbirth; it is to espy stained-glass windows featuring a sable-skinned Jesus; it is to marvel at Saint Thomas United Baptist Church in North Preston and to appreciate that the aforementioned beatified is none other than Rev. James Thomas, a Welshman elected to sainthood by his devoted Black congregants; it is to be astonished by the AUBA's poets, musicians, singers; but also by the percussion of the pianos, the chiming of the tambourines, the brass-instrument-hollering of the organs; and by the absence of hymnals and the overwhelming presence of Living Memory, whereby songs are descanted by heart, the Holy Bible chanted by heart.

I now salute Brothers Dudley Brown and Gordon Heath! Behold the good work they've wrought! Their assembly of scholars, parsing the *Black Baptist Experience in Canada*, let no trouble pass undiagnosed, let no mercy pass uncited, let no miracle pass unwitnessed. Across Canada, a spirited Muse has travelled, summoning the theologians and the elders, the witnesses and the delivered, to chronicle those called to uplift the downtrodden as well those called to upbraid the downpressor.

There is much illumination—much enlightenment—herein. Open these pages and be dazzled! But to those wary of disrupting their benighted condition, we answer thus: Only to the blind ensconced in darkness is Light ever a threat.

George Elliott Clarke
E.J. Pratt Professor of Canadian Literature
University of Toronto

1

Introduction

GORDON L. HEATH AND DUDLEY A. BROWN

THE EXPERIENCES OF PEOPLE of African descent in Canada are inextricably linked to the Christian church. The foundations of the African Canadian Christian church lay in the experiences of American Blacks who sought to secure their freedom (although not escape racism) during different eras and iterations of the North American enslavement saga. In the western provinces of Canada, African American immigration was the result of Blacks fleeing repressive segregation (Jim Crow); in Upper Canada, it was the result of the Fugitive Slave Acts in the years after the American Revolution and leading to the American Civil War; and in the Maritimes, it was an unexpected product of the American Revolution and the War of 1812.[1] For many (particularly in Upper Canada), the harsh struggle of making a new life under a northern sun, coupled with the Emancipation Proclamation, precipitated a return home at the cessation of the American Civil War. An economic downturn in late-nineteenth century Canada only made matters worse and made leaving seem more appealing than staying. Those that stayed continued to build the Black church/community and add to the history of those of African descent in Canada. More recently, those from the Caribbean and sub-Saharan Africa have bolstered the numbers and vitality of the Black Canadian communities and churches.

---

1. For a helpful examination of the impact of the war on Black migration to what would become Canada, see Taylor, *Internal Enemy*.

As will be noted in the chapters that follow, the church played a critical role in the life of Black Baptists in Canada.[2] The origins of the Black Baptist church in Canada go as far back as the *Invisible Institution* of the American South where a significant number of Blacks who were enslaved were barred from worshipping in a church that was controlled by slaveholders and their White supremacist theology.[3] Those enslaved developed an affinity for the Baptist denomination that, marked by a Holy Spirit-led worship style, reflected African culture; it was also a faith that believed in the worth of each individual regardless of colour, and, moreover, Baptist congregational independence provided autonomy to a people desiring freedom, equality, and participation in the affairs of their own church.[4] This volume is envisioned as a history of the Black Baptist experience in all regions of Canada; it seeks to provide a much-needed summary and analysis of the subject matter. Chapters examine events/themes/organizations (e.g., Underground Railroad, civil rights, women, missionary work, or African Associations), key churches (e.g., First Baptist Toronto, New Horizons Halifax), and important persons (e.g., William Troy, William M. Mitchell, or Jennie Johnson).

RELEVANT SCHOLARSHIP

Delineating the experiences of Black Baptists in Canada, in all its complexities, is a formidable task. With that acknowledgment, this book seeks to document through stories of significant individuals and institutions the origins, travails, events, spirit, community, and culture of Black Baptists in Canada. It provides an examination of a portion of the African Canadian kaleidoscope while contributing to, and engaging with, an expanding field of African Canadian history within the larger Canadian historical narrative.[5] And our hope is that this work spurs further pathbreaking research.

The exploration of the Black Baptist experience acknowledges the rich tradition of Black Canadian literature relatively unknown before the seminal works of George Elliott Clarke, works such as *Odysseys Home:*

---

2. Just as it did in other Black communities in other denominations (see, e.g., Este, "Black Church").

3. Gerbner, *Christian Slavery*.

4. Of course, not all enslaved even sought out conversion. And some of those that did converted for more temporal reasons such as literacy or other social gains (see Fountain, *Slavery*; Smith, "Slavery and Theology"; see also "Authentic Account").

5. For instance, see Siemerling, *Black Atlantic*.

Mapping African-Canadian Literature and the outstanding and only anthology of Black historical writings in Atlantic Canada, namely, *Fire on the Water: An Anthology of Black Nova Scotian Writing* (2 vols.).[6] Moreover, Clarke's *Directions Home* documents the African Canadian church's steady chronicling of the Black religious experience in Canada, principally that of the Baptists, as an instrument to address past negative critiques (such as that articulated by Robin Winks in *The Blacks in Canada: A History*)[7]; and, in the words of Barrington Walker, embrace the "counterculture of modernity" and "principles of intersectionality" as they relate to "colonization, Blackness, fugitivity, and the modern Canadian racial state."[8] These foundational works have contributed to a Black Canadian historiography now fairly well developed on the Maritime experience, as in key works such as Harvey Amani Whitfield's *Blacks on the Border: The Black Refugees in British North America, 1815–1860* and *Black Slaves in the Maritimes*. In the former volume, Whitfield re-examines the problems of nationality, location, identity, and historical memory by highlighting the transnational experience of the lives of the Black Refugees through an analysis of how former American slaves from disparate backgrounds became a distinct group before the American Civil War. In *Black Slaves in the Maritimes*, Whitfield identifies not only the enslaved, but their enslavers, thus broadening the general understanding of the most neglected aspect of pre-Confederation Canadian history. James W. St. G. Walker's *The Black Loyalists: The Search for a Promised Land in Nova Scotia and Sierra Leone* examines the historical and cultural background of the Black Loyalists and notes their vital contribution to the Nova Scotian community that rejected the 1792 exodus to Sierra Leone. Lastly, in "Slaves and their Owners in Ile Royale, 1713–1760,"[9] Kenneth Donovan takes the reader into the specific lives of the slaves in Ile Royale, New France; enslaved alongside the African captives are the First Peoples (*Panis*). Elucidating the Catholic church's view of slavery, Donovan speaks to slavery's extent and reasons for its expansion in New France.

The Black experience in Upper Canada is detailed in Donald Simpson's *Under the North Star: Black Communities in Upper Canada Before Confederation*, Daniel Hill's *The Freedom-Seekers*, and Walker's *Racial*

---

6. See, Clarke, *Fire on the Water*; *Odysseys Home*.
7. See, Clarke, *Directions Home*, 46–57.
8. Walker, "Critical Histories of Blackness in Canada," 40, 46.
9. Whitfield, *Blacks on the Border*; Walker, *The Black Loyalists*; Donovan, "Slaves."

Discrimination in Canada: The Black Experience. Simpson's study examines how fugitive slaves and free Blacks used the Underground Railroad to create Black settlements and communities in Upper Canada. Hill incorporates the contributions made by the Black Loyalists in Nova Scotia, and Walker chronicles their treatment by the greater White community during their efforts to become full citizens. First-hand accounts of the Black immigrants to Upper Canada are found in William Still's *The Underground Railroad Records*, Benjamin Drew's *A North-Side View of Slavery*, Mary Ann Shadd Cary's *Provincial Freeman*, Henry Bibb's *Voice of the Fugitive*, and more recently, Hilary Bates Neary's *A Black American Missionary in Canada*.[10] These works highlight the ingenuity, strength, and determination of Black immigrants in their historical, cultural, and social context while also chronicling their day-to-day existence in Upper Canada.

To the West, must-reads on the Black experience include R. Bruce Shepard's "Diplomatic Racism: Canadian Government and Black Migration from Oklahoma," plus several articles in Michele Johnson and Funke Aladejebi's edited volume *Unsettling the Great White North*, including Paul Watkins's "Hogan's Alley Remixed," Adam Arenson's "A Forgotten Generation: African Canadian History Between Fugitive Slave and World War I," and Gillian Creese's "Creating Spaces of Belonging: Building A New African Community In Vancouver." All these accounts assess the Black community's struggles, religious institutions, leadership, and document the deep-seated intolerance and disparagement by the larger White community—but mention Black Baptists only in passing.[11]

A lacuna in the Black Canadian historical narrative is obvious when one considers the Black communities' relationship with the church. Winks's influential work, *The Blacks in Canada*, while offering a comprehensive and detailed assessment of African Canadian history, contained significant shortcomings that included his offensively pejorative depiction of the Black Canadian church, community, and leadership. Taking a different tack on the role of the churches in the Black community is Walker.[12] He argues that the churches played a vital role in the survival

---

10. Simpson, *Under the North Star*; Hill, *Freedom-Seekers*; Walker, *Racial Discrimination*; Still, *Underground Railroad Records*; Drew, *North-Side View of Slavery*; *Provincial Freeman*; Bates Neary, *Black American Missionary*.

11. Shepard, "Diplomatic Racism"; Watkins, "Hogan's Alley Remixed"; Arenson, "Forgotten Generation"; Creese, "Creating Spaces."

12. Winks, *Blacks in Canada*; Walker, *Black Identity*.

and thriving of the Black community in the face of intense economic, social, and racial pressures.¹³ Other helpful commentators are Black Nova Scotian-born theologian, Peter J. Paris, whose relevant work is *The Moral, Political and Religious Significance of the Black Church in Nova Scotia*, and Dorothy S. Shreve's *The AfriCanadian Church: A Stabilizer*.

Fortunately, researchers in previous generations began documenting the Black Baptist experience, such as Peter E. MacKerrow's *A Brief History of the Coloured Baptists of Nova Scotia and their First Organization as Churches A. D. 1832*, and its successor, namely, A. Pearlean Oliver's *A Brief History of the Coloured Baptists of Nova Scotia 1782–1953*. Both editions delineate the Black Loyalists and Black Refugee migrations to Nova Scotia and their resolve to establish the Black Baptist church.¹⁴

More recently (but over a generation ago!), works such as Grant Gordon's *From Slavery to Freedom: The Life of David George* and Savanah E. Williams's "The Role of the African United Baptist Association in the Development of Indigenous Afro-Canadians in Nova Scotia, 1782 to 1978" and Clarke's even more recent and aforementioned "The Church Narrative," began to document and analyze the Black Baptist experience; particularly their efforts to build a distinctive Black Baptist church and identity in Nova Scotia. But more must be done.¹⁵ Denominational histories such as the older Harry Renfree's *Heritage and Horizon* or the more recent Gordon L. Heath, Taylor Murray, and Dallas Friesen's edited volume *Baptists in Canada* are comprehensive treatments of Baptists in Canada but only briefly cover the topic of Black Baptists.¹⁶

However, recently there has been a renaissance of sorts on research into the Black Baptists of Nova Scotia. Jennifer Riley's "The Contribution of the African United Baptist Association to Public Education, 1854–1940" is an example of a renewed interest in the African United Baptist

---

13. For a helpful (though a bit dated) summary of commentary on both sides of this concern over the impact of the churches on the Black community, see Este, "Black Church," 4–7.

14. It should be noted that Frank Boyd's Black Nationalist re-interpretation of the church in his edition of McKerrow's history has an "Afrocentrist" view of competing "integrationist" (McKerrow) versus Black Nationalist tensions in the African Baptist community.

15. See also a brief chapter on David George in Rawlyk, *Canada Fire*.

16. Mackerrow, *Brief History*; Oliver, *A Brief History*; Gordon, *From Slavery to Freedom*; Williams, "Role"; Renfree, *Heritage and Horizon*; Heath, Friesen, and Murray, *Baptists in Canada*. See also Canadian Baptist studies by scholars George Rawlyk and Barry Moody as well as Shreve, *AfriCanadian Church*.

Association (AUBA).[17] The most positive and prolific development has been the attention paid to Rev. William White, a popular Black Nova Scotia Baptist pastor, reformer, and military chaplain. There has been a current surge of research into his life, culminating in a recent doctoral dissertation.[18] This attention has been a boon for our knowledge of White and is a model to follow for research into other Baptist leaders. Of course, the study of prominent personages must not replace research into the views from the pews—research studies of the lives of the nameless and relatively powerless working classes that invigorated the Black Baptist churches.

While not the primary focus of their works, Jerome Teelucksingh's *The Lost Gospel: Christianity and Blacks in North America*, Karolyn Smardz Frost and Veta Smith Tucker's edited volume, *A Fluid Frontier: Slavery, Resistance, and the Underground Railroad in the Detroit River Borderland*, and Linda Brown-Kubisch's *The Queen's Bush Settlement: Black Pioneers 1839–1865* all provide a helpful summary of Black Baptists in Upper Canada. And Wendy Porter's chapter "A Quartet and an Anonymous Choir: The Remarkable Lives and Ministries of Four Black Baptist Women in Late Nineteenth-Century Ontario" in *Canadian Baptist Women* provides a glimpse into the life of a cadre of women musicians. These works are the harbingers of a robust view of the Black Baptist adherents in Ontario.[19]

Attention to western Canada is the most problematic because the region is often treated as devoid of Blacks. David Este and Jenna Bailey's scholarship in "Shiloh Baptist Church: The Pillar of Strength in Edmonton's African American Community" in Johnson and Aladejebi's edited volume, *Unsettling the Great White North*, along with Crawford Kilian's *Go Do Some Great Thing: The Black Pioneers of British Columbia* chronicles the Black Baptists from a western provincial perspective.[20] But there is much more to be done for the story of Black Baptist history as it moved from east to west (and south to north, and north to south).

The aforementioned works notwithstanding, little else has been published on this subject, and no book or edited volume currently exists

---

17. Riley, "Contribution."

18. Brown, "William Andrew White Jr."; see also Heath, "Wartime Diaries."

19. Teelucksingh, *Lost Gospel*; Smardz Frost and Tucker, eds., *Fluid Frontier*; Brown-Kubisch, *Queen's Bush Settlement*; Porter, "Quartet."

20. Este and Bailey, "Shiloh Baptist Church."

on the Black Baptist experience in Canada. This volume seeks to rectify this shortcoming, as well as inspire more work to follow.

SOURCES AND RESEARCH ISSUES

The stumbling block for historians of the Black Canadian experience has always been the limited availability of both secondary and primary sources; with the opening of local archives and research centres, the discovery of new sources, the microfilming and digitization of both documentary and published collections, and the availability of genealogical information, historians now have access to resources that make it possible to explore the history of Black Canadians in greater detail. Using primary source material as its foundation and the interaction of secondary sources as interpretive guides, this volume explores the similarities and differences among Black Baptists across the nation. That said, the arrival of Black Baptists in Canada varied from region to region. The eastern colonies (Maritimes) were the first to experience a large influx of Black immigrants followed by central Canada (then Upper Canada/Canada West) and finally the western provinces. That being the case, the creation of the Black Baptist church takes place between the early to the late nineteenth century in the central and eastern portions of what became Canada and in the early twentieth century in the western provinces. More recently, the Black Baptist church has been bolstered by the arrival of immigrants directly from the Caribbean and Sub-Saharan Africa, thus illustrating how each era possesses a new set of circumstances for the Black community. Readers will quickly note, however, that there are gaps in our coverage of regions in Canada. Sadly, despite our best and repeated efforts, we were unable to recruit more people to do research on the western Black Baptist experience. Our only consolations related to that disappointing point are that, first, perhaps this omission will spur others on to undertake the essential excavations, and, secondly, a recent chapter published elsewhere examines Shiloh Baptist Church in Edmonton, Alberta.[21] Even so, this book is primarily about the experience of Black Baptist communities in the nineteenth and early-twentieth century. Still, we can forecast that, while Black Baptist congregations continue to flourish, new scholars will arrive to document their persistent miracles of faith and works.

---

21. Este and Bailey, "Shiloh Baptist Church."

We recognize that terms used to describe a people are often contested, and some can be outright offensive. This book on the history of people of African descent inevitably brings up issues of vocabulary used in the discourse surrounding race. The terms "Africadians," "Afro-Canucks," "Africanadians," and "African Canadians" have been used in the Canadian context. However, we have opted to use "Black Canadians." Every term is problematic, this one included. However, in the Canadian context, "Black" is deployed by advocacy groups, governments, and scholars. We have also chosen to use the term "White," instead of "European," "British," or some other nationality from Europe. We have made this usage uniform throughout all chapters. There is no entirely satisfactory solution to this question of nomenclature (even the various authors of this book differ on the matter), and things are in flux even as we go to press. At the moment, however, this is where we editors stand.

A few comments are in order related to historical research, race, identity, and method. Much of the work of historians is that of discovering artifacts (literary and other) and then weaving together a narrative that tells the story of the past and its impress on current identity. In fact, while *storytelling* may not always garner the respect of some professional academics, it is widely known that individual and communal identity is shaped by the stories told at the bedside, in history books, around the table, and from the pulpit. That process of weaving together history and personal (and communal) identity formation is often called narrative identity.[22] For Black Baptists, that storytelling included not only the hope of the biblical narrative (sighting Black history in the narrative of Moses and the liberation of the enslaved) but also the trials and triumphs of the more modern Black experience. There is a reason why Black History Month focuses on getting people to read stories of Black history; there is a reason why we value having a Black Poet Laureate[23] put into prose the Black experience; there is a reason why universities add Black history to curricula; and there is a reason why children and families huddle around dinner tables listening to grandma and grandpa tell (once again) the stories of a by-gone era. No community can survive without a narrative

---

22. Setran, "Sowing the Story"; Fabius, "Toward an Integration." In regard to psychological aspects to healing and resistance through storytelling, see Chioneso et al., "Community Healing." For a theological discussion of memory, healing, and reconciliation, see Volf, *End of Memory*.

23. George Elliott Clarke, who so graciously agreed to write a Foreword to this book.

that makes sense of past and present and points to a positive telos for the future. And it is for that reason much of these pages are story telling—doing the work of discovery and identity as it relates to past, present, and future. In many ways, this volume is simply a continuation of the work of previous historians and narrators of the Black experience. That said, we wish to avoid the pitfalls of merely or simply storytelling and myth-making, eschewing a critical analysis, an approach that Barrington Walker cautions against.[24] In varying ways, the chapters in this book fuse storytelling with three aspects of modern feminist research—the "Three Rs" noted by Chad Bauman: Retrieval, Reconstruction, and Retheorization.[25] As Bauman notes, others have explained the same process as "rereading, reconceiving, and reconstructing" or "deconstruction, reconstruction, and construction of theory." In all cases, the telos of research is (1) to uncover and preserve voices (especially marginalized ones) from the past that have become lost or ignored, to (2) that of developing a new narrative that carefully tells a more nuanced and accurate story of the marginalized, to (3) producing a more conscientious historiography through utilizing methodologies and theoretical assumptions that further aid to foreground marginalized figures or movements. For us, we will ponder the Black Baptist congregations.

The Black Baptist experience intersects with racism, and that requires a critical reading of texts and events that takes into account seen and unseen realities of racism and implicit or explicit threats of violence. How does one take those grim realities into account? Much has been written on and theorized about how to think about race, and the older among us might remember James Cone and Black Liberation Theology whereas the younger may be more familiar with Critical Race Theory (CRT) (even though CRT has its roots back in the 1970s).[26] Authors in this volume have been left to chart a course on such methodological and theoretical matters in a way that best suits their research aims. Suffice it to say here that the way forward for historians dealing with race is much like that of travellers in the ancient myth of Scylla and Charybdis; there were dangers on both sides of the passage that must be avoided. On one side perches the danger of naivety; that is, to foolishly ignore the oppressive culture of racism just because a historical artifact does so. Black Baptists

---

24. Walker, "Critical Histories," 37–38.
25. Bauman, "Redeeming," 7. See also O'Connor, "Rereading."
26. Cone, *Black Theology*. For CRT, see Delgado and Stefancic, *Critical Race Theory*.

were aware of just how quickly things could go wrong and even turn violent if mistakes were made (or if even mistakes were *perceived* to have been made) or because Blacks did not placate White supremacist nostrums with adequate aplomb. Historians must read with eyes wide open, reading responsibly against the grain, trying their best to decipher code and identify implicit assumptions so often undetectable on first reading. In sum, while stories may be simply told, we need to recognize that history is never *simple*—especially when race and power are involved.

However, an equal danger is that of imposing modern assumptions on the past. We must be careful not to take away the agency of Black Baptists by assuming motives that are ours, not theirs. Good historians must understand cultures in their own setting— anything less is to do a sort of violence to a people once again. This is especially difficult when looking back on religious communities like Black Baptists, for modern historians not sympathetic to and/or conversant in the worldview of Christianity may pass over, impugn, or misinterpret the religious motivations of the Black Baptist Christians. In varying degrees and ways, the contributors have sought to avoid these two dangers, weaving together evidence into arguments and stories, while taking into account–as much as possible–complex issues of race, power, and oppression. Yet incontestable is the agency of the Black Baptists. Some accounts of Black history view the Black community as always being acted upon, as if its members were impotent or simply accepted their underclass position (thus reinforcing stereotypes of inferiority and passivity). While the Black community did endure racism and deliberate insult, the stories in these pages reveal Black Baptists were fully aware of their social location yet resisted its restrictions. They were the "central actors"[27] in their own story—and this volume's authors affirm that truth.

Of course, local, provincial, and national archives contain vital and often untapped material on the history of the Black experience. Yet for our purposes, the Canadian Baptist Archives at McMaster Divinity College, Hamilton, Ontario, and the Esther Clarke Wright Archives/Atlantic Baptist Archives at Acadia University, Wolfville, Nova Scotia, contain primary sources regarding organizations, persons, and local churches.[28]

27. Walker's expression (see Walker, "Critical Histories of Blackness," 33). For another helpful example of taking Black agency seriously, see Zaami, "Strategizing."

28. At present, there is no western Baptist archives, although there are western records in storage that hopefully someday will be catalogued and made available to researchers.

For instance, two key Black Baptist organizational structures were the African United Baptist Association of Nova Scotia (AUBANS, 1854) and the Amherstburg Association in Ontario (AAO, 1841). In both cases, the archives contain original and digital records of the minutes of those two bodies—a veritable treasure chest of information. Records are also held in trust for ongoing churches, whereas those of closed churches remain preserved in perpetuity. The weekly denominational papers also contain reports from churches, statements from pastors, and decisions of associations, all of which yield context and details on Black Baptist life. Diaries and personal papers of Black Baptist leaders can also be discovered on the shelves.

That said, there is a need for the ongoing gathering of materials for archival collections. Local churches often neglect or forget to save, organize, and submit primary source material to archives, risking the tragic loss of socio-historical memory. Research methods focused on sources outside of traditional archival labours have also shown themselves to be useful. For instance, family shoe boxes of letters in attics can be resourced for unknown treasures. Oral histories allow for those who are elderly to preserve memories of trials and triumphs for future generations.[29] Ethnographical work has also shown promise for examining Baptist communities.[30] As have architectural and social history.[31]

CHAPTERS

The chapters of this volume are individual efforts, but there are a number of interesting and intersecting themes throughout. For instance, East to West migration (and South to North—and vice versa) is a familiar factor in the birth of churches. Related to migration is the matter of cross-border relations, primarily across the US border but also *via* overseas voyages to Britain.[32] Those cross-border contacts were a reflection of family ties, but also an indication of how the Black evangelical community viewed Christian kinship (the notion of "brothers and sisters in Christ") as

---

29. For a good example of Black history relying on oral history, see Spencer, "Black Oneness."

30. For instance, see Duncan, *This Spot of Ground*.

31. For instance, see chapter below by Jennifer Cousineau on First Baptist, Amherstburg.

32. For instance, see Sawallisch, *Fugitive Borders*.

transcending political, national, and even racial identity.[33] The development of literature (letters, tracts, books, official denominational statements) is also a factor in the maturing of the Black Baptist community, both in Canada and abroad. Primary leaders—both male and female—play an outsized role in the churches and wider community. The essential function of the church—both local and associations—in the formation of community, but also dissemination of religious and political views, is widely recognized. And the motivation to live as Christians and carry out the work of the church by establishing structures, building churches, and spreading the gospel preferably with–or, if necessary, without–the assistance and/or partnership of the White Baptist churches is the heartbeat of the Black Baptists surveyed herein. And finally, the racism endured and the resiliency to withstand such insidious pressures is recorded herein, as is the recognition of Black agency for the promotion of justice and egalitarianism in the church and in society.

Of course, further research should focus on significant personages (including Rev. Dr. William White Jr., Rev. David George, Rev. Richard Preston, Pearleen Oliver, Peter E. McKerrow, Peter J. Paris, and Viola Desmond), vital institutions (like Black Baptist churches in segregated settlements like Dawn, Wilberforce, Africville, and the western provinces), and Black Baptist publications (including the theological texts of the clergy, the de facto intelligentsia), and comparative situations like the Canadian Black Baptist versus American Black Baptist history or the Black Canadian Methodist juxtaposed with the Black Canadian Baptist experience. We expect that this book will inspire others to take up those, and other, projects.

Denise Gillard opens this volume with an examination of how Black Christianity's evolution in an environment dominated by racism, classism, and sexism necessitated a separation from the mainstream (White) church to afford its members the full participation in all church (spiritual) and community (secular) affairs. Gillard's study describes the Black church's experience within the context of three major periods in Canadian history—the French regime, the British regime, and the settling of the Prairies. This chapter's identification of some common themes within the Black church tradition is enlightening as to the current situation of Black Christianity in Canada.

---

33. For an example of transnational evangelicalism among Baptists, see Heath, "'Great Association Above.'"

Dudley Brown's chapter on the Underground Railroad and its intersection with the Black Baptist church contends that there are two Underground Railroads, the legend and a factual history that has yet to be fully realized. The real Underground Railroad was neither subterranean nor an actual railroad; the metaphor described a coordinated system of civil disobedience directed and supported by thousands of people committed to what they saw as a just cause. The fugitive slaves who "rode" the railway brought with them the one institution that was truly theirs, the Black church.

In chapter four, Paul Wilson maintains that the mid-nineteenth century controversy over supporting resistance by soliciting aid for Black fugitive slaves was one of the most challenging issues that Black Regular Baptists in Canada West encountered in the period from 1850 to 1865. Two crucial participants in this charitable endeavour were Reverend William Troy of Amherstburg and Windsor, and Reverend William Mitchell of Toronto. On the one hand, their fund-raising advanced the causes of Black Regular Baptist resistance and self-reliance. On the other hand, the credibility of some Black British fund-raising and anti-slavery efforts were compromised and hampered by Mitchell's deceitful actions and fraudulent fund-raising behaviour in 1863 and 1864.

In chapter five, Nina Reid-Maroney looks at Black Baptists and the Theology of Print in Nineteenth Century Canada West. Her focus is on the same two individuals that Wilson canvasses: Reverend William Mitchell and Reverend William Troy. From narratives published by Baptist ministers such as Troy and Mitchell, through periodical literature, ephemera, and newspapers (including Henry and Mary Bibb's *Voice of the Fugitive*), the primary materials of Black Baptist print constitute one of the most important archives of Canada's abolitionist tradition. Situating this material within scholarship on African American print, the history of the book, and the work of the Black press in Canada, the chapter reconstructs networks of writers, editors, publishers, printers and readers, to understand their cultural insurgency in a transatlantic context. Offering a reading that attends to the material condition and publication histories of texts as well as their content, the chapter traces the role of textual production as testimony and witness, arguing that the antislavery world of Black Baptist communities was shaped by a theology of print.

Gordon L. Heath in chapter six is concerned with the formation and evolution of national identity among the Black Baptist community in Nova Scotia in the latter half of the nineteenth century and the dawn of the twentieth. What becomes quickly apparent when reading the AUBA minutes is that much of the national identity expressed in the Black Baptist community mirrored that of the rest of English-speaking Canada: Anglophile, loving Empress Victoria, and backing British imperialism. Yet there were critical differences, for the evolution of Black Baptist discourse was shaped as well by history, race, and religion, factors that together forged a unique perspective. And that originality was marked most notably by an urgent motivation for faithful citizenship, an orientation well known by those whose ethnicity or religion could not mirror the dominant cultural narrative.

In chapter seven, Jennifer Riley discusses the history of New Horizons Baptist Church (formerly Cornwallis St. Baptist) and its impact on the African Nova Scotian community. For the African Nova Scotian Baptists, the church is more than just a spiritual anchor; it is the place where its members seek to better their circumstances in all ways. From their arrival in Nova Scotia, the church has been the place where African Nova Scotians banded together to fight injustices. Like other African Nova Scotian churches, New Horizons has opposed systemic racism and the disenfranchising effects of colonialism. Fortunately, its heritage of resilience and fortitude ground a firm belief that through faith and advocacy, anything is possible. New Horizons is not just a church that stands in solidarity with those who are marginalized, it is also a church founded by a marginalized community that has fought not-stop for justice and equality.

In chapter eight, Jennifer Cousineau offers an architectural and social history of Amherstburg First Baptist Church and its congregation; it is adapted from research undertaken in support of a National Historic Site designation for the First Baptist Church in 2013. It takes the church building as its principal historical source and object of analysis. The chapter rests on the conviction that artifacts (including buildings) can be as revealing of the past as texts and other forms of historical evidence. As products of human ingenuity and collective action, buildings open a window onto the past and into the lives of the people who built and used them. This is particularly important for people whose history is not well-served by the documentary record. One of the few capacious, quasi-public spaces available to Black people in Amherstburg, the church immediately became a place of refuge and part of the infrastructure of the Underground Railroad. Many found their first physical and spiritual home in Upper Canada at the First Baptist Church. Its leaders ensured that those who followed them would find relief in the social and architectural body of the church.

Glenn Tomlinson in chapter nine posits that Washington Christian's story and that of the church he founded are not well documented. In fact, some of the details have been chronologically misplaced, spurring on spurious conclusions. To clarify the historical record, this chapter argues that the First Coloured Calvinistic Church was founded by Washington Christian in 1834, and not in 1826 as many contend. Tomlinson documents Christian's frustrations with the lack of progress regarding the emancipation of his African brothers and sisters; his dissatisfaction prompted his immigration to the "Promised Land" of Canada. Intending to minister to the destitute—those who escaped slavery—Christian settled in the administrative capital of the British colony of Upper Canada, i.e., the town of York (later Toronto); Tomlinson scruples to chronicle the significant difficulties that Christian encountered in founding, maintaining, and consolidating his Toronto church, while also planting churches in St. Catharines and Niagara.

In chapter ten, Taylor Murray holds, in his examination of Black Baptists in Victoria, British Columbia, that the Black experience is an inextricable piece of the history of Baptists in British Columbia. When the First Baptist Church of Victoria was founded in 1876, it was the first Baptist church in Canada west of Winnipeg and had the unique distinction of being comprised almost equally of Black and White members. That racial dynamic continued for a time, but in 1881, the Black members withdrew from the church, and just over two years later, the church was dissolved. Various historians have either mentioned or chronicled the formation of this church and the schism. This chapter retraces these events with the purpose of documenting a different perspective: the Black Baptist preference for self-chosen independence rather than tolerate segregated worship.

In chapter eleven, Késa Munroe-Anderson reimagines the African United Baptist Association and its education of the Black Nova Scotian community through the intersection of race and gender. As the oldest African Nova Scotian organization, the AUBA has demonstrated stalwart advocacy, provision of academic and leadership programming, and other tangible means of educational support—filling gaps in otherwise absent community services. Although the AUBA has a tradition of predominantly male leadership, all who served valiantly as civil rights activists, the vital role of the AUBA's women in leading educational advancement in female-dominated congregations cannot be overstated. This chapter examines the history of the AUBA through the lens of a male-female leadership partnership as critical to the educational development and success of African Nova Scotian communities.

In chapter twelve, Nina Reid-Maroney revisits her biography *The Reverend Jennie Johnson (1868-1967)*, published in 2013. Attending to Johnson's reflections on fragmentary textual sources, community memory, and Baptist history, this chapter has Reid-Maroney re-imagining Rev. Johnson in light of this emerging historiography. It presents a new introduction to her life, arguing that Johnson's approach to the struggle for women's ordination was linked to the Black abolitionist culture in which she was raised, and resonated in crucial ways with African Canadian freedom struggles in the twentieth century.

The final chapter has Hannah Lane discussing David George, Cultural Memory, and Public History. Fusing foundational studies with new approaches in current Black scholarship, Lane provides clarifications and a deeper context to the life of David George. Lane seeks to address topics, such as agency and historical impact, as they pertain to George's ministry in Nova Scotia and Sierra Leone. This chapter offers a critical history that moves beyond inspirational storytelling while making local Black history accessible to lay readers.

Finally, a few words of thanks are in order. Much of the research in this volume would not be possible without the aid of archivists Adam McCulloch (Canadian Baptist Archives, Hamilton, Ontario) and Pat Townsend (Baptist Archives, Wolfville, Nova Scotia), who provided digital access to records in the midst of the COVID-19 pandemic. Catherine Fancy at the archives at Acadia also provided some very helpful assistance with records. The authors of the various chapters are to be commended for taking on additional research tasks in the midst of the pandemic. It is never easy to research and write with a deadline (and COVID) looming, but everyone pulled it off while being irenic in the process. Thank you as well to George Elliott Clarke for the kind foreword, and for the much-needed input on critical issues and publications that we missed or misread. It is truly an honour to have such an accomplished figure associated with this project. The anonymous external readers provided much needed input at a very busy time of year, and they deserve thanks as well. And lastly, thanks to our families who supported our vision for the book and were willing to see less of us in order for that vision to come to pass.

BIBLIOGRAPHY

Primary Sources

ARCHIVES

"An Authentic Account of the Conversion and Experience of a Negro." *The New York Public Library Digital Collections.* Online: https://digitalcollections.nypl.org/items/c93f6270-1612-0134-7d57-00505686a51c.

MONOGRAPHS

Drew, Benjamin. *A North-Side View of Slavery. The Refugee; or the Narratives of Fugitive Slaves in Canada. Related by Themselves, with an Account of the History and Condition of the Coloured Population of Upper Canada.* Boston: John P. Jowett and Company, 1856.

MacKerrow, P. E. *A Brief History of the Coloured Baptists of Nova Scotia and their First Organization as Churches A. D. 1832.* Halifax, NS: Nova Scotia Printing Company, 1895.

NEWSPAPERS

The Provincial Freeman (Windsor, Toronto, Chatham, ON), 1853–1860.
Voice of the Fugitive (Sandwich, Canada West), 1851–1854.

Secondary Sources

Arenson, Adam "A Forgotten Generation: African Canadian History between Fugitive Slave and World War I." In *Unsettling the Great White North: Black Canadian History*, edited by Michele A. Johnson and Funké Aladejebi, 115–39. Toronto: University of Toronto Press, 2022.

Bates Neary, Hilary. *A Black American Missionary in Canada: The Life and Letters of Lewis Champion Chambers.* Montreal: McGill-Queens's University Press, 2022.

Bauman, Chad M. "Redeeming Indian 'Christian' Womanhood? Missionaries, *Dalits*, and Agency in Colonial India." *Journal of Feminist Studies in Religion* 24 (2008) 5–27.

Brown, Dudley. "William Andrew White Jr.: Portrait of an African Canadian Pastor, Chaplain, and Activist." PhD diss., McMaster Divinity College, 2022.

Brown-Kubisch, Linda. *The Queen's Bush Settlement: Black Pioneers 1839–1865.* Toronto: Natural Heritage, 2004.

Chioneso, N. A., et al. "Community Healing and Resistance through Storytelling: A Framework to Address Racial Trauma in Africana Communities." *Journal of Black Psychology* 46 (2020) 95–121.

Clarke, George Elliott. *Directions Home: Approaches to African-Canadian Literature.* Toronto: University of Toronto Press, 2012.

———. *Fire on the Water: An Anthology of Black Nova Scotian Writing.* 2 vols. Lawrencetown Beach, NS: Pottersfield, 1991–1992.

———. *Odysseys Home: Mapping African-Canadian Literature.* Toronto: University of Toronto Press, 2002.

Cone, James H. *A Black Theology of Liberation.* Maryknoll, NY: Orbis, 1970.

Creese, Gillian. "Creating Spaces of Belonging: Building A New African Community in Vancouver." In *Unsettling the Great White North: Black Canadian History*, edited by Michele A. Johnson and Funké Aladejebi, 383–401. Toronto: University of Toronto Press, 2022.

Delgado, Richard, and Jean Stefancic. *Critical Race Theory: An Introduction*. 3rd ed. New York: New York University Press, 2017.

Donovan, Kenneth. "Slaves and their Owners in Ile Royale, 1713–1760." *Journal of the History of the Atlantic Region* 25 (1995) 3–32.

Duncan, Carol B. "'Out of the Bitter Sea': The Black Church and Migration in North American." In *The Black Church Studies Reader*, edited by Alton B. Pollard and Carol B. Duncan, 237–44. London: MacMillan, 2016.

———. *This Spot of Ground: Spiritual Baptists in Toronto*. Waterloo: Wilfrid Laurier University Press, 2008.

Este, David C. "The Black Church as a Social Welfare Institution: Union United Church and the Development of Montreal's Black Community, 1907–1940." *Journal of Black Studies* 35 (2004) 3–22.

Este, David C., and Jenna Bailey. "Shiloh Baptist Church: The Pillar of Strength in Edmonton's African American Community." In *Unsettling the Great White North*, edited by Michele Johnson and Funké Aladejebi, 169–93. Toronto: University of Toronto Press, 2022.

Fabius, Chanee D. "Toward an Integration of Narrative Identity, Generativity, and Storytelling in African American Elders." *Journal of Black Studies* 47 (2016) 423–34.

Fountain, Daniel L. *Slavery, Civil War and Salvation: African American Slaves and Christianity, 1830–1870*. Baton Rouge: Louisiana State University Press, 2010.

Frost, Karolyn S. "African American and African Transnationalism along the Detroit River Borderland: The Example of Madison J. Lightfoot." *Journal of American Ethnic History* 32 (2013) 78–88.

Gerbner, Katharine. *Christian Slavery: Conversion and Race in the Protestant Atlantic World*. Philadelphia: University of Pennsylvania Press, 2018.

Gordon, Grant. *From Slavery to Freedom: The Life of David George, Pioneer Black Baptist Minister*. Hantsport, NS: Lancelot, 1992.

Heath, Gordon L. "'The Great Association Above:' Maritime Baptists and the War of 1812." *Pacific Journal of Baptist Research* 7 (2011) 1–22.

———. "The Wartime Diaries of Canadian Baptist Military Chaplain William A. White, 1917–1918." *Baptist Quarterly* (2017) 165–81.

Heath, Gordon L., Dallas Friesen, and Taylor Murray. *Baptists in Canada: Their History and Polity*. McMaster Ministry Studies Series 5. Eugene, OR: Pickwick, 2020.

Hill, Daniel G. *The Freedom-Seekers: Blacks in Early Canada*. Toronto: Stoddard, 1992.

Kilian, Crawford. *Go Do Some Great Thing: The Black Pioneers of British Columbia*. Madeira Park, BC: Harbour, 2016.

MacKerrow, P. E. *A Brief History of the Coloured Baptists of Nova Scotia (1783–1895)*, edited and annotated by Frank Stanley Boyd, Jr. Halifax, NS: Afro-Nova Scotia Enterprises, 1976.

O'Connor, June. "Rereading, Reconceiving, and Reconstructing Traditions: Feminist Research in Religion." *Women's Studies* 17 (1989) 101–23.

Oliver, Pearleen. *A Brief History of the Colored Baptists of Nova Scotia:1782–1953*. Halifax: McCurdy, 1953.

Paris, Peter J. *The Moral, Political and Religious Significance of the Black Church in Nova Scotia*. Dartmouth, NS: Black Cultural Centre for Nova Scotia, 1989.

Porter, Wendy. "A Quartet and an Anonymous Choir: The Remarkable Lives and Ministries of Four Black Baptist Women in Late Nineteenth-Century Ontario." In *Canadian Baptist Women*, edited by Sharon M. Bowler, 89–112. McMaster General Studies Series 8. Canadian Baptist Historical Society Series 3. Eugene: Pickwick, 2016.

Rawlyk, George A. *The Canada Fire: Radical Evangelicalism in British North America, 1775–1812*. Montreal/Kingston: McGill Queen's University Press, 1994.

Renfree, Harry A. *Heritage and Horizon: The Baptist Story in Canada*. Eugene, OR: Wipf and Stock, 2007.

Riley, Jennifer. "The Contribution of the African United Baptist Association to Public Education, 1854–1940." In *Atlantic Baptists and their World: A Festschrift in Honour of Dr. Robert S. Wilson*, edited by Taylor Murray and Gordon L. Heath, 269–86. Kentville, NS: Gaspereau Press, 2020.

Sawallisch, Nele. *Fugitive Borders: Black Canadian Cross-Border Literature at Mid-Nineteenth Century*. Bielefeld, Germany: Transcript, 2018.

Setran, David. "Sowing the Story: Narrative Identity and Emerging Adult Formation." *Christian Education Journal* 17 (2020) 92–109.

Shepard, R. Bruce. "Diplomatic Racism: Canadian Government and Black Migrationfrom Oklahoma." In *African Americans on the Great Plains: An Anthology*, edited by Bruce Glasrud and Charles Braithwaite, 162–83. Lincoln: University of Nebraska Press, 2009.

Shreve, Dorothy S. *The AfriCanadian Church: A Stabilizer*. Jordan Station, ON: Paideia, 1983.

Siemerling, Winfried. *The Black Atlantic Reconsidered: Black Canadian Writing, Cultural History, and the Presence of the Past*. Montreal/Kingston: McGill-Queen's University Press, 2015.

Simpson, Donald. *Under the North Star: Black Communities in Upper Canada before Confederation (1876)*. Trenton, NJ: African World, 2005.

Smardz Frost, Karolyn, and Veta Smith Tucker, eds. *A Fluid Frontier: Slavery, Resistance, and the Underground Railroad in the Detroit River Borderland*. Detroit: Wayne State University Press, 2016.

Smith, Timothy L. "Slavery and Theology: The Emergence of Black Consciousness in Nineteenth-Century America." *Church History* 41 (1972) 497–512.

Spencer, Elaine A. Brown. "The Black Oneness Church in Perspective." PhD diss., University of Toronto, 2009.

Still, William. *The Underground Railroad Records: Narrating the Hardships, Hairbreadth Escapes, and Death Struggles of Slaves in Their Efforts for Freedom*. New York: Random House, 2019.

Taylor, Alan. *The Internal Enemy: Slavery and War in Virginia, 1772–1832*. New York: Norton, 2013.

Teelucksingh, Jerome. *The Lost Gospel: Christianity and Blacks in North America*. Newcastle, UK: Cambridge Scholars, 2020.

Volf, Miroslav. *The End of Memory: Remembering Rightly in a Violent World*. Grand Raids: Eerdmans, 2006.

Walker, Barrington. "Critical Histories of Blackness in Canada." In *Unsettling the Great White North: Black Canadian History*, edited by Michele A. Johnson and Funké Aladejebi, 31–49. Toronto: University of Toronto Press, 2022.

Walker, James W. St. G. *Black Identity in Nova Scotia: Community and Institutions in Historical Perspective*. Dartmouth, NS: Black Cultural Centre for Nova Scotia, 1985.

———. *The Black Loyalists: The Search for a Promised Land in Nova Scotia and Sierra Leone 1783–1870*. Toronto: University of Toronto Press, 1992.

———. *Racial Discrimination in Canada: The Black Experience. Historical Booklet No. 41*. Ottawa: Canadian Historical Society, 1985.

Watkins, Paul. "Hogan's Alley Remixed." In *Unsettling the Great White North: Black Canadian History*, edited by Michele A. Johnson and Funké Aladejebi, 455–87. Toronto: University of Toronto Press, 2022.

Whitfield, Harvey Amani. *Blacks on the Border: The Black Refugees in British North American, 1815–1860*. Burlington: University of Vermont Press, 2006.

Williams, Savanah E. "The Role of the African United Baptist Association in the Development of Indigenous Afro-Canadians in Nova Scotia, 1782–1978." In *Repent and Believe: The Baptist Experience in Maritime Canada*, edited by Barry M. Moody, 46–65. Hantsport, NS: Lancelot, 1980.

Winks, Robin. *The Blacks in Canada: A History*. 2nd ed. Montreal: McGill University Press, 1997.

Zaami, Mariama. "Strategizing to Strengthen Social Inclusion: The Agency of Black African Immigrant Youth in Alberta, Canada." *Canadian Ethnic Studies* 52 (2020) 87–106.

2

An Introduction to the Black Church in Canada, 1663–1867

Denise Gillard

Gordon de La Mothe claims, "Religion plays a large part in the life of Black people all over the world."[1] His statement is as true of Blacks in Canada as it is of anywhere else. Wherever spirituality or spiritual expression took the form of Christian belief in the Canadian context, the Black religious experience evolved in the context of past, and ongoing, European imperialism with its institutional and ideological trappings of White supremacy and the accompanying practices of multiple oppressions. As a result, for the most part, wherever Christianity took root among settlement communities of Black people in Canada, the Black Church most often found it necessary to separate from mainstream culture to afford its members the full participation, lay empowerment, leadership development, and spiritual dignity essential to those who unite as the body of Christ.

Lawrence H. Mamiya writes,

> "The Black Church emerges from the religious, cultural, and social experience of Black people. With its roots on the continent of Africa and the Middle Passage, the Black Church provided structure and meaning for African people and their descendants

---

1. de La Mothe, *Reconstructing*, 71.

in the Americas who struggled to survive the ravages and brutality of slavery and racial oppression."[2]

Echoing Mamiya, Carol Duncan notes that "the roots of Black churches in Canada are as diverse as the people who occupy them."[3]

To demonstrate the nature of these various and diverse experiences and set some context for the chapters in this collection of essays, what follows below is a brief outlining of three major periods in Canadian history in correlation with key episodes of the Black experience, namely the French Regime (1536–1763); the early British Regime (1763–1792); and Upper Canada/Canada West (1791–1867). Following this outline will be a brief discussion of some common themes within the Black Church experience.

A few words of clarification are necessary. First, it is important to note that this chapter was originally published in 1998. Since that time, the world has undergone significant changes, and I am acutely aware of the influence of current events and contemporary scholarship on this revised work. It is worth mentioning that primary source material is still emerging and may not always be readily available or easily accessible. Additionally, the production and promotion of secondary material continues to pose challenges for scholars studying the Black Canadian experience. Notably, it is essential to acknowledge the fundamental differences between the writing and study of the Black Experience in Canada and the United States, respectively. While the US has long acknowledged Black studies as a legitimate field of historical inquiry, the same in Canada is still in its early infancy stage of development. That said, Jenna Benchetrit outlines recent positive announcements from four Canadian universities of Black studies programs with more of such programs in discussion by other institutions.[4] The disruption to status quo knowledge-making for the Black Church historian presents exciting, if not overwhelming, implications and opportunities.

Secondly, it is important to note that the dominant historical vision of Canada has generally been disseminated in terms of English and French culture. Today, some Canadians continue to think of Blacks only in terms of new immigrants, forgetting, denying, or remaining ignorant of the fact that Blacks account for 4.3 percent of Canada's total population

2. Floyd-Thomas et al., *Black Church Studies*, xxiii.
3. "Freedom and Resistance."
4. Benchetrit, "Wave."

and 16.1 percent of the racialized, and have been a recorded part of the Canadian experience at least since the year 1608.⁵ Blacks who can trace up to eight or more generations in Canada can still be asked, "And what Island do you come from?"⁶ As a result of this ignorance or denial, while most students of American history know that Christopher Columbus arrived at American shores in 1492, and many also know that a free Black man, Pedro Alonso Nino, accompanied him on this journey, very few Canadians by comparison know who the first Black was to arrive in Canada. Why is this so? Robin W. Winks names the relatively small size of the population as the main reason why the realities of Blacks in Canadian history have been ignored.⁷ While Winks's work was considered as one of the most comprehensive of the 1970s, more recent scholarship disputes his reasoning. For example, when noting Black history as missing from the pages of mainstream Canadian history, the authors of *We're Rooted Here and They Can't Pull Us Up* state, "Black people in Canada have a past that has been hidden or eradicated, just as racism has been deliberately denied as an organizing element in how Canada is constituted."⁸ While there has been some improvement in this area, writers such as Afua Cooper and Shannon Lodoen offer insight into the ways in which knowledge-making continues to be co-opted to support the dominant narrative.⁹ It is important that historians pull on every loose thread that contributes to the erasure or sanitization of the Black experience in Canada.¹⁰

Thirdly, it is also important to note that early interpretations of the Black experience, both secular and religious, have often been depicted in ways which are degrading, presumptuous and/or simply inaccurate. For instance, expressions of Christian belief are sometimes depicted as exotic in their Black articulation and adaption of the faith, seen as embodying the African tradition of music, dance, emotionalism, and immorality in the celebration of its practice as if primitive or uncivilized.¹¹ As Dionne

---

5. Thomson, *Blacks in Deep Snow*, 95.

6. I have experienced this on several occasions. Black people, such as second-generation Canadian Africans and South Americans, are now telling tales of the same experiences.

7. Winks, *Blacks in Canada*, ix.

8. Bristow, ed., *We're Rooted Here*, 3.

9. Cooper, *Hanging of Angélique*; Lodoen, "Myths."

10. For another example, see Cooper, *Hanging of Angélique*.

11. de La Mothe, *Reconstructing*, 71, 73. See also Evans, *Burden of Black Religion*, 65–104.

Brand warns, "to live in the Black Diaspora is to live as a fiction—a creation of empires, and also self-creation."[12]

NEW FRANCE

Although not a permanent resident, the first recorded Black person to come to Canada was Mathieu d'Acosta, a member of Canada's oldest club (the Order of Good Cheer), and an interpreter for Sieur de Monts, Governor at Port Royal (1605).[13] The first recorded Black resident of the nation in 1628 was a Black child from Madagascar, the property of the famous privateer David Kirke whose sale of the boy (later baptized as "Oliver LeJeune") in New France was Canada's first recorded European slave sale.[14] Since the time of Samuel de Champlain (1567–1635), the enslavement of Africans was commonplace in New France and, by 1760, records tell us that New France had a Black slave population that totaled nearly 1,200.[15]

At the time of Oliver LeJeune's arrival, the colony was run by the Company of New France. In 1663, however, the company gave up its charter and King Louis XIV appointed a Governor and Intendant to the colony hoping to strengthen it. Under new leadership, the colony flourished to the point that many of the colonists began to complain about the shortage of servants and workers. These settlers petitioned the Governor, Jacques-Rene de Brisay and the Intendant, Jean Bochart de Champigny, for permission to purchase Black slaves.[16] Daniel G. Hill documents the King's response: "His majesty finds it good that the inhabitants of Canada import negroes there to take care of their agriculture, but remarks that there is a risk that these negroes, coming from a very different climate, will perish in Canada; the project would then become useless."[17] In 1709, after the King failed to clarify his position on the matter, Intendant Jacques Raudotin passed the "Ordinance Rendered on the Subject of the Negroes and the Indians called Panis" legitimizing the enslavement of both Indigenous and Blacks brought to the colony.[18]

12. Brand, *Map*, 6.
13. Hill, *Freedom-Seekers*, 3.
14. Hill, *Freedom-Seekers*, 3.
15. Alexander and Glaze, *Towards Freedom*, 37.
16. Hill, *Freedom-Seekers*, 3.
17. Hill, *Freedom-Seekers*, 3.
18. "Enslavement."

With authorization granted, enslaved individuals were brought in and, alongside Panis (Native Americans who migrated to New France as household servants, primarily in Montreal), utilized as laborers. Like their counterparts in America, Canadian settlers encountered challenges in monitoring Indigenous North American slaves, who seemed to effortlessly vanish into the wilderness or were perceived unable to endure arduous labor with the same lucrative productivity attributed to Black slaves. Consequently, the enslavement of Blacks became the prevailing practice. Carole Pigler Christensen and Morton Weinfeld assert that in order to keep control over slaves in frontier Canada racism was institutionalized through the Code Noire of New France, a measure originally promulgated for use in the West Indies.[19] The original Code of 1685, as well as the revised one of 1728 (which merely added a statement forbidding intermarriage), were originally issued by France to protect colonists from slave actions such as theft, revolt, and escape.[20] Since the slaves of New France, for the most part, worked indoors as isolated labourers (as opposed to the popular gang-labour/plantation-style economy of other colonies), the protective statutes of these Codes were only enforced when the need arose.[21] Furthermore, Winks reports that in New France no steps were taken to prevent intermarriage.[22] What the Code did strongly assert in New France, however, was the understanding of Blacks as mere chattel, a sub-human species with no attachment to the land.

Blacks and the Church in New France

The colony of New France was, for the most part, Roman Catholic. In New France, the Catholic Church did not oppose or speak out against slavery. Secular priests, religious communities (including the Jesuits, Dominicans, and Franciscans), the Ursulines in Louisiana (which were within the Diocese of Quebec), the Brothers of Charity at Lewisburg, and the benevolent Mother Marie d'Youville (who ran the Hospital-General), all owned slaves. Yet historians like Winks portrayed the Roman Catholic slave-holding of New France and other Roman Catholic colonies as somewhat "humane and familial" in contrast to that of the English colonies since their practices were assessed as ones which seem to "soften"

---

19. Christensen and Weinfeld, "Black Family in Canada," 30.
20. Winks, *Blacks in Canada*, 7.
21. Alexander and Glaze, *Towards Freedom*. 37.
22. Winks, *Blacks in Canada*, 7.

the brutality of the institution in several ways.[23] For instance, the Roman Catholic Church practice of allowing slaves to participate in some sacraments with baptism, communion, and burial as regular ministries afforded them, is cited as evidence of its gentler nature; baptisms were often celebrated as a special social occasion for the slaves, and in French society the owner often claimed the honor of being godfather to his slave. Upon baptism, the slave was given his or her master's family name, with given names often based on family tradition.[24] When a slave died, it was normal for the owner to witness the act of burial. Marriage was only permitted with the owner's permission, since with the sacrament of marriage the slaves were granted their freedom. Winks sees these examples as evidence of Roman Catholic slave-owners thinking of their property in more humane terms than those of colonies in which slaves were given no more intrinsic value than that of horses.[25]

The demythologization of the slave experience in New France necessitates a more meticulous examination. It is important to note that all children born of slave marriages belonged to the mother's master. If a Black or Panis slave married with the partner remaining ignorant of their enslaved condition, this was deemed sufficient grounds for immediate annulment. Most notably, Bishop St. Vallier, in his Catechism of 1702, excluded slaves from taking Holy Orders or becoming Priests.

Furthermore, within the context of the "race, gender and power relations intrinsic to slavery," the 1734 trial, torture, execution, and humiliation of Marie-Joseph Angélique, an enslaved Black woman in Montreal, reveals the cruel and brutal nature of enslavement in New France in particular, and ultimately, Canada.[26] Accused of arson and on the basis of circumstantial evidence, she "was sentenced to make honorable amends, to have her hand cut off, and to be burnt alive. When the case was appealed, the Consiel Superieur . . . mitigated somewhat the horror of the punishment." After being tortured, "she was to be taken in a rubbish cart to the church door, where she was to make a formal confession of guilt; then she was to be hanged, before her body was burned . . . and her ashes were cast to the winds."[27]

23. Winks, *Blacks in Canada*, 176–77.

24. As opposed to British slaveholders who gave their slaves classical names such as "Othello" or chose names at random.

25. Winks, *Blacks in Canada*, 13–15.

26. Cooper, *Hanging of Angélique*, 289.

27. Vachon, "Marie-Joseph-Angélique."

One may wonder if the historians who share Wink's viewpoint think her story an anomaly or distortion of the realities of slavery in Canada, as despite its horror he holds to his articulation as it being "among the most benevolent expressions of the institution in North America."[28] He exposes his confliction in that he also states, "nonetheless it was slavery with accompanying potentialities toward the dominance of one man, and one race, over another."[29] In effect, the alliance between imperialistic pursuits coupled with the Roman Catholic Church's endorsement of this brand of slavery, in all its complexities, effectively smothered any real self-directed expression of a Black Church in the Black slave community of New France.

THE EARLY BRITISH REGIME

In 1713, the French territory of Acadia was handed over to the British by the Treaty of Utrecht. Settlers from New England poured into Acadia, renaming the new acquisition Nova Scotia. Since it is recorded that slaves helped build Nova Scotia when it was founded in 1749, historians conclude that settlers brought slaves with them.[30] With the conquest of New France, the Articles of Capitulation ensured the existing French slave system remained intact and fitted neatly into the new British regime. Once again, the leading colonists increased their demand for slave labor.[31] British General James Murray, Governor of Quebec, a slave-owner himself, felt more slaves would help the colony's economy.[32] The slave trade was brisk among Church of England ministers, government officials, and merchants, most notably in Quebec and Detroit (the British having taken Detroit from the French in 1760).[33]

The Loyalists

At the end of the Seven Years' War, the British government found itself weighed down by debt and began a program of tax reforms which rapidly led to the rebellion of its thirteen American colonies. With the Stamp Act

---

28. Winks, *Blacks in Canada*, 13–15
29. Winks, *Blacks in Canada*, 13–15.
30. Alexander and Glaze, *Towards Freedom*, 41.
31. Hill, *Freedom-Seekers*, 6.
32. Thomson, *Blacks Deep in Snow*, 18.
33. Hill, *Freedom-Seekers*, 9.

of 1765, the British tried for the first time to tax the colonists directly. But upon meeting swift American objections, the Act was repealed. Tempers flared on both sides and the final crisis began with protests against the Tea Act of 1773. While most Americans opposed the British reform measures, there were those who, despite their opposition, remained loyal to King George and wanted to find a way between dependence and independence.[34] These people are commonly referred to as Loyalists.

The Loyalists represented the whole range of society, although the rich, urban, official, conservative, and the recent immigrant all contributed proportionally more than other segments of the population.[35] As for the Christian faith being a motivating factor in their allegiance to Britain, Wallace Brown and Hereward Senior state, "Religion was not usually the key, although loyalty had an Anglican tinge in New Jersey, New York and especially New England, where Anglicans were a beleaguered minority (everywhere, the Loyalist elite was largely Anglican)."[36] Churches, marriages, partnerships, families and friendships split over the issue; people were also motivated for personal, political, financial and sometimes irrational reasons.[37] In 1775, the American colonies rebelled against Britain's King George III, the War of Independence began, and when the war was lost United Empire Loyalists moved northward out of American territory. Encouraged by British government promises of military commissions, administrative positions, generous grants of land and permission to bring their slaves, Loyalists left with their families to start new lives in the Maritimes and Quebec.[38]

As the war began, the British developed a divide-and-conquer strategy against the Americans by offering freedom to any rebel-owned slaves who would join their ranks. This led to slave holders passing laws and taking actions to protect their slaves from fleeing, yet despite those efforts thousands tried to escape to the north.[39] Ironically, British offers of freedom did not include the slaves of Loyalists. However, rebel slaves and Free-Blacks who fought for the British were promised the same reward as White Loyalists. While most slaves were transported to the Caribbean,

---

34. Brown and Senior, *Victorious in Defeat*, 5–8.
35. Brown and Senior, *Victorious in Defeat*, 10.
36. Brown and Senior, *Victorious in Defeat*, 14.
37. Brown and Senior, *Victorious in Defeat*, 15.
38. Hill, *Freedom-Seekers*, 9.
39. Hill, *Freedom-Seekers*, 9–10.

the Free-Blacks were given their choice of destination for economic reasons. Wanting to avoid areas dominated by large scale slavery, most Free-Blacks chose to go Nova Scotia.[40]

In 1783, peace was declared, and Britain recognized the birth of the US. Daniel G. Hill reports that at this period Quebec west of Montreal (soon to become Upper Canada, then Canada West, and finally Ontario), was for the most part still wilderness, with fringes of settlement along the Upper St. Lawrence and Lower Great Lakes. Approximately 10,000 Loyalists were resettled there by the British.[41] As previously stated in the discussion of New France, slavery on a small scale was already in place in British North America. It was most prominent in New France, although there are no clear statistics on the number of new slaves brought into Quebec by the Loyalists.

Nova Scotia

The rest of the Loyalists (approximately 30,000) were transported to Nova Scotia by ships carrying both Free Blacks and White Loyalists with their slaves, those slaves commonly referred to as "servants for life."[42] James Walker estimates that including free and enslaved Blacks, there were about 3,550 men, women, and children. The slaves who were brought to Nova Scotia found themselves distributed widely throughout the Maritimes, especially to Saint John, New Brunswick and Shelburne, Nova Scotia, with a few going to Prince Edward Island. The most important of the Free-Black settlements in Nova Scotia was Birchtown, named after Colonel Samuel Birch, the official who had issued the certificate allowing them to leave New York.[43] Birchtown was located near the boom town of Shelburne, where over 40 percent of the White Loyalists had settled.[44] The other two all-Black communities established by Black Loyalists were Brindley Town, with over 200 settlers (near Digby), and Little Tracadie (on St. George's Bay), with approximately 170 settlers. There were also important settlements of Blacks segregated within White communities, including Halifax and its surrounding area (400 Blacks in Halifax, 300 in Preston near Dartmouth), Chedabucto (350), Shelburne

---

40. Brown and Senior, *Victorious in Defeat*, 173.
41. Hill, *Freedom-Seekers*, 10.
42. Boyd, Introduction to *A Brief History*, xiv.
43. Niven, *Birchtown Archaelogical Survey*, 2.
44. Brown and Senior, *Victorious in Defeat*, 175.

(200), Annapolis (100), Liverpool (50), and Saint John, New Brunswick (180).[45]

The British promises to Loyalists—of all races—had included land, supplies and citizenship, land being the most important for survival. When many of these promises were broken, the disappointment of many of the Whites was significant; the disappointment for most of the Blacks was enormous. Brown and Senior sum up the Black situation in Nova Scotia as follows:

> The majority got no land; the minority who did, received smaller, poorer, less accessible grants than whites. By November 1786, when grants to whites had been completed in Shelburne, none of the Birchtown Blacks had received farms, although a few town lots had been issued. Two years later when the Birchtown grants were completed only about a third of the settlers had been awarded farms.[46]

Obviously this predicament contributed to the physical and economic decline of Blacks in Nova Scotia. Furthermore, while they were required to fulfill their duties as citizens (such as paying taxes), the slave-holding mentality of their White counterparts denied them their fair share of the land, relegated them to positions of sharecropping, day labourers and indentured servants, all of whom were often exploited and cheated.[47]

With the denial of land, the physical and economic decline of Blacks in Nova Scotia became deeply concerning. In a further blow to their already dire circumstances, the government ceased issuing rations in 1787, prompting several owners to emancipate their slaves to avoid the responsibility of providing for them. However, an even more poignant event that encapsulates their plight occurred in July 1784: a ten-day race riot engulfed Shelburne and Birchtown, pitting Blacks against Whites. Disgruntled disbanded soldiers, feeling threatened by the availability of cheaper labor offered by Free-Blacks, sought to drive them out of town. To restore order, Governor Parr had to deploy military forces. The Black loyalists had arrived in Nova Scotia with hopes of finding a home, a place of equality and freedom—a proverbial Promised Land. Instead, their overall experience was marred by distressing accounts of neo-slavery, violence, and oppression.

---

45. Brown and Senior, *Victorious in Defeat*, 175.
46. Brown and Senior, *Victorious in Defeat*, 175.
47. Brown and Senior, *Victorious in Defeat*, 176–77.

Blacks and the Church in Nova Scotia

Brown and Senior state, "The Blacks' greatest success was religious organization, by which they developed as a distinct and separate community."[48] When the Black Loyalists arrived in Nova Scotia in 1783, the Church of England, the established church, was immediately fortified with the arrival of White Anglican Loyalists. As with their secular experience, the Loyalist Black settlers (who were predominantly Anglican, Methodist, and Baptist) found themselves relegated to a distinctly second-class status in the church.

For example, most Blacks believed that baptism in the Anglican Church would make them "one and equal with whites."[49] However, even when Dr. John Breynton, Rector of St. Paul's, baptized many hundreds of them, Blacks found that while they could attend services and receive communion, they were segregated from White parishioners and forced into galleries set apart for Blacks, the poor, and soldiers. By 1815, Black worshippers were kept behind a partition.[50] Ultimately, Blacks were excluded when White parishioners grew in numbers. Furthermore, they were advised to gather in their own private homes.[51] This displacement left Black lay leaders with little supervision or instruction. To add insult to injury, in 1784 the Anglican-related Society for the Propagation of the Gospel had some Blacks displaced because, after years of waiting for the property promised to them, they had settled on an area of land reserved for church and school.[52]

Since it was obvious that they were neither welcomed nor nurtured in the Church of England, the Nova Scotian Blacks found their spiritual needs best met by their own lay preachers and teachers, in their segregated communities, and in independent churches only nominally affiliated with the White-dominated parent churches.[53] Their religious meetings became important spiritual and social outlets. Without them they would have been swallowed up by broken promises and dreams. The autonomous development of the Black Church in Nova Scotia coincided with

---

48. Brown and Senior, *Victorious in Defeat*, 178–79.
49. Wetmore and Sellick, eds., *Loyalist*, 74.
50. Brown and Senior, *Victorious in Defeat*, 179.
51. Wetmore and Sellick, eds., *Loyalist*, 75.
52. Wilson, *Loyal Blacks*, 120.
53. Blind Moses Wilkinson and Boston King were two of the significant Black preachers/pastors.

the Nova Scotian counterpart to the revivalism of the Great Awakening, which Ellen Gibson Wilson describes as "a revival which undermined the fashionable and formal churches and created a democratic and hot-blooded frontier religion."[54]

The Welsh Calvinistic Methodists, British Wesleyan Methodists, and the Baptists—all of whom were strongly affected by the New Light trend sparked by Henry Alline—gained many Black converts whose needs had not been met by the dominant church. Characterized by opponents as "a wild, emotional, Bible thumping madman, dashing around the country shouting the gospel from horseback and ignorantly condemning those who were more intellectually oriented and committed to an orderly, formal type of worship," Alline preached a message of freedom to all who would listen.[55] His direct, emotional, extemporaneous preaching in colloquial language stressed the idea that preaching did not depend on one's education or training since the aim was to uncover the spiritual rather than the literal meaning of the text.[56] In this message, all frontier Nova Scotians saw the release of what D. G. Bell calls, "long gathering religious energies," and while the lack of education on the part of many who either taught or preached was an affront to most traditionalists, the liberating power of the gospel broke through the harsh realities of frontier life.[57]

The revivalist zeal had huge ramifications for the Black Loyalists, particularly regarding dissenter and nonconformist popularity among them. As Gibson states, "The teaching that everyone was capable of imbibing and interpreting the Christian Gospel was ideal for a community thrown upon its own resources of leadership."[58] Such leadership came, for instance, from the Reverend John Marrant, the Welsh Calvinistic Methodist missionary to Nova Scotia and Black Loyalist, converted by George Whitefield in colonial Charleston. Marrant, who had served in the British army during the Revolutionary War, was persuaded by his brother (who lived in Birchtown) to come over from England in 1785. Assisted by William Furmage, another Black Loyalist, Marrant converted over forty families and ordained Black settler Cato Perkins.[59] As another example, Catherine Abernathy was a Welsh Calvinistic Methodist teacher placed

54. Wilson, *Loyal Blacks*, 18.
55. McCormick, *Faith Freedom and Democracy*, 13–14.
56. Bell, *Henry Alline*, 14.
57. Bell, *Henry Alline*, 15.
58. Wilson, *Loyal Blacks*, 126.
59. Brown and Senior, *Victorious in Defeat*, 179.

in charge of the Black settlement school at Preston under direction of the Society for the Propagation of the Gospel. She was suspended in 1789 for "embracing some Strange religious tenets."[60] In matters of religion and education, the Black church became the one institution where such Loyalists could develop dignity, pride, and leadership skills.

Of the Black preachers who began to arrive in the 1780s, the most important was the Baptist reformer David George (1743–1810). George, born a slave in Virginia, went on to become a Baptist preacher there, escaped with his family to Nova Scotia at the end of the American Revolution and led a group of Nova Scotians in their attempt to resettle in Sierra Leone.[61] While still illiterate and uneducated due to his status as a slave, George was gripped by what can only be described as an experiential faith in God. Soon after his conversion, George began to pray and exhort among other Blacks. Since he could not read at first, other Black preachers encouraged him in the Word. When reading his story in Grant Gordon's *From Slavery to Freedom*, one cannot help but note that for George the Scriptures were first validated by his experience as a runaway in search of freedom.[62] According to Gordon, George, who had already established the first continuing Black Baptist Congregation in Silver Bluff, South Carolina, "came into this volatile and primitive situation, hopeful of finding a new home and ministry."[63]

George's story provides us with helpful insight into the role, experience, and significance of the Black church in the lives of frontier Nova Scotians. He organized his first congregations at Shelbourne, and later in St. John, Fredericton, and Preston.[64] When he arrived in Shelbourne (1784), his ministry had immediate success with Blacks and Whites alike. But as Gordon states, "In every setting, his life and ministry were disrupted by racial prejudice, religious opposition, or political upheaval."[65] George recalls an event which illustrates the challenges he faced:

> Many had been baptized by Mr. Chipman of Annapolis... It was a mixed communion church. I preached there. We then returned with Mr. Holmes, when he and his wife sent me to Shelburne, and gave their experiences to the church on Thursday, and were

60. Wilson, *Loyal Blacks*, 130.
61. Gordon, *From Slavery to Freedom*, xiii–xv.
62. Gordon, *From Slavery to Freedom*, 7–30.
63. Gordon, *From Slavery to Freedom*, 50.
64. Murphy and Perlin, *Concise History*, 116.
65. Gordon, *From Slavery to Freedom*, 163.

baptized the next Lord's Day. Their relations, who lived in the town, were very angry, raised a mob, and endeavoured to hinder their being baptized [especially Mrs. Holmes's sister]. She laid hold of her hair to keep her from going down into the water, but the justices commanded peace and said that she should be baptized, as she desired it. Then they were all quiet. Soon after that the persecution increased and became so great it did not seem possible to preach, and I thought I must leave Shelbourne.[66]

Soon after this incident, his chapel was attacked by disbanded soldiers in the riot of 1784. George fled to Birchtown, where he continued his ministry, but encountered more opposition at the hands of both Black and White Anglicans. George expanded his mission to New Brunswick and had great success among the Blacks of Fredericton and Saint John. When telling of his experience there he recalled, "Some of the people . . . were so full of joy they ran out from waiting at tables on their Masters, with the knives and forks in their hand, to meet me at the water side."[67] Of George's preaching, Brown and Senior state, George was a classic, rousing revivalist, the most influential Black preacher, offering a message that went beyond salvation from sin to salvation from White domination. His revivalist energy and the success he had with a few Whites led to White opposition, which left him as a strictly Black spokesman.[68]

With the continuing decline of hope for viable, safe, respected, and prosperous communities, the frustration amongst Blacks and their leaders began to increase. Thomas Peters of Birchtown, formerly a sergeant in the regiment of Black Pioneers, sought justice by delivering to the British government in London a petition of complaint that articulated the disgusting condition of life in Nova Scotia. While in England, Peters met with representatives of the Sierra Leone Company who in 1787 had founded a colony on the peninsula of Sierra Leone in West Africa.

Originally, the British had founded the Sierra Leone colony for the purpose of establishing a homeland for freed slaves repatriated to Africa from Britain and the New World. Originally called the Province of Freedom, the colony of Sierra Leone was Britain's answer to the impending abolition of the slave trade and its inevitable clash with White concepts of race and economy. With large numbers of free yet impoverished Blacks seeking refuge in Britain and certain parts of the New World, the British

66. Mckerrow and Bill, *A Brief History*, 4.
67. Mckerrow and Bill, *A Brief History*, 5.
68. Brown and Senior, *Victorious in Defeat*, 180.

government was on several fronts challenged to find a solution to the "Black problem."⁶⁹ Thus, the climate was right for the British government to agree with Henry Smeathman's proposal to settle the poor London Blacks in Sierra Leone.

The colony was to be first of all a capitalist venture, in that its supporters hoped to develop trade in African products to supposedly replace the slave trade.⁷⁰ Secondly, philanthropists such as Granville Sharp hoped for a kind of eighteenth-century utopian venture and "experiment in 'freedom' for the Blacks of the diaspora who were the casualty of European enslavement."⁷¹ To suit their complementary vision of things, both groups expected the London Blacks to somehow transmit their concepts of Western civilization to Africa. This, however, was not to be, as many of the London Blacks and White settlers who accompanied them died from illnesses such as malaria and yellow fever, deserted, or were frustrated by the indigenous Africans repeated burning of the Freetown settlement.

As Headly Tulloch states, "The new colony needed fresh settlers if it was to survive."⁷² Who better for the Sierra Leone company to recruit so that they could reestablish their capitalist-philanthropist vision? To that end, Peters returned to Nova Scotia, joined by John Clarkson, agent of the Sierra Leone Company. Upon hearing of the venture, significant numbers of Blacks were extremely open to Clarke's promises of freedom of religion, free passage, free land, and racial equality for all.

Of the 3,550 Black Loyalists who had come to Nova Scotia, 1,196 joined the exodus to Sierra Leone, which set sail on January 15, 1792. This third included all the preachers and teachers, plus many more who were not forced to stay because of outstanding debts or slave obligations.⁷³ It is ironic that there was strong opposition to their leaving, since they had continuously been treated like second class outsiders, even, and perhaps most painfully, by the mainstream church. It seems that the colonists protested their departure mainly because of the impending loss of cheap labour. However, as Robin W. Winks states, "None could counter

---

69. For instance, with regards to the "Black poor," Campbell argues, "the British wanted to get rid of them by any means necessary" (see *Back to Africa*, iv).

70. Wilson, *Loyal Blacks*, ix.

71. Wilson, *Loyal Blacks*, iv.

72. Tulloch, *Black Canadians*, 83.

73. Pachai, *Beneath the Clouds*, 15.

the influence of the [Black's] own religious leaders, all of whom had fallen into line behind Clarkson and his assistants."[74]

Included on board the ship to Sierra Leone were Thomas Peters, David George (Baptist), Moses Wilkinson (Methodist), John Ball (Methodist), Cato Perkins (Welsh Calvinistic Methodist), Joseph Leonard (Anglican), Boston King (Methodist), and Adam and Catherine Abernathy (Anglican). Bridglal Pachai characterizes them as "The very people who provided hope and relief to the Black immigrants through the church institutions of the Anglican, Methodist and Baptist denominations."[75] In *Towards Freedom*, Ken Alexander and Avis Glaze state, "Unfortunately, their departure left a leadership vacuum in the fledgling Black community which remained. It also fueled the notion that Blacks were ill-suited to the Canadian climate and the tough realities of frontier life."[76] Along with Gordon, one cannot help but wonder what might have happened if the Black Loyalists had been treated more fairly in Nova Scotia: "Certainly fewer would have gone to Sierra Leone and the Nova Scotian Black community would not have been weakened. And the Baptist church in the Maritimes, particularly the Black Baptist church, would have become much stronger."[77] Instead, faced with the gap between what Nova Scotia promised and what Nova Scotia delivered, they left in hope of finding freedom, equality, and the promised land they were looking for elsewhere.

UPPER CANADA/CANADA WEST

In 1791, the reformer William Wilberforce introduced a bill to stop the importation of slaves into British colonies. This was the same year that one of his supporters, Colonel John Graves Simcoe, became the first Lieutenant Governor of Upper Canada.[78] It is said that after becoming acquainted with the brutality of slavery still present in Upper Canada, Simcoe began to work ardently for its abolition. Only two years later, in 1793, Simcoe and the slave-holding Chief Justice Osgoode reached a compromise and passed The Act to Prevent the Further Introduction of Slaves and to Limit the Term of Enforced Servitude, a bill which freed children of slaves after they reached the age of twenty five, and prevented

---

74. Winks, *Blacks in Canada*, 71.
75. Pachai, *Beneath the Clouds*, 20.
76. Alexander and Glaze, *Towards Freedom*, 50.
77. Gordon, *From Slavery to Freedom*, 164–65.
78. Hill, *Freedom-Seekers*, 15.

new settlers from bringing slaves into the province.⁷⁹ At the turn of the eighteenth century, the abolitionist movement picked up great momentum and several bills to abolish slavery were introduced but subsequently defeated. Then in 1803, Osgoode, by that time Chief Justice of Lower Canada, ruled that slavery was incompatible with British law. This historic judgment, while it did not abolish slavery, set free 300 slaves and marked the rapid decline of the enslavement of Blacks in Lower Canada.

The decline in slavery was also inevitable in Upper Canada. Hill explains that slaves were not a necessary prop for the economy of eighteenth-century Upper Canada: "The Canadian climate with its short agricultural season ruled out crops such as cotton, which required cheap, plentiful labour. Besides it was expensive to keep slaves fed, clothed, and housed through a long, unproductive winter."⁸⁰ While the rights of slave-holding citizens remained intact, many of them began to set their slaves free and join the abolitionist cause; others simply set their slaves free for economic reasons. While slavery was not completely outlawed in the British Empire until 1833, Canada was now a more secure haven for American refugee slaves seeking freedom.

Prior to the Act of 1793, there was no significant movement of Blacks into Upper Canada, but from that moment on Black immigration began to increase.⁸¹ After the War of 1812, Upper Canada's Attorney General, John Beverly Robinson, declared that residence in Canada made Blacks free and that Canadian courts would therefore uphold that freedom. This gave American soldiers stationed at Fort Malden during the war great incentive and they quickly brought news home of a country that welcomed Blacks.⁸² By the 1820s, fugitive slaves were trickling into Canada, the first major wave of them coming between 1817 and 1822.⁸³ The second wave of Black immigration came when the American Congress passed the Fugitive Slave Act of 1850, making escape more dangerous and expensive. This Act brought a dramatic increase to the Black population of Upper Canada: conservative estimates suggest that 30,000 fugitives may have reached Canada between 1800 and 1860. By the 1860s, Blacks were

---

79. Alexander and Glaze, *Towards Freedom*, 52–53.
80. Hill, *Freedom-Seekers*, 18.
81. Hill, *Freedom-Seekers*, 48.
82. Hill, *Freedom-Seekers*, 48.
83. Hill, *Freedom-Seekers*, 52.

engrossed in the difficult task of setting up and developing new communities throughout Canada West.[84]

Until the late 1840s, Whites did not find the Black presence in Upper Canada to be a cause of concern: there was lots of work, civil rights were afforded them, and they were able to live in peace as law-abiding citizens. However, as their numbers increased—as was the case in Colchester County, where by 1849 they comprised about one-third of the population—Whites became increasingly alarmed.[85] In her examination of the situation, Dorothy Shadd Shreve shows that several Blacks and Whites of that era understood socio-economic concerns to be at least one cause for the growing hostility. Racist policies, such as low wages and denial of access to education (later legislated segregation), quickly developed to keep Blacks "in their place."[86]

The Church in Canada West/Upper Canada

Coincident with these events was the fact that the circumstances of the British North American churches had changed dramatically in the second decade of the nineteenth century.[87] The first was the growing wedge between the British colonies and the United States, coupled with a growing sense of identity in British North America. The second was the development of a more decisively British character, imported into Canada with the swelling numbers of Scots, Irish, English, and Welsh immigrants.[88] For the Church, those factors contributed to a strengthened evangelical movement, which continued to gather momentum through the 1840s, and blossomed in the form of full-scale evangelical coalitions. Thus, the White Protestant churches experienced a surge in growth, cooperation, and vitality at the same time more Blacks were coming into the country via the Underground Railroad.

In their discussion of the early response to this influx of destitute refugees, Terence Murphy and Roberto Perlin state, "Evangelical Protestants responded to their arrival in typically philanthropic fashion, providing material aid and launching projects to facilitate resettlement."[89] The most

---

84. Hill, *Freedom-Seekers*, 32.
85. Shreve, *AfriCanadian Church*, 26–27.
86. Shreve, *AfriCanadian Church*, 27–29.
87. Murphy and Perlin, *Concise History*, 137.
88. Murphy and Perlin, *Concise History*, 137.
89. Murphy and Perlin, *Concise History*, 180.

noteworthy of those ventures was organized by William King near Chatham in 1849. Supported by the Free Church and managed by the Elgin Association (a stock company formed especially for this purpose), the Buxton Mission provided the escaped slaves with land, education, and Christian nurture. It was an evangelical venture with religious and educational aspects supported by the Presbyterian church. A very successful brick factory and an excellent gristmill are attributed to the Mission's endeavours.[90] Other such missionary organizations did likewise as they sought to provide care for Black refugees.[91] They funded and encouraged the development of Black congregations and while most of these were Methodist or Baptist, the evangelical spirit of cooperation flourished and other denominations such as Presbyterians and Congregationalists, supported the work among them.

But with the establishment of Black congregations, several layers of problems arose. On the one hand, the philanthropists rationalized the establishment of White-supervised all-Black congregations by appealing to "the preference of Blacks for passionate sermons, hymn-singing and other expressions of spiritual religion."[92] By using this as an excuse, Shreve observes, "It could be maintained, with a clear conscience, that Blacks were unfavorably disposed towards regular services and should be encouraged to form their own churches."[93]

By way of example, consider the case of Elder Browning and William Wilkes. Wilkes, a fugitive slave who came to Amherstburg in 1818 via the Underground Railroad, started preaching and exhorting almost the moment he landed. Wilkes was later able to purchase forty acres of land and build a log meeting house on one corner of the property, where he could share the Gospel with other Blacks who had settled in the area. Hearing of his religious endeavour, a White Baptist deacon from Detroit, Francis F. Browning, decided that Wilkes should be ordained. In 1821, he and two Regular Baptist ministers formed themselves into an ecclesiastical council and ordained Elder Wilkes to the Gospel Ministry. It was then necessary to re-baptize the entire congregation to meet their Regular Baptist requirements; after all necessary procedures carried out,

---

90. Shreve, *AfriCanadian Church*, 36–37.
91. Hill, *Freedom-Seekers*, 130.
92. Shreve, *AfriCanadian Church*, 42.
93. Shreve, *AfriCanadian Church*, 42.

the congregation became the First Africa Baptist Church.[94] This type of relationship seemed helpful for the evangelical cause.

On the other hand, Shreve states, "Before 1840, individual Blacks mingled with Whites at church services. As previously stated, with the large influx of fugitive slaves in the 1840s and 1850s, however, it was obvious that White tolerance of social intercourse with their coloured neighbours, even in the presence of God, was being strained to the limit."[95] One should consider that in the early years White Protestants did not find slavery inconsistent with Christianity. For example, the Reverend John Stuart, the first chaplain of the Legislative Council of Upper Canada and the first Anglican priest in what is now Ontario, who is further noted for building the first church in what is now Kingston, Ontario, and for opening the first grammar school in Upper Canada, was himself a slaveholder.[96] As well, in 1793 the baptisms of many slave children were recorded at St. Mark's Anglican Church, Niagara.[97] As Murphy and Perlin state, "Increased numbers [of Blacks] combined with the persistence of racist attitudes in white churches, reinforced the trend towards the formation of independent Black congregations."[98]

As soon as fugitive slaves reached freedom they immediately assembled for worship.[99] Since Blacks were only accepted into White churches on very unequal terms and many philanthropic ventures failed due to poor management, corruption, or tight reigned paternalism, the trend towards the establishment of separate African Christian denominations and churches continued to develop.[100]

In Upper Canada, the history of the African Churches began with the formation of Salem Chapel in St. Catherines in 1820.[101] In 1838, the African Methodist Episcopal Church arrived from the US. In the late 1830s or early 1840s, Jesse Coleman, a fugitive slave from Baltimore, founded the African Methodist Episcopal Zion Church and, by 1854, had

---

94. Shreve, *AfriCanadian Church*, 42–43.
95. Shreve, *AfriCanadian Church*, 41.
96. Millman, "Stuart John (1740/41–1811)."
97. Hill, *Freedom-Seekers*, 127; Millman, "Stuart John (1740/41–1811)"
98. Murphy and Perlin, *Concise History*, 149.
99. Shreve, *AfriCanadian Church*, 42; Hill, *Freedom-Seekers*, 130.
100. The disappointing result of Wilberforce is an excellent example of the philanthropic-capitalistic vision gone sour. See Shreve, *AfriCanadian Church*, 32–34.
101. Murphy and Perlin, *Concise History*, 149.

five sister churches in other areas of Upper and Lower Canada.[102] Baptist and Methodist churches were predominant. At first, Black-initiated churches in Upper Canada were interracial (Colchester after 1830, Niagara in 1831, and Toronto until 1829), but few remained inter-racial past the 1840s.[103] In describing the Black churches that sprang up in the settlements, Shreve states

> The cornerstones of their communities were the religious institutions, which ministered to their spiritual needs, performed social and educational functions, and supplied most of the administrators. Religion, indeed, was fundamental to the Black experience: in slavery, it was the only consolation; in freedom, it inspired exultation and gratitude. When they were denied full participation in the regular churches, they were prepared to follow a separate path to Christian salvation.[104]

An excellent example of this separate path is the Amherstburg Regular Baptist Association, founded in October 1841. Originally, Canadian Baptist trans-congregational polity found its expression in an associational pattern which was derived from a model established by their British and American counterparts. By the 1820s, all of the Baptist churches in Upper and Canada West were associated for practical as well as theological reasons, the general purpose being the edification and comfort of associated Baptist churches.[105] According to Eugene M. Thompson, early associations, while non-legislative, were called upon to give guidance and definite settlement over a variety of topics, including church polity, discipline, and political as well as social concerns.[106] Black churches, while included in association, felt marginalized by association policies and decisions that seemed to ignore rather than edify or comfort the needs and concerns of the Black church. The first paragraph of the summons issued by Second Baptist Church of Detroit to the Black Baptist churches of Canada West is helpful for understanding their perceptions:

> Believing that the time is now come that we should form ourselves into an Association because we cannot enjoy the privileges we wish as Christians with the white churches in Canada: centuries having rolled along since our fathers were organized

102. Murphy and Perlin, *Concise History*, 180.
103. Winks, *Blacks in Canada*, 341.
104. Shreve, *AfriCanadian Church*, 38.
105. Thompson, "Status."
106. Shreve, *AfriCanadian Church*, 99.

as a church; and believing that many of our fathers have gone down to the grave not enjoying their privileges and rights in the Christian churches among the whites, we invite all the Christian churches of the same faith and order to unite with us in the great Celestial cause.[107]

Hill states that the goals of the Association were "to promote unity among Black Baptists, to exchange ideas and to meet the religious needs of Blacks that had been neglected by the white churches of the area."[108] Over the next years this Association drew up their Constitution, Rules of Order, Articles of Faith, and Covenant, elected a moderator and a treasurer, established traveling missionaries to support smaller Baptist churches and scattered settlements, advised their churches on matters such as the institution of temperance meetings, Sundays Schools and Bible classes, raised funds, and passed Bylaws.[109] By 1861, the Association had grown from the original 47 members to 1,060.

The Association, however, also experienced much difficulty. Just as the Nova Scotians were opposed when they sought to leave the hardships of life in Canada, despite not having been embraced by White congregations, so likewise paternalistic White Church leaders were offended by the seeming haughtiness of the refugees who ventured out on their own. Accordingly, states Shreve, the formation of an independent association at Amherstburg in 1841 was a matter of grave offense to the Long Point Baptist Association of Canada West, which passed a resolution in 1843 to the effect that "an Association lately formed in the Western District composed of African churches, is not recognized as being in fellowship."[110] After much hostility and maneuvering around the issues, the two Associations resolved their differences, although the Amherstburg group was shaken by much internal division in the process.

SOME THOUGHTS TOWARDS THE INTERPRETING OF CANADIAN BLACK CHURCH EXPERIENCE

To honour the essence of the Black Church in Canada, it is crucial to consciously adopt an Afrocentric lens.[111] This lens serves as a guiding

---

107. Shreve, *AfriCanadian Church*, 47.
108. Hill, *Freedom-Seekers*, 140.
109. Shreve, *AfriCanadian Church*, 47–48.
110. Shreve, *AfriCanadian Church*, 66.
111. "Africentric lens" is defined as "Promoting the cultural, social and historical

principle for identifying the sources of interpretive themes that actively celebrate the cultural, social, and historical contributions of individuals with African heritage. Additionally, it ensures the acknowledgement of the persistent legacy of anti-Black racism, while cultivating a dynamic environment that fosters the pursuit of reparations. It is from this vantage point that we can delve into the following questions: First, where do these interpretive themes originate? Secondly, how do they support and highlight the rich cultural, social, and historical contributions of people of African heritage? Thirdly, in what ways do they acknowledge and address the ongoing impact of anti-Black racism? Fourthly, how can these interpretive themes provide space for the type of comprehensive analysis needed to foster the achievement of reparations? For the answers to these questions, we must go to what I propose as the primary source of Canadian Black Church empowerment—the biblical story. In doing so, the perspective of James Cone is helpful:

> The theme of liberation expressed in story-form is the essence of black religion. Both the content and form were essentially determined by black people's social existence . . . When Christianity was taught to them and they began to read the Bible, blacks simply appropriated those biblical stories that met their historical need. This is why some themes are stressed and others are overlooked . . . They did not debate religion on an abstract theological level but lived their religion concretely in history.[112]

This *lived religion* was curated within the Black space of the Church, outside of the controls of, and in opposition to White supremacy and the accompanying practices of multiple oppressions. Simply put, the appropriation of biblical story and in turn, relevant biblical symbols empowered the implicit and explicit tools of resistance inherent to the Black Church in Canada. Let us briefly examine some of these.

Egypt

What did Egypt mean to the Black Church? In the context of this survey, it had more than one meaning. When used on its own, Egypt was used to

---

contributions of people of African heritage, recognizing the ongoing legacy of anti-Black racism, and providing spaces to work towards achieving reparations" as noted in "By-law Considerations and Operational Factors," January 31, 2023, DownTheMarsh Community Land Trust, Truro, Nova Scotia.

112. Cone, "Story Context," 144.

symbolize enslavement and captivity described in the biblical text (Exod 1:11–14; 3:7; 5:1). In view of the atrocities of the Trans-Atlantic slave trade and their lived experiences in colonial Canada, Egypt was raised as a symbol of oppression from which one must be delivered or escape from and the Pharaoh of Egypt representative of the seat of power situated in the midst of an evil, unjust system. The enslavement of the Hebrews in Egypt was akin to the slavery of Blacks throughout the Americas and became a vocalization of the emancipation struggle.

The Black experience in New France is particularly relevant to this theme. It is ironic that some historians describe Roman Catholic influenced slavery as the most humane, yet clearly no significant Black Church movement in Canada rose out of the so-called humane and familial traits of that slave-holding system. In a sense, remaining stuck within the domain of Egypt is tantamount to being suppressed. For there to be any freedom of religious expression, it seems there needed to be some sort of escape.

Egypt and Ethiopia

In the early Canadian Black Church experience, an interesting shift occurred when the scriptural pairing of Egypt and Ethiopia were expounded upon (Ps 68:1). A new hermeneutic of identity, empowerment, and even separation from the European and the Continental African "other" was utilized to disconnect Egypt from the symbolism of enslavement. This transformative motif is particularly evident in the minutes of the African United Baptist Association (AUBA), established in 1854 with the aim of connecting Black Baptist churches throughout Nova Scotia. Under the visionary leadership of Rev. Richard Preston, these minutes provide substantial evidence of the identity and empowerment that were fostered within this context. Passed down through an oral tradition that can be traced even today, the appropriation of scripture to root the community's identity in Africa as Motherland and to lift such, as a scriptural place of honour despite their prevailing experience in Canadian society, is woven throughout preaching and decision-making practices, setting Nova Scotian Blacks apart from their oppressors and clearly placing their destiny in the hands of "God who rules Nations and governs Empires."[113] Heroes and Sheroes such as Ebed-melech the Ethiopian who rescues the prophet Jeremiah (Jer 38:7–13), the Queen of Sheba (2 Chr 9:8; 1 Kgs

---

113. Minutes of the Eighth Session (1861), 7.

10:9), the Ethiopian Eunuch (Acts 8:26–40), and any other biblical texts that confirmed the wisdom, prosperity and significance of the African kingdoms in God's salvific story long before the appearance of European missionizers were employed to affirm the Black Church's responsibility to reclaim the rightful position of its people.

Exodus, Promised Land, and Diaspora

In the Canadian Black church experience, three closely related themes emerge, whether expressed implicitly or explicitly. These themes include the sense of leaving one place to go somewhere else, the experience of claiming a home but never truly feeling at home, and the realities of a dispersed community. These themes are intricately interwoven with the migration experience of Black individuals escaping American enslavement and seeking refuge in Canada. Regardless of where they settled in Nova Scotia or Canada West, Blacks faced specific conditions and geographical circumstances that were shaped by powerful relationships and institutions. Consequently, all efforts aimed at self-actualization, arising from the exodus to Canada, were strongly centred around achieving social justice and uplifting the race through various means.

An examination of various resolutions in The Minutes and Proceedings of the General Convention for the Improvement of the Coloured Inhabitants of Canada (1853) provides a clear demonstration of the hopes associated with Canada:

> Canada is the first place that presents itself to our consideration. Here is the Asylum of the Refugees from American Slavery, and here the impartial laws of Great Britain have full sway. Here is a vast unoccupied area of soil, equal to the best Agricultural lands in the Western States of the American Union, and here are plenty of irrigating and navigable streams . . . Here we can literally hang as a threatening black cloud over the American Union, waiting and praying for the Lord's day of vengeance, when we may be the humble instruments of his hands, to do the terrible work, of his settling, for centuries of oppression, wrong and blasphemy . . . it is these things that make Canada a more beautiful country to the refugee from the plains of Carolina then the sunny home where he has left his chains, and though are goodly heritage here was as cold and Bleak as the rugged hills of Greenland, these considerations above would render it as pleasant to the mind as the sunny clime of delightful Italy. But we can thank God, that our Province is no unhospitable place. A

pleasant temperate climate, and a fertile soil invites the honest toiler to abundant rewards.[114]

Here we see the sincere hope for Canada as a refuge from enslavement; a land of milk and honey, and a place where with hard work anyone should be able to thrive. However, according to DeRose, Hannah, Hepburn, and Nagy, this was not the case: "On the surface, life appeared to be much better in Canada; however, this newfound freedom had limits. Although slaves were granted freedom in Canada, they still faced racism, oppression, and segregation. Over time these sentiments pushed blacks away from Canada."[115] After the abolition of slavery in America (1863), a second exodus occurred with about two thirds of the Black refugees in Canada returning home to the United States, having experienced life in Canada, and concluding that they could achieve more there.

An analysis of the earlier experience of the Nova Scotian Blacks reveals a common pattern of a second exodus resulting from the inherent tension between the concepts of exodus, promised land, and diaspora. Black church leaders, in their quest to address the needs of their own people and liberate themselves from structural oppression, made the choice to separate and embark on a journey of empowerment. For instance, in 1792, when several influential Black Christian preachers and leaders departed for Sierra Leone, the Canadian church missed out on the invaluable resource of their leadership. This departure marked a significant exodus from the mainstream, symbolizing their commitment to forging their own path.

An examination of the current growth (or decline) of all-Black churches in Canada, as well as those of many other ethnic groups, compels us to ask some difficult questions. Are people of colour still or once again experiencing the exclusionary attitudes and practices encountered when Blacks first attempted to join mainstream churches in the early days of our common history? What other factors may be at work? Do people of colour truly feel welcomed and embraced, or are they simply passing time in mainstream churches, waiting for a real home? As we seek to live out God's will in this nation, historians must point out the signposts from the past along the way, the aforementioned themes, whether named or unnamed, implicit or explicit, can be useful in helping evaluate the way Black Canadian history has been framed. Moreover, these themes possess

---

114. Minutes and Proceedings, 13–14.
115. "To Canada and Back Again"

the potential to hold individuals, organizations, and communities accountable, provide empowerment, and foster an Africentric perspective regarding the role and mission of the Black Baptist Church in Canada. Such insights can be instrumental in navigating future study of the Black Church in Canada.

BIBLIOGRAPHY

Primary Sources

Archives

Minutes of the Eighth Session of the African Baptist Association of Nova Scotia, 1861, 1872.

Minutes and Proceedings of the General Convention for the Improvement of the Coloured Inhabitants in Canada, 1853.

Monographs

MacKerrow, P. E. *A Brief History of the Coloured Baptists of Nova Scotia and their First Organization as Churches A. D. 1832*. Halifax, NS: Nova Scotia Printing Company, 1895.

Secondary Sources

Alexander, Ken, and Avis Glaze. *Towards Freedom: The African-Canadian Experience*. Toronto: Umbrella, 1996.

Bell, D. G. *Henry Alline and Maritime Religion*. Historical Booklet 51. Ottawa: Canadian Historical Association, 1993.

Benchetrit, Jenna. "Wave of Black Studies Programs at Canadian Universities, a Long Time Coming, Scholars Say." *CBC News*, October 31, 2021. No pages. Online: https://www.cbc.ca/news/canada/new-black-studies-curriculums-1.6229321.

Brand, Dionne. *A Map to the Door of No Return: Notes to Belonging*. Toronto: Doubleday, 2001.

Bristow, Peggy, ed. *We're Rooted Here and They Can't Pull Us Up: Essays in African Canadian Woman's History*. Toronto: University of Toronto Press, 1994.

Brown, Wallace, and Hereward Senior. *Victorious in Defeat: The Loyalists in Canada*. Toronto: Methuen, 1984.

Campbell, Mavis S. *Back to Africa: George Ross and the Maroons from Nova Scotia to Sierra Leone*. Trenton, NJ: Africa World, 1993.

Cooper, Afua. *The Hanging of Angélique: The Untold Story of Canadian Slavery and the Burning of Old Montréal*. Toronto: HarperCollins, 2006.

Christensen, Carole Pigler, and Morton Weinfeld. "The Black Family in Canada: A Preliminary Exploration of Family Patterns and Inequality." *Canadian Ethnic Studies* 25 (1993) 26–44.

Cone, James H. "The Story Context of Black Theology." *Theology Today* 32 (1975) 144–50.

"Enslavement of Indigenous People in Canada." *The Canadian Encyclopedia.* No pages. Online: https://www.thecanadianencyclopedia.ca/en/article/slavery-of-indigenous-people-in-canada.

Evans, Curtis J. *The Burden of Black Religion.* Oxford: Oxford University Press, 2008.

Floyd-Thomas, Stacey, et al. *Black Church Studies: An Introduction.* Nashville: Abingdon, 2007.

"Freedom and Resistance: Laurier Researcher Carol Duncan on the History of Black Churches in Canada." *Laurier* (February 22, 2021). No pages. Online: https://www.wlu.ca/news/spotlights/2021/feb/freedom-and-resistance-laurier-sociologist-carol-duncan-on-the-history-of-black-churches-in-canada.html.

Gillard, Denise. "The Black Church in Canada." *McMaster Journal of Theology and Ministry* (1998). No pages. Online: http://cblte.org/mjtm/1-5.htm.

Gordon, Grant. *From Slavery to Freedom: The Life of David George, Pioneer Black Baptist Minister.* Hantsport, NS: Lancelot, 1992.

Hill, Daniel G. *The Freedom-Seekers: Blacks in Early Canada.* Toronto: Stoddard, 1992.

Lodoen, Shannon. "The Myths That Make Us: An Examination of Canadian National Identity." MA thesis, University of Western Ontario, 2019.

McCormick, Ronald K. *Faith Freedom and Democracy: The Baptists in Atlantic Canada.* Tantallon, NS: Four East, 1993.

Millman, T. R. "Stuart John (1740/41–1811)." *Dictionary of Canadian Biography.* No pages. Online: http://www.biographi.ca/en/bio/stuart_john_1740_41_1811_5E.html.

Mothe, Gordon de La. *Reconstructing the Black Image.* London: Trentham, 1993.

Murphy, Terence, and Roberto Perlin. *A Concise History of Christianity in Canada.* Toronto: Oxford University Press, 1996.

Niven, Laird. *Birchtown Archaelogical Survey (1993): The Black Loyalist Settlement of Shelburne County, Nova Scotia, Canada.* Lockerport, NS: Roseway, 1994.

Pachai, Bridglal. *Beneath the Clouds of the Promised Land: The Survival of Nova Scotia's Blacks. Volume II: 1800–1989.* Hantsport, NS: Lancelot, 1990.

Shreve, Dorothy S. *The AfriCanadian Church: A Stabilizer.* Jordan Station, ON: Paideia, 1983.

Thompson, Eugene M., et al. "The Status of Transcongregational Polity." In *Canadian Baptist History and Polity: The McMaster Conference*, edited by Murray J. S. Ford, 83–107. Hamilton, ON: McMaster Divinity College, 1983.

Thomson, Colin A. *Blacks in Deep Snow: Black Pioneers in Canada.* Don Mills, ON: J. M. Dent and Sons, 1979.

"To Canada and Back Again: Immigration from the United States on the Underground Railroad (1840–1860)," *Canadian Museum of Immigration at Pier 21.* No pages. Online: https://pier21.ca/research/immigration-history/immigration-from-united-states-on-underground-railroad.

Tulloch, Headley. *Black Canadians: A Long Line of Fighters.* Toronto: NC, 1975.

Vachon, André "Marie-Joseph-Angélique." *Dictionary of Canadian Biography.* No pages. Online: http://www.biographi.ca/en/bio/marie_joseph_angelique_2E.html.

Wetmore, Donald, and Lester B. Sellick, eds. *Loyalist in Nova Scotia.* Hantsport, NS: Lancelot, 1983.

Winks, Robin. *The Blacks in Canada: A History.* 2nd ed. Montreal: McGill University Press, 1997.

Wilson, Ellen Gibson. *The Loyal Blacks: The Definitive Account of the First American Blacks Emancipated in the Revolution, their Return to Africa and their Creation of a New Society There.* New York: Capricorn, 1976.

3

The Underground Railroad and its Intersection with the Black Baptist Church in Upper Canada

Dudley A. Brown

When Georgia native John Henry Jackson came to Toronto in 1960 (to become the quarterback of the Toronto Argonauts), he and his Argo teammate Dave Mann longed for the food of home.[1] What was referred to as *soul food* was cooking born of necessity in the days of slavery; during that period of human bondage, Blacks crafted a homegrown cuisine out of the discards of the plantation master's kitchen—this type of fare was not served at any restaurants in Toronto.[2] In an attempt to amend the situation, Jackson and Mann opened Canada's first *soul food* restaurant—they named it *The Underground Railroad*. Lit by antique-style railroad lanterns, the co-owners sought to recreate the type of wayside hideaway where escaped slaves took refuge on their journey

---

1. It is interesting to note that Jackson (an American) came to Canada to play quarterback (CFL) because the professional league in his native United States (NFL) did not allow Blacks to play quarterback.

2. Sadlier, "BLACK IN TORONTO," para. 6; Plummer, "Historicist," para. 7; open in early 1969, The Underground Railroad became one of the city's best-known and popular restaurants for over 20 years. Locals took out-of-town guests to rub elbows with professional athletes and celebrities from Harry Belafonte to Magic Johnson; Salsberg, "Spice Up your Eating," para. 2–4.

north;³ it was said, "You could not be Black in Toronto and not know of The Underground Railroad Restaurant."⁴ The restaurant was a comfortable introduction to a historical reality most were aware of but few fully understood—Black or White.⁵

The saga of the Underground Railroad looms large in the national Canadian consciousness and identity. Canada views itself, especially when juxtaposed with the United States, as a bastion of freedom for fugitive slaves and free Blacks looking to preserve their liberty. This national identity rests largely on Canada being one of the primary destinations on the Railroad. In fact, there are two Underground Railroads, the legend and a factual history that has yet to be fully realized. For most people today—as for those in the 1830s and 1850s—the phrase Underground Railroad conjured images of "trapdoors, flickering lanterns, and moonlit pathways through the woods."⁶ The real Underground Railroad was neither a quaint eatery in Toronto, nor was it underground, or an actual railroad; the metaphor described a coordinated system of civil disobedience directed and supported by thousands of people committed to what they saw as a just cause.⁷ The Black fugitives that rode the railway brought with them the one institution that was truly theirs, the Black church. To determine the relationship between the Black Baptist church and the Underground Railroad, one must attempt to separate fact from legend. This chapter will use the histories of the Underground Railroad and the Black Baptist church to discover how they intersected in Upper Canada. This will not be an exhaustive list of churches or the entire story of the Railroad, but it will highlight those towns and churches that played a significant role in the Underground Railroad saga in Upper Canada. Let us begin with a brief introduction to the Black Baptist church in North America.

Birthed in the woods of the American slave south by a race of people desperate for hope,⁸ the Black church became the most important

---

3. Plummer, "Historicist," para. 7; Sadlier, "BLACK IN TORONTO," para. 3.

4. Sadlier, "BLACK IN TORONTO," para. 1; Plummer, "Historicist," para. para 2, 7.

5. Plummer, "Historicist," para. 7; Sadlier, "BLACK IN TORONTO," para. 3.

6. Goodheart, "Secret History," para. 6; Bordewich, *Bound for Canaan*, 4.

7. Foner, *Freedom*, 15; Malaspina, *Underground Railroad*, 5; Bordewich, *Bound for Canaan*, 4.

8. Hicks, *Images*, 27–28; Cone, *Black Power and Black Theology*, 95; Montgomery, *Under their Own Vine and Fig Tree*, 33–34; it was a result of the merger of the slaves' *invisible institution* of the South and the free Black church of the North.

institution in the Black community; it provided spiritual care, education, and the social and economic organizations necessary for building new communities.[9] The Great Awakenings of the eighteenth and nineteenth centuries opened American Protestantism to the African American slave by shifting the emphasis of the church from human impotence to human possibility for redemption.[10] In the British colony of Upper Canada, the Anglicans, Methodists, and Baptists initially allowed Blacks to worship within their confines but they did not permit them to mingle with the White congregants.[11] Through immigration, accessing vehicles like the Underground Railroad, the number of Blacks in White churches steadily increased; in time, this became problematic resulting in Blacks being asked to leave and gather in their own homes—this scenario was played out in nearly all "integrated" parts of Upper Canada irrespective of denomination. Having developed an affinity for the pneumatological focus of the Baptist faith[12] and benefiting from its congregational independence,[13] the newly banished would create a Black Baptist church in Upper Canada—and the Underground Railroad played a crucial role in its growth.

THE UNDERGROUND RAILROAD: ORIGINS

The appellation "Underground Railroad" did not exist in 1838—it is unclear exactly when the name originated. One account attributes its first use to an article in a Washington newspaper (in 1839) quoting a young slave who said he hoped to escape on a railroad that "went underground all the way to Boston."[14] Another account stems from the bewilderment of the pursuers of an escaped slave; upon losing the whereabouts

---

9. Gillard, "Black Church in Canada"; Cousineau, "First Baptist Church," 8.

10. Montgomery, *Under their Own Vine and Fig Tree*, 19; Glenn, "Negro Religion," 629.

11. Gillard, "Black Church in Canada"; Walker, *Loyalists*, 67; a special gallery was constructed in St. Paul's Church to confine the Blacks during worship services; Heike, "Out of Chatham," 175–77; Roger Hepburn, *Crossing the Border*, 1–3.

12. Huggins, *Black Odyssey*, 72–73; Glenn, "Negro Religion," 629; Montgomery, *Under their Own Vine and Fig Tree*, 14.

13. MacKerrow, *Brief History*, 8–14; Walker, *Loyalists*, 74; Clifford, *From Slavery to Freetown*, 21; George, "Life," 475–76; Davidson, *Birchtown*, 65; this independence provided autonomy to a people desiring freedom, equality, local democracy, and participation in the affairs of their church.

14. Smedley, *History*, 35; Walters, *Underground Railroad*, viii; Foner, *Freedom*, 6.

of their quarry, they declared, "there must be an underground railroad somewhere."[15] Still another story believes the name was coined following the arrival of the steam-powered locomotives in the United States.[16] The speed of railroads during the 1830s revolutionized travel across the United States and Canada; it is this speed that was thought to have inspired the term "Underground Railroad." The most common story about the name revolves around a fugitive slave named Tice Davids; pursued by his master, Davids took to the river and swam across disappearing so quickly that his astonished master was supposed to have said that Davids must have "gone off on an underground road." The retelling of this tale turned the "underground road" into the "Underground Railroad" and the name was born.[17] No matter its origin, the name soon became ubiquitous; in 1842, an Albany abolitionist newspaper reported that twenty-six fugitives had passed through the city "all by the underground railroad."[18] By 1853, the *New York Times* observed that the Underground Railroad had "come into very general use to describe the organized arrangements made in various sections of the country to aid fugitives from slavery."[19]

Most North Americans understand that this aid came via a vast, highly structured, and tightly coordinated network of hidden passages and safe houses that extended deep into the slave states and terminated in the free northern states and Canada—with selfless White Railroad workers helping vulnerable Blacks. This was not the whole truth. Regarding the Railroad workers, it failed to speak to the contributions of the Black Church, the Black community, and the fugitives' who rode the Railroad;[20] it also failed to mention that its coordination varied by necessity and that its tracts rarely if ever extended into the slave states. Furthermore, scholars, like Eric Foner and Kerry Walters, believe it is more accurate to think

15. Smedley, *History*, 35; Walters, *Underground Railroad*, viii; Foner, *Freedom*, 6.

16. Smedley, *History*, 35; Walters, *Underground Railroad*, viii; Foner, *Freedom*, 6; Gara, *Liberty Line*, 45; Gillard, "History"; Roger Hepburn, *Crossing the Border*, 1–3.

17. Walters, *Underground Railroad*, 5; Foner, *Gateway to Freedom*, 6; Gara, *Liberty Line*, 45.

18. Walters, *Underground Railroad*, 5; Foner, *Gateway to Freedom*, 6; Gara, *Liberty Line*, 45.

19. Walters, *Underground Railroad*, 5; Foner, *Gateway to Freedom*, 6; Gara, *Liberty Line*, 45.

20. Foner, *Gateway to Freedom*, 6, 11–13; Gara, *Liberty Line*, 9; Walters, *Underground Railroad*, 4–5; the adept nomenclature of the Railroad undoubtedly contributed to the perception that the system was centralized, nationwide, and precisely mapped out.

of the Underground Railroad in terms of function rather than organization; it should be understood not as a single entity but as an umbrella term for local groups that employed a wide range of techniques to assist fugitives slaves in escaping the *slave* South and protecting them once they were in the *free* North. It was less like the Internet and more cell-like in structure.[21]

As to its management, the Underground Railroad could be a well-coordinated enterprise in some places and a loosely linked chain of individuals in another. Participants in the work came and went, as did techniques; by necessity, there was adaptability because the railroad and its worker could not afford to be settled on a specific route or safe house to stay ahead of law enforcement or slave catchers. Although its origins remain unknown, what is unquestioned is that the Underground Railroad was up and running in the three decades before the Civil War—paralleling the emergence of the abolitionist movement and the *Fugitive Slave Act of 1850*.[22] Like the real railroad, the metaphorical variety had termini—it is at this juncture that it would intersect with the Black Baptist church. During the eighteen and nineteenth centuries, African Canadian and African American Baptists traditionally held reciprocal relationships; both communities transcended territorial borders, physically and ideologically, to develop a collective identity that coalesced around the shared struggle for freedom and equality rather than state and country.[23] When the northern states introduced restrictive regulations and laws in the 1830s and 1840s, many fugitive and free Blacks left for the province

---

21. Bordewich, *Bound for Canaan*, 5; Foner, *Gateway to Freedom*, 15; Walters, *Underground Railroad*, 4; Gara, *Liberty Line*, 9; defining the Underground Railroad in this manner makes it difficult to determine a definitive date for its origin since slaves were assisted in their escape from bondage since the earliest days of slavery in North America.

22. Walters, *Underground Railroad*, 4, 56–57, 64; Gara, *Liberty Line*, 93, 97; Foner, *Gateway to Freedom*, 21; there were two main land routes, one east and one west of the Appalachian Mountains; additionally, major water routs included Ohio, Missouri, Illinois, and the Mississippi rivers. A few of the more famous stationmasters were William Still of Philadelphia, Thomas Garrett of Delaware, Jacob R. Gibbs, John Rankin of Ohio, and Levi Coffin of Indiana.

23. Amherstburg Baptist Association (ABA) Minutes (October 8, 1841), 1–2; the Amherstburg Baptist Association (ABA) contained both American (Second Baptist Detroit) and Canadian Black Baptist churches. In 1841, the Association was named Amherstburg Baptist Association (ABA). In 1857, it was called Amherstburg Antislavery Regular Baptist Association (AARBA). Finally, in 1861, the name changed to Amherstburg Regular Missionary Baptist Association (ARMBA).

of Canada via the Underground Railroad—they brought with them the Black Baptist church.[24]

TERMINUS: COLCHESTER, TORONTO, ST. CATHARINES, AND HAMILTON STATIONS

Towns like Colchester, Upper Canada, spawned Black communities and Baptist churches due to their vicinity to terminals on the Underground Railroad. Possessed of fertile land that was easily accessible, the town of Colchester made it comparatively easy for freedom seekers to come directly from terminals of the Underground Railroad that were along the shores of Ohio or by way of Amherstburg. Elder William Wilks was one such freedom seeker. Initially unordained, Wilks ministered to and built a log cabin that served as a house of worship for former slaves who had taken up residence in Colchester. Wilks later obtained his ordination in Colchester and, on the first Friday of October 1821, he founded the First Africa Baptist Church of Colchester—likely the first Black Baptist church in Canada, they joined the Amherstburg Baptist Association (ABA) in 1847.[25]

Further east, Blacks in Toronto (then York) were composed of descendants of slaves of British Nationals, White Loyalist settlers, and West Indians from the Caribbean but the majority were made up of immigrants from the United States—both fugitive slaves from the American South and Northern free Blacks of means wishing to preserve their freedom.[26] Toronto was the safest city in the safest colony from a fugitive slave and free Black perspective; its distance from the border and its role as the business and cultural capital of the colonies made it a natural terminus on the Underground Railroad. In 1825, Washington Christian came to Toronto to serve among his Black brothers and sisters; a former Virginia slave, he and twelve other former slaves, after they were not welcomed in

---

24. Robinson, *Race*, 26, 28; Lewis, "Fugitive," 126; these 'Black Codes' limited Black employment, education, housing, and political engagement; Drew, *Refugee*, 244.

25. ABA Minutes, 21–22 September 1842, 1–2; Shadd, "Extending the Right Hand of Fellowship," 121; Elder Wilks is considered the first ordained Black man in Canada; ABA Minutes, 20 August 1847, 51; Sheffield, "Background," 47.

26. Shadd et al., *Underground Railroad*, 2–3.

the White church, decided to get together to worship[27]—they established the First Baptist Church of Toronto.[28]

Like Toronto, St. Catharines and Hamilton would also see Rev. Christian establish a Black Baptist congregation composed of fugitive slaves from the Underground Railroad.[29] He established the Baptist cause in St. Catharines on March 22, 1838. Still living in Toronto, Christian was thought to have established the Baptist church in Hamilton (between 1837 and 1838) on his way back and forth from St. Catharines—the principal conduit of Harriet Tubman's activities in Canada. In 1847, the Baptist Church in Hamilton sought admission into the ABA under the leadership of Elder A. Brown and thirty-six members. The early years of Zion Baptist Church in St. Catharines saw it affiliate itself with the Niagara Association until 1881 when, with its twenty-five members, it became a part of the ABA.[30] Many of the small Black settlements that were established in Upper Canada (by 1841 Canada West) spawned Black Baptist churches that became active in the Underground Railroad saga—some, like the First Baptist Church of Amherstburg, were the result of the town being a primary terminus on the Underground Railroad.[31]

TERMINUS: AMHERSTBURG STATION

The great abolitionist, Levi Coffin, wrote of Amherstburg, "this was the great landing point, the principal terminus of the Underground Railroad to the west."[32] So prominent is Amherstburg in the fugitive slave saga that in Harriet Beecher Stowe's novel, *Uncle Tom's Cabin*, two of the main

---

27. ABA Minutes, 21–22 September 1842, 3; Haldimand Baptist Association Minutes (1837), 5; Haldimand Baptist Association Minutes (1841), 67–68; Duncan, "'Out of the Bitter Sea,'" 241.

28. Shadd et al., *Underground Railroad*, 2–3; Toronto quickly developed a Black middle class; Walters, *Underground Railroad*, 105–6; Lewis, "Fugitive," 30.

29. Amherstburg Baptist Association (ABA) Minutes (September 21–22, 1842), 4; Shreve, *Pathfinders*, 95; Lewis, "Fugitive," 46, 49; these cities were the northern point of destination for the eastern section of the Underground Railroad. This is based upon the fact that all the letters published in William Still's book are from these three locations.

30. Hill, *Freedom-Seekers*, 39; Amherstburg Baptist Association (ABA) Minutes (September 21–22, 1842), 4; Amherstburg Baptist Association (ABA) Minutes (August 20, 1847), 51; Haldimand Baptist Association Minutes (1841), 68.

31. Calarco et al., *Places of the Underground Railroad*, 259; Cousineau, "First Baptist Church," 3; Robinson, *Race*, 28.

32. Coffin, *Reminiscences*, 249–50; Cousineau, "First Baptist Church," 7.

characters start their new lives as freemen in Amherstburg.³³ Blacks in Amherstburg go as far back as 1817 when Captain Charles Stuart, an ardent abolitionist, reports that 150 fugitive slaves entered Amherstburg between 1817 and 1822; very little is known about the ex-slaves between that time and 1838 but by the mid-1840s this congregation of Blacks desired a formal place of worship.³⁴ Among the fugitives was a young, energetic, and charismatic Anthony Binga. Pastor Binga began to preach, without formal ordination, about a year after he arrived in Amherstburg.³⁵ Local tradition dates the beginnings of the First Baptist Church to between 1836 and 1838. For a decade, the congregation met in the homes of congregants as church construction is and was an expensive endeavour—so much so for the once enslaved. Counting only nineteen members in 1841, pastor Binga set out to raise funds for the construction of the church by taking the role of an itinerant preacher. He travelled throughout Canada West in the hope of soliciting funds to help build the church—a goal he reached on December 21, 1849.³⁶

By 1841, Black colonies were scattered throughout the area bordered by Toronto, Niagara Falls, and Windsor; consequently, Black Baptist churches were springing up spontaneously. Since most of the Black immigrants entered through the Amherstburg area, especially in the early and formative years of migration, it was natural for its Black inhabitants to feel responsible for their welfare. They aided thousands who passed through their confines. The Amherstburg First Baptist Church recognized its responsibility, and, seeing the need for a closer fellowship among the scattered churches, many of which were small and in need of aid, sought a form of organization so that Baptists in the area might be properly prepared to serve the ever-increasing number of fugitives. To meet this growing need, meetings were held on October 8, 1841 at the home of John Liberty in Amherstburg to organize an association of

---

33. Beecher Stowe, *Uncle Tom's Cabin*, 351–52.

34. Lewis, "Fugitive," 53; taken from the original deed on file in the Fort Malden Museum, Amherstburg; Cousineau, "First Baptist Church," 5, 8; Landon, "Amherstburg," 2.

35. Cousineau, "First Baptist Church," 8, 9; Shreve, *Pathfinders*, 4; Lewis, "Fugitive," 53; Bibb, *Fugitive*; Schadd, *Freeman*; the church evolved from a mission set up by the White Presbyterian minister Isaac J. Rice, however, Mary Ann Schadd and Henry Bibb both wrote about the prosaic act of Blacks being pushed out of White churches—in the Amherstburg case it was done by minister Isaac J. Rice.

36. Amherstburg Baptist Association (ABA) Minutes (September 21–22, 1842), 5; Shreve, *Pathfinders*, 4; Cousineau, "First Baptist Church," 9.

Black Baptist churches—this was the origin of the Amherstburg Baptist Association (ABA).[37] As a principal stop on the Underground Railroad, Binga and the First Baptist Amherstburg church continued to aid and welcome fugitive slaves—the Black church/community, and the fugitives themselves, became very active workers on the Railroad.[38]

THE UNDERGROUND RAILROAD: STAFF

Initially, the work of the Underground Railroad was thought to be controlled by White abolitionists—Whites wrote most accounts (often making themselves the central character), contemporaneous or later, and often emphasized, even if unintentionally, White involvement leaving out Black contributions.[39] The once enslaved often stated that "I escaped without the aid . . . of any human being," the activist minister James W. C. Pennington wrote in 1855, "Like a man, I have emancipated myself."[40] Historians are beginning to appreciate the significant partnership between the Black Baptist church and the Underground Railroad. Numerous stationmasters and conductors were Black and the Black church and community created organizations for the general welfare of the newly free.[41] Once in the North, fugitive slaves were not only assisted by White

---

37. ABA Minutes, 21–22 September 1842, 1–5; ABA Minutes, 4–5 September 1851, 113.

38. Cousineau, "First Baptist Church," 4; it became the mother church of the ABA (later Amherstburg Regular Missionary Baptist Association, ARMBA); Walters, *Underground Railroad*, 108; the newly arrived fugitive needed aid that came from generous abolitionists and Railroad supporters back in the U.S.—usually through churches, abolitionist societies, and private individuals. The practice of soliciting funds created a controversy between two rival Black newspapers, Henry Bibb's *Voice of the Fugitive* and Mary Ann Shadd's *Provincial Freeman* (the first Black newspaper in Upper Canada); the latter believed that the solicitation of funds from White philanthropists would both perpetuate Black servility and feed into the bias that Blacks were incapable of taking care of themselves.

39. Foner, *Gateway to Freedom*, 11–14, 3–7; Gara, *Liberty Line*, 98; Goodheart, "Secret History," para. 6–7; a generation after the Civil War, one historian (White) interviewed surviving abolitionists (most of them White) and described a "great and intricate network" of agents, 3, 211 of whom he identified by name (nearly all of them White).

40. Foner, *Gateway to Freedom*, 19; Gara, *Liberty Line*, 18, 42; LaRoche, *Free Black Communities*, 138.

41. Foner, *Gateway to Freedom*, 5, 13; Walters, *Underground Railroad*, 6, 9; many ex-slaves were active in Northern abolitionist societies and were some of the most daring and dedicated Railroad agents.

Railroad agents but by Black residents; most escapes could not have been successful without the support of the Black communities and churches. However, the greatest credit for successful escape should go to the fugitives themselves.[42] It would be wrong to assume that freedom seekers could not succeed without the Railroad; in fact, knowledge of the Underground Railroad was not often known to the fugitive and was available only after the most difficult and dangerous part of the journey was accomplished.[43] To make it to a free state and access the Underground Railroad, fugitive slaves had to rely on their initiative, ingenuity, and courage. These slaves had to plan their escape, evade slave patrols and slave catchers, avoid illness and accidents, and stave off hunger and exposure all the while navigating to safe harbour with only the North Star as a guide. Under these extraordinary circumstances, it is a wonder that 1,000 to 2,000 slaves manage to escape each year in the three decades leading up to the Civil War—many others tried and failed.[44] Again, one of the first things those successful freedom seekers would do was build churches like the First Baptist Churches of Sandwich, Windsor, and Chatham.[45]

TERMINI: SANDWICH, WINDSOR, AND CHATHAM STATIONS

Located on the Detroit River, about two miles west of Windsor, the town of Sandwich was an active transit hub for fugitive slaves riding the Railroad; those that stayed in "this beautiful and quiet town" found its good soil and proximity to the city of Detroit ideal for the business of market gardening.[46] In 1840, a group of fugitive slaves met at the foot of Huron Line Road where they hewed logs from which to build a cabin to serve as a place of worship—this was the general pattern for the origin of the Black Baptist church; i.e., it often began with outdoor prayer meetings (harkening back to the *invisible institution*) and then moved to the homes

---

42. Foner, *Gateway to Freedom*, 18; Gara, *Liberty Line*, 18; Malaspian, *Railroad*, 6.

43. Foner, *Gateway to Freedom*, 19; Gara, *Liberty Line*, 18, 42, 61.

44. Walters, *Underground Railroad*, 6; Foner, *Gateway to Freedom*, 5, 13; Bakan, "Reconsidering," 6.

45. Hill, *Freedom-Seekers*, 130.

46. Lewis, "Religious Life of Fugitive Slaves," 62–63; Drew, *Refugee*, 341; ABA Minutes, 21–22 September 1842, 4; Mitchell, *Underground Railroad*, 151; geography and economics were the principal determining factors in the creation of communities—this included distance from the border and slave catchers, rich soil for farming, and proximity to economic centres.

of the different parishioners. At its inception, Sandwich First Baptist Church had eleven members in its congregation; by August 1, 1851, its first reverend, Madison J. Lightfoot, saw to the needs of twenty-three congregants in a new brick building.[47] To the east, in Windsor, the seeds of the Baptist church had not yet germinated.

Windsor, Ontario, was the most accessible place of refuge to thousands of fugitives fleeing bondage—beginning before 1803 but seeing a deluge by 1851. Slaves could stand on the shores of Detroit and almost see their exiled brothers and sisters beckoning them across the river.[48] Many did not stay in Windsor but, like Amherstburg and Sandwich, would stay for rehabilitation before moving further from the border. The Rev. William Mitchell, while visiting Windsor between 1858 and 1859, reported that a population of 2,500 contained seven to eight hundred members of the Black community. Despite the Black population, the Baptist church took some time to take root—only a Black Methodist church existed in 1851. Local tradition has Rev. William Troy journeying to Windsor for a brief ministry—while still the minister at Amherstburg—where he held prayer meetings and services among the unorganized Baptist people of Windsor. Seeing the potential of the growing Baptist movement in Windsor, Troy left his post at Amherstburg to give his full attention to the new church—the First Baptist Church of Windsor sought admittance into the ABA in 1856.[49]

By 1832, Blacks had made their way to Chatham via the Thames River tracks of the Underground Railroad. The extent of the fugitive slave migration caused Blacks to become one-third of the city's population by 1856. This large Black population resulted in the establishment of three Black Baptist churches in Chatham before 1856—Union Baptist, Second Baptist, and First Baptist Church. These three churches would eventually merge in 1856 under the leadership of Rev. Richard Duling—using the First Baptist building and taking the name First Baptist Church Congregation of Chatham.[50] Chatham was a natural terminus

47. ABA Minutes, 21–22 September 1842, 4–5; ABA Minutes, 4–5 September 1851, 113; Shreve, *Pathfinders*, 91; Frost, "African American and African Transnationalism," 32.

48. Mitchell, *Underground Railroad*, 145; Lewis, "Religious Life of Fugitive Slaves," 117–20; Shadd, *Freeman*.

49. Lewis, "Religious Life of Fugitive Slaves," 119–20; Shreve, *Pathfinders*, 97.

50. Mitchell, *Underground Railroad*, 141; Drew, *Refugee*, 234; ABA Minutes, 10 September 1857, 189; *Provincial Freeman*, 75, 79; ABA Minutes, 09 September 1853,

for the Underground Railroad because of the steamboats that ran regularly from Detroit to Chatham; since this natural thoroughfare provided nearly every Black community in the area direct contact with Detroit, Chatham became the "headquarters of Negroes in Canada"[51]—a natural meeting place for Black and White abolitionists. Legendary names like Mary Ann Shadd, William King, Martin Delany, and John Brown met in Chatham to ponder future possibilities for the people of African extraction in North America while the Railroad continued to ferry its cargo.[52] Some fugitives were content to end their clandestine trip on the Railroad and remain just inside the border between Canada and the United States; they settled in places like Cayuga, London, New Canaan, Shrewsbury, and Mount Pleasant—but they, and the churches they built, would not all stand the test of time.

THE UNDERGROUND RAILROAD: OBSCURE AND ABANDONED STATIONS

Many Black Baptist churches were created by the Railroad's tracks but later disappeared with little record of their existence. The following is not an exhaustive list but highlights some little-known Black Baptist churches and those Black Baptist churches that initially benefited from the Railroad's influx of passengers only to later suffer extinction due, in part, to its loss. The African Baptist Church in St. Thomas and Gosfield Baptist Church were two such churches. Located near Kingsville in Essex County, little is known about the origins of the Gosfield Baptist Church but its origins are thought to coincide with the founding of Colchester and Toronto Baptist churches. Situated on Kettle Creek, African Baptist Church in St. Thomas was received into the Western Association in 1837 with twelve members—St. Thomas's African Baptist Church became extinct between 1860 and 1865 and Gosfield Baptist by the 1920s.[53] Mount Pleasant Baptist would suffer a similar fate; situated about five miles east of Amherstburg, just south of the Pike Road, representative Henry

---

141; ABA Minutes, 09 September 1844, 18.

51. Lewis, "Religious Life of Fugitive Slaves," 96; Heike, "Out of Chatham," 165, 170.

52. Lewis, "Religious Life of Fugitive Slaves," 96; Heike, "Out of Chatham," 165, 170; John Brown plotted his rebellion at Harper's Ferry during the "Chatham Convention"—hoping to recruit Blacks living in Canada for his attempt to found a Black state on US soil.

53. Lewis, "Religious Life of Fugitive Slaves," 45, 48–49; Western Baptist Association Minutes (1845–1865); Shreve, *Pathfinders*, 19, 41.

Nettles and ten congregants comprised its membership when it entered the ABA (likely in 1843). In 1851, Mount Pleasant left the ABA because it preferred to fellowship with the American Baptist Free Mission Society and the Canadian Anti-Slavery Baptist Association (CASBA)—it would return to the ABA in 1857 with Anthony Binga as its pastor.[54]

Fugitive slaves accessing the Railroad started to arrive in the town of London around 1830; however, the early beginnings of the Baptist cause in London are obscure—the Rev. Daniel A. Turner is usually credited with beginning the London church. The church property on Horton Street, just west of Wellington Street, was purchased in 1845 by Abel Bedford Jones and donated to the congregation. The Second Baptist Church of London was a member of the Canadian Anti-Slavery Baptist Association (CASBA) and came into the ABA in 1857; a steady drop in membership over the years caused the church to become extinct on October 8, 1929.[55] Founded just after Second Baptist London, the First Baptist Church of North Cayuga was formed on August 22, 1848 with ten members in the small log cabin of Deacon Stephney Street. Situated near the Grand River, several miles inland from Lake Erie, First Baptist was not in communion with the other Black Baptist churches, in fact, it was never intended to be a church solely for Black members but to serve the entire community. The church was received into the Niagara Baptist Association and never joined the ABA.[56]

Like some of the previous churches, New Canaan Baptist Church/Settlement had been short-lived; founded in 1850 (by Rev. E. Kirkland) it was admitted into the ABA in 1854 but became extinct before 1875. Located near Harrow, about ten miles east of Amherstburg and five miles from the Colchester Baptist Church, the name given to this settlement represents what the American fugitive slaves thought of their new country; however, like nearly every other rural Black community, the people moved away (at the end of the American Civil War) and the church is believed to have become extinct in 1872.[57] Another member of the

---

54. Amherstburg Baptist Association (ABA) Minutes (September 21–22, 1842), 2; Shreve, *Pathfinders*, 10, 75; Lewis, "Religious Life of Fugitive Slaves," 108–9.

55. Amherstburg Baptist Association (ABA) Minutes (September 21–22, 1842), 200; Lewis, "Religious Life of Fugitive Slaves," 113–16; Shreve, *Pathfinders*, 84–85.

56. Lewis, "Religious Life of Fugitive Slaves," 110–11; North Cayuga Baptist Church Minutes (1848).

57. Amherstburg Baptist Association (ABA) Minutes, 151; Lewis, "Religious Life of Fugitive Slaves," 116–17; *Voice of the Fugitive*.

CASBA, Shrewsbury Baptist Church, was a refuge for fleeing slaves that crossed the river at Detroit, followed the Thames River to Chatham, and drifted southward toward Lake Erie. Addison Smith was the first Black to settle in the area; Smith built a school/meeting place that became the early church (organized between 1850 and 1856). Guided by the pastor Rev. Stephen White, the thirteen members of Shrewsbury Baptist church applied for admission into the ABA in 1857.[58] Not all Railroad patrons tried to establish themselves in new rural or urban settlements, others journeyed to the well-established and funded segregated Black settlements like Wilberforce, Dawn, and Elgin.

Colonization was always a contentious issue among northern free Blacks. At the turn of the nineteenth century, Black leaders envisioned migration to places such as Haiti, Liberia, or other British colonies in Africa—and those attempts were met with limited success. Because of Upper Canada's (and Nova Scotia's) willingness to accept Blacks after the Revolutionary War and the War of 1812, coupled with the fact that the British Crown had parcels of land set aside to sell exclusively to Blacks, the idea of the planned Black settlements in Upper Canada took root.[59] The Black settlement was conceived as a philosophy of separation from the dominant White culture to allow Blacks the opportunity to own land, pursue financial independence, engage in educational opportunities, and establish other social institutions independent of external White control—the settlements were constituted as a haven from racial oppression and an attempt to exact a measure of control over Black destinies.[60] The two known Baptist chapels that were built on the property of one such settlement, the Refugees' Home Society,[61] were the Little River Baptist Church, located on the Third Concession of Sandwich East Township, and the First Baptist Church at Puce River. In 1858, the village of Puce, which already possessed a thriving community of Blacks, erected a structure, built of logs (1864), that served as both a school and its church. Its first minister, Elder Foot, taught school during the week and preached

---

58. Amherstburg Baptist Association (ABA) Minutes, 193; Shreve, *Pathfinders*, 93; Lewis, "Religious Life of Fugitive Slaves," 121–22.

59. Steward, *Twenty-Two Years*, xx; Roger Hepburn, *Crossing the Border*, 1.

60. Roger Hepburn, *Crossing the Border*, 3–7, 10.

61. Pease and Pease, *Black Utopia*, 109; the last, and least successful, Black colony was the Refugees' Home Society (1852), the others were the Colonial Settlement at Wilberforce (1829), Dawn Settlement in Dresden (1842), and Elgin Settlement at Buxton (1849).

on Sundays—the congregation had joined the ABA in 1963 with twelve members. Unfortunately, Little River Baptist did not fair as well; the Rev. Israel Campbell and the eight members of his congregation joined the ABA in 1855, however, the church's lack of a permanent minister led to its extinction in 1881.[62]

Lastly, although it is not the focus of this chapter, it is important to note that, while the Underground Railroad also extended into the Black church/community of Lower Canada and the Maritimes, not all termini on the Railroad created Black Baptist communities/churches. In the Maritimes, Nova Scotia and New Brunswick's Black Baptist churches existed shortly after the American Revolutionary War.[63] This meant that the fugitive slaves that rode the Underground Railroad to the Maritimes did not have to create Black Baptist communities/churches; on the contrary, the existing Black Baptist churches/communities laid the tracks that allowed the Railroad to ferry its passengers to their churches/communities.[64] However, there is still the question of what caused the growth of the legend of the Underground Railroad.

THE UNDERGROUND RAILROAD: THE LEGEND

After the American Civil War, the secrecy surrounding the Railroad tended to encourage fanciful folklore and legend. This was due in part to the paucity of written documentation and an overreliance (often uncritically) on anecdotal and oral history; scholars like Wilbur H. Siebert and Robert Smedley asked participants to share their stories decades removed

---

62. ABA Minutes, 09 September 1864, 251; ABA Minutes, 13 September 1855, 165; Lewis, "Religious Life of Fugitive Slaves," 161–62.

63. MacKerrow, *Brief History*, 8–14,15–17; Clifford, *From Slavery to Freetown*, 21; George, "Life," 475–76; Davidson, *Birchtown*, 65; Renfree, *Heritage and Horizon*, 32–33; Walker, *Loyalists*, 53, 57, 75; Whitfield, *Blacks on the Border*, 1, 20; Baptist preachers like David George and John Burton founded Black Baptist churches in Nova Scotia and New Brunswick; David George was among the group of slaves and free Blacks who founded the Silver Bluff Baptist Church in South Carolina, said to be North America's first Black church. Davidson, "Burton, John," para 3; Burton became known as "an apostle to the coloured people."

64. Boyd, "Preston, Richard," para 6–9; Love-Joy, "Richard Preston," 3–5; Fosty and Fosty, *Black Ice*, 28–30; Siebert, "Underground Railroad," 460; Richard Preston, the first pastor and founder of African Baptist Church (becoming Cornwallis Street Baptist Church in 1832 and today New Horizons Baptist) founded Black Baptist churches in districts such as Dartmouth, Preston, Beechville, Yarmouth, and Hammond Plains.

from the event—an act that readily spawned imaginative embellishments.[65] Writers of fiction and historical novelist (like Harriet Beecher Stowe) then and today have borrowed from, added to, and popularized the legend that was given early credence by Siebert's original research on the Railroad—however, recent scholarship has taken these embellishments into account when taking a second reading of Seibert and Smedley's accounts supplementing them with new findings.[66] Furthermore, both abolitionists and proslavery journalists, who tended to exaggerate the scope and activities of the Railroad, aided in distorting the facts surrounding the Underground Railroad. It is impossible to say how many slaves escaped to freedom in the decades before the Civil War—scholars like Eric Foner, Larry Gara believe the numbers using the Railroad are a guess at best.[67]

65. Gara, *Liberty Line*, 2; *Freedom*, 13, 15; Siebert's research set out questionnaires (interviews, scoured local newspapers, and retraced routes taken by fugitives) to dozens of surviving abolitionists asking for their recollections about the operations of the Railroad. His publications before 1896-1951 portrayed a highly organized system involving thousand of northern agents and a "great intricate network" of stations leading to Canada. His work influenced both scholarly and popular conceptions of the Railroad influencing public history; for Siebert's account of the Underground Railroad see Siebert, *Underground Railroad*. For the Robert Smedley interview of abolitionists like Robert Purvis and Marianna Gibbons (member of the White abolitionist family) see Smedley, *History*.

66. Gara, *Liberty Line*, 11-12; LaRoche, *Free Black Communities*, 9; recently historians have begun to question the sweeping nature of Gara's (and other scholars) revisionism when it comes to Siebert's and Smedley's gathering of reminisces from former Railroad agents and fugitives; while acknowledging the exaggerations, their accounts cannot be entirely discounted. Historians have re-read Siebert's documents and supplemented them with in-depth local research, a close examination of pre-Civil War abolitionists' correspondence (White and Black), and antislavery newspapers; Foner, *Gateway to Freedom*, 12-15; scholars have also begun the difficult task of exploring covert systems of aid to fugitives within the slave states as well as lines of communication between enslaved communities. Far more needs to be done in analysing how vigilance networks functioned on the local level and how they built connections with groups across the antebellum North.

67. Goodheart, "Secret History," para. 6-7; Walters, *Underground Railroad*, 3; Foner, *Gateway to Freedom*, 4, 14-15, 42; Roger Hepburn, *Crossing the Border*, 10; estimates—Foner calls guesses—suggest somewhere between 1,000 and 5,000 per year between 1830 and 1860; hardly enough to affect the growth of the slave population (which approached four million in 1860) but sufficient to cause alarm in the slave states, create contention between North and South, and a significant monetary loss for affected stakeholders; Gara, *Liberty Line*, 18, 98, 30; manumitted slaves were far more common than is generally assumed especially in the context of the Railroad legend. Census reports for 1850 and 1860 indicate that more slaves were manumitted than ran

Both abolitionists and slave owners had a vested interest in exaggerating the number of fugitives—the former to emphasize the Black desire for freedom and their efforts as noble heroes and the latter as evidence of a northern conspiracy to undermine the institution of slavery and their economic welfare. Southern slave owners believed that Blacks had a "natural disposition to insurrection."[68] New Orleans physician Samuel Adolphus Cartwright lent credence to this ideology with his discovery of a previously unknown medical condition that he called "Drapetomania, or the disease causing Negroes to run away."[69] Drapetomania seemed on the verge of becoming a fatal contagion in the summer of 1851 when Cartwright's articles appeared. Worst of all, the exodus could no longer be blamed on scattered outbreaks of Drapetomania;[70] rather, it was an organized network, vast and sinister, that actively encouraged and abetted the fugitive. Another support of the legend was the Railroad's clandestinity, that is, it was thought to be extremely secret and only travelled under cover of night.

The fact is the Railroad increasingly operated not under cover of darkness but in broad daylight. In states farther north, the operation of the Railroad was less clandestine and the routes were more publicly known. The presumption was that the farther north the lines ran the safer fugitives were from pursuit and capture. Agents boasted of their connection with the Railroad and newspapers, with abolitionist sympathies, wrote glowingly of the routes in their locales.[71] A former slave in Syracuse, Jermain W. Loguen, announced himself in the local press as the city's "agent and keeper of the Underground Railroad Depot"; he held "donation parties" to raise money, while newspapers published statistics

---

away—1850 had 1,011 fugitives and 1,467 manumissions; 1860 had 803 fugitives and 3078 manumissions; for stories of passengers of the Underground Railroad see Still, *Underground Railroad Records*. Still, a Philadelphian who helped oversee one of the most competent liberty lines in the nation, kept the only systematic contemporaneous record of the Railroad.

68. Walters, *Underground Railroad*, 12; Foner, *Gateway to Freedom*, 4; Gara, *Liberty Line*, 7.

69. Goodheart, "Secret History," para. 1–5.

70. Goodheart, "Secret History," para. 1–5; Walters, *Underground Railroad*, 30; the term is derived from the ancient Greek meaning either a fugitive slave or for *runaway* and *madness*; Foner, *Gateway to Freedom*, 5.

71. Walters, *Underground Railroad*, 54–55; Goodheart, "Secret History," para. 9; Malaspian, *Railroad*, 5.

on the number of fugitives he helped.⁷² Abolitionist groups made little secret of assisting runaways—in fact, they trumpeted it in pamphlets, periodicals, and annual reports. In 1850, the New York State Vigilance Committee publicly proclaimed its mission to "receive, with open arms, the panting fugitive."⁷³ Underground Railroad bake sales became common fund-raisers in northern towns and cities, and bazaars with the slogan "buy for the sake of the slave" offered donated luxury goods and handmade knickknacks before the winter holidays—a far different picture than the clandestine image prevalent in Railroad lore.⁷⁴

At times secrecy was also broken by Underground Railroad workers jubilantly crowing about extraordinary escapes; such as Henry "Box" Brown's imaginative shipment of himself from Richmond to Philadelphia or the Crafts' daring masquerade as master and manservant. This tended to make the work of the Underground Railroad more difficult. Leaders like Frederick Douglas complained, "the practise of publishing every new invention by which a slave is known to have escaped from slavery has neither wisdom nor necessity to sustain it."⁷⁵ Douglas worried that the "very public manner" in which some locales advertised their liberty lines transformed the Underground Railroad into the "upper-ground railroad."⁷⁶ Douglas was correct in his fear but overestimated the flow of information to the public since most routes remained so clandestine that they are still difficult to trace today. As time passed, Underground Railroad workers realized that to protect the fugitive slaves, and because they were breaking the law, it was prudent to operate as clandestinely as possible.⁷⁷ Then came the Fugitive Slave Act of 1850. The Act granted slave catchers permission to recapture runaway slaves anywhere on American soil—the northern states, previously a place of refuge for fugitives escaping southern slavery, were no longer secure. Ultimately, the Fugitive Slave Act made all Blacks aliens in the land of their birth. The Act did not distinguish between fugitives, the previously or recently free, freeborn, or Blacks legally freed, all now feared being kidnapped and sold into

---

72. Goodheart, "Secret History," para. 10.
73. Foner, *Gateway to Freedom*, 9; Goodheart, "Secret History," para. 10.
74. Goodheart, "Secret History," para. 10.
75. Malaspian, *Railroad*, 8; Walters, *Underground Railroad*, 55–56.
76. Malaspian, *Railroad*, 8; Walters, *Underground Railroad*, 55–56.
77. Goodheart, "Secret History," para. 9–11, 17; Walters, *Underground Railroad*, 3.

slavery.[78] The Act fueled the engines of the Railroad and increased the number of American Blacks looking for refuge in Upper Canada. This period would enhance future Canadian Railroad lore by highlighting Canada's part in the unfree and free's quests to obtain or sustain their freedom. This was partly due to the belief that destitute American Blacks longed to escape the United States for a chance at Canadian freedom and acceptance.

In truth, immigration to Canada was intended as a last resort. Harriet Tubman commented: "We would rather stay in our native land, if we could be as free there as we are here."[79] Most American Blacks wanted to stay in the United States, however, while not all Black leaders agreed that relocation to Canada was prudent, some Black leaders began advocating that Blacks immigrate to Canada as a temporary refuge until the racial situation improved in the United States. The words of a fugitive made plain the gravity of the choice to board the Underground Railroad when she bemoaned, "We were comfortably settled in the States, and were broken up by the fugitive slave law, compelled to leave our home and friends, and . . . into a foreign country among strangers."[80] Another fugitive laments, "I had been in comfortable circumstances, but all my little property was lawed away. I was among strangers, poverty stricken, and in a cold country."[81] Lastly, Henry Bibb wrote, regarding the influx of fugitive slaves, "We are happy to inform our friends that we are having fresh arrivals of this class almost every day . . . men of capital . . . with good property . . . now settling among us from the northern states."[82] Bibb's statements point to the fact that many of the new arrivals were free people living good lives in the northern states; but, after the passage of the Fugitive Slave Act of 1850, feared for their freedom and lamented the need to move further north contradicting the image of the destitute fugitive, their need of the Railroad to procure their freedom, and, as stated

---

78. Bibb, *Fugitive*; Pease and Pease, *Black Utopia*, 7; Walters, *Underground Railroad*, 103; Bakan, "Reconsidering," 12; Canada did not capitulate with the US when it came to the return of fugitive slaves.

79. Simpson, *Under the North Star*, 132; Drew, *Refugee*, 3; Bakan, "Reconsidering," 14.

80. Simpson, *Under the North Star*, 132; Drew, *Refugee*, 3, 31, 4, 38.

81. Simpson, *Under the North Star*, 132; Drew, *Refugee*, 3, 31, 4, 38.

82. Lewis, "Religious Life of Fugitive Slaves," 119–20; Bibb, *Fugitive*; Shreve, *Pathfinders*, 97.

previously, puts into question the actual number of patrons that travelled on the Railroad.

Northern Blacks generally were much less driven to relocate to Canada. As many northern Blacks were either born free or had been living as free persons for a long time—the novelty of freedom was not the same for northern Blacks as it was for southern fugitives. As a result, northern Blacks were much less eager to abandon their lives in the United States. However, increasing racial hostility toward Blacks in the United States throughout the 1830s and 1840s (through enforcement of the Black Codes in the northern states) forced many American Blacks to reconsider relocation to Canada. Although most southern fugitives recognized that prejudice existed in Upper Canada, the majority did not see prejudice in Canada as either overwhelming or unavoidable. Most felt they lived well, certainly in comparison with their American experience. Northern Blacks were often disappointed by the racism they encountered. This was perhaps because their main motivation for immigrating to Canada was to live free from racism and discrimination; they had been led to believe Canada offered such a refuge—they found the reality of the situation disheartening.[83] This disappointment ensured that not all African American passengers on the Railroad stayed to become African Canadians.[84] Those that did found that one of the Canadian heirlooms of the Underground Railroad was the role it played as an icon of Canadian beneficence in the North American slave saga.

THE UNDERGROUND RAILROAD: CANADA'S MYTHS

The legacy of Canada as a haven of freedom for destitute southern fugitive slaves and a promised land of freedom and equality for northern African Americans remains pervasive in the Canadian imagination. This can reinforce a sense of superiority among Canadians (especially when juxtaposed with their American counterparts). Yet this popular myth always fails to consider the actual experiences of fugitive slaves once they arrived in Canada; specifically, the discrimination they faced in their daily lives and their exclusion from social institutions such as schools and churches. This myth was often tied to the journeys of the fugitives, disregarding the prejudices and racial tensions faced in Canada once they crossed the

---

83. Rhodes, "Contestation," 178; Vinci, "Between Blacks and Whites," 9–10.

84. Siebert, *Underground Railroad*, 461; Fosty and Fosty, *Black Ice*, 27, 30; Barss, "'African' Churches," 3.

border.⁸⁵ This belief became a part of the Canadian identity and perpetuated what James Walker called the "North Star Myth." Walker, along with scholars like George Elliott Clarke, speak to a Canadian acceptance that migration to its shores freed the fugitive from the racism they experienced in the United States and garnered them full citizenship.⁸⁶ In fact, in Toronto, legislation was pasted preventing African American immigrants from becoming naturalized in Upper Canada—without naturalization Blacks could not exercise their rights under British colonial law.⁸⁷

The experiences of the northern free Blacks, the enforcement of Black codes, and the Fugitive Slave Law of 1850 showed Canada was less the magnet of freedom to fugitives slaves and northern free Blacks as the United States was a propelling force from subjugation.⁸⁸ As far as the Underground Railroad is concerned, Michigan's incorporation as a Territory in 1805, and its Ordinance against slavery, saw the number of slaves in Upper Canada decline as many Black Canadian slaves made their way from Canada to Detroit and freedom.⁸⁹ The realization of racism in Canada helped precipitate the *Great Exodus* of African Americans back to the US after its Civil War. In 1861, shots fired at Fort Sumter heralded the beginning of the American Civil War—by 1862, the Union Army started recruiting Black soldiers. Hundreds of Black settlers returned to the US to join the fight; their departure signalled the slow decline of many Black settlements, urban and rural Black communities, and the Railroad. The Union victory saw many Blacks return to re-join family and friends with

---

85. Winks, *Blacks in Canada*, 1; Duncan, "'Out of the Bitter Sea,'" 239; Gillard, "Black Church in Canada."

86. Walker, *Racial Discrimination*, 6; Cooper, *Hanging of Angélique*, xii; Roger Hepburn, *Crossing the Border*, 10.

87. "Edwoods," 172; Frost, "Escaped Slaves"; while the "Edwoods and Others Naturalization Bill" passed in the Upper Canadian legislature (1837), it excluded from the list the names of every Black person who had applied, denying them full citizenship in the Empire—no grounds were given in the Journal of the House of Assembly to account for this omission.

88. Rhodes, "Contestation," 178; Walters, *Underground Railroad*, 10, 99, 101; along with the Act of 1850, Eli Whitney's invention of the cotton gin, which led to greater slave numbers, and the passing of the 1793 Emancipation Act by Governor John Graves Simcoe, ostensibly banning slavery in Upper Canada, caused the Railroad to extend into Canada.

89. Riddell, "Slave," 260–61; Bakan, "Reconsidering," 5; so many Black Canadian slaves escaped via the Railroad that a Company of Black militia—composed entirely of escaped slaves from Canada—was formed in Detroit in 1806 to assist in the general defence of the Territory.

a renewed hope of better race relations and signalled the demise of the Railroad.[90] The Underground Railroad was an exercise in the day-to-day resistance of the slave system but without a system to resist, it simply ceased to be; like its beginnings, no one knows when the last train pulled into the station, helped found and sustained its last Black Baptist church, or was assisted by the Black Baptist community.[91]

CONCLUSION

Many legends are based on facts that later succumb to embellishment; like these legends, the Underground Railroad's complete history has yet to be discovered. It was the first large-scale interracial collaboration in North America. Black and White, rich and poor, women and men, all possessed a shared conviction that slavery was a moral abomination and that the laws that governed such inhuman endeavour should be disobeyed whenever possible; moreover, it was a vital component in the establishment of the Black Baptist church in Upper Canada.[92] The Black church emerged as a central institution in the development of Black cultural life in Canada. The socio-historical context of legalized racial segregation and the resulting political and economic hegemony based on whiteness influenced the development of the Black church as a religious and social institution. The church was the first Black institution in North America; it provided solace, empowerment, and hope to its people—particularly to those of the Baptist faith. In the British colony of Upper Canada the Underground Railroad's tracks brought freedom seekers to areas where they had opportunity, could build communities, and birth Black Baptist churches. The churches grew where the terminals of the Railroad allowed its passengers to find freedom and hope for a better life; reciprocally,

---

90. Walters Walters, *Underground Railroad*, 115–17; Rhodes, "Contestation," 175–78; Vinci, "Between Blacks and Whites," 11, 20; Henry Bibb died in Windsor, Ontario (1854) firmly supporting the settlement of Blacks outside North America while the one-time staunch advocate of permanent settlement of Blacks in Canada, Mary Ann Shadd, eventually, disillusioned, returned to the United States during the Civil War; Bakan, "Reconsidering," 14; after 1863's slave emancipation, two-thirds of the Blacks in the colony of Canada returned to the US.

91. Walters, *Underground Railroad*, 117–21; Goodheart, "Secret History," para. 20.

92. Walters, *Underground Railroad*, 6–7; Foner, *Gateway to Freedom*, 15; Bordewich, *Bound for Canaan*, 4.

the church and its congregants became active members of the Railroad's staff.[93]

BIBLIOGRAPHY

Primary Sources

ARCHIVES

Amherstburg Baptist Association (ABA) Minutes, Volume 1 (October 8, 1841–September 14, 1877).
"Edwoods and Others Naturalization Bill." *Journal of the Legislative Council of Upper Canada: First Session of the Thirteenth Provincial Parliament* (1837).
Haldimand Baptist Association Minutes, 1837, 1841, 1850–1865.
North Cayuga Baptist Church Minutes, 1848.
Western Baptist Association Minutes, 1845–1865.

MONOGRAPHS

Drew, Benjamin. *A North-Side View of Slavery. The Refugee; or the Narratives of Fugitive Slaves in Canada. Related by Themselves, with an Account of the History and Condition of the Coloured Population of Upper Canada.* Boston: John P. Jowett and Company, 1856.
MacKerrow, P. E. *A Brief History of the Coloured Baptists of Nova Scotia and their First Organization as Churches A. D. 1832.* Halifax, NS: Nova Scotia Printing Company, 1895.
Shreve, Dorothy S. *Pathfinders of Liberty and Truth.* Merlin, UK: Merlin Standard, 1940.
Siebert, Wilbur H. *The Underground Railroad from Slavery to Freedom.* New York: MacMillan, 1898.
Smedley, Robert Clemens. *History of the Underground Railroad in Chester and the Neighboring Counties.* Lancaster, PA: John A. Hiestand, 1883.

NEWSPAPERS AND MAGAZINES

Barss, Gordon P. "'African' Churches in Nova Scotia: The Standing Today." *Maritime Baptist*, January 16, 1946.
Goodheart, Adam. "The Secret History of the Underground Railroad: Eric Foner Explores How It Really Worked." *The Atlantic*, March 15, 2015. No pages. Online: https://www.theatlantic.com/magazine/archive/2015/03/the-secret-history-of-the-underground-railroad/384966.
Love-Joy, Vivian. "Richard Preston, Ex-Slave: Religious Leader and Organizer of the Coloured Baptist of Nova Scotia, 1832–1861." *Atlantic Advocate*, April 1915.

---

93. Taken together with the circumstance of the Maritime Black Baptist churches—that built the tracks from their church door to the main trunk of the Railroad—the Black Baptist church and the Railroad could be said to have a relationship of procreative reciprocity.

Plummer, Kevin. "Historicist: The Food Is Soul Good: The Underground Railroad's 20-Year Run Serving Soul Food in Toronto." *Torontoist*, February 2014. No pages. Online: https://torontoist.com/2014/02/historicist-the-food-is-soul-good.

The Provincial Freeman (Windsor, Toronto, Chatham, ON), 1853–1860.

Salsberg, Lanny. "Spice Up your Eating." *Toronto Star*, November 21, 1969.

OTHER

Rippon, John. "An Account of the Life of Mr. David George, from Sierra Leone in Africa; Given by Himself in a Conversation with Brother Rippon of London, and Brother Pearce of Birmingham." *Baptist Annual Register* 1 (1790–1793) 473–84.

Sadlier, Rosemary. "BLACK IN TORONTO: Remembering Howard Matthews and the Now-Closed Underground Railroad Restaurant." *Toronto.com*. No pages. Online: https://www.toronto.com/news/black-in-toronto-remembering-howard-matthews-and-the-now-closed-underground-railroad-restaurant/article_f2cf5c5b-4340-52cb-ae54-d055dec661df.html.

Secondary Sources

Bakan, Abigail B. "Reconsidering the Underground Railroad: Slavery and Racialization in the Making of the Canadian State." *Social Studies* 1 (2008) 3–29.

Beecher Stowe, Harriet. *Uncle Tom's Cabin*. 1852. Reprint, New York: Bantam, 1981.

Bordewich, Fergus M. *Bound for Canaan: The Epic Story of the Underground Railroad, America's First Civil Rights Movement*. New York: Amistad, 2005.

Boyd, Frank S., Jr. "Preston, Richard." *Dictionary of Canadian Biography*. No pages. Online: http://www.biographi.ca/en/bio/preston_richard_8E.html.

Calarco, Tom, et al. *Places of the Underground Railroad: A Geographical Guide*. Santa Barbara, CA: Greenwood, 2011.

Clifford, Mary Louise. *From Slavery to Freetown: Black Loyalists After the American Revolution*. Jefferson, NC: McFarland, 2005.

Coffin, Levi. *Reminiscences of Levi Coffin*. Richmond, IN: Friend United, 2001.

Cone, James H. *Black Power and Black Theology*. New York: Seabury, 1969.

Cooper, Afua. *The Hanging of Angélique: The Untold Story of Canadian Slavery and the Burning of Old Montréal*. Toronto: HarperCollins, 2006.

Cousineau, Jennifer. "First Baptist Church, Amherstburg, Ontario." *Historic Sites and Monuments Board of Canada and Parks Canada* 4 (2011) 1–20.

Davidson, Stephen E. *Birchtown and the Black Loyalist Experience: From 1775 to the Present*. Halifax, NS: Formac, 2019.

———. "Burton, John." *Dictionary of Canadian Biography*. No pages. Online: http://www.biographi.ca/en/bio/burton_john_7E.html.

Duncan, Carol B. "'Out of the Bitter Sea': The Black Church and Migration in North American." In *The Black Church Studies Reader*, edited by Alton B. Pollard and Carol B. Duncan, 237–44. London: MacMillan, 2016.

Foner, Eric. *Gateway to Freedom: The Hidden History of The Underground Railroad*. Oxford: Oxford University Press, 2015.

Fosty, George, and Darril Fosty. *Black Ice: The Lost History of the Coloured Hockey League of The Maritimes, 1895–1925*. Halifax, NS: Nimbus, 2008.

Frost, Karolyn S. "African American and African Transnationalism along the Detroit River Borderland: The Example of Madison J. Lightfoot." *Journal of American Ethnic History* 32 (2013) 78–88.
Frost, Karolyn Smardz, "Escaped Slaves Helped Build T.O." *Toronto Star*, Feb 11, 2007.
Gara, Larry. *The Liberty Line: The Legend of the Underground Railroad*. Lexington: University of Kentucky Press, 1996.
Gillard, Denise. "The History of the Black Church in Canada." *Presbyterian Record* 123 (1999) 16–18.
Glenn, N. D. "Negro Religion and Negro Status in the United States." In *Religion, Culture and Society: A Reader in the Society of Religion*, edited by Louis Schneider, 623–38. New York: John Wiley, 1964.
Heike, Paul. "Out of Chatham: Abolitionism on the Canadian Frontier." *Atlantic Studies* 8 (2011) 165–88.
Hicks, H. Beecher, Jr. *Images of the Black Preacher: The Man Nobody Knows*. Valley Forge, PA: Judson, 1977.
Hill, Daniel G. *The Freedom-Seekers: Blacks in Early Canada*. Toronto: Stoddard, 1992.
Huggins, Nathan I. *Black Odyssey: The Ordeal of Slavery in America*. London: George Allen & Unwin, 1979.
Landon, Fred. "Amherstburg, Terminus of the Underground Railroad." *The Journal of Negro History* 10 (1925) 1–9.
LaRoche, Cheryl Janifer. *Free Black Communities and the Underground Railroad: The Geography of Resistance*. Urbana: University of Illinois Press, 2014.
Lewis, James K. "Religious Life of Fugitive Slaves and Rise of Coloured Baptist Churches 1820–1865 in What Is Now Known as Ontario." BDiv thesis, McMaster University, 1965.
Malaspina, Ann. *The Underground Railroad: The Journey to Freedom*. New York: Chelsea House, 2010.
Mitchell, William M. *The Underground Railroad from Slavery to Freedom*. London: William Tweedie, 1860.
Montgomery, William E. *Under their Own Vine and Fig Tree: The African-American Church in the South 1865–1900*. Baton Rouge: Louisiana State University Press, 1993.
Pease, William H., and Jane H. Pease. *Black Utopia: Negro Communal Experiments in America*. Madison: State Historical Society of Wisconsin, 1963.
Renfree, Harry A. *Heritage and Horizon: The Baptist Story in Canada*. Eugene, OR: Wipf and Stock, 2007.
Riddell, William Renwick. "The Slave in Upper Canada." *Journal of the American Institute of Criminal Law and Criminology* 14 (1923) 249–78.
Rhodes, Jane. "The Contestation over National Identity: Nineteenth Century Black Americans in Canada." *Canadian Review of American Studies* 30 (2000) 175–86.
Robinson, Julie Marie. *Race, Religion, and the Pulpit: Rev. Robert L. Bradby and the Making of Urban Detroit*. Detroit: Wayne State University Press, 2015.
Roger Hepburn, Sharon A. *Crossing the Border: A Free Black Community in Canada*. Urbana: University of Illinois Press, 2007.
Shadd, Adrienne. "Extending the Right Hand of Fellowship: Sandwich Baptist Church, Amherstburg First Baptist, and the Amherstburg Baptist Association." In *A Fluid Frontier: Slavery, Resistance, and the Underground Railroad in the Detroit River*

Borderland, edited *by* Karolyn Smardz Frost and Veta Smith Tucker, 120–32. Detroit: Wayne State University Press, 2016.

Shadd, Adrienne, et al. *The Underground Railroad: Next Stop Toronto*. Toronto: Dundurn, 2005.

Sheffield, Wilfred. "Background and Development of Negro Baptists in Ontario." BDiv thesis. McMaster University, 1952.

Siebert, Wilbur H. "The Underground Railroad in Massachusetts." *New England Quarterly* 9 (1939) 447–67.

Simpson, Donald George. *Under the North Star: Black Communities in Upper Canada before Confederation (1876)*. Trenton, NJ: Africa World, 2005.

Steward, Austin. *Twenty-Two Years a Slave and Forty Years a Freeman*. Syracuse, NY: Syracuse University Press, 2002.

Vinci, Alexandra. "Between Blacks and Whites over Issues of Schooling in Upper Canada, 1840–1860: White Prejudice, Black Anti-Slavery and School Reform." MA thesis, University Of Toronto, 2010.

Walker, James W. St. G. *The Black Loyalists: The Search for a Promised Land in Nova Scotia and Sierra Leone 1783–1870*. Toronto: University of Toronto Press, 1992.

———. *Racial Discrimination in Canada: The Black Experience*. Historical Booklet No. 41. Ottawa: Canadian Historical Society, 1985.

Walters, Kerry S. *The Underground Railroad: A Reference Guide*. Santa Barbara, CA: ABC-CLIO, 2012.

Winks, Robin. *The Blacks in Canada: A History*. 2nd ed. Montreal: McGill University Press, 1997.

4

"Begging" Baptists

Central Canadian Regular Baptists and the British Fund-Raising Activism of Reverend William Troy and Reverend William M. Mitchell, 1850–1865

Paul R. Wilson

Black Regular Baptists in Canada West, in the period from 1850 to 1865, faced many social, economic, political, and personal challenges. In the religious and education spheres, Black Baptists struggled to obtain the resources needed to institutionalize their Regular Baptist faith. In response to their resource challenges, two Black Regular Baptist Pastors, Reverend William Troy of Windsor and Detroit and Reverend William Mitchell of Toronto sought British aid. This chapter argues that Troy and Mitchell's initial solicitation of British aid, from 1859 to 1861, was an expression of resistance and "Black uplift activism" aimed at strengthening the Black Regular Baptist cause and the wider Black community through fund-raising for religious and educational institutions.[1] According to the available evidence, this venture achieved some of its intended ends. However, a second fund-raising initiative, undertaken by

---

1. Cooper, "*Voice of the Fugitive*," 148. The term used here expresses the nineteenth century Black definition of "uplift" that stressed Victorian values, such as, thrift, diligence, and self-help. This version of Black uplift also articulated and promoted a broad vision of collective social action that included resistance, advancement, and struggle. For a detailed analysis of Black uplift ideology see, Gaines, *Uplifting the Race*.

Mitchell alone, from 1863 to 1864, was driven by personal circumstances and objectives. Not only did this endeavour scandalize overseas Black fund-raising efforts, but also prompted additional fund-raising reforms.

Scholarly examinations of Black Regular Baptist fund-raising activism in Britain, on behalf of Black institutions in Canada West, are lacking. This chapter, with its specific focus on the fund-raising endeavours of William Troy and William Mitchell, strives to deepen our understanding of Black Regular Baptist efforts to obtain institutional resources for the communities they served. While the advancement of our knowledge about Black resistance, relocation, and resettlement in Canada has grown exponentially in the last few decades, understanding of Canadian resident Black Regular Baptist initiatives to solicit British aid remains relatively superficial. Notable professional and community historians have drawn attention to the background and work of Troy and Mitchell.[2] But, to date, no in-depth study has focussed exclusively on the British fund-raising activism of these two Regular Baptist figures. This chapter partially addresses this gap by offering a more fulsome exploration of Troy and Mitchell's solicitation of British aid.

BAPTIST TURBULENCE AND STRUGGLE FOR INSTITUTIONAL RESOURCES, 1850–1859

Turbulence and struggle are apt descriptions for the Baptist experience generally in the period from 1850 to 1860. Economically, Canada West experienced the effects of emerging industrialization including ongoing commercial volatility, a major depression in 1857, and a railway building boom.[3] Social change and challenge included an influx of Black Baptists after the passage of the Fugitive Slave Act of 1850.[4]

---

2. The starting point for autobiographical and biographical information about the lives and fund-raising activities of Troy and Mitchell is their published narratives (see Troy, *Hair-Breadth Escapes*, 1–9; Mitchell, *Underground Railroad*, iii–ix). For other biographical information about Mitchell see, Shadd et al., *Underground Railroad*, 30, 40–41, 46, 70–72; Ripley et al., eds., *Black Abolitionist Papers: Volume II*, 483; Green, *Black Americans*, 55, 65; Simpson, *Under the North Star*, 406, 411. For William Troy, see "REV. DR. WILLIAIM TROY LAID TO REST" in *Richmond Planet*, November 25, 1905; Ripley et al., eds., *Black Abolitionist Papers: Volume II*, 494–95; Smardz Frost and Tucker, eds., *Fluid Frontier*, 93, 108, 249; Simpson, *Under the North Star*, 275, 301, 305; Hill, *Freedom Seekers*, 144–45; Shreve, *AfriCanadian Church,* 57–60.

3. Bliss, *Northern Enterprise*, 175–81; Taylor and Baskerville, *Concise History*, 164–76; McCalla, *Planting the Province*, 199–243.

4. See Simpson, *Under the North Star*, 225–324; Heath, Friesen, and Murray, eds. *Baptists in Canada*, 41.

Baptists were certainly not immune to turbulence within their own religious community. For example, the mid-nineteenth-century debates over open versus closed communion and the struggle to achieve greater Baptist unity were troublesome issues for central Canadian Baptists. However, as Heath, Friesen, and Murray have recently observed, "Although Baptists in central Canada experienced turbulence in the mid-nineteenth century, many continued to work toward unity."[5]

Baptists also struggled to find the necessary resources to establish their institutions and expand their presence and influence in Canada West. Notations about the persistent lack of resources and calls for Baptists to practice God-honouring stewardship of time, talent, and property were a constant theme in Regular Baptist Association Minutes. For example, the Black Amherstburg Regular Baptist Missionary Association was established in 1841 "in part because of the racism they [Black Baptists] encountered on both sides of the border," and it struggled to obtain much-needed institutional resources.[6] The Circular Letter of August 19, 1850 from the Amherstburg Association to its member churches had as its theme "our leanness, our leanness."[7] This theme was chosen after the amount contributed by the churches to the Association's treasury was a paltry $2.54.[8] "We are pained," the letter noted, "when we contemplate the deplorably low state of the churches which compose this body."[9]

While they acknowledged that "various causes" were responsible for this sorry state, the letter writers argued that "a spirit of covetousness and strife for worldly gain" were the "paramount" causes that led "so many professed Christians among us, to look not at the things which are Christ's, but the things which are their own."[10] In response, the letter implored its readers to accept the biblical teaching about ownership and stewardship and put those truths into practice by following a series of actions. These actions included self-examination and the rejection of "covetousness," recognizing and accepting the Christian teaching that "we are not our own, we are bought with a price," adopting "practical and impartial benevolence," offering no excuses including lack of means, and

---

5. Heath, Friesen, and Murray. *Baptists in Canada*, 42.
6. Heath, Friesen, and Murray. *Baptists in Canada*, 41.
7. Amherstburg Baptist Association (ABA) Minutes (1850), 103.
8. Amherstburg Baptist Association (ABA) Minutes (1850), 98.
9. Amherstburg Baptist Association (ABA) Minutes (1850), 103.
10. Amherstburg Baptist Association (ABA) Minutes (1850), 104.

the entire consecration of one's person and possessions: "I consecrate to Thee, my time, my property, my talents, my life, my all. I keep nothing back."[11] Here was a commitment to the principles of sacrificial service and stewardship that, if practiced, would help to address the existing lack of institutional resources.

But despite such entreaties to its congregants, the Amherstburg Association continued to experience "leanness." Some outside help was forthcoming. Initially, the Amherstburg Association did receive practical assistance from the predominately White American Baptist Free Mission Society (hereafter ABFMS)—through the able and helpful efforts of ABFMS missionary William P. Newman.[12] In the 1850s, other ABFMS teachers served in the communities of Dawn, Hamilton, Chatham, and the Queen's Bush.[13] Black Baptists in the Amherstburg region also created and implemented self-help strategies such as a True Band Society where Blacks made regular contributions through dues that were used to mitigate hardship.[14]

Responses from White resident Regular Baptists to the broader anti-slavery cause and the Black Baptist need for institutional resources in Canada West contained far more sympathy than substance. For example, the predominately White Haldimand Association regularly passed resolutions opposing slavery but offered little regarding any direct financial aid to support their fellow Black Baptists.[15] When charges of pro-slavery tolerance or inaction were forthcoming, White Regular Baptists pointed to their many anti-slavery resolutions. In fact, as historians have noted, Baptists were the first to condemn slavery in the 1830s but Baptist belief in and practice of local church autonomy prevented them from speaking with one united voice against Black oppression.[16] Black critics remained unconvinced that White Canadian Regular Baptists were genuine supporters of the anti-slavery cause. In 1857, for example, an editorial in the

---

11. Amherstburg Baptist Association (ABA) Minutes (1850), 105–6, 109.

12. Ripley et al., *Abolitionist Papers*, Volume II, 302–3, fn. 2; Ripley highlights Newman's Baptist roots and his involvement in the anti-slavery movement in Canada West.

13. Ripley, et al., *Abolitionist Papers*, Volume II, 327, fn. 1.

14. Moore-Davis, "Canadian Black Settlements," 87; Shadd, "Extending the Right Hand of Fellowship," 127.

15. Haldimand Baptist Association Minutes (1852), 9–10.

16. Winks, *Blacks in Canada*, 219; Stouffer, *Light*, 166; Brown-Kubisch, *Queen's Bush Settlement*, 14.

Provincial Freeman, a leading Black weekly newspaper, claimed that the Canadian Regular Baptists' position on slavery was hypocritical:

> When the Regular Baptists of Canada can show that there is no fellowship, (with pro-slavery churches) then, and till then, shall it be worthwhile to refer to Resolutions against Slavery . . . for the present hypocritical position . . . does not entitle it to any consideration as a truth telling Body against slavery or as one that hates the iniquitous and accursed system—The southern attractions have, through New York and other mediums some power over the Regular Baptist Church in Canada.[17]

There were many reasons for White Baptist hypocrisy, such as lethargy and neglect of obligations to Black Baptists. Certainly "Yankee" attitudes of racial superiority, segregation, and prejudice, a tendency to favour independence, the polity of local church autonomy, and a strong focus among White Baptists on finding the resources they needed to achieve their goal of religious and middle-class respectability were key factors that shaped their responses.[18] As Donald Simpson has noted, however, "The Baptists record with regard to slavery was not completely negative by any means."[19] Some Canadian White Regular Baptist pastors and churches, such as the congregation led by "M. Gilmour in Peterborough," were unequivocal in their anti-slavery stance and demonstrated "a major concern for Blacks both in the United States and Canada."[20]

Still, tangible resource support from White Canadian Regular Baptists for their Black Baptist brothers and sisters fell far short of what was needed. In an editorial of November 10, 1855, published in the *Provincial Freeman*, William P. Newman, who was the editor of the *Provincial Freeman and Weekly Advertiser*, formerly enslaved, an ordained Baptist minister, "an itinerant missionary, within the bounds of the Canada Anti-Slavery Baptist Association," and a missionary with the ABFMS, chastised his White Baptist brethren for their inaction and their failure

---

17. *Provincial Freeman*, June 20, 1857.

18. For example, see the characterization of Blacks expressed by Robert Alexander Fyfe, who was the pastor of Bond Street Baptist Church, Toronto, for a second time from 1855–1860 (see Wells, *Life and Labors*, 241–49). As Gibson observed, Fyfe's stance "falls far short of the concepts widely held by Christians today" (*Robert Alexander Fyfe*, 192). For the White Baptist pursuit of middle-class respectability, see Wilson, "Caring for their Community."

19. Simpson, *Under the North Star*, 25.

20. Simpson, *Under the North Star*, 25.

to provide much-needed institutional resources: "It is a fact," Newman claimed, "that the colored people, of Canada, are almost entirely of Baptist or Methodist persuasion, and nearly all the teachers sent among them have been Presbyterians and Congregationalists."[21] After noting this failure Newman admonished his fellow Baptists: "But we must admonish our Baptist and Methodist friends, that they are sadly in fault, since they neglected their duty, and done but little or nothing for us, when they have been *earnestly entreated* to do something."[22] White Baptist neglect and inaction left Black Baptists in the position of having to fend for themselves, look for possible sources of institutional support outside of the Canadian Baptist domain, and make difficult decisions about what forms of fundraising were acceptable.

In sum, in the 1850s, when William Troy and William Mitchell became part of Black Baptist churches in Canada West, turbulence and struggle were certainly realities that generally characterized the Baptist experience. An ongoing lack of the resources needed to institutionalize Baptist faith and practice prompted Baptists to stress the need for better stewardship and search for additional funding sources and methods that would address their institutional needs. Despite the pleas from Black Baptists for White Baptist financial support, almost none was forthcoming. Given those conditions and circumstances, Black Baptists explored and pursued internal and external fund-raising initiatives. But adopting and executing fund-raising activism, particularly in the public domain, would prove to be both controversial and divisive.

BLACK REGULAR BAPTISTS AND THE "BEGGING" CONTROVERSY, 1850–1858

The question of whether public fund-raising appeals were an ethical and legitimate means of achieving institutional self-reliance was a complex and troublesome issue for Black Baptists in Canada West. Historians such as C. Peter Ripley, Robin Winks, Dorothy S, Shreve, Adrienne Shadd, and Donald Simpson have revealed the patterns and practices of Black fundraising activism generally and examined the "begging" controversies of the 1850s.[23] The specific focus here is on providing an overview of Black

---

21. *Provincial Freeman*, November 10, 1855. See also Shreve, *AfriCanadian Church*, 57; Annual Reports of ABFMS (1856), 13.

22. *Provincial Freeman*, November 10, 1855.

23. See Ripley et al., eds., *Black Abolitionist Papers: Volume II*, 29–32, 182, 183n2,

Regular Baptist positions on fund-raising and begging that preceded the British aid campaigns of William Troy and William Mitchell.

In short, two predominant positions were evident among Black Baptists. Some sided with the views expressed by Mary Ann Shadd Cary and her supporters. Essentially, Shadd Cary called on Blacks to be self-sufficient and favoured their assimilation into Canadian society. She also argued that the never-ending solicitation of resources (which she insultingly called "begging") for fugitives did more harm than good for Blacks.[24] In Shadd Cary's view, such charitable activities reinforced a culture of Black dependence and the stereotype of racial inferiority. The fund-raising process also undermined Canada's reputation as a haven and the Black community's role as an antislavery symbol.[25] Furthermore, Shadd Cary opposed the solicitation of resources from Whites and organizations where Whites and Blacks worked together on raising funds. In practice, Black Baptists that supported Shadd Cary's position often joined their local True Band or Vigilance Committee that had as their focus the care and support of Blacks who were struggling to survive.

In contrast, other Black Baptists sided with the views of Henry Bibb and his supporters. Essentially, as C. Peter Ripley has noted, these Blacks often "favored the Black settlements, separate institutions, and white philanthropy to support them."[26] Before 1852, Bibb was open to seeking and accepting aid for fugitive slaves from any quarter. But he clearly had strong views related to the objectives that begging should achieve: "If our people must beg," he stated, "we hope they may beg for something permanent."[27] Donald Simpson has pointed out that by 1852 Bibb had modified his view and, in an editorial, "he made a strong plea for self-help and against begging."[28] Black Baptists of this sort supported organizations like the Anti-Slavery Society of Canada, founded in Toronto in 1852, and the Refugee Home Society (hereafter RHS), founded on May 21, 1851. The RHS was subjected to relentless attacks from Mary Shadd

---

365n2; Winks, *Blacks in Canada*, 204–8, 227; Shreve, *AfriCanadian Church*, 38.

24. For Shadd's views see the Letter of Mary Ann Shadd Cary to George Whipple, December 28, 1852, in Ripley et al., eds., *Black Abolitionist Papers: Volume II*, 245–51. See also Ripley et al., eds., *Black Abolitionist Papers: Volume II*, 31. For Shadd's criticism of Baptists engaged in begging see *Voice of the Fugitive*, February 26, 1852.

25. Ripley et al., eds., *Black Abolitionist Papers: Volume II*, 32.

26. Ripley et al., eds., *Black Abolitionist Papers: Volume II*, 31.

27. As quoted in Tobin, *From Midnight To Dawn*, 91.

28. Simpson, *Under the North Star*, 85.

Cary who rightly accused RHS agents of engaging in abusive and corrupt begging practices.[29]

Philosophical divisions and disputes over what constituted acceptable fund-raising activism and the acrimony that this issue precipitated in Black Baptist communities was a major challenge. For example, the Amherstburg Association both condemned and condoned fund-raising activities. On the one hand, the Association condemned begging and attempts by predominately White mission agencies, missionaries, and their agents to impose, as historian Linda Brown-Kubisch has noted, "their ideal model of middle-class Christians" on the Black communities.[30] In his circular letter of 1851, Elder Horace H. Hawkins of Chatham, Ontario, noted that "ravenous wolves have roamed through our midst" and he lamented that "a few [churches] have consented to bow again under prejudice of color, and suffer a foreign body to manage through paid agents and by proxy your church matters."[31] Hawkins' reference to "paid agents" expressed the dismay and disapproval of Black Baptists who witnessed or knew of fraudulent actions by those who claimed to raise funds for fugitive slaves, but, in fact, sometimes kept the money raised for themselves.

On the other hand, the Association supported some fund-raising and missionary efforts particularly when those efforts involved one of their own. For example, in 1854, the Amherstburg Association initially defended the character and fund-raising efforts of the eccentric and controversial Isaac Rice. A White former Presbyterian minister, and for a time a Baptist member and leader in Amherstburg, an organizer of the Refugee Home Society, and the leader of the Union Border Mission (commonly known as the "Begging Society"), Rice claimed that all Canadian Blacks were "poor, starving, destitute fugitives."[32] He was soon accused of misrepresentation for the purpose of enabling his "begging" to raise more money from the public.[33] Nevertheless, in 1854, the Amherstburg Association unanimously passed a resolution in support of Rice's character and fund-raising efforts: "We recommend this brother to your affection and ask your care for his wants, defend his character, and

---

29. See Winks, *Blacks in Canada*, 205–7.
30. Brown-Kubisch, *Queen's Bush Settlement*, 11.
31. ABA, Minute Book, 1854, 122–23.
32. Hill, *Freedom Seekers*, 131.
33. Hill, *Freedom Seekers*, 130–31.

encourage him in his labors."[34] When Rice subsequently failed to account for a seven hundred dollar grant that he received, many Blacks became angry and Rice's involvement in the Association and its support for him quietly faded away.[35]

By the time Mitchell and Troy departed on their fund-raising mission to Britain in 1859, Black Regular Baptists in Canada West had experienced ongoing controversy regarding begging and what constituted acceptable fund-raising activism. Troy and Mitchell's arrival, their relationship, and the decision in the face of the begging controversy to undertake a British fund-raising venture, now requires our attention.

TROY AND MITCHELL'S CANADIAN ARRIVAL, THEIR RELATIONSHIP, AND THEIR DECISION TO SOLICIT BRITISH AID, 1854–1858

William Troy and William Mitchell arrived in Canada West in the mid-1850s. William Troy, a free Black Baptist, was a native of Virginia. He relocated from Cincinnati to Canada West in 1854, and soon began his ministry at the First Baptist Church in Amherstburg.[36] He quickly extended his ministry to Windsor in the form of prayer meetings, and he moved to that city in 1856 with the objective of founding a Black Baptist church.[37] He accomplished this goal while he also served as the fifth pastor of the Second Baptist Church in Detroit.[38] In addition to his pastoral work, Troy was also highly active in the work of the ABFMS and Amherstburg Association. In fact, he became Moderator of the Amherstburg Association in 1855 and a paid missionary for the ABFMS for about six months between 1858 and 1859.[39]

William M. Mitchell was a free Black born in Guildford County, North Carolina, around 1826 to an African American father and a Native American mother. He was orphaned and then indentured for twelve years as an apprentice to a slave owner in North Carolina where, as a

---

34. ABA, Minute Book, 1854, 122–23.

35. This conclusion follows that put forward by other historians (see Shadd, "Extending the Right Hand of Fellowship," 127); Moore-Davis, "Canadian Black Settlements," 87; Shreve, *AfriCanadian Church*, 73.

36. Hill, *Freedom Seekers*, 145; Troy, *Hair-Breadth Escapes*, 7–8.

37. Hill, *Freedom Seekers*, 145.

38. For more details see Hughes-Smith, "Worship Way Stations," 108.

39. ABA, Minute Book, 1855, 162; Annual Reports of ABFMS (1862), 23.

plantation manager, he ordered and witnessed the atrocities perpetrated on Black slaves. After he had served his apprenticeship, he experienced a conversion and became a Baptist minister. He moved to Ohio where he became actively involved in the anti-slavery cause as a conductor in the Underground Railroad doing all in his power "to aid fugitives from slavery in escaping to Canada."[40]

Around 1855, he "became a missionary to the escaped fugitives in Toronto, Canada West, in the service of the American Baptist Free Mission Society."[41] In 1858, the letter to the Haldimand Association from the Coloured Regular Baptist Church, located at the corner of Terauley (Bay Street) and Edward Streets in Toronto, noted "We have given a call to Elder Mitchell as our pastor, who has ministered to us very acceptably."[42] Mitchell was also involved in the social and political life of Toronto. Perhaps his most notable social involvement was his active role in the creation of the Constitution for The Association for the Education and Elevation of the Coloured People of Canada.[43]

Troy and Mitchell had connections at both the personal and professional levels. Both were devoted to the cause of abolition, helping fugitive slaves, the survival and elevation of their Black Baptist brethren, and the strengthening of the Black Baptist community and culture through their pastoral ministries and institutional fund-raising efforts. Troy and Mitchell also had a mutual interest in the advancement of the Black communities in Windsor and Detroit.[44] They were both missionaries for the ABFMS, and they shared similar uplift goals related to Black education and the establishment of Black Baptist churches.[45]

Although there is no direct evidence for how or when the idea of a joint fund-raising excursion to Britain emerged, Mitchell's fact-finding trip to Windsor, on behalf of The Provincial Association for the Education and Elevation of the Coloured People of Canada in 1858, likely

---

40. Mitchell, *Underground Railroad*, v; Shadd et al., *Underground Railroad*, 30, 40–41, 46, 70–72; Ripley et al., eds., *Black Abolitionist Papers: Volume II*, 483.

41. Mitchell, *Underground Railroad*, vi.

42. HRBA, *Minutes, 1858*, 8.

43. Mitchell, *Underground Railroad*, 158.

44. Finkenbine, "Community," 160–61.

45. That education was a focus for Mitchell is evident in his comments about Chatham, ON (see Mitchell, *Underground Railroad*, 141). For Troy's views on education see *Bristol Mercury*, September 15, 1860.

played a role.[46] In any case, Troy and Mitchell were able to secure support for their proposed mission from their Baptist brethren. Daniel Hill and Barbara Hughes-Smith have noted that the members of the Baptist church in Windsor "pooled their resources and sent Troy to England to raise funds" for a church building.[47] In 1859, at a lecture given in Manchester, Troy claimed that "the Rev. Mr. Mitchell . . . had been deputed to this country to raise funds."[48] The object of the mission was extended to include the building of schools, as the need for education was a persistent emphasis of the Amherstburg Association and a primary personal concern for Troy and Mitchell.[49]

PHASE ONE OF TROY AND MITCHELL'S FUND-RAISING MISSION TO BRITAIN, 1859–1860

The two men embarked on their fund-raising journey in the early spring of 1859. By March, they were in Britain and had begun the pre-publication, pre-Civil War phase (between 1859 and 1860) of their fund-raising lecture and sermon tour throughout Ireland, Scotland, Wales, and England. A second phase that began with the publication of Mitchell's narrative in 1860, would take on a different tone and cover new subject matter.

The purpose and motivation for Troy and Mitchell's visit was expressed in a short news summary of their lectures given in Glasgow on March 8, 1859: "The visit of these gentlemen from Canada is for the purpose of collecting a sufficient sum to complete the building of two chapels and school houses already commenced, but stopped for want of funds; and after fruitless efforts at endeavouring to obtain assistance in Canada, they have left their families to test the sympathies of British Christians."[50] Richard Blackett has noted that this venture was after the peak period, from 1848 to 1854, for such missions.[51] Nevertheless, their timing was fortuitous as both Scotland and Ireland, two places that they visited extensively, were experiencing an evangelical revival from 1859 to 1861.[52] In fact, the presence of Mitchell and Troy was noted in a report about a

---

46. Simpson, *Under the North Star*, 301.
47. Hill, *Freedom Seekers*, 145; Hughes-Smith, "Worship Way Stations," 108.
48. *Manchester Times*, 17 December 1859.
49. ABA Minute Book, 1857, 199; Shreve, *AfriCanadian Church*, 27–29.
50. *Glasgow Sentinel*, March 12, 1859.
51. Blackett, *Building an Antislavery Wall*, 145.
52. For information about revival in both Scotland and Ireland see Lennie, *Scotland Ablaze*.

revival union prayer meeting held at the Botanic Gardens in Belfast on 29 June 1859 where "the number present at any one time could not have been less than 10,000 to 15,000 individuals."[53]

Newspaper content that promoted and summarized Mitchell and Troy's lectures and sermons was a critical factor in realizing fund-raising success. Advertising in a local newspaper played a key role in creating public awareness, attracting interest, and giving notice that funds would be solicited. For example, the advertisement printed in Bristol's *Western Daily Press*, on 3 October 1860, was typical:

> *Fugitive Slaves in Canada*
>
> A lecture on Fugitive Slaves in Canada West will be delivered in Counterally Chapel, by Rev. William Troy (Coloured Minister), of Windsor, Canada West, This Wednesday evening. Chair to be taken at Seven O'clock.
>
> Many interesting facts and anecdotes will be given, connected with the Underground Railway and the escape of Fugitive Slaves to Canada, their perils, sufferings during the journey, and destitution in their arrival—the relief afforded—their industrial, mental, and moral condition.
>
> A collection will be made after the Lecture in aid of Building a Chapel and School Room for the Fugitive Slaves now resident at Windsor, C.W.[54]

The hope, of course, was that a large audience would attend and give generously to Mitchell and Troy's causes. Collections after a lecture were certainly a key method of acquiring funds. For example, after Troy delivered a lecture at Mossley on 8 February 1860, which included "a number of photographic likenesses of some of his relatives and fugitive brethren," a collection yielded the sum of "£11.8s."[55]

Other fund-raising collection methods were also utilized. Donations were also made by subscription or directly by a person or organization. After lectures by Mitchell and Troy in Glasgow on March 8, 1859, for example, those desirous of providing aid were informed that "subscriptions may be forwarded to any of the Ministers of Glasgow or elsewhere, who will have no difficulty in communicating with them [Mitchell and

---

53. *Guardian*, July 5, 1859.
54. *Western Daily Press*, October 3, 1860.
55. *Ashton and Stalybridge Reporter*, February 11, 1860.

Troy]."[56] According to Daniel Hill, Troy received a "donation from Queen Victoria who granted him an audience."[57] A 1967 history of First Baptist Church, Windsor, noted that "Rev. Troy journeyed to England to gain the [church land] Grant from Her Majesty, Queen Victoria."[58] Mitchell also had some fund-raising success. The 1859 letter from the Coloured Baptist Church in Toronto to the Haldimand Association recorded a key early outcome of Mitchell's efforts: "Are building a new Chapel—have it up and enclosed. Our pastor is in England, collecting, with considerable success."[59] Clearly, Mitchell and Troy's fund-raising activism utilized a variety of collection methods that were effective and wide-reaching.

Troy and Mitchell delivered lectures and sermons together and separately. As Richard Blackett has noted, a venture such as this followed well-established patterns including the offering of informative and persuasive "resistance" lectures designed "to evoke revulsion at American repression."[60] Topics covered by Mitchell and Troy in the first phase of their mission in 1850–1859 included a history of slavery in America, the vagaries of slavery, riveting accounts of escapes from slavery, and the moral, religious, socio-economic, psychological, and physical condition of fugitive slaves in Canada West.

On topics such as deprivation, loss, moral character, and the current amount of economic hardship experienced by fugitive slaves, which often generated charges of begging against fund-raisers, Mitchell and Troy walked a fine line in their lectures. On the one hand, they informed their audience that many fugitives had suffered pain and loss. In his lecture, delivered at Berry Street Church in Ulster on June 20, 1859, Mitchell underscored the losses and painful experiences of fugitive slaves seeking freedom in Canada. He "showed the feeling that prevailed among the Negro population of the Southern States for liberty; he depicted their struggles for freedom and the sufferings which they had undergone to obtain that object."[61]

Mitchell and Troy also openly shared the hardship stories of others and their personal experience of injustice. For example, in his Bristol

56. *Glasgow Sentinel*, March 12, 1859.
57. Hill, *Freedom Seekers*, 145.
58. Perry, *Long Road*, 122.
59. HRBA, *Minutes*, 1859, 8.
60. Blackett, *Building an Antislavery Wall*, 15–16.
61. *Banner of Ulster*, June 21, 1859.

lecture of September 13, 1860, Troy focussed on the denial of Black access to education in both America and Canada. He argued that, when it came to education, Blacks were treated with "contempt," and he admitted, "that not having opportunities for education, they were ignorant, and his great wonder was that they were not worse than they were."[62] Troy went on to illustrate the persistence of injustice by citing his own experience of mistreatment. For "even in the town of Windsor, in Canada West, where he resided," he noted, "the prejudice against people of colour had so followed them from the States, that his children were not allowed to attend the schoolhouse, for which he, in company with others in the coloured population, paid taxes."[63]

On the other hand, in their comments about economic hardship, both Mitchell and Troy emphasized the industry and success of the fugitive slaves. In his address at the Manchester Independent Chapel on December 15, 1859, for example, Troy noted that before his tour of Canada in 1850, "He had . . . been led to suppose the coloured people were in distress, but [he] was agreeably surprised to find the contrary. Many of the people followed various trades, and large numbers were farmers, and generally prosperous."[64]

Furthermore, the need for money to erect religious and educational institutions was consistently pressed upon the audience. For example, in the summary of Mitchell's lecture delivered on Monday June 20, 1859, in Belfast "to a public meeting" in "Dr. Cooke's Church" where "the attendance was very large," *The Northern Whig* emphasized his solicitation of funds: "Mr. Mitchell concluded a speech of great eloquence by appealing to the audience for pecuniary support to aid in the erection of schools and churches for the use of the poor Africans who are 'forced from home and all its treasures.'"[65] Similarly, at the end of his lecture about "the moral and religious condition of the fugitive slaves of Canada," given in Bristol, a traditional Baptist stronghold, on September 13, 1860, at the Old King Street Baptist school room, Troy "concluded by appealing to his audience to assist the fugitive slaves of Canada in building schools and places of worship, where they might be educated and taught the blessings to be

62. *Bristol Mercury*, September 15, 1860.
63. *Bristol Mercury*, September 15, 1860.
64. *Manchester Weekly Times*, December 17, 1859.
65. *Northern Whig*, June 21, 1859.

derived from the knowledge of the Gospel of Christ."[66] Clearly, a strong fund-raising appeal was a staple in Mitchell and Troy's presentations.

Mitchell and Troy's attempts to avoid the begging label were not entirely successful. Their fund-raising activism was characterized as "begging" by Julia Griffiths-Croft, a prominent British abolitionist with strong ties to the paragon of Black American abolitionists, Frederick Douglass. Griffiths-Croft did not mince words, in her letter of September 12, 1860, regarding her concerns about Mitchell and Troy's fund-raising and an onslaught of other solicitations for British aid:

> The subject of slavery is certainly being brought before our people at this time, and subscriptions towards some branch of the cause are being levied in all directions. In one town we have Mr. Mitchell begging for a chapel and school in Toronto. In another, Mr. Troy, collecting for a similar object in Canada West. *Here*, there is Rev. W[illiam] King, asking contributions for Buxton settlement; and *there* is Mr. Day, raising funds towards starting a newspaper. Then we have a host of coloured friends going up and down the country east, west, north and south, collecting money to buy their various relatives out of slavery.[67]

In contrast, other notable abolitionists expressed their support for Mitchell and Troy's fund-raising efforts and their objectives. For example, the testimonial in support of William Mitchell's fund-raising activism offered by the ardent and well-known abolitionist MP George Thompson on August 20, 1860, carried considerable weight:

> I can with confidence recommend you [Mitchell] to the Abolitionists of Great Britain, having made myself acquainted with your credentials, knowing, also, that you are the authorized agent of the Free Mission Society, and that you possess the esteem and good opinion of those whom you represent in Canada. The work in which you are engaged is a most important one, both in connection with the welfare of those who are fortunate enough to escape from slavery into the British dominions, and the progressive improvement and elevation, morally and religiously, of the coloured community of Western Canada.[68]

A long list of such commendations and expressions of support from other prominent British abolitionists, and in news reports about

66. *Bristol Daily Post*, September 14, 1860.
67. *Douglass Monthly*, November 1860.
68. Mitchell, *Underground Railroad*, 186.

the fund-raising work of Mitchell and Troy, provided a counter-weight to Croft's charge of begging. As the report about Mitchell and Troy's fund-raising efforts that appeared in the January 2, 1860 issue of *Anti-Slavery Reporter* observed, "the ministers of several towns in England and Scotland have identified themselves fully with the object."[69]

The first pre-publication phase of Mitchell and Troy's Fund-raising mission to Britain in 1859 and 1860 was generally well received by British audiences. Based on the available evidence, their lectures and sermons often persuaded those who heard them that their causes were worthy of support. Collections, subscriptions, and donations for the building of churches and schools in Windsor and Toronto did generate funds. However, changing circumstances in North America would soon change the tone, content, and status of their fund-raising activism.

PHASE TWO OF TROY AND MITCHELL'S FUND-RAISING MISSION TO BRITAIN, 1860–1861

While Mitchell and Troy certainly experienced their share of notoriety in 1859 and 1860, two events, in the second phase of their initiative in 1860 and 1861, brought more public attention to their efforts, more notoriety, and created a greater sense of urgency in their appeals for aid.

The increase in public awareness began in 1860 with the publication of William Mitchell's narrative entitled, *The Underground Railroad Slavery to Freedom*. The publication brought higher praise and added credibility to reports about Mitchell and Troy's fund-raising tour. The report that appeared in the December 1, 1860 issue of *The Luton Times and Dunstable Herald*, for example, noted Mitchell's narrative and was effusive in its praise: "A most attractive series of anti-slavery meetings have been held in Sheffield Nottingham," the report declared, "and several other towns, and addressed by the Rev. William Mitchell, of Toronto, author of 'The Underground Railroad,' and coloured minister of an American fugitive slave church."[70] Similarly, William Troy's 1861 publication of *Hair-Breath Escapes from Slavery to Freedom* drew its share of attention. For example, at an anti-slavery meeting held in Hull on April 21, 1861, the Chairman, Sheriff Dannatt, "read an extract, at some length, from Mr. Troy's little work, and called upon Mr. Troy to address the meeting."[71] Such public

69. *Anti-Slavery Reporter*, January 2, 1860.
70. *Luton Times*, December 1, 1860.
71. *Hull Packet*, April 26, 1861.

recognition of their published work put Mitchell and Troy's activism on a new level.

Other evidence of increased notoriety is found in news reports about Mitchell and Troy's fund-raising activism in this post-publication phase. For example, by 1861, William Howard Day, whom one report called "the most talented representative and advocate for the coloured race that has ever addressed an English assembly," made regular public lecture appearances with William Troy and, on occasion, William Mitchell.[72] Appearances with Day certainly enhanced the reach and reputation of Mitchell and Troy.

Furthermore, the association with Day also boosted Troy and Mitchell's fund-raising results. After one Day and Troy lecture was delivered in Hull, the *Hull Advertiser* of April 27, 1861, noted the response: "At the close of the meeting a strong appeal was made for subscriptions, when a very fair sum was collected."[73] A similar account was given later in the *Cheltenham Journal and Gloucestershire Gazette* of July 20, 1861: "An appeal was then made on behalf of the schools and chapel fund, which we understand was most liberally responded to."[74] On another occasion in Leeds, Troy disclosed, "he had been able to send £600, with which a chapel had been erected, a photograph of which he exhibited."[75] This evidence is important for two reasons. It demonstrates that some of Mitchell and Troy's fund-raising goals were achieved and that their efforts were substantially enhanced through the assistance offered by William Howard Day.

Of course, there was another key factor that reshaped this second phase. The start of the American Civil War, on April 12, 1861, altered both the content and level of urgency in Mitchell and Troy's appeals for aid. Their interactions in August 1861 with the Cork Ladies' Association, For the Religious and Moral Improvement of the Fugitive Slaves and Coloured Races in Canada, demonstrate how the Civil War altered the substance and tone of their fund-raising activism. Using extracts from their letters to and from home, Mitchell and Troy outlined the crisis that faced those in Canada who were trying to cope with an influx of fugitive slaves. Mitchell noted, "Emigration [of fugitive slaves] is more numerous since

---

72. See *Hull Packet*, April 26, 1861.
73. *Hull Advertiser*, April 27, 1861.
74. *Cheltenham Journal*, July 20, 1861.
75. *Leeds Intelligencer*, August 3, 1861.

the war in the United States than in any previous period." Troy noted that "At the town of Windsor, my home, within the last ten weeks not less than 500 have found shelter under the British flag, and many more are expected." Troy then made an appeal for more aid: "I cannot help," Troy declared, "but think that we shall have to put forth doubled effort for their physical wants." Similarly, Mitchell emphasized the urgent need for aid: "It is indeed earnestly to be hoped that the means will not be wanting to provide for the temporary sustenance and ultimate employment of these exiles from bondage."[76] Unfortunately, we do not have a record of how successful these appeals were in raising more funds. But the shift in both content and tone of Mitchell and Troy's appeals was palpable after the Civil War began.

The two phases of Mitchell and Troy's fund-raising mission to Britain, between 1859 and 1861, certainly caught the attention and imagination of those who listened to their appeals for aid. Clearly, the available evidence shows that, in the case of the Baptist chapel in Windsor, money did flow from Troy back to his church for the construction of that facility. The same appears to be true for Mitchell's chapel in Toronto. Unfortunately, specific information about whether funds raised in Britain were ever spent on a school in Windsor or Toronto was not found in the sources consulted for this study. One may reasonably conclude that Mitchell and Troy's fund-raising activism was at least partially successful in achieving its stated objectives of promoting resistance and Black social uplift through successful fund-raising for religious institutions. Of course, the story did not end here. Mitchell would subsequently undertake another fund-raising mission on his own.

A "PIOUS FRAUDSTER": WILLIAM MITCHELL'S DESPERATE AND DEVIOUS FUND-RAISING VENTURE, 1863–1864

Historians have noted and partially examined Mitchell's second fund-raising excursion to Britain. However, several important questions remain unanswered. Why did Mitchell make this trip? What did he actually do? How does one explain his behaviour? And what were the outcomes of his actions? While this short section does not provide complete answers to these questions, the material offered here does bring together

---

76. All of the quotations in this paragraph are taken from the *Constitution*, August 17, 1861.

the existing scholarship and provides new evidence that enhances one's understanding of what happened.

Based on a piecing together of the available evidence, it appears that Mitchell's decision to revisit Britain in search of funds was driven by tragedy and hardship at home. Adrienne Shadd, Afua Cooper, and Karolyn Smardz-Frost have noted, "Reverend Mitchell's daughter Eliza, who had been born in Ohio, died of inflammation in 1861 at the age of six years eleven months."[77] Furthermore, Mitchell was no longer pastor of the coloured Baptist church in Toronto by 1863. In fact, the church was without "the services of a settled Pastor."[78] The church was experiencing considerable discord and its affairs were administered by Thomas Ford Caldicott, said to have a talent for peacemaking, who served as the pastor of the influential Bond Street Baptist Church.[79] By 1864, the letter from the Black Baptist church to the Haldimand Association reported that the situation had finally been resolved: "Difficulties have been settled by the separation of a number of brethren who have been organized into a church in another part of the city."[80] The letter also noted that the church still had "no pastor."[81] Although the details about the severing of Mitchell's pastoral relationship with his church are unclear, the loss of his position was one he could not afford. With a wife and four remaining children to support, Mitchell's situation was likely desperate. Whatever his circumstances or motivations were, he decided to return to Britain in April 1863 to raise more aid.[82]

Mitchell's actions and behaviour on his second fund-raising journey are documented in his own words found in numerous news reports and published denunciations. On the surface, Mitchell's venture had all the appearances of the second phase of his first visit with Troy. His public lecture topics included slavery, the Civil War, his aid to fugitive slaves in their fight to freedom as discussed in his published narrative, and the state of the fugitives in Canada.[83]

77. Shadd et al., *Underground Railroad*, 46.
78. HRBA, *Minutes, 1863*, 11.
79. HRBA, *Minutes, 1863*, 11; Wilson, "Baptists and Business," 170.
80. HRBA, *Minutes, 1864*, 9.
81. HRBA, *Minutes, 1864*, 9.
82. Ripley et al., eds., *Black Abolitionist Papers: Volume I*, 483.
83. See *Sussex Advertiser*, November 3, 1863; *Maidstone and Kentish Journal*, December 8, 1863; *Sussex Advertiser*, January 2, 1864; *Windsor and Eton Express Berks*, April 16, 1864.

But Mitchell's decisions and conduct were cast in the British abolitionist community as scandalous and "delinquent."[84] An early exposure of Mitchell's unethical behaviour came with the publication of J. Sella Martin's public denunciation of him in the London *Patriot* on June 25, 1863. Martin, a highly respected Black American pastor and abolitionist, had, in January 1863, become the pastor of London's nondenominational abolitionist Free Christian Church.[85] Sella denounced Mitchell for misrepresentation and fraud: "Rev. William Mitchell is pretending to be on intimate terms with me, and [he] has used my name to sanction his pretended mission." Furthermore, Sella declared, "I have never seen the said William Mitchell since I have been in England, and further from that I hear of him that he is not worthy of the confidence and sympathy of the Christian public."[86]

Following Sella's public denunciation, Mitchell's behaviour worsened. Historian Jeffery Green has recently claimed that Mitchell was "a pious semi-fraudster" who "obtained alms by begging but used 'old and fraudulent credentials' and kept no records."[87] While there is certainly evidence to support Green's claims, the offences he lists are only part of the story. In fact, Mitchell's failings also included the non-payment of lodging expenses, lying, deviousness, and deceit. While news sources substantiated these charges, Mitchell's own words also verified his committal of these offences.

Mitchell's nefarious exploits reached their peak in the spring and fall of 1864. News reports about his activities alerted the public and prompted confrontations with Mitchell and his confession. On March 15, 1864, after Benjamin Copeland Etheridge, Baptist Minister of Ramsgate, and John Edgar, Grocer of Canterbury, confronted Mitchell, he admitted in a written confession that he was guilty of serious wrongdoing: "I have, for some time past, travelled with old credentials such as I obtained on my first visit," Mitchell declared, "that have not been renewed." Mitchell then confessed to committing other offences: "I admit having taken apartments at Mr. Collard's and Mr. Smith's, Canterbury, and gone away without paying for the same. I admit having told many falsehoods to the parties herein named." Finally, Mitchell made the questionable claim

---

84. *Anti-Slavery Reporter*, May 2, 1864.
85. See Ripley et al., eds., *Black Abolitionist Papers: Volume I*, 1, 3, 534–35.
86. *Patriot*, June 25, 1863.
87. Green, *Black Americans*, 55, 65.

that he had "collected about 400L, which I have transmitted to Nathaniel Warren of Toronto, less my travelling expenses and salary, through banks at Reading, Plymouth, North America Bank, London." Mitchell also promised "to leave the country" immediately, but that did not happen.[88]

Unfortunately, Mitchell's confession and promise at Ramsgate did not alter his behaviour. His deception, falsehood, and failure to make payments continued. Eventually, charges were brought against Mitchell in Birmingham and Cardiff. When Mitchell was confronted in Penmark, Wales, about his past wrongdoing and asked if he was *Wm Mitchell*, he offered the following response: "No, but I know who you mean. I have never seen him, but I have heard of him. He is a vile imposter-a humbug-and has but just got out of Birmingham gaol, after twenty-one days of it! His name was William, but my name is Matthew." After his confronters noted that he was "exceedingly fortunate in being *Matthew*, and not *William*" and that they would "feel great pleasure in drawing you [if he was William] through the horse pond nearby," they warned Mitchell that he might be "taken by mistake" and that "the gentlemen who tried *William* on Monday last, lives not far off."[89] After he experienced these threats, intimidation, and public expressions of outrage, Mitchell had breakfast at his lodgings the next morning "and left-without settling his account."[90]

Mitchell's wrongdoing and fraudulent fund-raising activities produced four outcomes. First, Mitchell's actions brought out latent racist attitudes indicative of racial prejudice.[91] Secondly, on a personal level Mitchell was discredited and disgraced;[92] and his probable desperate financial situation was not alleviated.[93] Thirdly, the scandal and suspicion created by Mitchell's exploits did damage to the reputation and credibility of the abolitionist cause and made the task of fund-raising more challenging for legitimate Black fundraisers like J. Sella Martin.[94] Finally,

---

88. All of the quotations in this paragraph are taken from *Anti-Slavery Reporter*, May 2, 1864.

89. *Cardiff and Merthyr Guardian*, October 21, 1864.

90. All of quotations in this paragraph are taken from *Cardiff and Merthyr Guardian*, October 21, 1864.

91. See *Cardiff and Merthyr Guardian*, October 21, 1864; *Carmanthan Journal*, October 14, 1864; *Cardiff Times*, October 21, 1864.

92. *Anti-Slavery Reporter*, May 2, 1864.

93. According to one 1864 news report "on coming to Cardiff he [Mitchell] was very needy indeed" (see *Carmanthan Journal*, October 14, 1864).

94. Ripley et al., eds., *Black Abolitionist Papers: Volume I*, 556–64.

Mitchell's folly gave further impetus to British efforts to reform fund-raising through the rigorous application of a *certification system*. According to Ripley, this system "was designed to guarantee the character of a fundraiser, the nature of his request, and the integrity of collection procedures."[95]

In conclusion, fund-raising in support of Blacks in Canada West was a highly problematic issue for central Canadian Regular Baptists in the mid-nineteenth century. The British fundraising endeavours of William Troy and William Mitchell exhibited the best and the worst of attempts to secure aid for religious and educational institutions that were essential for realizing Black social uplift.[96] On the one hand, Troy and Mitchell's first fund-raising foray, between 1859 and 1861, resulted in the building of chapels in Windsor and Toronto. On the other hand, Mitchell's desperate and misguided second venture, in 1863 and 1864, did more harm than good for those Black abolitionists who continued to seek British aid for the creation and support of Black institutions.

More study of Canadian Regular Baptist fund-raising efforts on behalf of Blacks is certainly needed to deepen and widen our understanding of such endeavours. Future explorations need to examine, in far more detail, Canadian and American responses to Troy and Mitchell's fund-raising efforts, the role of women in fund-raising, the efforts and contributions of individual Canadian Regular Baptist churches, and activities and actions of the True Bands and Vigilance Committees. One hopes that this chapter has provided some answers to lingering questions and a stimulus for future studies focused on Regular Baptist fund-raising on behalf of Black causes.

BIBLIOGRAPHY

Primary Sources

ARCHIVES

Amherstburg Baptist Association (ABA) Minutes, 1841–1877.
Annual Reports of ABFMS (American Baptist Free Mission Society), 1855–1868.
Haldimand Baptist Association Minutes, 1850–1865.

---

95. Ripley et al., eds., *Black Abolitionist Papers: Volume I*, 561; Fishman, "Charitable Accountability."

96. If Mitchell was an example of the worst, it can be argued that Troy was one of the best Black Baptist fund-raisers. In 1863, the ABFMS commended his efforts "in England and Jamaica, in raising funds to complete his chapel" in Windsor (see Annual Reports of ABFMS [1863], 8).

Monographs

Mitchell, William M. *The Underground Railroad from Slavery to Freedom.* London: William Tweedie, 1860.
Troy, William. *Hair-Breadth Escapes from Slavery to Freedom.* Manchester, UK: W. Bremner, 1861.

Newspapers and Magazines

Anti-Slavery Reporter, 1859–1865.
Ashton and Stalybridge Reporter, 1859–1862.
Banner of Ulster, 1859–1862.
Bristol Daily Post, 1859–1862.
Bristol Mercury and Western Counties Advertiser, 1859–1862.
Cardiff and Merthyr Guardian, 1863–1864.
Cardiff Times, 1863–1864.
Carmanthan Journal, 1863–1864.
Cheltenham Journal and Gloucestershire Gazette, 1859–1862.
Constitution; or, Cork Advertiser, 1859–1862.
Douglass Monthly, 1859–1865.
Glasgow Sentinel, 1859–1862.
Guardian (Glasgow), 1859–1862.
Hull Advertiser, 1859–1862.
Hull Packet and East Riding Times, 1859–1862.
Leeds Intelligencer, 1859–1862.
Luton Times and Dunstable Herald, 1859–1862.
Maidstone and Kentish Journal, 1863–1864.
Manchester Weekly Times, 1859–1862.
The Northern Whig, 1859–1862.
Patriot (London), 1863–1864.
The Provincial Freeman (Windsor, Toronto, Chatham, ON), 1853–1860
Richmond Planet, 1905.
Sussex Advertiser & Weald of Kent Chronicle, 1863–1864.
Voice of the Fugitive (Sandwich, Canada West), 1851–1853.
Western Daily Press, 1859–1862.
Windsor and Eton Express Berks, Bucks, and Middlesex Journal, and West Surrey Gazette, 1863–1864.

Secondary Sources

Blackett, Richard J. M. *Building an Antislavery Wall: Black Americans in the Atlantic Abolitionist Movement, 1830–1860.* Baton Rouge: Louisiana State University Press, 1983.
Bliss, Michael. *Northern Enterprise: Five Centuries of Canadian Business.* Toronto: McClelland and Stewart, 1987.
Brown-Kubisch, Linda. *The Queen's Bush Settlement: Black Pioneers 1839–1865.* Toronto: Natural Heritage, 2004.
Cooper, Afua. "The *Voice of the Fugitive*: A Transnational Abolitionist Organ." In *A Fluid Frontier: Slavery, Resistance, and the Underground Railroad in the Detroit

River Borderland, edited *by* Karolyn Smardz Frost and Veta Smith Tucker, 135–53. Detroit: Wayne State University Press, 2016.

Finkenbine, Roy. "A Community Militant and Organized: The Colored Vigilant Committee of Detroit." In *A Fluid Frontier: Slavery, Resistance, and the Underground Railroad in the Detroit River Borderland*, edited *by* Karolyn Smardz Frost and Veta Smith Tucker, 154–64. Detroit: Wayne State University Press, 2016.

Fishman, James J. "Charitable Accountability and Reform in Nineteenth-Century England: The Case of the Charity Commission." *Chicago-Kent Law Review* 80 (2005) 723–78.

Gaines, Kevin K. *Uplifting the Race: Black, Leadership, Politics, and Culture in the Twentieth Century*. Chapel Hill: North Carolina University Press, 1996.

Green, Jeffrey. *Black Americans in Victorian Britain*. Barnsley, UK: Pen and Sword, 2018.

Gibson, Theo T. *Robert Alexander Fyfe: His Contemporaries and his Influence*. Burlington, ON: Welch, 1988.

Heath, Gordon L., Dallas Friesen, and Taylor Murray, eds. *Baptists in Canada: Their History and Polity*. McMaster Ministry Studies Series 5. Eugene, OR: Pickwick, 2020.

Hill, Daniel G. *The Freedom Seekers: Blacks in Early Canada*. Agincourt, ON: The Book Society of Canada, 1981.

Hughes-Smith, Barbara. "Worship Way Stations in Detroit." In *A Fluid Frontier: Slavery, Resistance, and the Underground Railroad in the Detroit River Borderland*, edited *by* Karolyn Smardz Frost and Veta Smith Tucker, 103–19. Detroit: Wayne State University Press, 2016.

Lennie, Tom. *Scotland Ablaze: The Twenty-Five Year Fire of Revival That Swept Scotland, 1858–79*. Geanies House, Scotland: Christian Focus, 2018.

McCalla, Douglas. *Planting the Province: The Economic History of Upper Canada, 1784–1870*. Ontario Historical Studies Series. Toronto: University of Toronto Press, 1993.

Moore-Davis, Irene. "Canadian Black Settlements in the Detroit River Region." In *A Fluid Frontier: Slavery, Resistance, and the Underground Railroad in the Detroit River Borderland*, edited *by* Karolyn Smardz Frost and Veta Smith Tucker, 83–102. Detroit: Wayne State University Press, 2016.

Perry, Charlotte Bronté. *The Long Road: A History of the Coloured Canadian in Windsor, Ontario, 1867–1967*. Windsor, ON: Summer, 1969.

Ripley, C. Peter, et al., eds. *The Black Abolitionist Papers: Volume I. British Isles, 1830–1865*. Chapel Hill: University of North Carolina Press, 2015.

———. *The Black Abolitionist Papers: Volume II. Canada, 1830–1865*. Chapel Hill: University of North Carolina Press, 2015.

Shadd, Adrienne. "Extending the Right Hand of Fellowship: Sandwich Baptist Church, Amherstburg First Baptist, and the Amherstburg Baptist Association." In *A Fluid Frontier: Slavery, Resistance, and the Underground Railroad in the Detroit River Borderland*, edited *by* Karolyn Smardz Frost and Veta Smith Tucker, 120–32. Detroit: Wayne State University Press, 2016.

Shadd, Adrienne, et al. *The Underground Railroad: Next Stop Toronto*. Toronto: Dundurn, 2005.

Shreve, Dorothy S. *The AfriCanadian Church: A Stabilizer*. Jordan Station, ON: Paideia, 1983.

Simpson, Donald George. *Under the North Star: Black Communities in Upper Canada before Confederation (1876)*. Trenton, NJ: Africa World, 2005.

Taylor, Graham D., and Peter A. Baskerville. *A Concise History of Business in Canada*. Toronto: Oxford University Press, 1994.

Tobin, Jacqueline L. *From Midnight to Dawn: The Last Tracks of the Underground Railroad*. New York: Anchor, 2008.

Wells, J. E. *Life and Labors of Robert Alex. Fyfe, D.D.* Toronto: W. J. Gage & Company, 1885.

Wilson, Paul R. "Baptists and Business: Central Canadian Baptists and the Secularization of the Businessmen at Toronto's Jarvis Street Baptist Church, 1848–1921." PhD diss., University of Western Ontario, 1996.

———. "Caring for their Community: The Philanthropic and Moral Reform Efforts of Toronto's Baptists, 1834–1918." In *Baptists and Public Life in Canada*, edited Gordon L. Heath and Paul R. Wilson, 219–62. McMaster General Studies Series 2. Canadian Baptist Historical Society Series 1. Eugene, OR: Pickwick, 2012.

Winks, Robin. *The Blacks in Canada: A History*. 2nd ed. Montreal: McGill University Press, 1997.

5

Black Baptist Print Culture in Nineteenth-Century Canada West

Nina Reid-Maroney

The Argyll Congregational Chapel in the city of Bath is built of cream-coloured stone and stands on Great Pulteney Street not far from the bridge over the Avon River. Across the Georgian cityscape, commemorative plaques mark Bath's links to the antislavery movement—noting sites associated with figures such as William Wilberforce and Hannah More. No outward signs mark the antislavery history of the Argyll Chapel. But in the winter of 1861, as the United States stood on the precipice of civil war, two Black abolitionists active in Baptist congregations in Canada West spoke at the Argyll Chapel to an audience eager to hear of their work. The lecture tour that brought Reverend William Troy of Windsor and the Reverend William Mitchell of Toronto to speak on the conditions and prospects of freedom seekers in Canada helps us to trace the vibrant Black abolitionist networks that linked the nineteenth-century communities in Canada West to the global movement to end racial slavery—even as it points to ways in which much of that history of transatlantic engagement has largely disappeared from public memory. While they were in England, however, both William Troy and William Mitchell wrote their presence into the historical record of the transatlantic antislavery movement by publishing books.[1]

---

1. William Troy and William Mitchell's presence in Bath is noted in the tours given by local historian Roger Holly. On the hidden histories of slavery and resistance in Bath

William Troy's *Hair-Breadth Escapes from Slavery to Freedom* and William Mitchell's *The Underground Railroad* joined the works of other Baptist ministers whose abolitionist activities centred on authorship and print culture—including figures such as Nathaniel and Benjamin Paul, Israel Lewis, William Newman, and Samuel Davis. Their works, published widely in the Black press and in other antislavery newspapers, can be placed in the wider context of Baptist-linked periodical literature—from Henry and Mary Bibb's *Voice of the Fugitive*, the first Black newspaper in Canada, to "phantom texts" like the Reverend Peter Stanford's *Christian Defender*, known only through its mention in other print works.[2] While important research on Black abolitionist thought and activism in nineteenth century Canada has included some of the individual works produced by Black Baptist writers and editors, the work of Black Baptist print culture has not been treated as a literary tradition produced in a specific theological context. Yet the materials of Black Baptist print constitute one of the richest archives in Canada's abolitionist past. The recent work of historians, including Derrick Spires, Eric Gardner, and Teresa Goddu, pointed to the rich possibilities of combining textual and literary analysis with the analysis of the material features of print—including printing history, illustration, inscription, annotation, advertisements, endorsements, and typography.[3] This body of scholarship offers new ways to examine familiar sources, and new ways to contextualize and read evidence that appears to be fragmentary and ephemeral. Examining the materials of Black Baptist print from the perspective of book history and attending to the material features and publishing histories of texts, as well as to their intellectual and political content, this chapter argues that antislavery books, newspapers, pamphlets, and articles produced by Black Baptists in the nineteenth-century Canada West gave material form to an activist theology of print.

The expression "theology of print" is rooted in studies of the Protestant Reformation. It enters scholarship on nineteenth-century abolition

---

and Bristol in relation to memory studies, see Otele, "Slavery and Visual Memory" (blog), August 29, 2016; Bell et al., "From Uncle Tom's Cabin to Countering Colston"; Mitchell, *Underground Railroad*; Troy, *Hair-Breadth Escapes*.

2. McCaskill and Serafini, eds., *Magnificent Reverend*, 7.

3. Jackson, "Talking Book"; Spires, *Practice of Citizenship*; Goddu, "Slave Narrative"; *Selling Antislavery*; Foreman et al., *Colored Conventions Movement*; Roy, "Cheap Editions."

through Kenyon Gradert's work on William Lloyd Garrison's *Liberator*.[4] Gradert argues that White New England abolitionists expressed a "theology of print" or a "theology of the press" by laying claim to the spirit of the Reformation and the role of print technologies in Protestantism's expansion. But if White abolitionists found in print culture the power to reconnect their cause to the radicalism of the Protestant Reformation, Black abolitionists engaged in something more than simply thinking about their activism in print as part of a theological tradition of protest. Their work invites consideration of a more expansive concept of a theology of print—one that can account for the ways in which Black authors tied their textual production to deep theological concepts of community, testimony, and of witness. Both William Troy and William Mitchell used such concepts to write books at once grounded in the historical experience contained within their pages and informed by a larger framework of meaning derived from their understanding of scripture, authorship, and textual study. Their works used a self-aware engagement in the culture of print to address epistemologies of erasure and the acts of anti-Black violence that extended into the forced silences of the historical record.[5] While examining their texts can help us trace writing, printing, reading practices, and map transatlantic networks of activism, the analysis also reveals the outlines of a self-reflexive approach to print imbued with a reverence for the central metaphor of the Word and inspired by biblical imagery that spoke of the redemptive power of acts of inscription.

During the period between the founding of the Wilberforce settlement in 1832 in Upper Canada and the establishing of the *Voice of the Fugitive* in 1851, Black Baptist abolitionists published short pieces interspersed through newspapers, political convention minutes, and pamphlet literature. Even fragments of this evidence reveal a theologically grounded and historically framed assignation of power to words-in-print. Figures such as Samuel Davis and William Newman, both of whom would minister in the Baptist congregation that grew up around the Dawn settlement, were known to communities in Canada West first through their published work and identified that work as a strategic component of abolitionist organizing. An 1843 speech of the Reverend Samuel Davis, for example, offers a glimpse of widely published textual

---

4. Mailloux, "Enactment History."

5. On historiography that counters silence on and erasure of Black presence in archives and other historical records, see Fuentes, *Dispossessed Lives*; Smallwood, "Politics"; Whitfield, "White Archives."

material that owed much to the rich aural cultures of the church and the political convention movement. Transcribed and published in the Minutes of the National Convention of the Colored Citizens Held at Buffalo, Davis's speech focused on the need for political action:

> It is our right, our duty, and, I hope I may say, our fixed determination, to make known our wrongs to the world, and to our oppressors; to cease not day nor night to "tell, in burning words, our tale of woe" and pour a flood of living light on the minds and consciences of the oppressor; till we change their thoughts, feelings, and actions towards us as men and citizens of this land.[6]

Davis uses an intertextual reference to tie his call of moral suasion to the poetry of the Welsh poet Felicia Hemans, and claims the metaphor of burning words for the abolitionist cause.[7] Davis's call for words that would "pour a flood of living light on the minds and consciences of the oppressor" evokes biblical imagery of inscription and proclamation, while connecting the language of prophecy to the immediate experiences of enslavement, disenfranchisement, and violence.

Useful parallels to Baptist engagement with print are found in Eric Gardner's transformative study of the *Christian Recorder*, the denominational paper of the African Methodist Episcopal Church. Gardner's work traces the relationship between the church and Black activist networks constituted in print, arguing that in the mid-nineteenth century, AME Church publications, including the *Christian Recorder*, extended the reach of the AME as an organization and expanded the influence of practical abolitionist theologies that ran through AME networks.[8] The role of print in the AME tradition reaches back to its founding documents and the work of Richard Allen; print production was promoted in the next generation of leadership under Bishop Daniel Payne. By contrast, Black Baptist history and church polity meant that a single denominational paper did not emerge in the same way from a central publishing house on the AME model until after the Civil War. Articles published in historically White Baptist churches and denominational newspapers,

---

6. Samuel Davis's speech printed in Minutes of the National Convention of the Colored Citizens. For biographical detail on Davis, see Ripley et al., eds., *Black Abolitionist Papers: Volume II*, 494.

7. The line "And tell in burning words thy tale of wrong" appears in Hemans, "Switzer's Wife." On this poem's transatlantic influence, particularly on African American poetry, see Lootens, *Political Poetess*, 183–89.

8. Gardner, *Black Print Unbound*.

including the *American Baptist*, were noted in the Black press in Canada, but were often controversial for the ways in which, as Henry Bibb noted, Black communities in Canada and their activities were misrepresented.[9] In 1893, Black Baptists in the National Baptist Convention set out the importance of funding their own print materials, arguing that "as a denomination we shall never attain to the broad influence and elevated dignity worthy of so vast a body of Baptists, so long as our literary productions remain unpublished, our work unsystematized, and its success remains dependent upon the option of our friends for prosecution."[10] The committee alluded to "hundreds of literary and theological productions from the pens of colored Baptists, eminently worthy of publication and issuance, and which should be published for the good of the people, but because our friends care not to publish them, they remain unpublished, hence are lost to the denomination and the world."[11] The call for a Black Baptist publishing house, including ownership of the presses and type, as well as the control over published content, addressed questions of racial equality and identity that resonated in new ways during the aftermath of Reconstruction but which dated back to the abolitionist period and to the concerns raised by the Black abolitionist and newspaper editor, William Howard Day. As a supporter and friend of William Mitchell and William Troy, Day accompanied them on their speaking tour, and made the case to British friends of antislavery that establishing a printing press in Black Canadian settlements was as important as establishing churches and schools.[12]

For Black Baptists in Canada West moving to and through the regional abolitionist culture of the Lake Erie borderlands, the absence of a denominational paper was part of a diasporic context that made access to the materials of print both urgent and uncertain. In response to the need for publications that could act, in Eric Gardner's words, as "a textual meeting place for geographically diverse voices," Black Baptists relied on the broader network of the Black press.[13] Henry Bibb and Mary Bibb's *Voice of the Fugitive*, the first Black newspaper to be published in Canada, highlights the relationship between the abolitionist network of print and

---

9. Bibb, "American Baptist."
10. Morris, *Sermons*, 59.
11. Morris, *Sermons*, 57.
12. "American Slavery."
13. Gardner, *Black Print Unbound*, 14.

the abolitionist network of Baptist churches.[14] A theology of freedom ran through the *Voice of the Fugitive*'s mandate to provide spiritual vision and support, to expose the trauma of enslavement, to decry racial prejudice in Canada, to trace the contours of the landscape of freedom, and call for action across lines of race, denomination, and geography. The theological strain of *Voice of the Fugitive* was in keeping with Henry Bibb's long engagement in the "Bibles for the Slave" movement, which interwove the strands of abolitionist action, print culture, and biblical reverence for the Word as an emancipatory agent in the world.[15]

The *Voice of the Fugitive* embodied Bibb's vision of modern print as the medium of his antislavery gospel, joining antislavery print to an emancipatory theology. For the Bibbs, as for their readers throughout the Great Lakes borderlands, the antislavery gospel and its life in print ran through and across shifting denominational boundaries of Black churches in Canada West. Published from the Bibb's offices next door to the Baptist Church in Sandwich, the *Voice of the Fugitive* was woven into the region's Black Baptist community. It joined the larger project of the Black press in the region, defined by the movement of editors, writers, readers, and publishers whose work reveals complex interplay among abolitionist movements on both sides of the Atlantic.[16] In the Great Lakes region, this included the *Provincial Freeman*, *Frederick Douglass' Paper* and the *North Star*, the *Aliened American* and the *True Democrat* published in Cleveland, as well the *True Royalist and Weekly Intelligencer*, and antislavery papers such as the *Signal of Liberty* and the *Anti-Slavery Bugle* to which the early leaders of the Baptist churches in Sandwich and Amherstburg contributed. Black Baptist print in Canada came into being within this broader intellectual geography as the voice of emigrationist communities and shared the Black press's wider concerns with speaking to the particularities of place—the details of space, geography, and political landscapes—even as it was fundamentally concerned with the issues raised by migration, movement, and mobility. Agents, writers, editors,

---

14. The authoritative account of Henry and Mary Bibb and the establishing of the *Voice of the Fugitive* in Cooper, "'Doing Battle in Freedom's Cause.'" Cooper notes the origins of the *Voice of the Fugitive* in the Convention movement, and discusses the Bibbs' ties to Methodists, Baptists, and Congregationalists of the American Missionary Association. See also Silverman, "We Shall Be Heard."

15. On Bibb's work with the American Missionary Association and the Bibles for the Slave campaign, see the detailed and nuanced discussion in Cooper, "'Doing Battle in Freedom's Cause,'" 85–92.

16. See "Editors' Introduction" in Bonner et al., eds., *Black Press*.

and readers of Black Baptist print related to one another as part of this set of highly fluid interconnections that ebbed and flowed across time and place. While print materials were meant to circulate, they also served to stabilize experience within the denominational diaspora grounding ideas in tangible texts that served as points of connection and sometimes as sites of memory. I have argued elsewhere that we might think of the materials of Black print culture as moveable archives, constructed to be repositories of knowledge about the African American and African Canadian pasts.[17] In literary scholar Ernest's formulation, Black print culture identified "the terms by which a fragmented community could understand itself historically, and by which history could be understood so as to identify moral responsibility and by which moral responsibility could be transformed into concrete action—this was the work of historical research and representation."[18] Ernest's central argument about African American writers and their crafting an activist historical consciousness from the materials of a past too traumatic to ever be fully recorded in a single narrative, invites us to reframe the texts of the Black Baptist tradition and to pay attention to the ways that their authors leveraged the medium of print to do the work of connecting word and deed, theological precepts, and abolitionist strategies.

In 1853, the Amherstburg First Baptist Church hosted the General Convention for the Improvement of the Colored Inhabitants of Canada, which drew together Black abolitionists from across Canada West, Michigan, and Ohio. The broad antislavery resolutions and actions undertaken by the Convention offer a sense of the scope and composition of this abolitionist network, which included those in attendance, as well as the trustees of the church who opened their doors to the convention and thereby identified their worship space as a site of activism. Their resolution to have Bibb print the proceedings at the *Voice of the Fugitive*, and the subscription list of those who took on the work of financing and distributing 500 copies of the material once printed, provides evidence of the delegates' concern with creating an historical record of their work, and points to the interconnections among Black Baptists and the Bibbs' print network.[19] In the following year, when the Amherstburg Association of Black Baptist churches moved to have their constitution and

---

17. Reid-Maroney, "Possibilities," 5–6.
18. Ernest, *Liberation Historiography*, 19.
19. Minutes and Proceedings, 1853.

bylaws printed, they too turned to Bibb. Both of these examples feature typographically complex title pages using no fewer than twelve different typefaces, including neoclassical serifs, medieval revivalist black letter, Egyptian slab serif fonts with decorative drop shadows, and display type with ornamental letterforms. They convey the range of Bibb's repertoire in his printshop, but there is also an emotional register to the typography of the title pages that frames the seriousness of purpose in the meetings recorded within. Both examples call to mind literary scholar Marcy Dinius' discussion of the "radical typography" of David Walker's *Appeal*, and the ways in which typographic innovation could signal changes of tone and expression to guide readers in speaking the texts aloud.[20] Bibb's title pages break from the constraints of typographic convention associated with the title pages of books, and draw instead from the typefaces and uses of type associated with the production of advertising and ephemera. Typographic experimentation in Bibb's work paid attention to the context in which texts would be read and circulated in abolitionist communities, and to the printed form as an act of agency that inscribed the lived experience of Baptist congregants into the historical record.

Across the Atlantic in 1860, William Troy and William Mitchell's narratives rolled off industrial steam presses in London, Birmingham, Edinburgh, and in Manchester at the offices of the Manchester Guardian; publishers and printers whose connections in the book trade dovetailed with their reformist interests supported the production of both books. In the close relationship between Mitchell and Troy's lecture tour and the books produced to support that work, we see both authors drawing on and contributing to culture of print in Baptist churches and communities closer to home. Read in the context of early Baptist print that was produced in fluid abolitionist communities, circulated through a diffuse Baptist church network Canada West, and focused on a combining of the practical and the prophetic, Mitchell's *Underground Railroad* and Troy's *Hair-breadth Escapes* emerge as part of a wider literary tradition in which a sharpened historical consciousness and a theological imperative met in the mediating space of print.

Troy's *Hair-Breadth Escapes from Slavery to Freedom* is a collection of brief narratives of survival and resistance; the experiences of seventeen formerly enslaved men, women, and their families who, using the activist network of the Underground Railroad, make their way to Amherstburg

20. Dinius, *Textual Effects*.

and Windsor. The book opens with an account of Troy's early life in Virginia, where he had been born into nominal freedom that afforded but a thin protection from the violence of slavery around him. Of his life after his Baptist conversion as a young man, he writes:

> I felt that I was in the midst of devouring human wolves... Though still in the land of my nativity, I was made a stranger. The law of the country knew me as a thing, the church knew me in the same way. I saw my fellow-countrymen sold out of the church to which I belonged. The pastor sold one after another of his flock. The deacons bought and sold slaves. Sermons were preached to justify these wicked deeds. I was made to keep silent; I heard, but I condemned them in my heart.[21]

His condemnation of the pro-slavery Baptist church he attended in Virginia prompted his move to Cincinnati, in 1848, where he joined the activist congregation of Zion Baptist Church, studied in preparation for ministry with the Reverend Wallace Shelton, and received a licence to preach. His call to ministry coincided with the passage of the 1850 Fugitive Slave Law. Troy joined Cincinnati's Vigilance Committee, willing to defy federal law by helping freedom seekers who crossed into Cincinnati. When he was called to Amherstburg, and then to Windsor, Troy continued in the work of active resistance. The British lecture tour and the publication of his book extended this work. As William Howard Day noted in a testimonial letter to Troy, printed as part of the book's introductory material, "It is an honour to you to have written this book, because of the difficulties which I know you have been obliged to surmount; but it is much greater honour that you have been an actor in the thrilling scenes described—that, disregarding a false law and a false gospel, you were able to point the traveller on his weary way to Liberty."[22] Troy brought his message of the violence and trauma of escape from enslavement to cities and towns across England that were deeply implicated in the economy that supported the conditions his book described. Press reports from their speaking tour indicate that English supporters often preceded Troy and Mitchell at the podium, urging audiences to recognize their own culpability and their own power to bring the system down. Published in this context on a tour in which aural and print culture converged, Troy's *Hair-Breadth Escapes* was in part a prophetic intervention that collapsed

---

21. Troy, *Hair-Breadth Escapes*, 6.
22. For Day's letter to Troy, see Troy, *Hair-Breadth Escapes*, 110.

the illusion of moral distance between the cotton fields of the enslaver and the cotton mills of the English industrial heartland.

Mitchell's work, titled *The Underground Railroad* also tells personal histories of enslavement and escape, which Mitchell heard and gathered from people among whom he ministered. The first section of the book sets out the details of the Underground Railroad, as Mitchell knew it from experience, and the second describes life in Canadian abolitionist communities. *The Underground Railroad* features a copperplate etching of the author. In the portrait, Mitchell is seated, with his gaze averted from the viewer in an expression that conveys reflection tinged with sorrow, and his hand at rest on the open pages of a large book. Sharp contrasts delineate Mitchell's portrait from contemporary antislavery images of reading, such as the one published in the 1850 *Facts for Baptist Churches* by Andrew Foss and Edward Matthews. In the latter volume, the illustration depicts Mahommah Gardo Baquaqua, formerly enslaved, self-emancipated, and a convert of the Free Baptist Mission in Haiti;[23] Baquaqua is seated beside a White missionary who points an extended finger toward the pages of the book, though the open book is tilted too far downward to suggest that either figure is reading it. *Facts for Baptist Churches* was an antislavery text that condemned churches in fellowship with enslavers, but its narratives traced White antislavery missions, cited White authors, and appealed to White readers. Baquaqua's biography, "written and revised from his own words" by Samuel Moore, and published in Detroit in 1854, also bears a complex relationship to Baquaqua's agency and autonomy as an author.[24] Mitchell's portrait of a Black Baptist clergyman in command of the open Bible seems a direct answer to the Baquaqua portrait, and to perhaps the most famous nineteenth century visual representation of literacy: Hammat Billing's illustration of Eva teaching Tom to read the Bible in the 1852 first edition of Harriet Beecher Stowe's *Uncle Tom's Cabin*.[25] The engraving of Mitchell places him in a position of agency with respect to both the book depicted in the engraving, and the book of Mitchell's authorship in which the visual image resides.

Both books' relationship to practical abolition is made clear in the front matter—letters of endorsement, a dedication, a preface, notices of speeches in the British press, lists of supporters, and concluding remarks

---

23. Foss and Mathews, *Facts*; Law and Lovejoy, *Biography*.

24. Moore, *Biography*.

25. Morgan, *Uncle Tom's Cabin*, 26–31.

from the author to his British friends. The endorsements in *Hair-Breadth Escapes* are interconnected with those in *The Underground Railroad* in a web of cross-referenced and overlapping material. The conversational endorsements between the two books speak to the ways in which they differed from slave narratives—neither Troy nor Mitchell had been born into slavery, and both wrote of escape from their perspective as Baptist ministers deeply engaged in the work of the Underground Railroad. Book historian Beth McCoy has argued that paratexts attached to nineteenth-century slave narratives were ambivalent spaces in which White abolitionists used their introductory remarks to claim a presumptive authority over the narrative that followed.[26] Troy and Mitchell's works were printed with endorsements and a formal preface from members of the British antislavery circles in which they moved—but Tory and Mitchell also used the space of the introductory endorsements to asset authorial control by locating their texts within their political lives as activists. Troy includes a dedication to William Howard Day, a Black abolitionist, newspaper editor, Oberlin graduate, and member of the abolitionist community in Chatham. Day, in turn, provided a testimonial letter for both Troy and Mitchell, and Troy added another layer to the intertextual construction to his work by linking text and paratext by quoting at length from one of Day's most powerful political speeches: "What is slavery, but a constant war on one and all? . . . *The first duty of the slave, then, is to be FREE. Being a man, he is a child of God. His servitude is a fiction, unrecognised by just enactment, human or divine.*"[27] Troy places this passage from Day at the conclusion of a chapter outlining a heartbreaking story in which Troy tried, unsuccessfully, to navigate the legal system on behalf of a family who had made their way to Cincinnati only to be returned to their enslavers. Day's words become an invocation and connect the story of the failed rescue and the individual's experiences—it relates to the broader political context and the antislavery culture of the Great Lakes region in which he participated. The paratextual material embeds both books in the practical operations and ideological structures of the Underground Railroad.

Both works are unflinchingly detailed in their account of how, when, and where Black abolitionists and their White allies created the system of resistance that the title of Mitchell's work identifies as the Underground

26. McCoy, "Race."
27. William Howard Day, quoted in Troy, *Hair-Breadth Escapes*, 85–86.

Railroad. *The Underground Railroad* and *Hair-Breadth Escapes* are unusual because they published detailed accounts of the inner workings of the Underground Railroad from the authorial perspective of Black activists; writing in ways that made plain the Underground Railroad's relationship to, and origins in, the larger work of Black abolitionists—including its links to the ongoing work of their congregations in Canada. Their works were written, printed, circulated, and read in the tumultuous interval between the execution of John Brown in December of 1859 and the outbreak of the Civil War in the spring of 1861—months in which the role of abolitionists in Canada West was the subject of an investigation by a Select Committee of the United States Senate.[28] William Still's *Underground Railroad*, perhaps the closest text to Troy and Mitchell for the purposes of comparison, was published in 1872; Still's work is an activist text, but was a work of history removed from the immediacy of the perils imposed by the Fugitive Slave Law that framed the abolitionist interventions it describes. Troy and Mitchell, however, wrote books of living history recording their engagement in the most significant movement of political resistance of their time, and did so while the perilous work was still going on. Immersed in the producing of their books as abolitionist practice, both authors understood that the material act of setting words down in print gave shape and boldness to the theological acts of proclamation, prophecy, and witness.

On the surface, the small narratives that Troy and Mitchell stitch together in their books resemble the biographical testimonies collected by Benjamin Drew and published in *Northside View of Slavery* (1856). But, while Drew, a White abolitionist, approaches his account of Black communities in Canada from the perspective of someone gathering data to bolster the abolitionist argument, the authors of *The Underground Railroad* and *Hair-Breadth Escapes* approach Underground Railroad narratives with a sense of pastoral regard and concern. All the people whose stories are gathered in the book were known to them; most were members of their churches. By placing narratives side by side in the pages of their books, Troy and Mitchell recreate community, and the relationships that form a congregation, with all of its complex associations and connections.

---

28. John Murray Mason and Jacob Collamer, *Report [of] the Select committee of the Senate appointed to inquire into the late invasion and seizure of the public property at Harper's Ferry* (Washington, 1860).

In addition to helping to reveal the networks of intellectual activism through which Troy and Mitchell travelled, and which they helped to create, *Hair-Breadth Escapes* casts light on the relationship between the book as a weapon in the antislavery struggle, and the abolitionist work that its pages describe. In their formal construction, both works use intertextual references and the reprinting of other works to create layers of meaning and a richness informed by cultures of reading, authorship, and study. *Hair-Breadth Escapes* frames each chapter with a concluding stanza of poetry. The excerpt from the poem *America*, by the Black abolitionist poet James Monroe Whitfield, for example, quotes a work first published in the 1853 edition of Julia Griffiths's *Autographs of Freedom*, published in Whitefield's *America and other Poems* later in the same year; it was reprinted in the *Anglo African Magazine* edited by Thomas Hamilton in 1860, and eventually quoted by characters in Martin Delaney's novel, *Blake*, serialized in the Anglo African Magazine and published as the bound volume of that periodical in 1860.[29] As literary scholar Ivy G. Wilson points out, the practice of reprinting Whitfield's poetry gestures to "African American literary production beyond the slave narrative."[30] Troy's framing of his narratives with poetry not only reaches outward to place his book within the context of Black activism in print, but directs readers' attention to a wider Black literary tradition—the literary practice of diasporic communities in which verses of poetry appeared as fragments reframed and resituated in richly allusive contexts. Troy's inclusion of Whitfield and other poets evokes the process described by Ellen Gruber Garvey as "writing with scissors."[31] Troy pieces literary fragments in place throughout his work, and stitches them together in an allusive pattern that creates new meaning even as it makes reference to a collective literary past.

The importance of print in building historical consciousness as a counter to the dehumanizing intentions and conditions of enslavement had been set out in the 1854 *Autobiography of a Fugitive Negro* by the Congregationalist minister Samuel Ringgold Ward. Ward's narrative, published in London, included a reflection on the erasing of history leaving only "scraps, patches, anecdotes" to serve as historical data for

---

29. Whitefield, *America and Other Poems*.
30. Wilson, "Periodicals," 134.
31. Garvey, *Writing with Scissors*, 4.

Africans in the diaspora.³² Both narratives of Mitchell and Troy respond to the same challenge and use their works to build a documentary record as an abolitionist intervention. Troy's account of his early life includes references to hiding his books as a child while attending a secret school arranged by his father near their home in Virginia. In his narrative of the life of an enslaved Virginian called Reuben, Troy notes that Reuban defied the laws of the state in his participation in worship—he would "sometimes venture to take a text in preaching, though it is positively against the law in that State for any coloured person, free or slave, to make use of a text." Recounting Reuben's escape, recapture, sale into Louisiana, and a subsequent debate at Reuben's church regarding whether or not he should be formally excluded from fellowship for having tried to escape, Troy reminded readers of the legal context in which "the liberty of a man's conscience is locked in" by unjust laws against literacy and education. He cited the Revised Statutes of Louisiana, which carried penalties including hard labour, imprisonment, or death for "whosoever shall knowingly be instrumental in bringing into this State any paper, pamphlet, or book" that might lead to "discontent" among enslaved or nominally free Black residents.³³ By the specific naming of the dangers associated with abolitionist print forms— "paper, pamphlet, or book"—Troy draws attention to the activist power of his work. Reflexive references to print culture run through *Hair-Breadth Escapes*—a "little book" intended, as the author of the preface noted, to "add another blow to drive home the wedge of abolition, till it splits the trunk of slavery asunder."³⁴

In a foundational work of textual studies, Jerome McGann argues for the importance of bibliographic codes—the meaning of the work that is embedded within its material form and in social, political, and cultural context. In their intentional construction of the bibliographic codes in their texts—intertextual reference, illustrations, typography, and layers of paratext—Black Baptist authors revealed the rich significance they attached to the printed word. In the process, they also produced closely drawn portraits of suffering and violence of such weight and magnitude that the power of words alone was tested, and yet that weight and magnitude compelled them to bear witness. Faced with the inadequacy of his words to fully convey the dehumanizing horror of slavery at the centre of

---

32. Ward, *Autobiography*, 269.
33. Troy, *Hair-Breadth Escapes*, 32.
34. Arthur Mursell, Preface to Troy, *Hair-Breadth Escapes*, ix.

his narrative, William Mitchell quoted the antislavery poetry of Jeremiah Holmes Wiffen ("Whate'er of crime, whate'er of woe / Europe has wrought and Afric wept, / In his recording volume, lo! / The Angel of the Court has kept") and followed Wiffen's textual metaphors back to the Bible: "The facts I narrate of the sorrows of the down-trodden may be considered exaggerations by the ignorant and unfeeling; but surely not by the recording angel, who drops a tear at every record made, nor can they be by the compassionate Saviour, who tells their wanderings, puts their tears into his bottle, and writes them in his book of remembrance."[35] Evoking the words of the Psalmist ("Thou tellest my wanderings: put thou my tears into thy bottle: are they not in thy book?"), the book of remembrance in Malachi, and the recording angels in the book of Revelation, Mitchell fuses the lexicon of print with the language of the Bible. Likening tears to ink and rendering narration as compassion, the passage positions acts of recording, of inscribing, of marking words, and of setting things down as acts of redemptive possibility. The metaphor positions both the material form of the book and the recorded histories it contains as the tool through which slavery can be dismantled.

Writing of Black abolitionist communities in the United States and the Vigilance Committees that supported Underground Railroad activism in urban centres, historian Jesse Olsavsky argues that Black activist-authored and published books, pamphlets, and newspapers constitute an "emancipatory archive of knowledge."[36] Written, published, and read in the twilight of the transatlantic antislavery movement, the works of Baptist authors convey an emancipatory theology, contributing reappropriation of print in the Black abolitionist tradition. Attending to their work can help to reshape and sharpen the critical edge of our understanding of the Underground Railroad and Black Baptist churches—revealing the contours of political resistance and the form and depth of African Canadian intellectual history. The narratives effect a reconstruction, tracing passages from slavery to freedom, binding experience, and pages together in an integrative act that used the material artefact of the book as a brave counterweight to enslavement's violence, disruption, and dispersal.

---

35. Mitchell, *Underground Railroad*, 79. On Jeremiah Holmes Wiffen's poetry and the antislavery anthology, *The Bow in the Could*, see Bird, "*Woman of Letters*."

36. Olsavsky, *Most Absolute Abolition*, 27.

BIBLIOGRAPHY

Primary Sources

ARCHIVES

Minutes and Proceedings of the General Convention for the Improvement of the Coloured Inhabitants in Canada, 1853.

Minutes of the National Convention of the Colored Citizens, Buffalo, NY, August 15–19, 1843.

MONOGRAPHS

Foss, Andrew, and Edward Mathews. *Facts for Baptist Churches*. Utica, NY: American Baptist Free Mission Society, 1850.

Mitchell, William M. *The Underground Railroad from Slavery to Freedom*. London: William Tweedie, 1860.

Moore, Samuel. *Biography of Mahommah G. Baquaqua, a Native of Zoogoo, in the Interior of Africa*. Detroit: Pomeroy, 1854.

Morris, E. C. *Sermons, Addresses and Reminiscences and Important Correspondence: With a Picture Gallery of Eminent Ministers and Scholars*. Nashville: National Baptist Publishing Board, 1901.

Troy, William. *Hair-Breadth Escapes from Slavery to Freedom*. Manchester, UK: W. Bremner, 1861.

Ward, Samuel Ringgold. *Autobiography of a Fugitive Negro: His Anti-slavery Labours in the United States and Canada*. London: Paternoster, 1855.

Whitefield, James Monroe. *America and Other Poems*. Buffalo, NY: James S. Leavitt, 1853.

NEWSPAPERS AND MAGAZINES

"American Slavery." *Cheltenham Chronicle*, 23 July 1861.

Bibb, Henry. "American Baptist." *Voice of the Fugitive*, 23 April 1851.

POETRY

Hemans, Felica D. "The Switzer's Wife." In *Records of Woman, with Other Poems*, 35–44. 2nd ed. Edinburgh: William Blackwood, 1828.

Secondary Sources

Bell, Amy, et al. "From *Uncle Tom's Cabin* to Countering Colston: Slavery, History and Memory in a Transatlantic Undergraduate Research Project." *International Public History* 2 (2019) 1–4.

Bird, Eleanor. "A Woman of Letters: Mary Anne Rawson's Letter Collection and her Compilation of the Anti-Slavery Gift. Book *The Bow in the Cloud*, 1826–1834." *Nineteenth-Century Gender Studies* 17 (2021). No pages. Online: http://ww.w.ncgsjournal.com/issue172/PDFs/bird.pdf.

Bonner, Claudine, et al., eds. *The Black Press: A Shadowed Canadian Tradition*. Toronto: University of Toronto Press, forthcoming.

Cooper, Afua. "'Doing Battle in Freedom's Cause': Henry Bibb, Abolitionism, Race Uplift, and Black Manhood, 1842–1854." PhD diss., University of Toronto, 2000.

Dinius, Marcy. *The Textual Effects of David Walker's Appeal: Print-Based Activism Against Slavery, Racism, and Discrimination, 1829–1851.* Philadelphia: University of Pennsylvania Press, 2022.

Ernest, John. *Liberation Historiography: African American Writers and the Challenge of History, 1794–1861.* Chapel Hill: University of North Carolina Press, 2004.

Foreman, P. Gabrielle, et al. *The Colored Conventions Movement: Black Organizing in the Nineteenth Century.* Chapel Hill: University of North Carolina Press, 2021.

Fuentes, Marisa. *Dispossessed Lives: Enslaved Women, Violence, and the Archive.* Philadelphia: University of Pennsylvania Press, 2016.

Gardner, Eric. *Black Print Unbound: The Christian Recorder, African American Literature, and Periodical Culture.* New York: Oxford University Press, 2015.

Garvey, Ellen Gruber. *Writing with Scissors: American Scrapbooks from the Civil War to the Harlem Renaissance.* New York: Oxford University Press, 2013.

Goddu, Teresa A. *Selling Antislavery: Abolition and Mass Media in Antebellum America.* Philadelphia: University of Pennsylvania Press, 2020.

———. "The Slave Narrative as Material Text." In *The Oxford Handbook of the African American Slave Narrative*, edited by John Ernest, 149–64. Oxford: Oxford University Press, 2014.

Jackson, Leon. "The Talking Book and the Talking Book Historian: African American Cultures of Print—The State of the Discipline." *Book History* 13 (2010) 251–308.

Law, Robin, and Paul Lovejoy. *The Biography of Mahommah Gardo Baquaqua: His Passage from Slavery to Freedom in Africa and America.* Princeton, NJ: Markus Wiener, 2009.

Lootens, Tricia. *The Political Poetess: Victorian Femininity, Race, and the Legacy of Separate Spheres.* Princeton, NJ: Princeton University Press, 2016.

Mailloux, Steven. "Enactment History, Jesuit Practices, and Rhetorical Hermeneutics." In *Theorizing Writing Histories of Rhetoric*, edited by Michelle Ballif, 25–40. Carbondale: Southern Illinois University Press, 2012.

McCaskill, Barbara, and Sedonia Serafini, eds. *The Magnificent Reverend Peter Thomas Stanford, Transatlantic Reformer and Race Man.* Athens: University of Georgia Press, 2020.

McCoy, Beth. "Race and the (Para)Textual Condition." *Publications of the Modern Language Association of America* 121 (2006) 156–69.

Morgan, Jo-Ann. *Uncle Tom's Cabin as Visual Culture.* Columbia, MO: University of Missouri Press, 2007.

Olsavsky, Jesse. *The Most Absolute Abolition: Runaways, Vigilance Committees, and the Rise of Revolutionary Abolitionism, 1835–1861.* Baton Rouge: Louisiana State University Press, 2021.

Otele, Olivette. "Slavery and Visual Memory: What Britain Can Learn from France." *Open Democracy* (August 29, 2016). No pages. Online: https://www.opendemocracy.net/en/beyond-trafficking-and-slavery/slavery-and-visual-memory-what-britain-can-learn-from-france.

Reid-Maroney, Nina. "Possibilities for African Canadian Intellectual History: The Case of 19th-Century Upper Canada/Canada West." *History Compass* 15 (2017) 1–9, DOI: 10.1111/hic3.12432.

Ripley, C. Peter, et al., eds. *The Black Abolitionist Papers: Volume II. Canada, 1830–1865*. Chapel Hill: University of North Carolina Press, 2015.

Roy, Michaël. "Cheap Editions, Little Books, and Handsome Duodecimos: A Book History Approach to Antebellum Slave Narratives." *MELUS: Multi-Ethnic Literature in the US* 40 (2015) 69–93.

Silverman, Jason. "We Shall Be Heard: The Development of the Fugitive Slave Press in Canada." *Canadian Historical Review* 65 (1984) 56–69.

Smallwood, Stephanie E. "The Politics of the Archive and History's Accountability to the Enslaved." *History of the Present* 6 (2016) 117–32.

Spires, Derrick. *The Practice of Citizenship: Black Politics and Print Culture in the Early United States*. Philadelphia: University of Pennsylvania Press, 2019.

Whitfield, Harvey Amani. "White Archives, Black Fragments: Problems and Possibilities in Telling the Lives of Enslaved Black People in the Maritimes." *The Canadian Historical Review* 101 (2020) 323–45.

Wilson, Ivy G. "Periodicals, Print Culture and African American Poetry." In *A Companion to African American Literature*, edited by Gene Andrew Jarrett, 133–48. Oxford: Wiley-Blackwell, 2013.

6

Sojourners and Citizens

National Identity in the African Baptist Association, 1855–1914

Gordon L. Heath

The minutes of the African Baptist Association in 1868 record the exhortation: "Dear brethren, knowing that this world is not our home, for we are strangers and sojourners as were our fathers, therefore we seek a country which the world by nature knows nothing about."[1] Yet a little more than a generation later that same Black Baptist community was pining for an opportunity for their young men to join with the rest of Canada and the empire in the conflagration in Europe.

The expression of sojourner has been shared at times by virtually all Christian communities in some way or another. Being a sojourner for Black Baptists meant living with dual citizenship, an Augustinian model of Christian participation in both church and society.[2] The usage of the term sojourners by Black Baptists in Nova Scotia was pressing and poignant—the hope of a spiritual kingdom had buoyed their spirits in the darkest days of enslavement and the biblical motifs of membership in the present kingdom of God as well as the future hope of heaven provided motivation and inspiration as they sought to establish themselves in their

---

1. Minutes of the African Baptist Association (1868), 7.
2. St. Augustine (345–430) detailed this two-fold citizenship in his *City of God*.

work of Christian service as newly freed men and women in Nova Scotia.[3] Yet, that very same community carried with it to Nova Scotia a loyalty to Crown and a willingness to be identified as citizens in the colony-but-soon-to-be nation; the sojourners had also found a temporal home.

Budding national identity in late-nineteenth century Canada was among British-background Protestants fused to a surging imperial identity tied to notions of Anglo-Saxon superiority.[4] But how did Canada's Black Baptists, a relatively small community on the margins, fit into that powerful and pervasive national vision? This chapter is concerned with the formation and evolution of national identity among the Black Baptist community in Nova Scotia in the latter half of the nineteenth century and the early years of the twentieth. What is quickly apparent when reading the association minutes is that much of the national identity expressed in the Black Baptist community mirrored that of much of their White neighbours. Yet there were critical differences, for the evolution of Black Baptist discourse was shaped as well by history, race, and religion, factors that together forged a unique perspective on matters of national identity. And that unique perspective was marked most notably by a pressing and urgent motivation for faithful citizenship, a type of motivation well known by those whose ethnicity or religion did not fit within the dominant cultural narrative.

The views expressed in the minutes—admittedly a limited sample of opinion—reveal a consistent public narrative of obligations and convictions shaped on the margins of a dominant Anglo-French (and British imperial) national identity. What is also apparent in the minutes is a fusion of patriotism, social reform, and race consciousness distinctly forged by religious convictions.[5] It is virtually impossible to pull those aspects apart, for they are intertwined and mutually supportive. What

---

3. For commentary in the usage of the Old Testament among Black communities, see the chapter entitled "'Let My People Go': Exodus in the African American Experience" in Kling, *Bible in History*.

4. See Berger, *Sense of Power*; Buckner, ed., *Canada and the End of Empire*; Buckner, ed., *Canada and the British Empire*; Penlington, *Canada*; Page, "Canada"; *Boer War*; "Carl Berger"; Cole, "Canada's 'Nationalistic' Imperialists"; Cook, "George R. Parkin."

5. Historians a century later must be careful to exercise historical imagination in order to see the world of the past as those in the past saw it so as to not miss how those religious communities imagined their identity and charted their course according to their own terms. As Peter Berger argues, religion must be taken seriously for it is the "sacred canopy" that is constructed to provide meaning and order to existence (see *Sacred Canopy*).

this chapter argues is that within the Black Baptist community there was among some an appreciation for the relative safety and opportunity provided in Canada when contrasted with the horrors of American slavery, and that gratefulness (but, as noted below, not naivety) nurtured a sense of loyalty to the nation. Their religious convictions also compelled them to engage in evangelism and social reforms to shape their vision of a Christian Canada. Yet, there was a pragmatic and strategic element to their loyalty, something born out of the optimism of the age as well as the need to demonstrate the abilities of the Black community in order to silence naysayers and doubters of their worth as equal citizens, as well as to gain "equality with whites, dignity in status, and justice in the public sphere,"[6] something coined the "politics of respectability."[7] While today the expression "respectability politics" is sometimes used pejoratively against any minority community (ethnic, religious, or other) that seems to be denying/downplaying its own identity or compromising its own values for the sake of acceptance (or assimilation) by the dominant group, it is not being used pejoratively in this case.[8] For a people at the end of the nineteenth century who had faced such profound adversity (and continued to face ongoing struggles) such a strategy seemed then to be the only and wisest way forward – to judge it differently today seems to minimize and even denigrate the agency and wisdom of the nineteenth-century Black community. This is also not to say that there was a static or monochrome view of nation and empire in the Black community (for as Winfried Siemerling's recent summary of Black literature indicates it is often best to speak in the plural of Black communities[9]). However, it is to say that the public record in the Baptist minutes is fairly consistent in how it speaks of and imagines national identity.[10]

The Black Baptist experience of national identity mirrored in some ways that of other minorities. Living on the margins required constant negotiation, and identity was often marked by fluidity and diversity.[11]

---

6. Fingard, "Race and Respectability," 172.

7. Gaines, *Uplifting the Race*, 45, 161–62, 259.

8. Higginbotham, *Righteous Discontent*; White, *Dark Continent*; Pitcan, Marwick, and Boyd, "Performing a Vanilla Self."

9. Siemerling, *Black Atlantic*.

10. Even among Anglo-Saxon Nonconformists in Britain there was no uniform opinion on empire (see Bebbington, *Nonconformist Conscience*).

11. For examples of religious (and ethnic) minorities on the margins in a time of surging imperial sentiment see Heath, ed., *Empire*.

Ties of blood and land could also lead to a plurality of loyalties, something that Blacks with their African, American, British, and Canadian identities experienced firsthand.[12] The problem for those on the margins was that what one calls plurality of loyalty another may label divided loyalty; thus the need for fluidity and negotiation. Identities on the margins were often "a concocted fictive construct and . . . a negotiated, improvised way of being in the world of nations."[13] The reading of religious national and imperial discourse on the margins must take into account how groups—whether consciously or not—strategically positioned themselves in relationship to national and imperial expectations, especially when they appeared to be disloyal. As other minorities knew, any displays of disloyalty (especially in time of war) could lead to ostracism or worse.[14] A glimpse of that concern with fostering "ill feeling to our brother in White" can be seen in the introduction of the African Baptist Association's secretary Peter E. MacKerrow's history of the suffering inflicted on Blacks by White racism.[15] That is not to say that discourse of loyalty was necessarily disingenuous (the ardent response to the Great War among the Black community suggests that it was sincere[16]), but it does mean an examination of those on the margins such as Black Baptists needs to include a recognition of the negotiation of a safe place on the margins so as to avoid any adverse reactions to what was perceived by others to be disloyalty.

The agency of Black Baptists also needs to be noted by taking seriously their lived experience and to recognize Black Baptist motives for decision-making in the midst of the birth of the nation, a growing empire, and uncertain international relations. As was the case with other Canadians, they navigated their own sense of belonging in the midst of a welter of assumptions in the age of the New Imperialism. Allen P. Stouffer claims that the "African British North Americans, like other

12. Whitfield, *Blacks on the Border*.
13. Yelin, *From the Margins of Empire*, 171.
14. For instance, see Heath, "'Boers.'"
15. "I trust that this book will create no ill feeling to our brother in White, but rather kindle a flame of love towards the memory of many of the names mentioned therein, thereby making it commendable to all, but more particularly to our Baptist brethren whose kind patronage I humbly crave." MacKerrow, *Brief History*, 6.
16. Armstrong, "Unwelcome Sacrifice"; Ruck, *Canada's Black Battalion*; Walker, "Race"; Joost, "No. 2 Construction Battalion"; Foyn, "Underside of Glory"; Heath, "Wartime Diaries."

settlers, in large measure were self-directed autonomous people who collectively identified their needs, established their goals, and devised means to achieve them."[17] In similar fashion, Black Baptist religious communities imagined their identity and charted their course on their own terms. They were acting within the general framework of a cross-border, multi-denominational evangelicalism, one with a history of an abiding loyalty to nation, missions, social reform, and social justice. In that sense, Black Baptists were mirroring the actions and discourse of their White coreligionists, however, with the added, and crucially important, reality that their marginalized status placed unique pressures on—and opened up possibilities for—the Black denomination. And those opportunities, it was frequently stated, were to be exploited to the fullest. The period under consideration was increasingly considered to be an "age of progress," one where opportunities abounded for race advancement. And, as argued elsewhere, it was eventually seen as a providential opportunity not to be missed.[18]

Finally, this research is not interested in definitions of what exactly is a "nation," rather it is concerned with how a sense of national (and/or civic) identity was forged in the midst of real-life real-time circumstances. Daniel Francis defines a nation as "a group of people who share the same illusions about themselves."[19] Stated more positively, each nation has its own "civic ideology, a framework of ideas and aspirations that expresses itself in allegiance to certain public policies and institutions," which has to be continually "recreated and reinforced."[20] In a similar vein Benedict Anderson argues that a nation is "an imagined political community."[21] In both cases the emphasis is on the imagination—how people individually and collectively imagined themselves in relationship with neighbours near and far, known and unknown, within the same political boundaries. My concern in this chapter is to explore what can be seen in the minutes with regards to how Black Baptists envisioned themselves within a nation as a minority. What type of *imagined community* did they construct that led to them sharing a sense of kinship and community with the wider Canadian (White and other) populace? And how (if at all) did it evolve over

---

17. Stouffer, "Towards Community," 204.
18. See Heath, "Opportunity."
19. Francis, *National Dreams*, 10.
20. Francis, *National Dreams*, 10.
21. Anderson, *Imagined Communities*, 6.

time? The answers to those questions will carry further the discussion of those such as Nele Sawallisch who are seeking to get a clearer sense of how Blacks with cross-border relations and experiences conceived and wrote about their own loyalties to nation(s).[22]

The language of imagined community intersects well with Peter Berger's concept of "plausibility structure." The symbiotic relationship between nation, justice, missions, and empire at the time provided a conceptual basis for thinking about the Christian life, shaped political commentary, focused prayers, inspired sermons, motivated actions, and made sense of a troublesome world. Here Peter Berger's concept of "plausibility structure" is helpful.[23] The socially constructed world of late-nineteenth century Canadian Black Baptists was one whereby God in his providence was understood to have established the nation and empire for his purposes. The fusion of justice, missions, and empire simply made sense of their experience, and was a concept bolstered by significant institutions such as church, schools, and government. Contemporary readers may look back aghast at some of the claims and assumptions made during the heyday of imperialism, recognizing the dynamic of socialization on Black Baptist spirituality. But in doing so contemporary readers do well to remember that recognizing past socialization is easy, recognizing it in the present is a different matter altogether. Of course, it also needs to be remembered that notions of empire were fluid and often contested. In fact, while there may have been widespread support for the empire among segments of Canadian society, there was no uniform idea of what belonging to the empire meant. "Imperialism" in late Victorian Canada enveloped a wide and diverse range of sentiments, and it was this ambiguity that was one of the reasons for its wide appeal.[24] Carl Berger notes this ambiguity, and it is one of the problems that confronts historians who attempt to make sense of the whole imperial movement.[25]

NOVA SCOTIAN BLACK BAPTISTS

As noted elsewhere in this volume, while there may have been individual Africans in the earliest years of European colonization, significant

---

22. See esp. Sawallisch, *Fugitive Borders*, 14–17, for Sawallisch's helpful summary of debates over the usages of the term "nation."

23. Berger, *Sacred Canopy*.

24. Miller, *Painting the Map Red*, 4. See also Page, *Imperialism and Canada*, 2.

25. Page, "Carl Berger," 40.

numbers only began to arrive with the waves of Loyalist migrations after the Revolutionary War. The proximity of Nova Scotia meant that it was a prime destination for Loyalists, although some also arrived in what became New Brunswick and Prince Edward Island. Churches were critical to the survival and success of Black loyalists, slaves, refugees, and freemen/women who migrated to Nova Scotia in the nineteenth century, and they were "for a very long and most crucial period, the most effective institution in the Black community. Only the family, perhaps, was more important."[26] Besides meeting spiritual needs, churches provided vital social links, economic assistance, and educational and leadership opportunities. Black religious organizations were formed to advocate for the elimination of slavery, with Black Baptists being the first to do so in the late 1830s.[27] While some churches were inter-racial, Blacks and Whites most often organized parallel institutions, something usually agreeable to both groups. The key Black Baptist organization in Nova Scotia was the African Baptist Association (ABA).[28] It was relatively small compared with their larger White Baptist counterparts, with roughly just over a dozen churches in the Maritimes.[29]

SOURCES

The chief archival sources for this research are the official minutes of the African Baptist Association, which are located at Acadia University, Wolfville, Nova Scotia.[30] While neither as intimate or personal as diaries or letters, nor as moving as sermons or poetry, the minutes do provide a degree of insight into the public activities and attitudes of the Black Baptist community in Nova Scotia. They also give a glimpse into self-organized

---

26. Bertley, *Canada*, 135. Other important institutions were schools and press. See Winks, *Blacks in Canada*, ch. 11.

27. Winks, *Blacks in Canada*, 219. Black Baptist pastor Richard Preston started the African Abolition Society (c.1846).

28. Established 1854. A similar organization existed in Ontario, the Amherstburg Association in Ontario (established 1841). The name was changed to the African United Baptist Association (AUBA) in 1919. For brief history of the association, see Williams, "Role."

29. For histories of the Black Baptist experience in Nova Scotia, see Oliver, *Brief History*; MacKerrow, *Brief History*; Pachai, *Nova Scotia Black Experience*.

30. Some years have not survived the ravages of time, and, as a result, there are a few gaps in the collection. The archival sources can be accessed online. See Acadia Archives, "African United Baptist Association."

and autonomous Black communities and how they served the purposes and needs of their Black constituents.

The annual two-or-three-day-long denominational meetings were public events at a local church (the location rotated around the association) comprised of clergy and church members, with some invited guests such as leaders from other denominations or local politicians. The minutes reveal the events and decisions of the deliberating bodies, but, like all minutes, they are necessarily brief—and selective—summaries of the event in question. That said, the richest vein of information is often the circular letter at the end of the minutes. It is a detailed summary of aspirations and ideals that provide a sense of the ethos and pathos of the Black Baptist community (or, at the very least, at least that of the writer, usually a prominent leader[31]). In fact, the circular letter at the end of each year's minutes often reads very much like a sermon, a key aspect of Black religious life used to shape communal hopes and convictions.[32]

The minutes were quickly printed and disseminated among the respective churches, but also circulated as far afield as the United States and Britain. Besides demonstrating the trans-national, cross-border relationships of the Black community (as well as transnational evangelical community),[33] that circulation suggests a didactic element to the minutes, moving beyond simply recording events for posterity to instructing readers as to the higher aims and attitudes of the Black communities.

DEVELOPMENT OF NATIONAL IDENTITY

National Identity

Black Loyalists who emigrated to Nova Scotia carried with them their loyalty to Britain, and their convictions surrounding the relative goodness of England and Canada made it easier to embrace a dual citizenship. Statements such as "this world is not our home"[34] were reminders of a better world in the life beyond, but they were not indications of

---

31. Peter E. MacKerrow was the secretary of the association for thirty consecutive years and had considerable influence in the community. During that time, he wrote a number of the circulars (see Fingard, "McKerrow").

32. Niles, "Rhetorical Characteristics," 15.

33. Heath, "'Great Association Above.'"

34. Minutes of the African Baptist Association (1867); Minutes of the African Baptist Association (1868); see "Circular Letter" in Minutes of the African Baptist Association (1869).

disengagement from the world or disinterest in earthly citizenship. Sojourners were to be active in engaging this world as well. Their doctrinal statement on civil government made clear the functions and limits of government authority,[35] a position that in no way contradicted being dual citizens. That being the case, there was a limit on state authority, and, as MacKerrow wrote, while the new arrivals fleeing slavery "transferred their allegiance to an earthly sovereign" the Lord Jesus continued to be the "Sovereign of their hearts."[36] Stated simply, they imagined themselves with dual identities as both sojourners and citizens. And that identity begins to explain the fact that Black soldiers fought in every major Canadian conflict leading up to (and including) the First World War.[37]

Richard Preston's appreciation of England provided a moral imprimatur of sorts for England and its empire. The Black Baptist community was well aware of the giants in their midst, those who had braved adversity and overcome hardship to establish Baptist churches in the province. Preston was the most iconic figure, and in the year of his death (1861) the minutes included an extensive summary of his life and contribution to Baptist work.[38] Preston's ministry had extended all the way to England, and, as the following comment on his death indicates, he had forged strong bonds with his White co-religionist that remained throughout his life: "Oh! how his heart was cheered, when receiving a letter from one of our English Ministers, a few weeks before his death; in that letter he heard from a number of his ministering brethren, and others of whom he had formed acquaintances with 30 years ago."[39] Elsewhere the minutes referred to those in "Old England" as "our dear friends across the broad waters."[40] That language of friendship went all the way back to the first year of the association, for in commentary on the financial aid given to Preston for money raised in England for the formation of Cornwallis Baptist it was declared "Old England, God bless her, forever!"[41] Decades

35. Minutes of the African Baptist Association (1869); Minutes of the African Baptist Association (1881). For details on Preston, see Boyd, "Preston, Richard."

36. MacKerrow, *Brief History*, 73.

37. See Green, "Upper Canada's Black Defenders"; Tulloch, *Black Canadians*; Ruck, *Canada's Black Battalion*; Newfield, "Upper Canada's Black Defenders?"; Armstrong, "Unwelcome Sacrifice"; Walker, "Race."

38. Minutes of the African Baptist Association (1861).

39. Minutes of the African Baptist Association (1861).

40. Minutes of the African Baptist Association (1865).

41. Minutes of the African Baptist Association (1855).

later, the links between Preston and England were once again raised, with similar commentary on the goodness of England towards Preston and the Black community: "And now, dear Brethren, in conclusion, what must I further say for him [Preston] who braved the mighty ocean and crossed to Mother England, that land whose laws have done so much for the African race in general and this Association in particular, which laid the first foundation for us to build upon. We say, unanimously in loud voices exclaim, 'God bless her! And protect her in all her troubles; defend her that she may overcome and vanquish her enemies.'"[42]

In tandem with those expressions of gratitude and endearment to England for aiding Preston were indications of a belief that there was something unique about England. Those convictions were not rooted in some Pollyanna naivety about a supposedly sinless England. Rather, it was the relative goodness that they had experienced in coming to Nova Scotia that convinced them that the Black community was without question relatively better off in Canada than the United States. For instance, in the eulogy of Richard Preston it was stated: "Our brother was converted in Virginia, United States of America, in the year of our Lord 1815, at this time he was held as a slave by American Slaveholders. But God had nobler work for him to do in a British and a free land; and in 1816, he was found clear gone and safely landed in Halifax, Nova Scotia."[43] Commentary on the experience of William Barrett echoes the sense that the arrival to Canada was markedly better than staying the United States: "Our brother [Willian Barrett] was converted while a young man, a slave, in Virginia, United States. But God made a way for his escape, and in the year 1820 he was safely landed in Halifax. He appreciated the freedom of man very much, and was ever found thanking God for his great deliverance."[44] Those well known testimonies of freedom played an important part in the formation of positive national identities and loyalty.[45] What would have also bolstered those positive feelings of appreciation was the Royal Navy's vigorous anti-slavery campaign on the high seas throughout the mid and late-nineteenth century[46] (as will be seen below, Britain imperial

42. Minutes of the African Baptist Association (1880).

43. See "Circular Letter" in Minutes of the African Baptist Association (1861).

44. Minutes of the African Baptist Association (1871).

45. The testimonies of many of the early Black Baptist leaders often included accounts of how their lot was bettered by escaping to English territory. For further examples, see MacKerrow, *Brief History*.

46. Grindal, *Opposing the Slavers*. Whether done for noble reasons or mixed

power and expansion in the latter part of the century was considered to be a boon for Africans under more oppressive rule such as by the Boers).

Along with the personal experience of those enslaved finding freedom in Canada, the record of Britain itself seemed to some to indicate something unique about the empire in which they found themselves.[47] Those perceptions of empire were not unique to the Black community, in fact, those perceptions of the empire were ubiquitous in popular culture at large. An exceptionally helpful indication of how Britain and its empire were imagined can be seen in a lengthy circular letter in 1878, written by association secretary MacKerrow.[48] The letter was entitled "The Bible and Its Social Influence in the Family." The letter starts by pointing out how the Bible was the guide provided to all God's people as they travel on the pilgrimage to the heavenly New Jerusalem. The need was for Christians to read the Bible, for without it they were lost without a trustworthy guide, and thus parents had "a great duty … incumbent upon [them] to instill in the hearts of the little ones the value and importance of the Bible, with its immense moral as well as religious influence." That importance of the Bible was then linked to the greatness of Britain and its empire. MacKerrow was referencing a supposed incident that was portrayed in a painting by Thomas Jones Barker, first displayed in 1863. The iconic image was reproduced widely in Britain and its empire and provided a powerful and persuasive moral argument for British imperial expansion, especially as it related to the spread of missions and the Bible. What is particularly noteworthy is how that theme that was a favourite among White Protestant supporters and preachers of empire had also captured the imagination of some among the Black community.

> I was quite amused some few years ago in perusing an English religious periodical, shortly after the siege of Magdala, an

---

motives such as suppressing the economies of Britain's opponents, the net result of the Royal Navy's efforts was a decline of the slave trade – and that would have been cause for rejoicing among the enslaved and those opposed to the slave trade.

47. The minutes lack criticism of empire and imperial advance. Of course, the lack of criticism in the Nova Scotia minutes does not mean none existed—it was just a matter of what made it into the minutes. However, the record of Black Americans at a time when America was engaged in imperial conquests at the turn of the century indicates a skepticism of the alleged "blessings" of US expansion (see Gatewood, "Black Americans"). However, there were those who supported the war effort against Spain as a way to not only liberate Blacks from Spanish oppression but also gain recognition as able and loyal citizens and soldiers (see Gatewood, "Kansas Negroes").

48. Minutes of the African Baptist Association (1878).

African Prince who was sent as an embassy, with costly presents for Queen Victoria, from an Ethiopian Court, preferred a modest request that our Beloved Sovereign would tell him the secret of England's greatness and glory. Her Majesty did not like Hezekiah show the Ambassador her diamonds and precious jewels, and her rich ornaments, but handed him a beautifully bound copy of the Holy Bible, saying, "Tell the Prince that this weapon is the success of England's greatness."[49]

MacKerrow did not take issue with the veracity of that account of an alleged encounter between Queen and Prince, rather he went on to provide evidence that, indeed, Britain was a unique nation due to the influence of the Bible on the empire. He reflected on nations such as France, Prussia, Spain, and Mexico and found them wanting due to their lack of access to the Bible. However, nations that had ready access to the Bible (and the literacy to read it) were deemed to be bastions of liberty: "Let us now return home to our own Continent, name the lands of the Bible, and you name the lands of constitutional freedom. England, Scotland, Switzerland, Holland and America, received their liberties from God's word." He concluded with an affirmation that the churches needed to "impart all the instruction you can from that good Book, for it is the necessary condition of a nation's prosperity." And as for the issue of race, the suffering of the Black community was due to failures to apply the teaching of the Bible, and the suffering would continue "until we put more value on it than we do."[50]

Like a number of other Canadian citizens, the Black Baptist community expressed the pride and jingoism of imperial zeal during the heyday of Canadian imperialism. Notions of the empire and its alleged blessings were readily apparent in some extensive commentary in the minutes during the South African War (1899–1902).[51] That commentary mirrored the commentary coming from other Canadian Protestant churches;[52] for instance, the war was deemed to be righteous due to the alleged Boer mistreatment of Black Africans, and a more favourable British

---

49. Minutes of the African Baptist Association (1878).

50. Minutes of the African Baptist Association (1878).

51. Also called the Boer War, Anglo-Boer War, or the Second Anglo-Boer War (the First Anglo-Boer War was from 1880 to 1881). Afrikaans call the war *Vrijheidsoorlog* ("freedom wars").

52. For Baptist, Anglican, Methodist, and Presbyterian churches and the war, see Heath, *War*.

rule was seen to be a remedy to such injustice. A prayer was offered to "Almighty God" for the "final overthrow of their enemy, the Boers" so that the Black peoples of Africa who had long suffered under the oppressive rule of "hypocritical Bible rulers [the Boers]" would be able to experience the same goodness as those Blacks in Nova Scotia who had been fortunate enough to have been "rocked in the cradle of an Anglo-Saxon Christianity."[53] The British (and Canadian) victory in 1902 was celebrated, and, as the following commentary indicates, the expansion of the "glorious Empire" was seen to inevitably lead to a boon for the Black community in the south of Africa:

> The establishment of the British Empire throughout the whole of South Africa means that the color mark will be no impediment to the rise of the colored race . . . Education will come as the Government becomes settled, and the colored people will . . . be free to be all that can be obtained for the in the direction of culture and Christianity; and as a result, we shall see for the first time in the history of South Africa, a people fresh from the soil, sprung as it were from primeval conditions out of the stagnant pools of Boer oppression, and like Orion rising from a midnight sky into the highest atmosphere of modern civilization.[54]

Such advancement for the empire's African subjects was considered to be supported by the new King Edward, and for that reason "no Canadian need be ashamed to belong to an Empire which embraces one-fifth of the inhabitable globe, and to know that this Dominion forms nearly half of the whole . . . we have a reason to be both thankful and proud."[55] It is hard to imagine such ardent statements of support emanating from the Black community if it was believed that imperial advance would make things worse. What is important to note is that undergirding such lofty imperial rhetoric was the conviction that imperial advance would bring about relief and advancement for their African brothers and sisters. In fact, both Black and White Baptists were caught up in the jingoistic imperial propaganda of the war that trumpeted that the imperial cause was just and one that would lead to a better rule than the Boers.

Not only was there a vision for partnership in imperial expansion, there was also a unique prophetic element to their sense of citizenship.

---

53. Minutes of the African Baptist Association (1901).
54. Minutes of the African Baptist Association (1902).
55. Minutes of the African Baptist Association (1902).

Their statement on eschatology was a widely and long-held Christian position on the return of Jesus and final judgement.[56] Second Timothy 2:3 was invoked to encourage members to work hard in this life and be rewarded in the next life: "Endure hardships as good soldiers, and the very God of heaven will bless you in this present world, and in the world to come will place the Crown of Glory upon your heads. Amen."[57] There was also the hope of final judgment, for a judgment of unjust rulers who misused their power to exploit and enslave would have been consoling for those long held in the grip of slavery. But there was another element to their view of the future of the nation that was tied to their own sense of national identity, one that was rooted in a particular interpretation of an Old Testament prophecy. The passage is Psalms 68:31 which reads "Princes shall come out of Egypt; Ethiopia shall soon stretch out her hands unto God" (KJV). One reference in the minutes applies the text in this manner:

> We thank God for this free salvation, that the day is fast approaching when "Princes will come out of Egypt and Ethiopia will stretch forth their hands unto God." And His mighty arm will not be shortened, nor those all-seeing eyes that can see in the distance will not be dimmed, nor will His ears be heavy to hear the cries of the poor and despised of all races, but as civilization increases, Africa will forge along the line of advancement, solving her own problem by industry, patience and perseverance, distaining even to strike back at her enemies, or to answer to their accusations, awaiting the righteous judgments of their blessed and glorious Redeemer.[58]

As Roy Kay notes, this application of Ps 68:31 had broad appeal among Black Christians. For some, it meant the Christianization and modernization of Black people in the United States and Africa, for others the promise of freedom for those enslaved and full citizenship, and yet for others the end of colonization and the start of African nation-states.[59] For Black Baptists in Nova Scotia, it was an optimistic vision of hope, one that provided a sense that the darkness of the past and the struggles of the

---

56. Minutes of the African Baptist Association (1869); Minutes of the African Baptist Association (1881).

57. See "Circular Letter" in Minutes of the African Baptist Association (1865).

58. Minutes of the African Baptist Association (1903). See also Minutes of the African Baptist Association (1861).

59. Kay, *Ethiopia Prophecy*.

present would, at some time soon, be replaced by a vibrant and surging African race, one fully engaged as equals in civic affairs.

As alluded to above, it is important to note that convictions about the goodness of Canada and the empire to which it belonged does not mean that Black Baptists had embraced a "North Star Myth"[60] of Canadian exceptionalism. It was simply a matter of relative good; in the decades of slavery and postwar unrest, the situation in Nova Scotia was deemed to be relatively better than in the United States. Canada seemed a promised land compared to the options available in the United States. That being the case, while the minutes often speak highly of relations with fellow White Baptists and neighbours,[61] there are clear indications that Black Baptists were well aware that racism still existed. Nova Scotia Blacks faced official and popular level prejudice that made life in the new land difficult and dangerous. Black settlers and citizens often faced government restrictions, and popular-level violence towards Blacks was often lurking in the shadows. For instance, the minutes of 1877 lament the ongoing struggles of the Black community in the face of injustices:

> Showing that it was the want of learning that kept our forefathers in slavery, and for to-day we are suffering, but he hoped that the day would soon dawn when the cloud of prejudice that now hangs over the descendants of "Africa" in this province particularly, will soon be dispersed, when we will be able to breathe a clearer atmosphere than we now do. The condition of the people of colour in this province he said, was deplorable, none worse throughout the Dominion, for although our votes are sought both in parliamental and civic elections, yet no recompense do we receive, but have to put up with the meanest of school houses that the province can afford, which deserves the greatest censure from the educated world.[62]

At the beginning of the new century, positive reports from the United States seemed to indicate that the Black community in the United States was better off than the one in Nova Scotia. And partially due to those reports, the ABA formed a Ways and Means Committee (1916) to explore ways to strengthen the Black Canadian experience. Such

---

60. Walker, *Racial Discrimination*.

61. Minutes of the African Baptist Association (1871); Minutes of the African Baptist Association (1873).

62. Minutes of the African Baptist Association (1877).

commentary and decisions are a reminder that the cross-border migration of the Black community was not always from south to north.[63]

The response to such racism—and other sins of the nation—was an indication of how Black Baptists imagined their place in society. Their identity as sojourners provided hope when things were dark, but that same identity as sojourners compelled them to engage in social reform as citizens. The laws of the land needed to be Christianized, and faithful citizens needed to act as Christians if the dream of a Christian nation was to become a reality. And in that manner, they were much like other White Baptists (and Anglicans, Methodists, and Protestants) who sought to participate in the surging movement of social reform in the late-nineteenth century.

Activism, Social Reform, and Race Advancement

There were multiple motives for dealing with social ills; the glory of God was thought to be on display when acting righteously,[64] the morality of the nation was considered to be critical for receiving God's blessing, and—a specific concern for the Black community—the corruption of character impinged on opportunities for race advancement. As the nineteenth century passed and the twentieth arrived there was a growing optimism in the Black community regarding what they could attain, echoing optimism such as found in Booker T. Washington's *A New Negro for a New Century*.[65] What was unique and most pressing was the need for the Black community to seize the day and take advantage of available opportunities. It was also deemed critical to avoid succumbing to social ills that could easily short circuit that process. Undergirding the desire for social reform and its positive impact on the churches and nation was a "politics of respectability," the assumption that they would

---

63. The falling short of Black opportunities in Canada was lamented by Baptists such as Baptist leader and historian MacKerrow. See MacKerrow, *Brief History*, 95, 101. See also Whitfield, *Blacks on the Border*.

64. "We acknowledge our everlasting and indispensable obligations to glorify God, by living a holy, righteous and godly life, in this present world, in all our several places and relations; and we engage by the assistance of the Divine Spirit, to improve our time, strength, talents, and advantages, to his glory and the good of our fellow men; promising, by Divine help, to walk in our houses as becomes those professing godliness, and to train up those under our care in the ways of religion and virtue" (see "Articles of Faith and Practice" in Minutes of the African Baptist Association [1869]).

65. Washington, *New Negro*.

gain recognition in society by their virtuous behaviour and exemplary conduct.[66]

Comments on social issues such as prohibition and education mirrored in many ways typical White Baptist and Methodist views. The commentary in the Black Baptist community on temperance was ubiquitous, with frequent exhortations to avoid the plague of alcohol.[67] The minutes of 1885 provide a helpful glimpse of the messages of three women on the issue of temperance, who "spoke admirably on the question at issue, showing the great influence that women have either for good or evil."[68] Stated simply, it was believed that there was nothing good to be gained by drinking, especially for a people that were seeking to rise to their full potential.

For decades the Black churches had also sought to advance themselves through a focus on education.[69] The minutes include exhortations for the Black community to educate itself or suffer the consequences. For instance, one meeting fused the issues of temperance and education, the linkage being the wastage of money, the harm to persons, and the hindering of the nation: the speaker "referred to the waste of money entailed by the use of intoxicating liquors. We are too poor to spend money for that which especially harms us. Without education we cannot be great; we cannot succeed. Education, temperance and morality are essential to good homes, to good communities, to good countries."[70] Discussion continued on the need for educated ministers, and how "progress [was] being made along educational lines in the United States, and of the opportunities offered in this way to the colored people of the province."[71]

Yet, another area of activism was that of missions. At that time home missions and foreign missions were under the same umbrella, and both had an evangelistic element as well as a social component. The nineteenth century was marked by a surging Protestant missionary enterprise, and Baptists in general were ardently involved in the movement. For, as Brian Stanley argues, "If you wish to mobilize Baptists (and evangelicals as a

---

66. Gaines, *Uplifting the Race*, 45, 161–62, 259.

67. Minutes of the African Baptist Association (1883); Minutes of the African Baptist Association (1885).

68. Minutes of the African Baptist Association (1885).

69. Riley, "Contribution."

70. Minutes of the African Baptist Association (1907).

71. Minutes of the African Baptist Association (1907). For mention of industrial schools, see Minutes of the African Baptist Association (1903).

whole) on an issue that divides the nation down the middle politically, the way to do it is to persuade them that liberty to preach the gospel is at stake."[72] The link with Baptist missionaries and the struggle against slavery made the call to missions even more compelling for Black Baptists.[73]

Not surprisingly, support for the missionary impulse can be seen in the minutes. Excitement was expressed over the fact that "within our own time the crusade has been pressed with such vigor that the hope has been kindled that we may see the complete evangelization of the world within our own generation."[74] The advance of Christianity in India was praised, as was the work of home mission among immigrants in the West, Roman Catholics in Quebec, and among the Black community in the Maritimes.[75] What is interesting to note is the commentary on missions to Africa in 1885, the year of the Berlin Conference and start of the "Scramble for Africa."[76] In the following comments it is clear that there were those in the Black community that had embraced the missionary spirit of the day:

> The Moderator made a brilliant speech regarding the Foreign Missionary field, inasmuch as we have done nothing for Foreign Missions it was not too late to make a commencement, as the mission which once blazed in Africa had somewhat subsided, yet he fully believed that the missionary angel was passing over from Asia to Africa. "Lott Carey," the pioneer missionary to Africa, was a Virginian by birth of African descent; he became converted in the early part of this century, having heard a sermon preached on the conversation that took place between our blessed Master and Nicodemus, he was deeply impressed, he straightway made a resolution to learn to read, which he did rapidly, which gave him a taste for missionary life, and in 1821 sailed for Sierra Leone, Africa. His career was short but effective, being at times priest and chieftain—his obstructions were numerous, ofttimes coming from unexpected sources. The Colonization Society proved most disastrous to his advancement, having to war both with the enemy of souls as well as that

---

72. Stanley, "Baptists."

73. Stanley, "Nineteenth-Century Liberation Theology"; "Baptists"; Lawes, "Historical Evaluation."

74. Minutes of the African Baptist Association (1913).

75. Minutes of the African Baptist Association (1913). See also Minutes of the African Baptist Association (1885).

76. See Pakenham, *Scramble for Africa*.

of civilization, it was up-hill work. He met his death by accident, and nothing now remains to mark his resting place but the usual piece of marble stone. The speaker impressed his hearers very much on this theme of Foreign Missionary work, which he hoped that the brethren present would use very effort possible and stir up that missionary spirit, let it be great or small. He informed us that the Congo field was now open to the world, and why should there not be young men in this very meeting decide to go there and labour for God—he had offered himself to go, and he wanted to see others do likewise.[77]

The comment on Congo is especially poignant, considering the horrors that would occur under Belgium rule.[78] Nevertheless, the discourse on missions reflected the optimism of the day and provides a sense of the alleged destiny of Canadians in what was considered to be a providential opportunity.

One further area of social reform was related to race. As can well be imagined, the Black community was cognizant of matters related to race. And, as noted above, the need was pressing for the Black community to rise to new heights in what was considered to be a period of great optimism and opportunity. Exhortations and official statements were made about the inherent equality of all peoples, Black, White, and others.[79] For instance, in a recasting of the notion of property, readers were reminded that all Christians were part of a global "brotherhood," and all Christians—Black and White—were God's "property."

> The Church is a holy brotherhood: every member is God's child, every member is Christ's brother . . . Brethren, here is equality—not that there are no distinctions or differences, for there are babes, young men and fathers; there are different gifts and different administrations; some are in office, and some are not; some are to guide, others are to follow; some are to feed, others are to be fed; some rule, others are ruled—but we have all the same nature, we all stand in the same relation to God and to each other, are all partakers of the same grace, and shall all meet in the same family mansion at the end of our journey. God having done so much for us, having conferred so much upon us, and having brought us into such a high and honorable connection

77. Minutes of the African Baptist Association (1885).

78. Hochschild, *King Leopold's Ghost*.

79. See "Articles of Faith and Practice" in Minutes of the African Baptist Association (1869); see "Circular Letter" in Minutes of the African Baptist Association (1876).

with Himself, we are not at our own disposal: we are absolutely His property, for we have put ourselves into His hands, that He may use us and dispose of us as He pleases.[80]

That equality being the case, there was a sense of urgency to the need for the Black community to advance. In fact, the social ills such as alcohol were readily criticized because they would keep the Black community down and out, thus justifying the racism of those who considered the Black community incapable of equalling that of Whites, or others.

Fortunately, the minutes provide some examples of exhortations to inspire Black Baptists to take advantage of the opportunities before them. The end of the century and the beginning of the new was deemed to be "the most important age of our World's History . . . we have a reason to believe that a mighty Breath of the Divine Spirit is now passing over the earth."[81] Elsewhere it was stated that the age was "an age of improvement and progress" where "science and religion, law and liberty must make progress."[82] And yet elsewhere the successes of the Black community as ministers, lawyers, politicians, and musicians were highlighted to show that advancement was possible.[83] In sum, it was deemed to be an age of progress and living in the future as in the past was not an option: "The world has progressed and is progressing and so should we."[84] William White, who was quickly becoming one of the key leaders of the Black Baptist community in Nova Scotia,[85] made it clear that the choice to advance was not an option: the "watchword should be 'Forward.' We must go ahead or die."[86] As for how the Black community could advance, it was argued that the ABA was vital in making it happen.

> It strikes at the very root of our usefulness as an Association; for I submit that the chief, if not the only reason that we are banded together is, that we can and should devise ways and means for the spread of the Gospel among and the general betterment of the condition of the colored people in Nova Scotia. If we fail to use of God-given powers in this direction then, as individuals,

80. Minutes of the African Baptist Association (1880).
81. Minutes of the African Baptist Association (1877).
82. Minutes of the African Baptist Association (1880).
83. Minutes of the African Baptist Association (1881).
84. Minutes of the African Baptist Association (1907).
85. Brown, "William Andrew White Jr."
86. Minutes of the African Baptist Association (1907).

we do not measure up to the standard of our true manhood, and as an Association we lose every vestige of our usefulness as an organization.[87]

That conviction regarding the usefulness of the association would lead to the formation of a Ways and Means Committee, a group that provided informative and inspiring information in the coming years, especially in the closing years of the Great War.[88]

Within the commentary in the minutes there was what some have coined a "race consciousness" developing in the Black Baptist community. Melissa Shaw argues that the First World War intensified that race consciousness,[89] but, as the minutes in the decades preceding the war indicate, there was a prewar sense that the Black community in Nova Scotia needed to take advantage of the opportunities before it. An implicit assumption not stated overtly in the prewar years, but seems clear in the war years to come, was a sort of *quid pro quo*; the expected dividend of responsible citizenship was "to both a rightful place in that wider democracy and ampler justice which are to be ushered in after the war."[90] In other words, much like other Black communities throughout the empire,[91] race advancement would not only lead to an improved community life for Blacks, but also, as the Black community rose to new heights, an improved relationship with Whites and an equal part to play in the nation.

CONCLUSION

While at times using the language of sojourners, the views expressed in the minutes reveal a fairly consistent public narrative of obligations and convictions shaped by being on the margins of a dominant Anglo-French (and British imperial) national identity. What is also apparent in the minutes is a fusion of patriotism, social reform, and race consciousness distinctly forged by religious convictions. It is virtually impossible to pull those aspects apart, for they are intertwined and mutually supportive. What this chapter demonstrates is how among Black Baptists there was an appreciation among some for the relative safety and opportunity of

87. Minutes of the African Baptist Association (1907).
88. See esp. Minutes of the African Baptist Association (1918).
89. Shaw, "'Most Anxious.'"
90. *African United Baptist Association*, 1918.
91. Killingray, "'Good West Indian.'"

Canada when contrasted with the horrors of American slavery, and that gratefulness nurtured a sense of loyalty to the nation. Their religious convictions compelled them to engage in evangelism and social reforms to shape a Christian Canada. Yet there was also a pragmatic and strategic element to their loyalty and social engagement, something born out of the optimism of the age as well as the need to demonstrate the abilities of the Black community in order to silence naysayers and doubters of their worth as equal citizens. While it is outside the purview of this chapter, it is worth noting that the Great War thrust upon Canadians in the summer of 1914 was seen as a once-in-a-lifetime opportunity to do just that.

BIBLIOGRAPHY

Primary Sources

Archives

Minutes of the African Baptist Association, 1855–1914.

Monographs

MacKerrow, P. E. *A Brief History of the Coloured Baptists of Nova Scotia and their First Organization as Churches A. D. 1832*. Halifax, NS: Nova Scotia Printing Company, 1895.

Secondary Sources

Anderson, Benedict. *Imagined Communities: Reflections on the Origin and Spread of Nationalism*. London: Verso, 1991.

Armstrong, John G. "The Unwelcome Sacrifice: A Black Unit in the Canadian Expeditionary Force, 1917–1919." In *Ethnic Armies: Polyethnic Armed Forces from the Time of the Habsburgs to the Age of the Superpowers*, edited by N. F. Dreisziger, 178–97. Waterloo, ON: Wilfrid Laurier University Press, 1990.

Bebbington, David. *The Nonconformist Conscience: Chapel and Politics, 1870–1914*. London: George Allen & Unwin, 1982.

Berger, Carl. *The Sense of Power: Studies in the Ideas of Canadian Imperialism, 1867–1914*. Toronto: University of Toronto Press, 1970.

Berger, Peter L. *The Sacred Canopy: Elements of a Sociological Theory of Religion*. New York: Doubleday, 1967.

Bertley, Leo W. *Canada and its People of African Descent*. Pierrefonds, QC: Bilongo, 1977.

Boyd, Frank S., Jr. "Preston, Richard." *Dictionary of Canadian Biography*. No pages. Online: http://www.biographi.ca/en/bio/preston_richard_8E.html.

Brown, Dudley. "William Andrew White Jr.: Portrait of an African Canadian Pastor, Chaplain, and Activist." PhD diss., McMaster Divinity College, 2022.

Buckner, Phillip, ed. *Canada and the British Empire*. Oxford: Oxford University Press, 2008.

———, ed. *Canada and the End of Empire*. Toronto: University of British Columbia Press, 2005.

Cole, Douglas. "Canada's 'Nationalistic' Imperialists." *Journal of Canadian Studies* 5 (1970) 44–45.

Cook, Terry. "George R. Parkin and the Concept of Britannic Idealism." *Journal of Canadian Studies* 10 (1975) 15–31.

Fingard, Judith. "McKerrow, Peter Evander." *Dictionary of Canadian Biography*. No pages. Online: http://www.biographi.ca/en/bio/mckerrow_peter_evander_13E.html.

———. "Race and Respectability in Victorian Halifax." *The Journal of Imperial and Commonwealth History* 20 (1992) 169–95.

Foyn, Sean Flynn. "The Underside of Glory: AfriCanadian Enlistment in the Canadian Expeditionary Force, 1914–1917." MA thesis, University of Ottawa, 1999.

Francis, Daniel. *National Dreams: Myth, Memory and Canadian History*. Vancouver: Arsenal Pulp, 1997.

Gaines, Kevin K. *Uplifting the Race: Black, Leadership, Politics, and Culture in the Twentieth Century*. Chapel Hill: North Carolina University Press, 1996.

Gatewood, Willard B., Jr. "Black Americans and the Quest for Empire." *The Journal of Southern History* 38 (1972) 545–65.

———. "Kansas Negroes and the Spanish-American War." *The Kansas Historical Quarterly* 37 (1971) 300–313.

Green, Ernest. "Upper Canada's Black Defenders." *Ontario History* 27 (1937) 365–91.

Grindal, Peter. *Opposing the Slavers: The Royal Navy's Campaign against the Atlantic Slave Trade*. London: I. B. Tauris, 2018.

Heath, Gordon L. "'The Boers Standing in the Way of Progress in Africa Must Be Swept Aside': Patriotism and Imperialism in the Canadian *Jewish Times* during the South African War." In *Empire from the Margins: Religious Minorities in Canada and the South African War, 1899–1902*, edited by Gordon L. Heath, 155–71. McMaster General Studies Series 11. Eugene, OR: Pickwick, 2017.

Heath, Gordon L., ed. *Empire from the Margins: Religious Minorities in Canada and the South African War, 1899–1902*. McMaster General Studies Series 11. Eugene: Pickwick, 2017.

Heath, Gordon L. "'The Great Association Above:' Maritime Baptists and the War of 1812." *Pacific Journal of Baptist Research* 7 (2011) 1–22.

———. "An Opportunity Not to Be Missed: The Black Baptist and Methodist War Effort on the Canadian Home Front, 1914–1918," forthcoming.

———. *A War with a Silver Lining: Canadian Protestant Churches and the South African War, 1899–1902*. Montreal: McGill-Queen's University Press, 2009.

———. "The Wartime Diaries of Canadian Baptist Military Chaplain William A. White, 1917–1918." *Baptist Quarterly* (2017) 165–81.

Higginbotham, Evelyn Brooks. *Righteous Discontent: The Women's Movement in the Black Baptist Church, 1880–1920*. Cambridge, MA: Harvard University Press, 1993.

Hochschild, Adam. *King Leopold's Ghost: A Story of Greed, Terror, and Heroism in Colonial Africa*. Boston: Houghton Mifflin, 1998.

Joost, Mathias. "No. 2 Construction Battalion: The Operational History." *Canadian Military Journal* 16 (2016) 51–59.

Kay, Roy. *The Ethiopia Prophecy in Black American Letters*. Gainesville: University Press of Florida, 2012.

Killingray, David. "'A Good West Indian, a Good African, and, in Short, a Good Britisher': Black and British in a Colour-Conscious Empire, 1760–1950." *Journal of Imperial and Commonwealth History* 36 (2008) 363–81.

Kling, David W. *The Bible in History: How the Texts Have Shaped the Times*. Oxford: Oxford University Press, 2004.

Lawes, Marvia E. "A Historical Evaluation of Jamaica Baptists: A Spirituality of Resistance." *Black Theology* 6 (2008) 366–92.

Newfield, Gareth. "Upper Canada's Black Defenders? Re-evaluating the War of 1812 Coloured Corps." *Canadian Military History* 18 (2009) 31–40.

Niles, Lyndrey A. "Rhetorical Characteristics of Traditional Black Preaching." *Journal of Black Studies* 15 (1984) 41–52.

Oliver, Pearleen. *A Brief History of the Colored Baptists of Nova Scotia:1782–1953*. Halifax: McCurdy, 1953.

Page, Robert. *The Boer War and Canadian Imperialism*. Ottawa: The Canadian Historical Association, 1987.

———. "Canada and the Imperial Idea in the Boer War Years." *Journal of Canadian Studies* 5 (1970) 33–49.

———. "Carl Berger and the Intellectual Origins of Canadian Imperialist Thought, 1867–1914." *Journal of Canadian Studies* 5 (1970) 39–43.

Pakenham, Thomas. *The Scramble for Africa: White Man's Conquest of the Dark Continent from 1876 to 1912*. New York: Avon, 1991.

Penlington, Norman. *Canada and Imperialism, 1896*. Toronto: University of Toronto Press, 1965.

Pitcan, Mikaela, Alice E. Marwick, and Danah Boyd. "Performing a Vanilla Self: Respectability Politics, Social Class, and the Digital World." *Journal of Computer-Mediated Communication* 23 (2018) 163–79.

Riley, Jennifer. "The Contribution of the African United Baptist Association to Public Education, 1854–1940." In *Atlantic Baptists and their World: A Festschrift in Honour of Dr. Robert S. Wilson*, edited by Taylor Murray and Gordon L. Heath, 269–86. Kentville, NS: Gaspereau Press, 2020.

Ruck, Calvin W. *Canada's Black Battalion: No. 2 Construction, 1916–1920*. Halifax: Society for the Protection and Preservation of Black Culture in Nova Scotia, 1986.

Sawallisch, Nele. *Fugitive Borders: Black Canadian Cross-Border Literature at Mid-Nineteenth Century*. Bielefeld, Germany: Transcript, 2018.

Shaw, Melissa. "'Most Anxious to Serve their King and Country': Black Canadians' Fight to Enlist in WWI and Emerging Race Consciousness in Ontario, 1914–1919." *Social History* 44 (2016) 543–80.

Siemerling, Winfried. *The Black Atlantic Reconsidered: Black Canadian Writing, Cultural History, and the Presence of the Past*. Montreal/Kingston: McGill-Queen's University Press, 2015.

Stanley, Brian. "Baptists, Antislavery and the Legacy of Imperialism." *Baptist Quarterly* 42 (2007) 284–95.

———. "Nineteenth-Century Liberation Theology: Nonconformist Missionaries and Imperialism." *Baptist Quarterly* 32 (1987) 5–18.

Stouffer, Allen P. "Towards Community: Black Methodists in Nineteenth-Century Nova Scotia." *Canadian Society of Church History* (2014) 195–209.

Tulloch, Headley. *Black Canadians: A Long Line of Fighters*. Toronto: NC, 1975.

Walker, James W. St. G. "Race and Recruitment in World War I: Enlistment of Visible Minorities in the Canadian Expeditionary Force." *Canadian Historical Review* 70 (1989) 1–26.

———. *Racial Discrimination in Canada: The Black Experience*. Historical Booklet No. 41. Ottawa: Canadian Historical Society, 1985.

Washington, Booker T. *A New Negro for a New Century*. Chicago: American, 1900.

White, E. Frances. *Dark Continent of our Bodies: Black Feminism and the Politics of Respectability*. Philadelphia: Temple University Press, 2001.

Whitfield, Harvey Amani. *Blacks on the Border: The Black Refugees in British North American, 1815–1860*. Burlington: University of Vermont Press, 2006.

Williams, Savanah E. "The Role of the African United Baptist Association in the Development of Indigenous Afro-Canadians in Nova Scotia, 1782–1978." In *Repent and Believe: The Baptist Experience in Maritime Canada*, edited by Barry M. Moody, 46–65. Hantsport, NS: Lancelot, 1980.

Winks, Robin. *The Blacks in Canada: A History*. 2nd ed. Montreal: McGill University Press, 1997.

Yelin, Louise. *From the Margins of Empire: Christina Stead, Doris Lessing, Nadine Gordimer*. Ithaca, NY: Cornell University Press, 1998.

7

New Horizons Baptist Church

A History of Spirituality, Perseverance, and Social Justice

Jennifer Riley

In May 2018, the congregation of Cornwallis St. Baptist Church, located in Halifax, Nova Scotia, announced its decision to formally change its name to New Horizons Baptist Church. Since 1831, the church has stood in its urban Halifax neighbourhood and served the people as Cornwallis St. Baptist. However, in the midst of protests regarding Lord Cornwallis[1] and his role in the oppression and abuse of indigenous peoples, the congregation felt that they could not serve in truth and solidarity with all people of colour while carrying the name Cornwallis. It was noted in the press release that in its nearly 200 years of existence, Cornwallis Street Baptist Church has "worked with community organizations and partnered with sister churches and city agencies in collaborative efforts to address poverty, education gaps, violence and social injustice."[2]

This statement encapsulates the role of the Black Baptist Church in Nova Scotia. For the African Nova Scotian Baptists, the church is more than just a spiritual anchor, it is the place where its members seek to better their circumstances in all areas of life. From their arrival in Nova

---

1. The Founder of Halifax and the governor of Nova Scotia, Edward Cornwallis, was well known for his Scalping Proclamation which offered a bounty for any indigenous person killed in Nova Scotia.
2. "Historic Cornwallis Street Baptist Church."

Scotia, the church has been the place where African Nova Scotians banded together to fight injustices in their communities. Like other African Nova Scotian churches, New Horizons Baptist[3] has the effects of systemic racism and of colonialism woven into its very fabric. Fortunately, there are also strands of resilience and fortitude combined with a firm belief that through faith and hard work anything is possible. New Horizons is not just a church that stands in solidarity with those who are marginalized, it is a church founded by a marginalized community that has fought for justice and equality since its founding.

The history of Nova Scotia cannot be written without including the Black population and their contributions. As the British began to colonize the province, Nova Scotian settlers depended on the Black Refugees, the Black Loyalists, and the Maroons for labour to build the province's infrastructure and its fortifications. The African Nova Scotians, as they are now called, were lured to the province, primarily from the American colonies, with promises of land grants, equal pay for equal work and a future for their children. However, the reality of life in the province was much different than the rosy picture that had been painted by those who brought the Blacks to Nova Scotia.

Because Nova Scotia was a British colony, most laws and regulations mirrored those of England. This meant that Black immigrants were not citizens and had no ability to participate in public life. In fact, life in Nova Scotia was so difficult that more than 1,000 Black people chose to travel to Sierra Leone in 1792 to begin a new life there. Those who remained struggled to find advocates in their fight to become equal participants in the building and governing of Nova Scotia. The church became a place of support, not just spiritual support but a place to have a voice, to be able to speak out about their circumstances and seek solutions to their problems.

As the Black population grew in the province, the church represented all that a new life of freedom could be for African Nova Scotians. As Pearleen Oliver so eloquently stated, the church represented the support system the people needed to embrace their new lives:

> Their escape, as refugees to Nova Scotia is the beginning of this story: of their healing and development as they sought spiritual help and guidance through their small churches where they could sing their spirituals of joy and sadness; where they could speak freely of their hard trials and great tribulations and where

3. This chapter will use the former name of the church Cornwallis Street Baptist as the history discussed took place while the church carried that name.

they could give comfort and support to each other. No more auction block, no more agony, no more whips to tear the flesh, no more incessant toiling without respite, here, they could reclaim their stolen humanity.[4]

Those small beacons of religious freedom that Oliver spoke of were hard won, and New Horizons Baptist Church is a portrait of the struggle for community that these new Nova Scotians faced; not just a spiritual community but a community that would provide the strength to see their dreams of a prosperous life in Nova Scotia fulfilled. With each new pastor and generation of congregants, the mission of the church to fight for social justice has grown. The foundation for this mission is found in the beginnings of the African Nova Scotian fight for a place of worship to call their own.

The Church of England was the sanctioned church in Nova Scotia in the late eighteenth century. Many Blacks were baptized into the Church of England, and, in fact, the Anglican Church considered itself very successful in converting the Black population to Christianity.[5] However, for the Black congregants, this church was not meeting its needs. The Anglican church perhaps lacked the understanding of what church and faith meant to the African Nova Scotian community or, perhaps more likely, the priests and bishops did not care about the welfare of these people once they had been baptized.

This lack of understanding of the purpose and function of the church in the African Nova Scotian community by the Church of England manifested in a myriad of unaddressed issues. The churches were often far from their homes making attendance difficult and the community role of the church impossible. There was often a language barrier, the sermons heard were not always understood. This is evidenced by the testimony of a man attending a service with a congregation including Jamaican immigrants. Upon leaving the service, he spoke with some of the Jamaican men: "Once, coming out of the church, a gentleman, who had attended the service, asked one of the Maroon captains, shivering with cold, if he knew what the clergyman had said. 'Me Sabby?' or 'How should I know?' was the answer. He had been smoking a pipe with some, while others were asleep."[6]

4. Oliver, *Song of the Spirit*, 13.
5. Walker, *Black Loyalists*, 70.
6. Fingard, *Anglican Design*, 68.

These men were perhaps outside the church because pew rents were often unaffordable. And, although these men were members of the congregation, they were denied leadership positions and seldom had contact with clergy outside of Sunday morning service. The Church of England appeared to have little interest in building the Black community or helping its members to better themselves.

African Nova Scotians longed to have church leaders, elders, preachers, and teachers that came from within their own community. Many began to gather in homes and conduct worship services that were more meaningful to them. As Anglican Church leadership saw this trend developing, lay leaders were appointed from within the communities. However, these leaders did not hold the same permissions as their White counterparts. It was assumed that Black people did not have the intelligence necessary to perform the spiritual duties of a lay leader in the Church of England. The Black lay leaders were only given permission to encourage the community not to meet at home but to attend services at the established church.[7]

Undeterred, Black lay leaders began performing weddings, funerals, and administering the sacraments. The reaction of the Church was far from positive. Black leaders who attempted to perform clerical duties were chastised. Joseph Leonard is a perfect example of this. As a lay leader in a community far from the established church, Leonard became a pastor to his people and established the church community that the people desired. He taught school, he led Bible study and performed all other pastoral functions. When the local bishop found out what Leonard was doing, he was removed from his position. The Church of England was unwilling to have people of colour providing spiritual care to its congregants, even if those congregants were Black.[8]

But African Nova Scotians were not willing to accept the status quo. Each family had come to this province expecting that the barriers of racism were going to be broken down in their new home. The people were unwilling to be subjected to a church hierarchy that did not afford them opportunities to grow both in their faith and in their life. Historians have long recognized the importance of faith in the development of the strong, socially minded African Nova Scotian communities. In his 2005 history, Whitfield noted:

---

7. Walker, *Black Loyalists*, 68.
8. Wilson, *Loyal Blacks*, 118.

The Black Refugees placed great importance on religion. Christianity allowed the refugees to make some sense of their lives. Early religious gatherings in Preston and Hammonds Plains served as the foundation for Refugee consciousness and community . . . spiritual gatherings and church meeting houses were not simply religious in nature . . . these churches represented the organizing principle around which life was structured. His church was his school, his forum, his political arena, his social club, his art gallery and his conservatory of music.[9]

Early in Nova Scotia's history, leaders emerged who worked through the church for equality for African Nova Scotians. David George was a Black pastor from the United States who fought for equal rights for African Nova Scotians through the church and civil disobedience. He is known to have preached to the Black communities at Preston and Halifax.[10] Those meetings were the beginnings of what would become the congregation of Cornwallis St. Baptist Church. George desired to be recognized as a pastor by Whites as well as Blacks and did have success in baptizing people of both races. However, this was not well received by many in the White community. George faced opposition that sometimes led to riots in towns where he was preaching and baptizing.[11]

David George spent years preaching to the Black communities throughout Nova Scotia and even into New Brunswick. His work was not only in the spiritual lives of the community, but in social justice. George fought for promised land grants and equal pay for employment, but the work was dangerous and extremely difficult with little success for the Black community. Those realities eventually forced George to make the difficult decision to join a large number of Black settlers who had chosen to leave Nova Scotia and form a new community in Sierra Leone, Africa. When he left for Sierra Leone in 1792, taking many leaders with him, there was a noticeable lack of leadership in the Black community that was felt throughout the province.

Burgeoning congregations in Halifax and other areas of the province were once again in need of strong leadership to continue to nurture their spirituality and lead the fight for equality in Nova Scotia. John Burton, a White pastor, stepped into these communities as that next preacher and leader. Burton arrived in Nova Scotia as an Anglican missionary but

9. Whitfield, *From American Slaves to Nova Scotia Subjects*, 95.
10. Gordon, *From Slavery to Freedom*, 71.
11. Gordon, *From Slavery to Freedom*, 60.

after a trip to the United States he returned to Nova Scotia as a converted Baptist in 1795.[12]

It is said that Burton had a heart for the African Nova Scotians and when he set up the first Baptist church in Halifax[13] he welcomed them as congregants and leaders. It was in this church and in meeting houses throughout the province begun by George, that African Nova Scotians began to worship in a manner that was consistent with their culture and understanding of God. Buoyed by their experience as leaders in the church, they also began to seek education and the betterment of their circumstances. Under Burton's leadership, the Black Baptists did experience growth in numbers, but he was still a White man in charge of the Black congregants. In fact, he was in charge not only as their church leader but also in civil affairs. He was given authority by the province to litigate disputes among the African Nova Scotians and even mete out punishment for crimes. In the *Christian Visitor* of 1856, David Nutter had this to say about John Burton:

> Brother Burton was just the man to have the care and management of this class of people, the coloured. There was something peculiar in them, and there was something in this preacher which qualified him to deal with them. Brother B. was a king among them, and they rendered unto Caesar the things which are Caesar's. He reigned with undisputed sway amongst them. He said come, and they came, go and they went, do this and they did it; but if he was king, he was a fatherly king; for in his government, he united the mildness and condescension of a father with the severity of a sovereign. Father Burton used to exercise his office of magistrate in connection with that of a pastor. He cited delinquent persons before him, heard witnesses, and without a jury, he gave his judgement against the evil doer. This was done not only with members of his church but with others, and all submitted to his decision. I heard it said in Halifax, that the justices and even the Governor of the province acquiesced in Mr. Burton's decisions and let him deal as he thought proper, with this class of her Majesty's subjects, and they were wise in doing so.[14]

---

12. Boyd, *McKerrow*, 12.

13. This congregation remained under Burton's leadership until his death in 1838.

14. Boyd, *McKerrow*, 10.

Echoes of the slave mentality are clear in this epitaph. Nutter called the Blacks "peculiar," likely meaning inferior or unwilling to do what was expected of them. He implied that the congregation needed someone to "deal" with them, much as their masters had dealt with them during slavery. There is also the implication that the appointed government officials of the city of Halifax and the province of Nova Scotia did not want to deal with issues arising in the Black community and were willing to let this "class" of people to be ruled by Briton, even calling Burton a king over the Blacks. Despite the promises that had been made to the Blacks, Nova Scotia had the mindset of a slave society: "American slavery, fundamentally, had meant the exploitation of black labour. To the Nova Scotian of European descent, therefore, blacks were usually considered to be nothing but a source of cheap labour."[15]

But the African Nova Scotians were not willing to be second-class citizens. They knew that they were able to lead, and they were determined to have their own voice. Much progress was made under the leadership of Burton during his years as pastor of the Halifax congregation, however, the African Nova Scotians would become the focus of a major dispute in 1824. The Anglican Church in Halifax experienced a leadership dispute that resulted in the Church splitting. A group of dissenters left the Anglican church and came to Burton's Baptist church, which was the only Baptist church in Halifax. The dissenters eventually fought to have the Blacks removed from the church and took their dispute to the Maritime Convention.[16] The former Anglicans lost their dispute and eventually started their own church.

This event made it clear to the Black congregants that their position in the church remained precarious at best. They determined that their own church was required, one free of White leadership and oversight. It was fortuitous that at that time a young former slave was proving his leadership skills to the congregation in Halifax. Richard Preston had been working with John Burton and had been preaching and teaching in many of the Black settlements. The African Nova Scotian leaders at John Burton's church saw in Preston a man who could guide and direct them as they moved forward with their own church. However, their experience with the religious authorities in the Anglican Church led the people to

---

15. Walker, *Black Loyalists*, 42.
16. Boyd, *McKerrow*, 9.

believe that Preston would have a difficult time becoming ordained and therefore legitimized as a church leader in Nova Scotia.[17]

The group raised enough money to send Preston to England to be trained and ordained under Baptist abolitionists. This was an amazing undertaking for both the community and Preston himself. To raise enough money to get Preston to England was an enormous task. But Preston thrived in England and proved himself to be a thoughtful and intelligent leader. Through his time with the abolitionist society, he grew in his resolve to have a church which would fight for the civil rights of the African Nova Scotian community. Preston was also able to raise funds for the building of a chapel in Halifax. The 1855 minutes of the African Baptist Association note that Preston raised 630 pounds for the construction.[18]

While Preston was in England, the leadership at home was moving forward with plans for the new church. In fact, a resolution had been drawn up on 14 April 1832, founding the first African Baptist Church in Halifax, even though the church did not yet exist physically. The resolution stated that Preston would be the pastor of the African Baptist Church that would have branches in Dartmouth, Preston, Beech Hill and Hammonds Plains.[19]

The church at Halifax, commonly known as the African Chapel, was completed by 1834 at which time the trustees, who had exhausted their funds on completing the building, petitioned the government for funds to hire a teacher. It was the congregation's stated desire that the building not only be used for Sunday morning worship but that a weekly school be held in the building where a teacher "taught the younger generation principles of morality and ordinary system of education".[20]

Preston was devoted to the cause of freedom and equality for the African Nova Scotian community. He preached often on the subject and organized an abolitionist society in Halifax in 1846. The list of officers for the society is evidence of the importance of the church in community organization. All were not only members of African Baptist churches but leaders in those churches; Prince William Sport, a trustee of the Halifax church, Septimus Clarke, who would become clerk of the not yet formed

---

17. Pachai, *Beneath the Clouds*, 58.
18. AUBA, *1855 Minutes*.
19. Boyd, *McKerrow*, 13.
20. "African Nova Scotians."

African Baptist Association, and William Barrett, treasurer of the Halifax church.[21] Leadership skills gained in the church were being put to use in the civic arena a mere thirteen years after the formation of the church. The church became the driving force for social justice almost immediately.

Preston recognized that when fighting systemic racism, numbers were important. The more people he could bring together, the better chance they had of effecting change. He had spent time going to many smaller Black settlements and preaching, teaching, and setting up congregations under the leadership of elders. In 1854, those churches were formed into an association. There were twelve churches in the original association that were served by three ordained ministers and four licentiates. In their first meeting, the influence of Cornwallis Street Baptist church in providing aid to other African Nova Scotians is clear in the following resolution:

> "The warmest thanks be given to Bro. Preston and Bro. Clarke for the able, diligent manner in which they have thus far fulfilled the trust committed to them, and for the admirable report in which they have unfolded plans that give promise to the benevolent efforts of the denomination. As well as the organization necessary for drawing from the philanthropic disposition and exertion of the African Baptists of Nova Scotia, the permanent effects and sustained action so much and so long desired."

The minutes also hold a resolution to make the Cornwallis Street church the mother church of the Association and recognize Richard Preston as the Bishop.[22] By 1855, there were 103 members at Cornwallis Street Baptist Church and members of the other churches in the Association totaled 205.[23]

Preston served as pastor of Cornwallis Street Baptist Church and Bishop of the African Baptist Association until his death in 1861. He had laid the foundation for a church that was concerned not only with spiritual matters in the Black community but also with bettering the situation for its people in Nova Scotia. Preston's vision of a community, which shared equality with its White counterparts in every area of life, was built upon by each new pastor and successive generation of congregants. The following are some notable pastors and their contributions to the church

---

21. Boyd, *McKerrow*, 22.
22. AUBA, *1855 Minutes*.
23. AUBA, *1855 Minutes*.

and the community in general in the late nineteenth and early twentieth centuries.

Upon the death of Rev. Preston, James Thomas became the pastor of Cornwallis Street Baptist[24] and its other charges.[25] Some felt that this was a move in the wrong direction as Thomas was a White man, not an African Nova Scotian. However, Thomas was married to a Black woman from Preston and had travelled with Richard Preston to many of the churches on evangelistic missions and was ordained by Preston in 1857. Although some leaders, particularly in the Preston area churches, objected to the appointment, overall, Thomas had a ministry worth noting in the Cornwallis Street history.[26]

The little chapel had fallen into some disrepair since its founding, and it was through the generosity of Rev. Thomas that repairs were made and eventually a vestry added. McKerrow notes that Thomas had such confidence in the congregation that he gave the loan for repairs without requiring any paperwork or mortgage from the church.[27] The repairs to the building were greatly needed and the funds appreciated by the congregation, but Thomas was not only remembered for his financial contributions. In 1868, Thomas was the preacher during a powerful time of revival when many professed faith in Jesus Christ. In that year, Thomas baptized seventy-two people. Then in 1874, forty-six more were baptized. These baptisms were from all of the pastoral charges, so it is impossible to say how many were members of the Cornwallis Street Baptist Church. However, the 1874 minutes of the Association show the membership of Cornwallis Street Baptist Church as 180 people, the largest in the Association.

As a foundation for social justice, education became a focus for Cornwallis Street Baptist Church. Before the government of Nova Scotia took over the regulation and funding of schooling for children of the province, education in the Black community was provided by Anglican benevolent societies. These societies felt that schooling for Black children should be solely for the purpose of training domestic servants and teaching religion. These societies did little to further the opportunities

---

24. McKerrow notes that Thomas was 'elected', but there is no evidence to back this claim.

25. AUBA, *1861 Minutes*.

26. Boyd, *McKerrow*, 32–33.

27. Boyd, *McKerrow*, 33.

for success outside of domestic service through their educational endeavours.[28]

A common secular education should have become available for all children in Nova Scotia when the province began funding education in 1811. However, politicians and public servants worked together to make a case for segregated schools.[29] The pastors of the Cornwallis Street Baptist Church objected to these schools and presented a petition to the Legislature in 1883. The signatories to this petition were Rev. Alexander Bailey, pastor 1879–1880, Rev. William Boone, pastor 1880–1881 and P. E. McKerrow, member of Cornwallis Street and clerk of the Association. In this petition, the petitioners noted that "a minute had been passed by the Council for Public Instruction, in defiance of the whole tenor and general spirit of the Act establishing free schools in Nova Scotia and which enabled the Commissioners of Schools for this city to exclude all colored children, so called, from the common school and establish separate schools for said children."[30]

With little progress made after this petition, a delegation from Cornwallis Street Baptist Church returned to the legislature in 1876. Rev. Henry H. Johnson, the pastor at the time, made an impassioned plea on behalf of Black children who, as British subjects, were entitled to equal education. He called segregated schooling "a relic of slavery"[31] and asked it to be abolished. The debate over segregated schools, known as the colour line, went on in the legislature for several years. In the end, it was made law that students could not be excluded from common schools in their district based on race. However, school inspectors retained the authority to erect a separate school where they felt it necessary.[32] This meant that because large Black communities, like Halifax, had enough children to warrant their own schoolhouse, education, particularly in the large urban communities, remained segregated well into the twentieth century.

Despite the difficulties in receiving a quality education in Halifax, members of the Cornwallis Street congregation became examples to other communities in what could be achieved even in such difficult

28. Pachai, *Beneath the Clouds*, 49.

29. The 1811 Bill held that communities would be responsible for building a schoolhouse and hiring a teacher before a subsidy would be provided.

30. Public Archives of Nova Scotia, Assembly Petitions—Education, 1883, RG-5, series P, vol. 78 pp 2–3, as cited in Boyd

31. Pachai, *Beneath the Clouds*, 83.

32. Pachai, *Beneath the Clouds*, 85.

circumstances. One such person was James R. Johnston. As a young member of the congregation, he held the positions of Sunday school superintendent, Church Clerk and the organizer of the Baptist Youth Provincial Union. In the secular world, he became the first African Nova Scotian to be admitted to Dalhousie University School of Law and, upon graduation, the first African Nova Scotian lawyer.[33]

Like many other African Nova Scotian leaders of his day, Johnston's thoughts were constantly occupied with finding solutions for the problem of receiving quality education faced by the majority of the community. In the United States, industrial schools for Blacks were beginning to have success. Johnston was aware of the Hampton Institute in Virginia that had influenced the Tuskegee Institute in Alabama, founded by Booker T. Washington.[34] Johnston believed that a similar type of schooling could be made available to African Nova Scotians if the community combined their resources.

Mention is made in the African Baptist Association minutes in 1903 of a committee being formed to consider an industrial school for the community. A few years later, Johnston presented his proposal for an Industrial School and the work began to plan and raise funds for the building of the school. Unfortunately, Johnston would never see his dream fulfilled as he was killed in 1915 in a family dispute.[35] However, the groundwork had been laid and, in 1921, the Nova Scotia Home for Colored Children opened its doors as a school and orphanage for African Nova Scotian children.

Johnston was not alone in his work to build an industrial school for African Nova Scotians. In 1909, a new pastor arrived to begin work at Cornwallis St. Since the end of Rev. Thomas' ministry in 1879, there had been a succession of pastors who stayed at the church for relatively short periods of time. Although these pastors advanced the work of the church in areas of social justice, the membership was down to ninety in 1907, and a new energy was needed. Rev. Moses B. Puryear would prove to be a force for good in the church and community.

Arriving from Pennsylvania, Rev. Puryear shared Johnston's belief in the use of industrial schools for the education of Black children and was familiar with the Hampton Institute on which Johnston had based his

---

33. Pachai, *Beneath the Clouds*, 72.
34. Saunders, *Share and Care*, 19.
35. Saunders, *Share and Care*, 25.

proposal.³⁶ Where Puryear differed from many Black leaders was in his willingness to enlist the help of Nova Scotians from outside of the Black community. He held a meeting at the Halifax Board of Trade in order to gain support for the project from Haligonians. Shortly after Johnston's death a committee was ready to present the proposal to the Nova Scotia Legislature. This committee drew from the congregation of Cornwallis Street, with J. A. R. Kinney as a member. Kinney became the clerk of the Association in 1916³⁷ and was involved in the planning and building of the school as well as sitting on its first board of trustees.³⁸

James R. Johnston's untimely death did not end his influence or his inspiration for the community.³⁹

The legacy of the Home fell well short of its intended purpose. See Taylor, Nova Scotia Home. In his short life, he began a project that would become a valuable resource for the community for years to come. The Nova Scotia Home for Colored Children provided a level of education to African Nova Scotian children that had been unavailable to the majority. The Home also provided a home for orphans and indigent children where they could learn the skills necessary to be successful citizens.

Setting the foundations for the home was a great accomplishment, but it was not Johnston's only legacy. In the years following his death, the Association recognized the value of the Baptist Young People's Union founded by Johnston at Cornwallis Street Baptist. Johnston's group became the model used in the churches of the Association to organize young people. This group, for the training and spiritual development of young people, was perhaps Johnston's greatest legacy. Still in existence today, now known as the Provincial Baptist Youth Fellowship (BYF), this branch of the Association holds its own conference each year inviting young people from all over the province to come together and worship and learn from each other. Most of the churches of the Association still have a BYF, as the groups are known. Youth in these groups develop leadership skills, public speaking abilities, and often go on to hold offices in the greater church body.⁴⁰

36. Saunders, *Share and Care*, 24.
37. AUBA, *1916 Minutes*.
38. Saunders, *Share and Care*, 27.
39. The legacy of the Home fell well short of its intended purpose.
40. The author of this chapter provided leadership to the Provincial Baptist Youth Fellowship and draws these opinions from personal experience.

In the early twentieth century, world and local events changed the focus of ministry at the mother church for a time. First, the Halifax explosion in 1917 devastated much of the city. The mother church was heavily involved in aiding survivors of the explosion who suffered physical injuries, loss of family members, as well as the loss of homes and employment. On the global front, World War I began in 1914. A future pastor of Cornwallis Street Baptist Church, Rev. William White, was instrumental in the fight to allow Blacks to serve in the military during the war.

White first became acquainted with the congregation at Cornwallis Street when he came as a supply minister in 1902, although he would not be officially called as the pastor until 1919. By that time, White was well known throughout the province's Black communities as he was a principal recruiter for the No. 2 Construction Battalion, the first all-Black unit to serve in the Canadian military.[41] White served as chaplain to the unit and was given the rank of honorary Captain.[42]

Like Puryear before him, White saw the importance of gaining support from the White community in building up the Black community. Rather than working with the secular community, White bolstered the standing of the Black churches within the wider Maritime Convention of Baptists. White received two degrees from Acadia University in Wolfville (Bachelor of Arts and a Bachelor of Divinity) and became the second Black minister ordained by the Maritime Convention. Before coming to Cornwallis Street Baptist, White served for the Home Mission Board of the Convention. He was the first Black person in that role and founded Second Baptist Church New Glasgow as part of his work during that time. As pastor of the mother church, he served as secretary of the Halifax and Dartmouth Ministerial Association;[43] both positions allowed him the voice to champion the cause of his people's needs and desires to the broader church community. He also began a radio ministry that was heard through eastern Canada and United States, giving him even greater reach for his cause nationally and internationally.[44]

Rev. White's dedicated service as pastor continued until his death in 1936. The minutes of the annual meeting of the African Baptist Association in 1936 mentioned the deep loss felt by the Association on the death

---

41. Cahill, "William Andrew White."
42. Pachai, *Beneath the Clouds*, 183.
43. Pachai, *Beneath the Clouds*, 184.
44. Pachai, *Beneath the Clouds*, 185.

of Rev. Dr. White. He was considered to have made stellar contributions as a great leader and was considered to be a wonderful man of God.[45] At that same meeting, the Sunday morning address was given by the pastor who would succeed White as pastor of the mother church.

Rev. William Pearly Oliver assumed the role of pastor of the mother church in 1937. Like White before him, Oliver had graduated from Acadia University with a Bachelor of Arts and Bachelor of Divinity. Beginning his ministry at the age of twenty-five, Oliver was the youngest pastor to serve at Cornwallis Street Baptist and would become its longest serving pastor since Rev. Preston. Rev. Oliver's deep commitment to the betterment of his people led him to become one of the greatest advocates for social justice of his day.

In his quest for equality for African Nova Scotians, Rev. Oliver was involved in the founding of several institutions. In 1945, the Nova Scotia Association for the Advancement of Colored People was formed and worked out of the Cornwallis Street Baptist Church.[46] One of the principal goals of the organization was to work in partnership with government agencies to improve the lives of African Nova Scotians. In 1945, in an article for the Halifax newspaper the *Chronicle Herald*, Rev. Oliver noted the church's role in this endeavour: "[It is your] Christian duty to fight against forces which foster religious persecution and racial hatred, and that the Negro must fight these forces with the same intensity as he showed as a soldier in battle."[47]

In 1968, Oliver became the chair of the newly formed Black United Front of Nova Scotia. This group was more controversial and had less support from the African United Baptist Association.[48] Oliver noted that it would be an organization with "a new firmness, dignity, aggressiveness, even militance."[49] However, Oliver felt the organization had a role to play as "an umbrella for the black family, an organization that would create unity through consensus, a kind of coordinating and catalytic body."[50] Although Oliver has great hopes for the organization, its work

---

45. AUBA, *1936 Minutes*.
46. Oliver, "Nova Scotia Association," 13.
47. Oliver, "Nova Scotia Association," 13.
48. Pachai, *Beneath the Clouds*, 298.
49. Pachai, *Beneath the Clouds*, 2.
50. Pachai, *Beneath the Clouds*, 249.

was plagued by controversy and it never reached the potential Oliver foresaw at its inception.

Oliver's devotion to the African Nova Scotian community continued after he left the pastorate in 1962. Although no longer the pastor, he remained involved with the church and Association until his death in 1989. As he continued his work in education through the new government departments he helped to create, Oliver continued to be recognized for his influence on the betterment of the African Nova Scotian community. He received the Order of Canada in 1984.

This short sketch of influential pastors and lay persons in the history of New Horizons Baptist Church is only a partial representation of the impact members of this church have had in social justice and the development of the African Baptists of Nova Scotia. From the formation of the African United Baptist Association by Rev. Richard Preston in 1854, congregants from New Horizons have held office in the Association. Those members, under the guidance and leadership of their pastors, have continually shaped the direction of the Association and participated in its efforts to improve the lives of all African Nova Scotians.

One such member was P. E. McKerrow, an active member of the church and the long-time clerk of the African Baptist Association. His written history of the church and community in the late-nineteenth century has become a staple of factual data for the time. He summarized the early years of the church in this way:

> The history of this church with its varied vicissitudes, would make a large volume in itself. Being one of the oldest in the Association, many of the old fugitives were its first members. They brought with them what is termed the old-time religion. Their preachers, although unlearned, were men of deep godly piety, whose labours were blest with lasting members in the church.[51]

The work of James Johnston and James Kinney Sr. have already been mentioned for their contribution in the early years of the church and community; the example of service set by these men has been an inspiration to those who have followed. Through its history, the church has produced leaders in the areas of education, law, human rights and sports and the arts. Portia White, daughter of Rev. White, before becoming famous as an opera singer, gained fame at home by sharing her talents for fundraising events and leading the church choir. As a teacher, White

51. Boyd, *McKerrow*, 40.

contributed to the education of the community at the Nova Scotia Home for Colored Children and in other communities.[52] The church has also been a place where future pastors have embraced their faith and honed their craft. Rev. Dr. Donald Skier (1926–1999) and Rev. Dr. Donald Fairfax (1919–2010) both began their faith journey at New Horizons Baptist Church. Both men were advocates for social justice in the communities they served.

These first preachers and members began a journey of faith, worship, and a fight for social justice that has continued to the present day. Perhaps one of the greatest legacies the founders of a church can hope for is to have its mission continuing, if not yet fulfilled, after many years of existence. Through the end of the twentieth century and beginning of the twenty-first century, there have been several pastors which served for varying amounts of time. Many continued to support and grow the organizations that the earlier pastors founded.

In 2022, New Horizons Baptist Church celebrated 190 years of continuous ministry to the African Nova Scotian community of Halifax. Rev. Dr. Rhonda Britton, the first female pastor of the church, also celebrated fifteen years of ministry at the church with a momentous achievement for the congregation. The government of Nova Scotia agreed to contribute 1.7 million dollars to the Richard Preston Centre for Excellence. This non-profit society, which was created and is housed in the church, is designed to nurture youth through tutoring, mentoring and other programs. It also serves a community hub for gatherings of every description. In announcing the funding, the Minister for African Nova Scotian Affairs, Pat Dunn, said this:

> Community hubs have the potential to improve the lives of community members through various activities, programs and services. It is the leadership of community organizations like New Horizons Baptist Church, the African United Baptist Association, and the Richard Preston Centre for Excellence who strive to make a positive difference for people through their culturally focused initiatives and projects.[53]

Rev. Dr. Britton added this response:

> New Horizons Baptist Church believes that the love of God means ministering to the whole person. As our non-profit arm,

---

52. Pachai, *Beneath the Clouds*, 179.
53. "Government Invests."

the Richard Preston Centre for Excellence facilitates programming from education upgrades to mental and physical health awareness clinics to life skills workshops. We are excited and grateful for this funding that affirms 190 years of the spiritual and social work of the church and builds on the church's legacy far into the future through the Richard Preston Centre for Excellence.[54]

Through its growth from the African Baptist Chapel, to Cornwallis Street Baptist Church, and now as New Horizons Baptist church, the work of this congregation has been a shining example of what people can accomplish with strong faith and unity of purpose.

BIBLIOGRAPHY

Primary Sources

ARCHIVES

"African Nova Scotians in the Age of Slavery and Abolition: Petition of Richard Preston for Money to Pay for a Teacher." *Nova Scotia Archives* (February 15, 1834). Online: https://archives.novascotia.ca/africanns/archives/?ID=105&Page=200402231.

Annual Meeting Minutes of African United Baptist Association, 1855, 1916, 1936, 1961.

Secondary Sources

Boyd, Frank S., Jr. *McKerrow: A Brief History of Blacks in Nova Scotia (1783–1895)*. Halifax: Afro Nova Scotian Enterprises, 1976.

Cahill, Barry. "William Andrew White." *Dictionary of Canadian Biography*. No pages. Online: http://www.biographi.ca/en/bio/white_william_andrew_16E.html.

Fingard, Judith. *The Anglican Design in Loyalist Nova Scotia, 1783-1816*. London: The Society for the Propagation of Christian Knowledge, 1972.

Gordon, Grant. *From Slavery to Freedom: The Life of David George, Pioneer Black Baptist Minister*. Hantsport, NS: Lancelot, 1992.

"Government Invests in Richard Preston Centre of Excellence." *Nova Scotia* (March 16, 2022). No pages. Online: https://news.novascotia.ca/en/2022/03/16/government-invests-richard-preston-centre-excellence.

"Historic Cornwallis Street Baptist Church Selects New Name." *New Horizons Baptist Church* (May 7, 2018). No pages. Online: https://newhorizonsbaptist.ca/2018/05/14/name-change-press-release.

Oliver, Jules R. "Nova Scotia Association for the Advancement of Colored People: An Historical Evaluation of the NSAACP and the Role It Has Played in the Area of Employment." MSW thesis, Acadia University, 1969.

Oliver, Pearleen. *Song of the Spirit: An Historical Narrative of the Beechville United Baptist Church*. Hantsport, NS: Lancelot, 1994.

---

54. "Government Invests."

Pachai, Bridglal. *Beneath the Clouds of the Promised Land: The Survival of Nova Scotia's Blacks. Volume II: 1800–1989*. Hantsport, NS: Lancelot, 1990.

Saunders, Charles R. *Share and Care: The Story of the Nova Scotia Home for Colored Children*. Halifax, NS: Nimbus, 1994.

Taylor, Wanda L. *The Nova Scotia Home for Colored Children: The Hurt, the Hope, and the Healing*. Halifax, NS: Nimbus, 2015.

Walker, James W. St. G. *The Black Loyalists: The Search for a Promised Land in Nova Scotia and Sierra Leone 1783–1870*. Toronto: University of Toronto Press, 1992.

Whitfield, Harvey Amani. *From American Slaves to Nova Scotia Subjects: The Case of the Black Refugees, 1813–1840*. Toronto: Prentice Hall, 2005.

Wilson, Ellen Gibson. *The Loyal Blacks: The Definitive Account of the First American Blacks Emancipated in the Revolution, their Return to Africa and their Creation of a New Society There*. New York: Capricorn, 1976.

8

Architecture and Experience at the First Baptist Church, Amherstburg

JENNIFER COUSINEAU

On December 21, 1849, the congregation of the First Baptist Church in Amherstburg, Ontario, proudly dedicated its new building.[1] The small congregation's first purpose-built church was hard won. Its members had settled in Canada West during the 1830s and 1840s, a majority having fled enslavement in the United States. Most were pre-literate, and none had great material wealth. Their bold young pastor, Rev. Anthony Binga, also known as "The Walking Preacher," had raised funds for the building during preaching tours of the region, which he called the "wilderness of bush and bog."[2] The congregation participated in every aspect of the church's construction, and its completion was a moment of celebration that marked a turning point in the lives of Black Baptists

---

1. I would like to thank my colleagues and former colleagues at Parks Canada, Nathalie Clerk, Bill Wylie, and Shannon Ricketts, as well as Karolyn Smardz Frost, Kenn Stanton of the North American Black Historical Museum, Jennifer McLeod at the Marsh Collection in Amherstburg, Dr. Barbara K. Hughes Smith, the great-great grandniece of Anthony Binga, and Agnes Ellsworth, historian for the Amherstburg Regular Missionary Baptist Association, for supporting my research for this project.

2. The titles commonly used among Baptists require some explanation. "Elder" or "Pastor" is the traditional titles given to clergy in the Baptist Church. Deacons, called "Brothers," are usually not ordained but assist the pastor in their duties. "Father," which was given to Anthony Binga in his later years, was not used in the same manner as the Catholic Church, rather, it reflected the affection of his congregants (see Amherstburg Regular Missionary Baptist Association, *Pathfinders*, 72).

in Amherstburg and its surrounding region. Moreover, Amherstburg's early Black Baptists would likely not have imagined that 160 years later their descendants would successfully petition the federal government of Canada to designate it a National Historic Site. Their petition was successful. Reflecting the methodological principle of reciprocity, the research for this chapter was conducted at the invitation of the current stewards and congregation of the First Baptist Church.[3] Leaders and long-time members of the First Baptist community gave generously of their time during an initial site visit—opening the church for two days of field research and interviews that culminated in the designation of the church as a National Historic Site in 2011.

National designation affirmed what the first congregation already knew: that this place—the centre of their spiritual and communal life—was meaningful beyond its immediate cultural and historical context. The First Baptist Church and the constellation of small Black churches in Southern Ontario are rare and eloquent remnants of the material production of early Black free people in the Detroit River region.[4] Why, then, does this compelling body of material culture remain largely unexamined in the voluminous literature on churches in Canada?

Almost forty years after architectural historians began to study vernacular architecture seriously, small, vernacular buildings in small towns or villages are still frequently overlooked because of their unassuming aesthetics, size, or because the communities to which they belong have historically been marginalized. Sometimes, they are overlooked by intent because their owners were understandably reluctant to draw attention to themselves, especially in places where immigrants, or people of colour, were not welcome. Recent scholarship in the United States, where African Americans form a larger proportion of the total population, has shown that the material record of historically marginalized groups has a great deal to contribute to our understanding of the past. In a 2021 article published in the online journal *Platform*, architectural historians Louis Nelson and Niya Bates explain why buildings, especially buildings like the First Baptist Church, are important as historical evidence: "Historians regularly complain about the limitations of archives; the documentary

---

3. For more on this principle, in the context of emerging practices for studying marginalized communities, see Bates and Nelson, "Race and Place."

4. The Reverend Nathaniel Dett, BME Church in Niagara Falls, built, in 1836, the Sandwich First Baptist Church in Windsor, in 1851, the Nazrey AME Church in Amherstburg, in 1851, and the BME Church or Salem Chapel in St. Catharines (1851).

record muffles stories of marginalized and oppressed populations and in rare instances of acknowledgement, the voices are usually those of the oppressors."[5] Nelson and Bates articulate a founding principle of the discipline of architectural history: the lives of the historically marginalized, oppressed, and displaced can often effectively be studied through the material record they leave behind in buildings and landscapes.

This chapter seeks to understand the religious experiences and ritual practices of Black Baptists in Southern Ontario from the mid-nineteenth century through the early twentieth century. These experiences represent a new departure in the already long history of Black settlement in Canada, which dates back to the early seventeenth century with the arrival of unfree African people. The settlement of self-liberated people in Southern Ontario brought new Protestant cultural and religious traditions to a region that had already experienced great cultural flux. Furthermore, this chapter considers the First Baptist Church at Amherstburg as a case study of the Black Baptist experience viewed through the lens of architecture, ritual objects, and the landscape. It further considers the church-centred activities of the people who built, used, and were formed by the church. From this evidence, a rich picture of early Black Baptists in Ontario emerges. Their church was the principal destination and refuge for Black settlers in nineteenth century Canada; where Baptists (and other Black settlers welcomed by the Baptists) broke from a hostile world and created a sanctuary from a hostile environment. It was a congregational structure that gave shape to, and was fashioned through, Black Baptist worship and ritual. Looking to the future, it was the seat of hope and a gathering place where Black Baptists created opportunities for professional advancement and social empowerment.

THE FIRST BAPTIST CHURCH AND THE UNDERGROUND RAILROAD

Between the 1820s and 1860s, thousands of self-liberated people of African descent found their first physical and spiritual homes on Canadian soil at Amherstburg's First Baptist Church. Among the church's earliest functions was as a shelter for people fleeing the slave system in the United States. Amherstburg and the First Baptist Church building were principal *termini* of the Underground Railroad; they formed part of what Karolyn Smardz Frost and Veta Smith Tucker have called the fluid frontier—the

---

5. Bates and Nelson, "Race and Place."

"Detroit River borderland" that "has been both a boundary and a passageway for people of African ancestry for more than three centuries."[6] The enslavement of Africans, and the flight from it, was nearly two centuries old in North America when newly-free people first began to appear in Amherstburg not long after the War of 1812. Over the course of the nineteenth century, tensions grew between slaveholders and abolitionists in the United States while increasing numbers of freedom-seekers escaped to the North. When the northern states introduced restrictive regulations and laws in the 1830s and 1840s, and when, in 1834, slavery was finally abolished in Upper Canada, unfree and free Black people alike left for British North America.[7] The stream became a flood after the enactment of the federal Fugitive Slave Law of 1850, which exposed Black people to the threat of enslavement regardless of whether they had previously been unfree.

In 1793, John Graves Simcoe, Lieutenant Governor of Upper Canada and a passionate abolitionist, set in motion the first major piece of

---

6. Smardz Frost and Tucker, eds., *Fluid Frontier*, 3. The nature and definition of the Underground Railroad have been subject to considerable debate over the past several decades. Larry Gara's *Liberty Line* sought to revise an outdated narrative of the Underground Railroad as a highly romanticized system operated by White people for the benefit of Black refugees—who were portrayed as passive rather than active agents in their rescues. More recent work stresses Black agency, initiative, and ingenuity. Frost and Tucker underscore the challenging idea of the Underground Railroad advancing the image of the United States as "the land of the free," while also creating an image of Canada as a haven for Black people that was not born out in the experiences of the refugees. Historian Shannon Ricketts offered a working definition of the Underground Railroad that "emphasizes the clandestine and multiracial network of abolitionists on both sides of the border who assisted those escaping slavery" ("Underground Railroad"). See also Gara, *Liberty Line*.

7. My usage in this chapter follows, in modified form, Barrington Walker, who, in his *Race on Trial* uses the term "Blacks" to describe people of African descent living in Canada and the United States; my preference is to use Black people, recognizing the humanity of subjects alongside their identity as people of African descent. Many researchers currently favour the terms "enslaved" and "enslaver." In *Cabin, Quarter, Plantation*, the architectural historian, and scholar of Black landscapes, Rebecca Ginsburg, uses the term "enslaved person/people" to replace the older term "slave." Karolyn Smardz Frost and other scholars have noted that this is grammatically incorrect usage, however, since an "enslaver" is the person who first takes another person into slavery, which is distinct from a slave-holder, who keeps people in slavery. Karolyn Smardz Frost, personal communication, September 2022; Ellis and Ginsburg, eds., *Cabin*. More recent scholarship has developed additional terms for expressing the experiences of people of African descent. Historian Tiya Miles uses the descriptive "unfree people," which I have also used in this paper.

anti-slavery legislation in the British Empire.[8] The legislation did not free a single slave at the time, but it modestly set a gradual course for the abolition of slavery in Canada.[9] By 1833, when slavery was abolished in the British Empire, there were only a small number of people still legally unfree in the province. The geographic proximity of Canada, the relative porousness of the border, the refusal of British North America to support slavery, and the burdensome impact of the Fugitive Slave Act created conditions under which Canada became a destination for many people of African descent. Although the exact number of refugees is impossible to determine, reliable contemporary witnesses believe that between 30,000 and 35,000 came to Canada before the outbreak of the American Civil War.[10] The successful escapes of even this tiny proportion of people living in bondage dealt an important symbolic blow to the slave system by showing that, even at great risk and cost, Black people were fully committed to a life of liberty.[11] The First Baptist Church of Amherstburg, and myriad other sites that became nodes of anti-slavery activity in the Detroit River Region, made a deep impression on slaveholders, the general public, and perhaps most immediately on the people who would benefit directly from the refuge these sites offered.[12]

TERMINUS AMHERSTBURG

Records exist to tell us how contemporaries viewed the town where the First Baptist Church was built, and perhaps the reason it was built. A few years prior to its construction, after visiting Amherstburg in 1844, the American Quaker abolitionist Levi Coffin described Amherstburg as "the great landing point, the principal terminus of the Underground Railroad

---

8. "An Act to Prevent the Further Introduction of Slaves and to Limit the Term of Contracts for Servitude within This Province." For a spatial perspective on Simcoe, see Bunch, "John Graves Simcoe's Weird Relationship with Slavery."

9. The Legislative Assembly and Legislative Council, through which Simcoe's anti-slavery Bill would need to pass, held a majority of slaveholders. Against his will, Simcoe was forced to compromise in order to ensure the Bill's passage (see Frost, *I've Got a Home*, 23–35).

10. Frost, *I've Got a Home*, xv. Michael Wayne gives a figure of 17,000 refugees during the same period ("Black Population"). Wayne's analysis, however, has proven controversial.

11. Quarles, *Black Abolitionists*, 143.

12. On the abolition movement in Canada see Wylie, "Abolition Movement," and Stouffer, *Light*.

to the west."[13] Coffin would have known Amherstburg well; he earned his informal nickname, "president of the Underground Railroad," by helping thousands flee the slave system. Such was the town's reputation that Harriet Beecher Stowe placed two of the main characters in her abolitionist novel *Uncle Tom's Cabin*, in Amherstburg, where they began their lives as free people.[14] Black settlement in Amherstburg, however, predates the mass movement of freedom-seekers into the region, by several decades. Karolyn Smardz Frost notes that people of African descent could be found in Amherstburg from the earliest days of French settlement (in the mid-eighteenth century). Among them were people held in bondage by the French and Indigenous people.[15] By the 1790s, the area was known as Malden, and the first British fort, Fort Amherstburg, was the most substantial built presence in the area.[16] United Empire Loyalists settled around Malden in the late eighteenth century—bringing the people they held in bondage together with their other possessions.[17] The first group, of approximately 150 self-liberated people, arrived after the War of 1812. Although there were a number of migration centres, in what is now the Detroit-Windsor corridor, including the small communities that became Sandwich and, later, Windsor, Amherstburg was the most accessible to refugees because it was the point the Detroit River was narrowest—with Grosse Ile and Bois Blanc Island as intermediate steps between Michigan on the one side and Upper Canada on the other. The strong current forced most to cross the river by raft or boat. In the winter, some freedom seekers walked across the ice into Canada.[18] Harrowing accounts of their arrival

13. Coffin, *Reminiscences*, 249–50; Coffin is recognized by the United States National Park Service as a person of significance (see "Levi Coffin").

14. When "The Fugitive Slave Movement" was designated a National Historic Event by the Historic Sites and Monuments Board of Canada in 1925, the Board recommended ". . . that the Fugitive Slave Movement be declared of national importance in the history of Canada, and that it be commemorated by the erection of a memorial in Amherstburg or elsewhere, action to be taken in due course" (see Russell, "Underground Railroad").

15. Communication with Karolyn Smardz Frost, March 20, 2021.

16. "Fort Malden."

17. By this time, slavery had existed in Canada for almost two hundred years. The first person known to have been brought into New France as a slave arrived in 1628; slavery was practiced until the end of the French Regime and "with renewed vigour" after the British conquest in 1763 (see Walker, *Race on Trial*, 4–5); Hill, *Freedom Seekers*, ch. 1. For the historical geography of the area, see Clarke, *Land*, 57–60; *Ordinary People of Essex*.

18. Simpson, "Negroes in Ontario," 306.

in Upper Canada described the dangers of the journey and the harshness of the landscape and climate. Possibly in order to encourage others who might be considering a similar journey, some accounts described rapturous people at the moment they left slavery behind forever. One man, for example, was said to have led his tired animal across the frozen Detroit river, and, "When he put his foot on the soil, the angel of freedom touched his heart, and it leapt for joy. Cold, cheerless, and unpromising as everything looked without him, he felt the divine hand within him, and he instinctively exclaimed, 'O Lord God, I thank thee!—I am free!'"[19] Most Black settlers made their first homes around a "small tract of land in the rear of the village" provided by the British would-be clergyman and abolitionist, Charles Stuart.[20] British merchants, who later built fine homes on Amherstburg's main streets, claimed access to waterfront plots and the front ranges of the town. French and Black settlers, among other non-elites, built their homes further from the waterfront. An early visitor reported that "the Negro village and the clearances were then but just begun . . . the huts [were] very indifferent affairs, but were thought to be palaces by the freemen who inhabited them."[21] This early Black migration helped make Amherstburg the centre of a flourishing, but short-lived, Canadian tobacco culture.[22] By 1832, just prior to the founding of the congregation that would later build the First Baptist Church, there were as many as 300 people of African descent in the Amherstburg area—not all were Baptists. With the town's population estimated at 400, this group made up a sizable proportion of the whole.[23]

MISSIONARY CHURCH

James K. Lewis, an early twentieth century historian of the Black Baptist experience in Ontario, observed that the first communal institution to be established by Black people in every settlement in the province was

---

19. Loguen, *Rev. J. W. Loguen*, 335.

20. Bigsby, *Shoe*, 48; see also Barker, *Captain Charles Stuart*.

21. Hill, *Freedom Seekers*, 48.

22. Winks, *Blacks in Canada*, 145; Amherstburg Bicentennial Book Committee, *Amherstburg 1796–1996*, 238–39.

23. Precise numbers for the Black population of the region are impossible to ascertain. The population of Amherstburg was in continual flux; newcomers passed through, staying for varying amounts of time before moving further inland (see Simpson, "Negroes in Ontario," 612–18).

a church.²⁴ In enslavement, this was the only institution they were allowed—some states and individual slaveholders denied them even this.²⁵ In Amherstburg, the earliest Black church, and the First Baptist, evolved from a mission previously established by the White Presbyterian minister, Isaac J. Rice—whose goal was to receive freedom-seekers from the United States. Prompted by the location of Amherstburg in the transborder region, and the fact that the Black community at the time was mostly made up of newly free people, mission and church functions may have converged as much from expediency as doctrine. Rice had instituted a non-denominational mission, but eventually, a critical mass of Baptist settlers sought to establish a formal church. In blending the functions of social mission and formal worship, the First Baptist Church participated in a widespread contemporary practice; hundreds of Black churches across the northern states and in Upper Canada assisted thousands of Black freedom-seekers during this period. The number of people in flight from slavery who passed through Amherstburg was initially modest, but it gradually increased. After the Fugitive Slave Law was enacted in 1850, contemporary sources claim that Amherstburg received up to thirty fugitives per day.²⁶ Anthony Binga described them in highly evocative biblical language as coming "by the fifties every day, like frogs in Egypt."²⁷ Some stayed, but many passed through; newcomers' immediate needs were food, clothing, shelter, and employment. This was the work of the small mission established in Amherstburg by Rice.²⁸ The newly free, young, energetic, and charismatic Anthony Binga soon joined Rice. Binga recalled how, in 1836, when he was about 18, "Isaac J. Rice . . . myself, and Hiram Wilson . . . would receive the fugitives and provide for them, distribute

---

24. Lewis, "Early Negro Migration."

25. All manner of variation could be found. In Richmond, Virginia, in the early-nineteenth century, unfree Black people were permitted to worship at the White First Baptist Church, but when their numbers grew dramatically the White leadership of the church allowed them to establish their church only if they had a White minister (see Brackney, *Baptists in North America*, 180).

26. Anthony Binga in Siebert, *Underground Railroad*, 194.

27. Ohio Historical Society, Columbus, Ohio, Wilbur H. Siebert Papers, MSS 116, Box 101. Binga, himself a Black refugee, certainly meant no offence to other refugees by comparing them with the biblical plague of frogs. His reference was meant to emphasize the high numbers arriving at the border.

28. Landon, "Work."

provisions; take care of them if they were sick, settle them among the white people who wanted to hire."[29]

About a year after his arrival in Amherstburg, Binga began to preach without formal ordination, a widespread phenomenon among Black *and* White Baptists at that time.[30] He probably gathered his first congregants during the course of his missionary work, for local tradition dates the beginnings of the First Baptist Church to between 1836 and 1838. For a decade, the congregation met in the houses of congregants in the neighbourhoods around King and George Street, in what was then the east part of Amherstburg, where both the First Baptist Church and the Nazrey AME Church are located. Church building in the early nineteenth century was a time-consuming and expensive endeavour and therefore not one easily undertaken by new settlers. Membership in the congregation was initially small; the First Baptist Church counted only nineteen members in 1841, and its pastor (Binga) was just twenty-four years old. A few years later, Binga set to work as an itinerant preacher in order to raise funds for the construction of the First Baptist Church. This was not unusual for Baptist preachers in Canada West at the time. Binga travelled "on foot or on horseback through wilderness of bush and bog, that he might solicit funds to help him build a church."[31] By around 1848, sufficient funds had been raised. Once completed, the congregation dedicated the church for a variety of purposes. Under Binga's leadership, the church welcomed freedom-seekers until the outbreak of the Civil War. In a letter from Amherstburg in 1856, L.G. Spears wrote that several refugees "had the privilege of hearing two able sermons preached in the land of freedom, one by Elder Binga, and one by Elder Troy."[32] Only a

---

29. Wilbur H. Siebert Papers, MSS 116, Box 101, n.p. Levi Coffin visited Amherstburg in 1844 and wrote: "While at this place, we made our headquarters with Isaac J. Rice's missionary buildings, where he had a large school for coloured children. He had laboured here, among the coloured people mostly fugitives, for six years. He ... believed that the Lord called him to this field of missionary labour among the fugitive slaves who came here by hundreds and by thousands, poor, destitute ... suffering from all the evil influences of slavery."

30. Brackney, *Baptists in North America*, 181. An earlier preacher from Amherstburg, William Wilks, had moved on to establish the First Baptist Church at Colchester, but without ordination. The pastor of the Second Baptist Church Detroit sought to remedy the situation and brought another ordained minister north with him to ordain Wilks and to re-baptize his entire congregation (see Sobel, *Trabelin' On*, 160–62).

31. ARMBA, *Pathfinders*, 72.

32. *Provincial Freeman*, February 23, 1856.

year earlier, a fellow citizen had expressed his gratitude for the reception he had been given in the town:

> We, the coloured people of Amherstburg, have the most of us fled from American Slavery, the vilest that ever saw the light, but through the good Providence of God, and by the means of friends, the North Star, the underground railroad, we have sought for freedom and found it in Canada, under her Majesty; and when many of us arrived here, we were literally naked, hungry, and penniless.[33]

In addition to receiving self-liberated people, the First Baptist Church prioritized the institution for Sunday or Sabbath schools. Sabbath schools supplemented the religious instruction of "the rising generation" of children; they also supported the education of adults, offering literacy skills to the "Missing Generation" of formerly unfree persons who had no formal education.[34] The architecture of the First Baptist Church—solid, capacious, familiar, welcoming, and situated far from the waterfront and the ever-present danger of slave-catchers—was, from its inception, an architecture of expediency and social service.[35] Its construction signaled the permanence and confidence of a young but thriving community.

33. *Provincial Freeman*, December 22, 1855.
34. Shreve, *AfriCanadian Church*, 50–51.
35. It was not uncommon for slave-catchers to cross the border between the United States and Canada West in an attempt to return fugitives to their masters. By the 1830s, there were several known cases of Kentucky-based slave-catchers who had kidnapped free people from the Detroit River district and sold them into Southern slavery. Such actions were deeply resented in a province not long since settled by British Empire Loyalists, who felt their sovereignty threatened by American expansionism and any perceived expression thereof. There were also notable cases of Americans seeking to return fugitives through the process of extradition. The British government consistently refused to extradite fugitive slaves, arguing that within the British Empire it was illegal for one person to own another and therefore the "self-theft" of which the fugitives were accused was by definition inadmissible as a crime. Karolyn Smardz Frost's analysis of one such case, that of Thornton and Lucie Blackburn (NHP, 1999) can be found in *I've Got a Home*. On aspects of fugitives' experience, see also Rebecca Ginsburg, "Escaping Through a Black Landscape." In Ellis and Ginsburg, eds., *Cabin*, 51–66; Finkelman, ed., *Fugitive Slaves*; Genovese, *Roll*; Franklin and Schweninger, *Runaway Slaves*.

MISSION AT THE CENTRE: THE MOTHER CHURCH OF THE AMHERSTBURG REGULAR MISSIONARY BAPTIST ASSOCIATION

Having a large building, in a busy regional centre, permitted Amherstburg's Black Baptists to lead in missionary work that went well beyond the reception of newcomers. The First Baptist Church is called the "Mother Church" of the Amherstburg Regular Missionary Baptist Association, an early and important regional Black institution. Its immediate predecessor, the Baptist Association for Coloured People, was founded under that name by another regional Black Baptist church, the Second Baptist Church of Detroit. Members of the organization changed its name to the Amherstburg Regular Missionary Baptist Association (hereafter ARMBA) and its headquarters to Amherstburg in October 1841. The group held its inaugural convention at the home of John Liberty, on George Street, in Amherstburg—a small 1.5-storey clapboard saltbox house that still fronts the sidewalk near the site of the church. It was not by coincidence that the congregation of the First Baptist Church also met in Liberty's home—there was significant overlap between the two groups. The congregation and the Association would meet in informal spaces until 1848 when their numbers warranted, and their finances could support, a larger meeting place.

Three churches were represented at the founding meeting of the ARMBA—the First Baptist at Amherstburg, with 19 members, the First Baptist at Sandwich, a small settlement outside Windsor, with 11 members, and the Second Baptist Church of Detroit, with 17 members.[36] The Association was unusual in its historical context, first, because it was a transnational organization and second, because a strong umbrella organization seems to run counter to the decentralizing tendencies of traditional Baptist doctrine and practice.[37] But the reason for its founding was clear: exclusion from White Baptist congregations in Canada and the United States on the basis of race. Early Association leaders convened its first conference with the following call to organize:

---

36. The first four, and the greatest number of, meetings of the Association took place in Amherstburg.

37. The doctrine of religious freedom implies, among other things, the independence of individual congregations from larger bodies or hierarchies (see Lewis, "Early Negro Migration," 119–21). On Baptist doctrine, see Brackney, *Baptists in North America*.

> Resolved that we the Second Baptist Church of the City of Detroit believing that the time is now Come that We ought to form ourselves into an association because We cannot enjoy the Privileges we Wish as Christians with the White Churches in Canada, that centuries have Rolled along Since our Fathers became organized as a Church, and believing that many of our Fathers have gone down the grave not enjoying their Just privileges and Right in the Christian Churches among the whites: We invite all the Christian Churches of the same faith and order to unite with us in the Great Celestial Cause union is Strength, united we Stand and Divided we fall. Come up Brethren from all part of the provinces and let us see what we can do for ourselves and our children.[38]

In the mid-nineteenth century Canada West, many White people would not commune with Black people in their churches. This became increasingly the case as the number of Black settlers in Canada increased. Black people were treated as an underclass across the religious spectrum. Separate and unequal seating was enforced, and some churches required Black people to attend entirely separate services. In some places, they were given communion only after all the White people had been to the altar. Some White Baptist churches would not baptize Black people; one camp meeting expelled Black people altogether.[39] No positions of clerical authority or secular power were open to Black people in White churches or religious organizations.[40] Such demeaning conditions must have been deeply resented by people who had demonstrated the character necessary to break free from slavery. Several decades earlier, the influential Black leader and minister, Richard Allen, had protested religious racism by leaving St. George's Methodist Church in Philadelphia and founding the all-Black African Methodist Episcopal Church.[41] Perhaps inspired by such examples, the fledgling churches of the ARMBA created an institution and later built a building that would support and affirm their efforts to provide a dignified and satisfying religious experience to people of

---

38. Minutes of Amherstburg (1841). For obvious reasons the Amherstburg Association could not meet in Detroit where such a meeting would be considered an invitation to controversy, not to mention the danger it would pose to delegates from Canada West. The Second Baptist Church in Detroit is listed on the National Register of Historic Places in the United States.

39. See Brackney, *Baptists in North America*, ch. 8.

40. Walker, *History of Blacks in Canada*, 135–40.

41. "Richard Allen."

African descent. They established a group to unite the small Black congregations that had begun to emerge in Michigan and Canada West.[42] Beyond even these functions, the Association aimed to offer avenues for advancement and training for future Black leaders.[43] By the end of its inaugural meeting, participants had already filled the roles of organizer, moderator, preacher, and secretary, extending the scope of their activities far beyond what they might achieve within a White-led organization. The Association was the "full expression of new-found freedom not available elsewhere."[44] Leaders with dignified titles like Deacon George French, Church Clerk Madison J. Lightfoot (both from the Second Baptist, Detroit), and Pastor Anthony Binga of Amherstburg, whose leadership was so strong that he earned the title "Father Binga," modeled what Black people could achieve.

The ARMBA was not universally well-received. A group of White-led local Baptist churches called the Long Point Baptist Association voted not to recognize "an association lately formed in the Western District composed of African Churches."[45] Horace Hawkins, a leader of the ARMBA and cousin of Anthony Binga, answered this rejection boldly and with the full force of nineteenth century religious rhetoric:

> The time has come when it becomes us as an Association composed as we are denominated "the people of colour," to stand like men of war, in defence of the truth . . . and to expose the base and ignominious misrepresentations of the Long Point or Western Baptist Association in Canada West. Since we have come out from them, and have formed ourselves into an independent Association and cast off the yoke of Antichristian bondage and no longer to be set at naught in their Ecclesiastical councils, to be looked upon with contempt, to be insulted whenever and wherever we meet with them as we suppose to worship the true and living God . . . We are no longer duped by those agents of the Arch-Necromancer of the infernal region of malignity and impetuosity.[46]

42. Lewis, "Early Negro Migration," 120. Prior to 1841, Black Baptist churches had been formed in Colchester, Toronto, Gosfield, Wilberforce, St. Thomas, St. Catharines, Amherstburg, and Sandwich largely through the efforts of the charismatic Reverend Washington Christian.

43. It did so for over a century after its founding.

44. Lewis, "Early Negro Migration," 121.

45. Minutes of Long Point Baptist Association (1842).

46. Amherstburg Baptist Association (ABA) Minutes (1843).

Hawkins's words reflected the common belief among Christians of African descent that slaveholders and their associates did not practice *true* Christianity because the practices of slaveholders conflicted so deeply with their understanding of biblical values. Despite the fervor of Hawkins' words, by 1856, the rift between the two Baptist associations had been healed—the groups sought to cooperate on a larger project: abolition.

BLACK ABOLITION: THE ARMBA AND THE FIGHT AGAINST SLAVERY

From its earliest days, a prime tenet of the ARMBA was opposition to slavery.[47] Henry Nettles of Amherstburg opened its inaugural meeting preaching a sermon where God spoke to Moses saying: "thou shalt say unto him, the Lord God of the Hebrews hath sent me unto thee, saying, Let my people go."[48] The churches of the ARMBA were unequivocal in their condemnation of American slavery. Individual churches, especially those closest to the border, such as the Amherstburg First Baptist, Sandwich First Baptist, and the Detroit Second Baptist, actively received refugees as part of the Underground Railroad network. As the conflict deepened across the border, and in particular after the passage of the Fugitive Slave Act of 1850, the Association repeatedly recommended that its churches hold regular monthly, Friday evening "anti-slavery prayer meetings." It also strongly urged member churches to "stand up against it [slavery] as strong opposers, wherever they meet it, whether in Church or State; and ever hold forth anti-slavery truth to the world, and not to tolerate any person or persons who will hold fellowship with slaveholders or their apologists."[49] A related resolution of the Association underlines the rationale for the establishment of separate Black churches, namely, that some White churches, both north and south of the international border, tolerated slaveholding on some level. As a countermeasure, the Association's member churches refused to accept the baptisms performed in churches that tolerated slavery and rejected their leadership, asserting that: "baptisms performed by slaveholding ministers, however sincere the candidate, be not considered lawful Bible baptism in the churches of this Association nor shall such ministers be considered as the children of

---

47. Shreve, *AfriCanadian Church*, 48–49.
48. Amherstburg Baptist Association (ABA) Minutes (1843).
49. Minutes of Amherstburg (1851).

God so as to be permitted to approach our communion, believing that he who will sell his brother or sister for gold or silver today is unfit to baptize tomorrow."[50]

A final anti-slavery measure taken by the ARMBA and its churches was to ally themselves with groups that existed to combat slavery. In this, as in its other endeavours, the ARMBA operated transnationally. In 1849, the Association became an auxiliary of the American Baptist Free Mission Society, a group based in the northern states and dedicated to helping formerly unfree people wherever they migrated.[51] Some member churches of the Amherstburg Association broke away to form a new abolitionist group, the Canadian Anti-Slavery Baptist Association. Slavery was an issue of such paramount importance to the Amherstburg Association that it changed its name to the Amherstburg Antislavery Regular Baptist Association to reflect this priority. By 1861, at the height of its success, the Amherstburg Association had a membership of over 1,000 in fourteen congregations in two countries.[52] After the Civil War, the Amherstburg Association saw a gradual decrease in membership but continued to serve the needs of its members to this day.[53]

THE FIRST BAPTIST CHURCH AND BLACK BAPTIST PRACTICE IN CANADA

The open commodious sanctuary of the First Baptist Church offered a space that helped to make participation in the abolition movement resistance to racism, and the settlement of refugees possible for Ontario's early Black Baptists. But Black Baptist identities were not limited to these outward-looking service-oriented activities. Their contribution to the formation of the Black Baptist church in Ontario, during what has been called its "Heroic Age," went deeper.[54] The physical fabric of the First

---

50. Minutes of Amherstburg (1853). It has been suggested that the term "slaveholding ministers" may have included those in northern churches having contact with southern churches. Anti-slavery exponents claimed that contact with the northern branches of such churches was wrong, even though their association with slavery was indirect (see Lewis, "Religious Life of Fugitive Slaves").

51. Shreve, *AfriCanadian Church*, 49–50.

52. Brackney, *Baptists in North America*, 185.

53. The ARMBA still exists. As of 2020, it had nine member churches.

54. Between 1800 and the Civil War, 168 Black Baptist congregations were formed in the United States and 19 in what is now Ontario (see Brackney, *Baptists in North America*, 179).

Baptist Church reveals the nature of Black Baptist spirituality in Canada West during its formative years.

Approximately half of the newly free Black people who came to Upper Canada are believed to have been Baptists.[55] This Christian denomination has its origins in the English Reformation. It was part of the Puritan movement, which sought to shed what was perceived as the excesses of Roman Catholicism and the Church of England. Baptists settled in the American Colonies in the seventeenth century, and in, what would become, Canada in the eighteenth century. The religious revivals known as the First (1740–1760) and the Second (1800–1830) Great Awakening attracted many converts among the unfree population.[56] Baptists believe in the authority of Scripture above church traditions, in the separation of church and state, in the interconnection between evangelism and social justice, adult baptism (called the "baptism of believers"), and in a personal relationship with God that pervades every aspect of the lived experience.[57] In general, Black Baptist practice was distinguished by its experiential and emotive qualities, and by the singing, dancing, and other ecstatic activities that often occurred at services and revivals.[58]

For early Black Baptists in Canada West, religion was all-encompassing. Freedom-seekers of all denominations described, the journey to, and, arrival in, Canada in the language of the Hebrew Bible, specifically, that used in the book of Exodus—referencing the departure of the Israelites from Egypt; Harriet Tubman was known as the "Moses of her people," Canada was referred to as "the Promised Land," or "Canaan," or the "other side of the Jordan," and "Deliverers" were people who helped feed, clothe, and house fugitives.[59] In light of the Baptist worldview, in which a personal God was ever-present, and the recent experiences of self-liberated people, it made sense that the church would be considered

---

55. Shreve, *AfriCanadian Church*, 42.

56. Brackney, *Baptists in North America*, 8–23; Also see Heath, Friesen, and Murray, *Baptists in Canada*; Torbet, *History*; Zeman, *Baptist Roots*; Zeman, ed., *Baptists in Canada*; McBeth, *Baptist Heritage*; Renfree, *Heritage and Horizon*; Griffin-Allwood et al., *Baptists in Canada*.

57. Brackney, *Baptists in North America*, 8–23.

58. Mechal Sobel argues that although White Baptists also emphasized the experiential over the intellectual experience, White Baptists' expression became more subdued and "professionalized" in the generation after the Second Great Revival (see *Trabelin' On*, ch. 6). See also Shreve, *AfriCanadian Church*, 42–44.

59. This linguistic formulation comes from Matt 25:34–46 (see Lewis, "Early Negro Migration," 119); and Bradford, *Harriet*.

the most important building in the Black community. S. G. Howe, a prominent Bostonian abolitionist who visited Black settlements across Canada West just after the American Civil war, observed that "whenever a few refugees congregate together, the first thing they do in common is to provide for public worship. They have a passion for a church. Not merely a church spiritual, but a church material; and it must be good looking, too."[60]

Howe's description accurately reflects the aspirations and experiences of members of the First Baptist Church congregation with respect to their building. To interpret the relatively small size and simplicity of decoration in the First Baptist Church as a reflection of the material poverty or lack of sophistication of its builders would be to misunderstand the intentions and needs of Black Baptists as they remade their lives in their new environment. The Black Baptists in Amherstburg did not aspire to what they might have considered the ostentatious architectural posturing of their French Catholic neighbours,[61] they valued simple beauty, comfort, and utility for their congregational rituals and the demands of the wider community. A letter published in the *Provincial Freeman* praised the efforts of the Amherstburg First Baptist Church and captured the architectural and spiritual aspirations of its users: "We want good and comfortable meeting houses almost in every direction...places of attraction for all classes, where the high praises of Jesus may be sung. We want food for our souls and clothing for our minds and suitable houses for the work of God's praises."[62] The members of the church clearly sought attractive buildings in which they could congregate comfortably and where they could perform the rituals they had developed over time and brought to Amherstburg.

The first Black churches, like the earliest houses in Black Canadian communities in Canada, were commonly of log construction and they were usually replaced as soon as possible with something more permanent.[63] The First Baptist Church at Amherstburg, however, was a solidly

60. Lewis, "Early Negro Migration," 119; Bradford, *Harriet*.

61. Hill writes that, in general, the Roman Catholic Church in the 19th century had a more "moderating influence" on slavery than Protestant denominations, which were more supportive of the institution. The Catholic Church certainly had no problem baptizing, marrying, and burying Black people when slavery was in force under the French regime (*Freedom Seekers*, 127).

62. Howe, *Report*, 89–90.

63. The First Baptist Church in Sandwich is an example. They began to gather in

constructed timber frame church of white pine cut from local forests. The original clapboard siding was covered over with vinyl siding in the mid-twentieth century only after almost 150 years of use. It was a substantial building, made to last. Its 28.6-foot ceiling was triple the height of the houses in the area. At 259 square metres, it was many times larger than the standard two, three, and four-room dwellings that still surround it. The approximately 100 congregants who attended services through the 1850s would have entered into what, by contrast with their homes, would have been a lofty generous interior space.[64] The church's congregants may not have been familiar with the English architect A. W. Pugin's claim that Gothic architecture was Christian architecture par excellence but they knew that the elegant pointed arch windows, so characteristic of these types of churches across Ontario, set their building apart from the mundane world and expressed its ecclesiastical function without ambiguity. By the standards of its users, the First Baptist Church was comfortable, attractive, and suitable for their spiritual work. This may be why they were willing to "expend an undue and unreasonable part of their time and substance in building churches."[65] The seriousness with which this congregation took its church building was evident even before the first tree was cut. The first pastor of the First Baptist Church, Elder Anthony Binga, spent the better part of four years, between 1845 and 1849, raising funds for its construction.

TO HEAR THE WORD: THE FIRST BAPTIST AS AUDITORY CHURCH

A charismatic leader, Anthony Binga was a familiar type among Baptists. As early as 1784, the fiery David George was preaching or "exhorting" to Black Nova Scotians, as he had in North Carolina.[66] In nineteenth century Canada, the preacher was a key figure in Black Baptist religious life; his sermon was the experience on which Baptist services turned. This would have been particularly true for what members of the Amherstburg

---

homes, built a log church, and finally built the current brick and frame structure. See Ricketts, "Sandwich," 9.

64. Benjamin Drew interviewed the Pastor of the First Baptist Church, Rev. William Troy, in 1855. Troy reported that about 100 "colored" people attended his services at the First Baptist Church. Drew, *North-Side View of Slavery*, 353–54.

65. Drew, *North-Side View of Slavery*, 90.

66. Brackney, *Baptists in North America*, 177.

Association called "the Missing Generation" who could not read but were highly attuned to oral culture. In addition to the fact that many congregants were illiterate, liturgical books were expensive and rare; and for an experientially oriented religious culture like that of Black Baptists, a formal written service would have been out of place. Rare examples of Black Baptist preaching in Canada West attest to its animated nature; sermons were said to be "rich in the use of metaphors and emotional devices, much more so than even white revivalist preachers."[67]

The vernacular designers of the First Baptist Church created a plan that gave priority to the preacher and to "the Word" he preached. The church plan, and the seating within it, was oriented toward an elevated pulpit so that the entire congregation could hear *and* see the preacher at all times.[68] It stood at the west end of the church directly opposite the main entrance. At approximately thirty-three feet wide and forty-four feet long, just slightly longer than it was wide, the First Baptist Church could accommodate about 100 congregants comfortably. Its ceiling was high enough to carry the sound of a strong voice but not so high that it would be lost. With no balconies, piers, interior columns, beams, or rafters, congregants could both hear and see their preacher. The placement of the two most westerly windows closer to the pulpit and slightly more distant from the other two pairs on the side elevations suggests the importance of the preaching function for the congregation. The preacher undoubtedly benefited from the illumination provided by the pair of windows closest to the pulpit, and the congregation would also have benefited from being better able to see the person attempting to inspire and instruct them. We know that this church was a centre of local preaching. In addition to Sunday sermons, the annual meetings of the Amherstburg Association, both before and after the church was constructed, featured at least three sermons. Each was inspired by a biblical verse that is recorded in the meeting minutes—along with the name of the preacher,

---

67. Brackney, *Baptists in North America*, 181.

68. The popularity of this configuration has often been linked to the urban churches of the post-Reformation period. After the Great Fire of London in 1666, the English architect Sir Christopher Wren was charged with rebuilding London's churches. Wren considered the proportions of the compact auditory plan to be ideal because they would enable "all to hear the Service, and both to hear distinctly and see the preacher." Christopher Wren, *Parentalia, or, Memoirs of the family of the Wrens*, (1710), as cited in Nelson, *Beauty of Holiness*, 74. My use of the term "compact auditory" church or plan reflects current, widespread scholarly usage (see Nelson, *Beauty of Holiness*, 71–76; Upton, *Holy Things*).

and occasionally a brief description. As an early space purpose-built to accommodate communal gatherings for worship, the simple, uncluttered, auditory church participated in the development of a critical dimension of Black Baptist practice in Canada.

BAPTIZING BAPTISTS

Baptists are named for one of the hallmarks of their denomination, the *baptism of believers*; i.e., adults who choose to become members of the church through full immersion in water. Baptism was important to the early congregants of Amherstburg's First Baptist Church. Every year, its leaders reported the number of baptisms at the meetings of the Amherstburg Association Conference. There was rejoicing at the *spiritual awakening* that was believed to have occurred when the number of baptisms rose above the norm. For the first half-century of its existence, people who sought baptism at First Baptist were baptized by full immersion in the Detroit River, in both winter and summer.[69] Although the evocative river setting may have heightened the occasion in certain respects, it had the disadvantages of being very public and, in winter, quite uncomfortable. Church historians claim, "it was not unheard of to break a hole in the ice to baptize ... Large crowds were brought by ferry from Detroit and many from Windsor came to the baptismal site which is located just opposite Bois Blanc Island."[70]

For a combination of reasons, including comfort, privacy, safety, and autonomy, a baptismal pool was installed at the First Baptist Church in 1907. The pool was built beneath the floor behind the pulpit, the most public and visible space in the church. This change to the fabric of the church altered the baptismal ritual dramatically for the foreseeable future. Not only were baptisms brought inside the church property but they were also given a place of utmost significance. Architecturally, the addition of the baptismal pool placed baptisms on par with the preaching of God's Word. Baptisms were performed below the pulpit but within the same vertical space—at the west end of the church, directly opposite the main entrance. When the pool was not in use, hinged wooden doors close over it recreating the flat solid surface of an extended pulpit. The

---

69. The oldest member of the current congregation, Donald Harris, also spoke of a baptismal tub in the back yard of the church but corroborating sources for this have not yet been located.

70. Lewis, "First Baptist Church of Amherstburg," 3.

year the baptismal pool was constructed was considered one of "spiritual awakening"; thirty-three baptisms were performed that year. The pastor reported, "We have noticed during the past year that on the whole prosperity has been showered upon us. From the spiritual standpoint, God has worked marvellously as the result of the prayer of his followers."[71] Photographs of adult baptisms from the 1950s, 1980s, and 1990s record visibly moved participants deeply involved in a pivotal spiritual experience.[72] Though the baptismal pool was a later addition to the original structure of First Baptist, it tracks the development of an integral religious practice for Canada's Black Baptists.[73]

BUILDINGS AND BAPTIST PRACTICE

In her award-winning 2021 book, *All That She Carried: The Journey of Ashley's Sack, a Black Family Keepsake*, historian Tiya Miles writes of the importance of owning things for unfree Black people:

> Having things . . . undermined the logic of slavery in a society in which it was formally illegal for "property" to own property. As possessors of stuff, Black people demonstrated their personhood, reflecting dignity inwardly to themselves and outwardly to others. Possessing things inspired pride and challenged the belief that Black people were unworthy of property's privileges. Having things was a salve that reinforced a sense of self-worth in a society that demeaned Black people by equating them with objects.[74]

Unlike the people in Mile's story, nineteenth century Black Baptists in Canada were legally free. As the voices that call out from the Amherstburg Association's minutes attest, they were agents of their destinies.

71. Minutes of Amherstburg (1907).

72. These images can be seen in the Alvin McCurdy Collection, Archives of Ontario.

73. Of the nine churches that are currently members of the ARMBA in Ontario, eight have Baptismal pools. Dates of construction have not been located for all of these pools. According to the historian of the Association, Agnes Ellsworth, those that have pools are the Windsor First Baptist Church in Windsor (1862), the Sandwich First Baptist Church in Windsor (1851; NHS, 1999), the Puce First Baptist Church in Puce River (1964), the First Baptist Church in Chatham (1853), the Union Baptist Church in Chatham (1849), the First Regular Baptist Church in Dresden (1857–59), the Shrewsbury Baptist Church in Shrewsbury (late 1850s), and the First Baptist Church in Amherstburg (1848–49). Oral communication with Agnes Ellsworth, historian of the ARMBA, March 2011.

74. Miles, *All That She Carried*, 129.

Nonetheless, having once lived in bondage, they valued their possessions greatly and their possessions included the communal buildings made by the work of their hands. Today, buildings like the First Baptist Church offer compelling evidence for understanding what early Black Baptists believed and how they practiced their faith in ways that were both distinctive and broadly shared. Stewardship of their own dignified, purpose-built, space was a novel experience for the Baptists of Amherstburg. Their provision of a haven and shelter for newly freed people encouraged others to flee along the networks of the Underground Railroad. As the Mother Church of the ARMBA, the church helped foster an important Black organization in the province; enabling its members to participate fully in church activities and to achieve the agency denied them in the broader White-dominated society. In a material expression of the vibrant ritual practices of the region's early Black Baptists, the church made visible what some historians have called "the invisible institution"—a reference to the Black church in North America under slavery.[75] Though a full picture of the history of Black Baptists in Canada will only emerge through further research and new scholarship, it is hoped that this chapter has offered some insight into a fascinating time and place deserving of greater attention. Equally as important, it has argued for the potential of material culture, and in particular, of buildings, as a source for the histories of marginalized people everywhere.

BIBLIOGRAPHY

Primary Sources

Archives

Minutes of Amherstburg Regular Missionary Baptist Association (ARMBA), 1841, 1851, 1853, 1907.

Minutes of Long Point Baptist Association, 1842. Wilbur H. Siebert Papers, MSS 116, Box 101. Ohio Historical Society, Columbus, OH, US.

Monographs

Bigsby, John J. *The Shoe and the Canoe*. London: Chapman and Hall, 1850.

Drew, Benjamin. *A North-Side View of Slavery. The Refugee; or the Narratives of Fugitive Slaves in Canada. Related by Themselves, with an Account of the History and Condition of the Coloured Population of Upper Canada*. Boston: John P. Jowett and Company, 1856.

75. Sobel, *Trabelin' On*, xvii.

Siebert, Wilbur H. *The Underground Railroad from Slavery to Freedom.* New York: MacMillan, 1898.

Newspapers and Magazines

The Provincial Freeman (Windsor, Toronto, Chatham, ON), 1855, 1856

Secondary Sources

Amherstburg Bicentennial Book Committee, *Amherstburg 1796–1996: The New Town on the Garrison Grounds.* Amherstburg, ON: Amherstburg Bicentennial Book Committee, 1996.

Amherstburg Regular Missionary Baptist Association. *Pathfinders of Liberty and Truth: A Century with the Amherstburg Regular Missionary Baptist Association.* Buxton, ON: Amherstburg Regular Missionary Baptist Association, 1940.

Barker, Anthony J. *Captain Charles Stuart: Anglo-American Abolitionist.* Baton Rouge: Louisiana State University Press, 1986.

Bates, Niya, and Louis P. Nelson. "Race and Place in the United States: Toward Repair." *Platform* (April 26, 2021). No pages. Online: https://www.platformspace.net/home/race-and-place-in-united-states-toward-repair.

Bradford, Sarah H. *Harriet: The Moses of her People.* New York: J.J. Little, 1901.

Brackney, William H. *Baptists in North America: An Historical Perspective.* New York: Wiley-Blackwell, 2006.

Bunch, Adam. "John Graves Simcoe's Weird Relationship with Slavery." *Spacing* (September 5, 2017). No pages. Online: http://spacing.ca/toronto/2017/09/05/john-graves-simcoes-weird-relationship-slavery.

Clarke, John. *Land, Power, and Economics on the Frontier of Upper Canada.* Kingston and Montréal: McGill-Queen's University Press, 2001.

———. *The Ordinary People of Essex: Environment, Culture, and Economy on the Frontier of Upper Canada.* Montréal and Kingston: McGill-Queen's University Press, 2010.

Coffin, Levi. *Reminiscences of Levi Coffin.* Richmond, IN: Friend United, 2001.

Ellis, Clifton, and Rebecca Ginsburg, eds. *Cabin, Quarter, Plantation: Architecture and Landscapes of North American Slavery.* New Haven: Yale University Press, 2010.

Finkelman, Paul, ed. *Fugitive Slaves.* New York: Garland, 1989.

Franklin, John Hope, and Loren Schweninger. *Runaway Slaves: Revels on the Plantation.* Oxford: Oxford University Press, 1999.

Frost, Karolyn Smardz. *I've Got a Home in Glory Land: A Lost Tale of the Underground Railroad.* Toronto: Thomas Allen, 2007.

Frost, Karolyn Smardz, and Veta Smith Tucker, eds. *A Fluid Frontier: Slavery, Resistance and the Underground Railroad in the Detroit River Borderland.* Detroit: Wayne State University Press, 2016.

"Fort Malden National Historic Site: History of the Fort." *Government of Canada* (Sep 16, 2022). No pages. Online: https://www.pc.gc.ca/en/lhn-nhs/on/malden/culture/histoire-history.

Gara, Larry. *The Liberty Line: The Legend of the Underground Railroad.* Lexington: University of Kentucky Press, 1996.

Genovese, Eugene D. *Roll, Jordan, Roll: The World the Slaves Made.* New York: Vintage, 1972.
Griffin-Allwood, Philip G. A., et al. *Baptists in Canada, 1760-1990: A Bibliography.* Wolfville, NS: Acadia Divinity College, 1989.
Heath, Gordon L., Dallas Friesen, and Taylor Murray. *Baptists in Canada: Their History and Polity.* McMaster Ministry Studies Series 5. Eugene, OR: Pickwick, 2020.
Hill, Daniel G. *The Freedom Seekers: Blacks in Early Canada.* Agincourt, ON: The Book Society of Canada, 1981.
Howe, S.G. *Report to the Freedmen's Inquiry Commission 1864: The Refugees From Slavery in Canada West.* 1864. Reprint, New York: Arno Press and the New York Times, 1969.
Landon, Fred. "The Work of the American Missionary Association Among Negro Refugees in Canada West, 1848-64." *Ontario Historical Society Papers and Records* 21 (1924) 198-295.
Lewis, James K. "Early Negro Migration and the Amherstburg Baptist Association." *Ontario History* 58 (1966) 117-31.
———. "Religious Life of Fugitive Slaves and Rise of Coloured Baptist Churches 1820-1865 in What Is Now Known as Ontario." BDiv thesis, McMaster University, 1965.
"Levi Coffin," *National Park Service.* No pages. Online: https://www.nps.gov/people/levi-coffin.htm.
Loguen, J. W. *The Rev. J.W. Loguen, as a Slave and as a Freeman.* Syracuse, NY; Truair, 1859.
McBeth, H. Leon. *The Baptist Heritage: Four Centuries of Baptist Witness.* Nashville: Boardman and Holman, 1987.
Miles, Tiya. *All That She Carried: The Journey of Ashley's Sack, a Black Family Keepsake.* New York: Random House, 2021.
Nelson, Louis P. *The Beauty of Holiness: Anglicanism and Architecture in Colonial South Carolina.* Chapel Hill: University of North Carolina Press, 1988.
Quarles, Benjamin. *Black Abolitionists.* New York: Oxford University Press, 1969.
Renfree, Harry A. *Heritage and Horizon: The Baptist Story in Canada.* Eugene, OR: Wipf and Stock, 2007.
"Richard Allen and the Origins of the AME Church." *US National Archives* (June 9 2021). No pages. Online: https://rediscovering-black history.blogs.archives.gov/2021/06/09/richard-allen.
Ricketts, Shannon. "Underground Railroad Canada/US Joint Initiative." *Historic Sites and Monuments Board of Canada* (Submission Report OB-7), 1998.
Russell, Hilary. "The Underground Railroad." *Historic Sites and Monuments Board of Canada* (Agenda Paper), 1996.
Shreve, Dorothy S. *The AfriCanadian Church: A Stabilizer.* Jordan Station, ON: Paideia, 1983.
Simpson, Donald. G. "Negroes in Ontario from Early Times to 1870." PhD Diss., University of Western Ontario, 1970.
Sobel, Mechal. *Trabelin' On: The Slave Journey to an Afro-Baptist Faith.* Princeton, NJ: Princeton University Press, 1988.
Stouffer, Alan P. *The Light of Nature and the Law of God: Anti-Slavery in Ontario, 1883-1877.* Montréal and Kingston: McGill-Queens University Press, 1992.
Torbet, Robert G. *A History of the Baptists.* 3rd ed. Valley Forge, PA: Judson, 1973.

Upton, Dell. *Holy Things and Profane: Anglican Parish Churches in Colonial Virginia.* New Haven: Yale University Press, 1986.

Walker, Barrington. *Race on Trial: Black Defendants in Ontario's Criminal Courts, 1858-1958.* Toronto: University of Toronto Press, 2010.

Walker, James W. St. G. *A History of Blacks in Canada: A Study Guide for Teac\hers and Students.* Ottawa: Minister of State for Multiculturalism, 1980.

Wayne, Michael. "The Black Population of Canada West on the Eve of the American Civil War: A Reassessment Based on The Manuscript Census of 1861." In *A Nation of Immigrants: Women, Workers and Communities in Canadian History, 1840s-1960s,* edited by Franca Iacovetta et al., 58-82. Toronto: University of Toronto Press, 1998.

Winks, Robin. *The Blacks in Canada: A History.* 2nd ed. Montreal: McGill University Press, 1997.

Wylie, William. "The Abolition Movement in British North America." *Historic Sites and Monuments Board of Canada* (Framework Study), 2003.

Zeman, J. K. *Baptist Roots and Identity.* Etobicoke, ON: Baptist Convention of Ontario and Quebec, 1978.

Zeman, J. K., ed. *Baptists in Canada.* Arlington, MA: American Baptist Historical Society, 1980.

9

Washington Christian (1776–1850) and the Founding of the First Coloured Calvinistic Baptist Church of Toronto

Glenn Tomlinson

The name Washington Christian is well known in the annals of the Black Baptist experience in the city of Toronto. However, his story and the story of the church he founded are not well documented.[1] In fact, some of the chronological details have been misconstrued leading to some erroneous conclusions.[2] To clarify the historical record, this chapter argues that the First Coloured Calvinistic Church was founded by Washington Christian in 1834, and not in 1826 as many contend.

Washington Christian was born enslaved in the Commonwealth of Virginia in 1776. He escaped to the northern states and became a Christian and a preacher of the Christian faith serving in various African-American contexts for six years from approximately 1826 to 1832, with his ordination occurring in 1829. Frustrated with the lack of progress concerning the emancipation of his African brothers and sisters, he decided to remove to what many enslaved Blacks considered to be the "Promised Land," arriving in Canada likely sometime in 1832. It is here we pick-up the story.[3]

---

1. "Christian, Washington."

2. For a summary of those conclusions, see footnote 12.

3. For a full account of Christian's life and ministry, see Tomlinson, *Washington Christian*. This chapter is adapted from that work.

1833–1841

With a view to ministering to the destitute Black Christian community, he settled in the administrative capital of the British colony, the town of York—a town that would shortly change its name and be incorporated as the city of Toronto in 1834.[4] Christian became a member of the Baptist Church on March Street, likely sometime in the year of 1833.[5] As was the practice of Baptist churches of the day, Christian presented a letter of transmission from his previous church stating he was a member in good standing, then interviewed by two of the leading men of the society, recommended by them to the church, and finally received by experience at the church. Before an exploration of his experience in this church is undertaken, something needs to be said about the history of York's Baptist witness.

The Baptists first established a church in "muddy" York on October 25, 1818, under the ministry of a Scotsman, Alexander Stewart (1774–1840).[6] The church continued for approximately a year-and-a-half, whereafter, it was formally dissolved when Stewart and several of its members obtained their settlement allotments northwest of the capital. It is clear, however, that Baptists remained in York and informally practiced their faith. Moreover, it is probable that Stewart continued to minister to them. In 1826, however, Stewart returned to York to settle permanently. At this time, he also reconstituted the church. The church first met in his home, then in a schoolhouse, then in a Masonic lodge located in Market Lane for five years, and then finally in their building, on March Street, by the spring of 1832. This was the skeletal framework of the church's early days, but what was it actually like?

Division marked the first quarter century of the March Street Baptist Church's existence. Matters of opinion were held as intransigently as fundamentals of the faith. This situation was exacerbated by a congregation composed of a variety of groups with particular prejudices. Thus,

---

4. *York Commercial Directory* (1837), 9; *York Commercial Directory* (1843–1844), 27; *York Commercial Directory* (1846–1847), 12; Christian is not listed in the *York Commercial Directory* (1833–1834).

5. "Colored Baptists' Church." The only minute book for March Street Baptist Church that is extant for this period covers from 16 October 1829 to 3 July 1832. As Christian is not mentioned as being received into membership during this time, it must have been sometime after (see Minutes of the Baptist Church at York).

6. For a history of this church, see Tomlinson, *From Scotland to Canada*; "Hard Beginning."

Highland Scots could not get along with Lowland Scots, let alone with Welshmen or Englishmen; American patriots could not get along with Canadian Loyalists and free people of colour could not get along with those who had recently escaped slavery. Christian was well acquainted with the want of homogeneity.[7] Nevertheless, rather than stand aloof from formal fellowship and commitment to the body of Christ, he chose to enter.[8] But how did this lack of unity manifest itself in this church with regard to his group particularly?

Before this question is answered, it is important to state that there were other men and women of African descent who were received into the membership of March Street Baptist Church before Washington Christian. For example, the minutes of the Baptist Church at York, Upper Canada, recorded that John and Agnes Fels, of the "African Baptist Church in New York," were received into membership on September 11, 1831.[9] However, difficulties began when not all of Christian's brothers and sisters in the faith could produce letters of transmission, particularly if they were among those who arrived via the Underground Railroad. Further, the leadership of March Street Baptist Church required something more of these recently escaped church attendees. One early chronicler explains, "They welcomed their southern brethren of colored blood but demanded that they produce letters of dismissal from their old churches and that they at once repay their former masters the loss sustained by their escape from slavery."[10]

Given their impoverished state, none of the former slaves could fulfill such a requirement. The congregation at March Street had reached an impasse. What was to be done? "The runaways decided to have a church of their own,"[11] and Christian led the way: "Washington Christian, an ex-slave and a man of commanding personality and excellent education, who was a member of the March Street congregation, saw the situation

---

7. Tomlinson, *Washington Christian*, 8.

8. March Street Baptist Church often designated men, with the necessary qualifications, as preachers of the Gospel. However, a record of sermons preached is only extant for part of 1833 and none of 1834. Therefore, it is not known whether Christian was among March Street's licentiates (see Stewart, "Register of Sermons").

9. Minutes of the Baptist Church at York.

10. "Colored Baptists' Church."

11. "Twas Sixty Years."

and gathered his brethren around him for the inception of (a) separate church, which came into being in 1834."[12]

Father Christian, as he would become affectionally known, constituted Toronto's second Baptist church with twelve charter members.[13] Many accounts indicate that these men and women were the destitute of his people—recently escaped slaves.[14] To start a church is difficult, to begin it without material means is daunting. Nevertheless, the pastor and his people worked hard, looked to God, and set about to consolidate the work. They secured a church home by affiliating with churches of like faith and by replicating themselves—planting churches, ordaining ministers, and fighting for righteousness in society. Though the first seven

---

12. "Colored Baptists' Church."

For examples of the year 1834 being corroborated by the earliest published histories of the church see the following: (1) 1904: "About the year 1834 a few coloured people met for services in a little frame building on March (now Lombard) street. A frame building on Richmond Street, where the Hebrew synagogue now stands, was then leased by them and here they continued to worship until 1841 when the present site was purchased and a small church erected. At this time Elder Christian was pastor" (Robertson, *Robertson's Landmarks of Toronto*, 471). (2) 1907: "The congregation was first organized in 1834 by Father Christian." ("New Church"). (3) 1914: "University Avenue Baptist Church."

Confusion on dates is understandable, for there were likely some members of the *daughter work* who had also been members of the *mother church* at March Street, which was consolidated in 1826 and secured its first long term home in 1827.For examples of many later published histories that cite the inception of the church as 1826 or 1827 see the following: (1) 1926: "One hundred years ago the congregation now known as the First Baptist Church of Toronto came into being . . . In 1826 a small group of Baptists, several of whom were colored, began to worship together, though there is no record of where their services were held. The following year the colored members of the church were holding separate services, and this body grew until in 1834, simultaneously with the naming of Toronto, the present church was organized" ("Colored Baptists' Church"); (2) 1934: "Centennial Year"; (3) 1940: Amherstburg Regular Missionary Baptist Association, *Pathfinders*, 3-4; (4) 1957: "Founded by Slaves"; (5) 1972: "In the early 1820s a number of escaped slaves who had come to Canada via the "underground railway" gathered in Toronto—then the Town of York—to "praise, sing, and thank God for their escape from bondage. At first they worshipped outdoors an in each other's homes. They were formed into a congregation under the leadership of an itinerant evangelist from the Southern United States, Elder Washington Christian, in 1826, thus becoming Toronto's first Baptist church and first black institution" ("Church Founded by Slaves"); (6) 1981: "First Baptist Church"; (7) 1996: Mascoll, "Downtown Church"; (8) Winter, "Connected."

13. "Twas Sixty Years."

14. "Church was Founded," *The Globe*.

years of Christian's ministry were ones of struggle, eventually it led to a revival and a new building.

It is not known where Christian's new church gathered together for worship during the first two years of its existence.[15] During that time, the March Street church experienced further division. By the spring of 1836, Alexander Stewart stepped aside; an exodus of some of the members formed a third Baptist church under the leadership of John Eglinton Maxwell (1803–1876).[16] The trustees of March Street shuttered the doors to what remained of its membership and rented out their facilities—first to John Jennings (1814–1876) of the United Presbyterian Church (likely in the summer of 1836), and then to Christian's congregation in the fall.[17] Christian's church made use of the building until the end of the year.[18] Further, he likely saw the March Street accommodation as only temporary, assuming the March Street congregation would eventually return. His church family, therefore, sought long-term accommodation and finally secured facilities in a frame building on Richmond Street, a place where they would worship for four years.[19] Interestingly, some of the members of the March Street church came to Christian's church, at the new location, and sat under his ministry. James Gillespie Birney (1792–1857), a Kentucky slaveholder-turned-abolitionist, visited Toronto and Christian's church in 1837 and described it as follows:

> In the afternoon, I went to a Baptist Church, the pastor of which is Mr. Christian, a colored man, a native of Virginia and formerly a Slave. The Congregation, which was larger than the building could well accommodate, was composed of about an equal number of whites and colored persons. There was no distinction

---

15. Rolph, *Brief Account*, 178; on a visit to Toronto, in 1836, Thomas Rolph makes reference to visiting an "African Church." However, this is likely a reference to the African Methodist Episcopal Church which was founded in 1833, i.e., "the colored inhabitants of Toronto also have an African Church, which is well attended—it is very gratifying to bear testimony to the good conduct of the negroes residing in this city—they have most of them escaped from Slavery, they are well protected and kindly used, and appear to evince a sense of gratitude at their treatment, and show that they duly appreciate the inestimable blessing of freedom."

16. The church ceased to exist by 1839. For more information, see Tomlinson, *From Scotland to Canada*, 220–21.

17. See Jarvis Street Baptist Church, 53. See also "Colored Baptists' Church."

18. Thereafter, Maxwell's church took up the tenancy from January to April 1837.

19. *The City of Toronto*, 31. See also Robertson, *Robertson's Landmarks of Toronto*, 471.

in seats, nor any, the least recognition, so far as I could discern, of a difference made by complexion or any other cause. There is a considerable number of the members of the Church that are whites. I never saw a better looking or more orderly Congregation assembled. In their persons they were neat - in their attention to the services decorous and exemplary.[20]

However, while happy to minister to all, Christian detected a spiritual lethargy in his March Street brethren.[21] Desirous of seeing the mother church revive, he encouraged the March Street Baptist church to wake up and start meeting again. They heeded his counsel and secured the agent for the Upper Canada Baptist Missionary Society, Samuel Tapscott (1804–1888).[22] Tapscott ministered from May 1837 into the autumn of the same year—when the Rebellion threw everything into confusion. Nevertheless, Christian's exhortation had its effect, and the church eventually reconstituted itself on October 31, 1840.[23] A later writer described the far-reaching effect of Christian's church upon the Baptist cause in the city,

> A few coloured people sixty years ago organized themselves into a Baptist church, stimulated a few white people that attended their services to start out for themselves; from the latter the old Bond street church originated, and from that the present magnificent and wealthy Jarvis street church, and from thus, again, all the other Baptist churches of the city. The coloured people may well feel proud that their humble beginning more than half of a century since has resulted in such a magnificent consequence.[24]

---

20. Birney, *Letters*, 396.

21. *Canadian Baptist Magazine* (1.8), 180–81. This indifference was well-described by another: "DEAR BROTHER—A Christian Brother, travelling during last summer in the Upper Province, came to a place where was a Baptist Church, the members of which were all asleep in Divine things; and when that brother reasoned with some of the leading members on this unnatural state of things, they said they were only taking a 'Spiritual nap,' and that they would wake up presently and go on their way again. Active religion must indeed be at a low ebb where such sentiments are held and acted on."

22. Tapscott, "Journal," 65–68. While ministering at March Street, Tapscott also had the opportunity to preach the Lord's Day afternoons "for Elder Christian, the Pastor of the colored Church."

23. *Canadian Baptist Magazine* (1.6), 144.

24. From an 1887 history cited in Robertson, *Robertson's Landmarks of Toronto*, 471.

The next evidence of Christian's consolidating efforts comes to light in the church's affiliation with the Haldimand Baptist Association.[25] This likely occurred late in 1835.[26] Though they had separated from their brethren at March Street, they deemed communion with their brethren essential. At each annual gathering of this fellowship, reports from each member church would be given by their appointed delegate and then summarized for publication. Such reports shed light on the progress of each congregation. From 1834 to 1841, two of these published reports survive. They read as follows:

> Report for the year 1836: TORONTO. This church expresses a deep sense of the all-important subject and cause of the kingdom of the Redeemer, as being one worthy of the highest consideration, and deserving our utmost attention. It expresses its gratitude to the author and giver of all spiritual blessings, for the manifestations of his love and mercy; that, although in its infant state, has been subject to frequent vicissitudes, yet the hand of the Lord has sustained it with peculiar prosperity and increase.[27]

> Report for the year 1839: First Toronto Church blesses God for preserving them through surrounding difficulties and trials which have come upon them during the past year. The Lord has dealt mercifully with them and filled their hearts with hopes of better things to come. This church, though the poorest in the Association, has formed a Missionary Society, and has collected one pound five shillings for Missionary purposes. They are determined to go for the word. They have a Sabbath School but want a library. They pray that God will give them more of the grace of self-denial—that their offerings may henceforth bear a greater proportion to the magnitude of his claims upon them.[28]

---

25. In 1819, Upper Canada was divided into four regional Baptist associations: Eastern and Western, west of York, Haldimand and Johnstown, and east of York.

26. Allen, *Triennial Baptist Register*, 288. At the time, the Haldimand Association, report for 1835, printed that no African or coloured Baptist Church in York was reported as a member, however, the report for 1836 lists the church and states, "Voted, that the church in Toronto shall have the minutes this year gratis, in consequence of their not receiving their part last year—being miscarried"; indicating they must have joined sometime after the 1835 report went to print, likely late in 1835; Haldimand Baptist Association Minutes (1837), 4.

27. Haldimand Baptist Association Minutes (1837), 15.

28. See "Haldimand Baptist Association" in *Canadian Baptist Magazine* (1.12), 284.

So committed was he to the welfare of his sister churches that his church agreed to host the annual association meetings of 1838—though the report for this year is lacking.[29] One further anecdote relating to his commitment to fellowship is worthy of comment. While participating at the convention held at Whitby, from January 27 to 29, 1837, he had the opportunity to minister God's word to his brethren at a private house on the Saturday,[30] and it is here a rare glimpse is caught of his giftedness as a preacher: "'Father' Washington Christian was evidently a remarkable man. In the records of the Whitby Association there is a note that tells how the announcement of his engagement to preach had drawn the crowds miles around and the (place) was too small to hold them so that two other ministers had to hold overflow meetings under "'the canopy of heaven.'"[31]

The third evidence of Christian's consolidating effort can be seen in his desire, and the church's, to multiply disciples. It is amazing to consider that while his church struggled during its early days—with vicissitudes, difficulties, and trials, even fighting for its very existence—he and the church possessed the spiritual wherewithal to replicate themselves thus advancing the Baptist cause (Matt 28:18–20). Christian's name is linked with a couple of churches and a couple of men in this vein. First, it is well attested that he planted an African Baptist church in St Catherines and presided over a second one in Niagara—though details of their founding are lacking.[32] The details notwithstanding, when one considers the primitive modes of transportation and road network in the province of Upper Canada, his accomplishments are impressive. Second, Christian, now into his sixties, and giving thought to the future of the church, obeyed the apostolic command to entrust the Gospel to faithful men (2 Tim 2:2) by presiding over the ordination of two men during this period, Samuel H. Davis (1810–1907)[33] and Stephen Dutton (1785–1855). Concerning Dutton, Christian made a report to the *Canada Baptist Magazine and Missionary Register*:

29. Haldimand Baptist Association Minutes (1837), 4–5.

30. Haldimand Baptist Association Minutes (1837), 5.

31. "Colored Baptists' Church." Also, "Hearing him speak in Whitby in 1837, an observer noted that 'while truth fell from his lips it reached many hearts and suffused many eyes with tears'" (see "Christian, Washington").

32. Biography in the *Amherstburg Association Minutes*; *Canadian Baptist Magazine* (5.3), 69.

33. Amherstburg Regular Missionary Baptist Association, *Pathfinders*, 3.

Designation of an Evangelist

Dear Brother—At a meeting of the first Baptist Church of this city, convened for the purpose of setting Brother Dutton apart to the work of ministry, the ordaining council was as follows: Elder Christian, Pastor of the same church, was chosen Moderator, and James Johnson was chosen Clerk. Elder James Mitchell, Pastor of Yonge Street Church and brethren Williams, Dark, Goodenham were present. After Brother Dutton related his experience, his call to the ministry, and his views of divine truth, the council agreed to ordain him as an Evangelist. After singing and prayer by Elder Christian, Elder Mitchell preached from 2 Tim. ii. 15. Elder Christian gave the charge from 2 Tim. iv. 2; Elder Mitchell offered the ordination prayer, and the meeting separated after singing and benediction by the candidate.

Washington Christian
Pastor of the 1st Baptist Church in Toronto.
Toronto, 19 August 1841.[34]

The influx of destitute African Americans must have been a challenge to cope with for both the city and Christian's church. Indeed, there is evidence that the church was struggling to meet the material needs of its pastor. A report of the Canada Baptist Missionary Society in 1838 indicates: "A grant of thirty dollars has been made to Elder Christian, of Toronto, to aid in the preaching of the Gospel among the coloured inhabitants of the city."[35] Even beyond the cause of the Baptist faith, and the care of his brethren, Christian set an example for his flock by seeking the welfare of his fellow citizens. This love of justice and kindness (Mic 6:8) can be seen in two ways: first, he became part of the short-lived Upper Canada Anti-Slavery Society founded by Methodist minister Ephraim Evans (1803–1892) in 1837;[36] second, and in the same year, he ensured his name was affixed to "Edwoods and others Naturalization bill"—a petition to the provincial Legislative Assembly.[37] Regarding this latter initiative, one modern writer explains this was:

---

34. *Canadian Baptist Magazine* (5.4), 89.
35. *Canadian Baptist Magazine* (2.4), 92.
36. Price, *Slavery in America*, 207–9.
37. "Edwoods," 172. William Henderson Edwoods (1809–1862) was a member of Washington Christian's church and one of four trustees of the church's first building at Queen and Victoria Streets.

a subtle protest to highlight the unspoken racial discrimination on the part of civil servants and legislators that prevented African American immigrants from becoming naturalized in Upper Canada. Black people were entitled, under British colonial law, to all the rights and privileges of full civil participation, but could not exercise those rights without taking this important step... The bill to naturalize the applicants passed the Upper Canadian legislature . . . but with an amendment that excluded from the list the names of every black person who had applied . . . No grounds were given in the Journal of the House of Assembly to account for the omission, of these very respectable men, and the substance of the preceding debate was not recorded. The circumstances certainly suggest that the applicants expected to be refused. That they applied at all could be construed as a statement of protest against the exclusion of black immigrants from their full rights as British subjects.[38]

While the naturalization petition did not achieve its ultimate end, it laid the groundwork and elevated both the pastor and the church in the eyes of Toronto's populace. Washington Christian's church experienced a revival that eventually allowed them to erect a church building. The revival began in the fall of 1839 and lasted until the spring of 1840. Evidently, Christian relayed his rather mixed 1839 report to the Haldimand Association sometime before the revival. The *Canada Baptist Magazine and Missionary Register* published three separate entries on the revival:

Upper Canada.

Toronto, 9 December 1839

Baptism of Seventeen Persons in The Bay

To a Christian mind a finer spectacle was never presented on the shores of Lake Ontario, than was exhibited yesterday in the baptism of fourteen females and three males, on a profession of faith, in the blessed Redeemer. They were all members of the congregation of coloured people in this city, under the pastoral care of Brother Christian. The public services of the day were conducted in the Chapel in Richmond-street, by brethren Bosworth and Mitchell. After the morning service, which ended about half-past eleven, the whole congregation, with the candidates and ministers, proceeded in order, to the bottom of Bay-street, where a convenient place for the interesting rite was selected, near the new bathing-house. After a short address

38. Frost, "Escaped Slaves."

from the pastor, Mr. Christian, singing, and prayer, the first candidate was led by him into the water, and baptized by him in the scriptural manner of immersion. The other candidates were successively led in by the deacons; and it was pleasing to witness the calm yet joyful manner in which they submitted to the ordinance, and the cheerful greetings which, by their looks and smiles, the advancing and retiring parties exchanged with each other. After each baptism, a line or two of praise to God were sung by the members on the shore, while the next was proceeding to the appointed spot. A numerous concourse of spectators were assembled on the shore and riding bank, and behaved with the greatest respect and decorum, many of them impressed with the solemnity as well as novelty of the scene.

The afternoon service commenced at three o-clock, and towards the conclusion of it the newly baptized persons, with two others who had obeyed the ordinance previously, were fully admitted into the church, each of them receiving a short but appropriate address from the gratified pastor, in the presence of a crowded congregation who participated in his pleasure, and united in the prayer that the favour of God might often 'renew the wonders of the day.'

About nine months ago the church was in a very declining state. Two or three of the more lively and spiritual members endeavoured to excite a greater concern among their brethren; prayer meetings were more frequently held, attended with more regularity and ardour, and continued with increasing fervency, until the church, being prepared to receive the blessing, it was bestowed upon them in answer to their earnest prayer. Many others are under great concern; and there is strong hope that further accessions will soon be made to this Christian society.[39]

Baptism of Thirteen Persons

Toronto, 4 May 1840.

Dear Sir—Since you published the account of the baptism in January last, the work of God, in the conversion of souls, has still been going on through the winter; and on the 12th of April last we had the happiness of witnessing the solemn and impressive ordinance of baptism administered to thirteen joyful candidates in the Bay, at the usual place. The morning of the day was ushered in by a copious fall of rain, which continued till

39. *Canadian Baptist Magazine* (3.7), 162.

eleven o'clock, A.M., when the sun broke through the clouds, and shone till the conclusion of the ceremony. But although the day was so unfavourable, there was a vast concourse of spectators and friends from the country to witness the ordinance. The use of the Methodist Episcopal Meeting-house was kindly lent for the occasion. The morning discourse was preached by Elder Mitchel (sic), who came with all the members of his church and many others, from the surrounding country. The house was filled. In the afternoon, the candidates received the right hand of fellowship, with a short address from Elder Christian, and with the friends and brethren partook of the emblems of our dying Lord. There were nearly 200 who sat down, which is a great number for this place—some of them coming from a distance of fifty miles. W. C. Boyd.[40]

In the Haldimand Association, the church in the city of Toronto, under the care of Elder Christian, has had thirty added to its number by baptism since the last meeting of the Association; and the church in Yonge Street, under Elder Mitchell, has lately received eight by baptism. Yours sincerely, John Oakley.[41]

The addition of thirty persons to the membership of the church, an increase of over forty percent, moved the dream of building a church into the realm of possibility—there was still the matter of land and building.[42] Concerning the land, a prominent member of the provincial government, and a Church of Scotland man, Peter McCutcheon (1789–1860), known as Peter McGill after 1821, who owned much property in the centre of the city, set aside a parcel of land for Christian's congregation—lot number 2 on the northeast corner of Lot, now Queen, and Victoria Streets.[43] With the land secured, the congregation could set about the business of erecting an edifice. During the building's construction, Christian sought to raise funds to offset the financing debt. Late in 1840, he deployed two of his leaders, Stephen Dutton and John Randolph, to scour New England for the funds. The *Liberator* of Boston published the church's appeal:

40. *Canadian Baptist Magazine* (3.12), 285.

41. *Canadian Baptist Magazine* (3.12), 283.

42. The church had reported a membership of seventy-three to the Haldimand Association before the revival (see "Haldimand Baptist Association: Twenty-First Anniversary" in *Canadian Baptist Magazine* [3.12], 284).

43. "Colored Baptists' Church."

Upper Canada. Our colored Baptist brethren in Toronto, having escaped from this slavery ridden country, to a retreat where they can worship God according to the dictates of their own consciences, with none to molest or make them afraid, are now endeavouring to procure the means for erecting a meeting-house, and have partially succeeded. Messrs. Stephen Dutton and John L. Randolph have been deputed by them to collect funds for this purpose, and are now in this city and vicinity. Those who feel disposed to aid them can send their donations to 25, Cornhill.[44]

The two men met with some success—though McGill continued to hold the deed to the land until 1845 when the remaining debt was paid off. The Baptist church at Queen and Victoria Street opened its doors in the first days of spring 1841. The *Magazine* printed an account of the joyous occasion:

Dear Sir—I send you a short account of the opening of the new chapel in Toronto, belonging to the church under the pastoral care of the Rev. W. Christian. The place was opened for divine service Lord's day, March 28, by a series of services, commencing at 6 A.M., when the church and friends met for prayer. The Dedication Sermon was preached at 11 A.M. by our esteemed friend Elder Mitchell of Yonge Street, from these words—"I will glorify the house of my glory." Isa. LXX. 7. The Rev. Mr. Roaf preached again at 6 in the evening. The house was well filled during the services, and the collections amounted to £12 13s. The size of the building is 50 feet by 36, and it has cost about £550 including the ground. We have collected and paid £250. Trusting that God, our Heavenly Father, will enable us to discharge the remaining debt, and praying that he will fill it with faithful and devoted servants, I remain, your's in the best of bonds, W.C. Boyd. Toronto, 19 April 1841.[45]

Years later, a description of the church building was preserved in John Ross Robertson's monumental work *Landmarks of Toronto*:

The church stands north and south with the front gable on Queen street, a little belfry, but no bell above. A porch rounds out to the sidewalk but the entrance is at one side of the porch and is only reached after passing through a gate in the low picket fence running around the building and then up four steps. Above this porch is a small shield containing this inscription:

44. *Liberator*, 3.
45. *Canadian Baptist Magazine* (3.12), 289.

> First Baptist Church
> Erected. A.D. 1841.
> Rebuilt. A.D. 1873.
>
> There are three gothic windows of frosted glass on each side of the church, and two in front. A slender chimney rises above the north gable. At this end is a brick, low-set Sunday school room, and beyond this the parsonage of the minister.[46]

Christian must have looked upon the formative years of 1833 to 1841 with an immense amount of personal satisfaction. It should be noted that he, like any pastor, was not alone in the work; the congregation laboured with their gifts and prayed diligently alongside him. At the youthful age of sixty-one, Washington Christian entered the bonds of holy matrimony marrying Ann Randall (d. 1862)[47] on March 15, 1837. The ceremony was officiated by the Wesleyan Methodist minister Matthew Lang (1798–1850) and witnessed by his friend William Henry Harris (1809–1881).[48]

1842–1850

Even with their increased membership, Christian's church still lacked resources to offset the remaining debt. A census taken of the Black population of Toronto, in the spring of 1841, showed that the bulk of Christian's congregation lived on subsistence-type occupations. Christian responded by seeking affiliation with the African-focused American Baptist Missionary Convention—Christian likely secured an annual stipend.[49] Consequently, it is not surprising that by the fall of 1841 he made this appeal to his Canadian co-religionists:

> 1st Toronto—This church reviewing their progress during the past year, see that God has done great things for them whereof they are glad. He has enabled them to erect a neat and

---

46. Robertson, *Robertson's Landmarks of Toronto*, 471.

47. "DIED"; sources are unanimous in citing Ann Randall's birthplace as the United States. However, one source places her birth year as 1800, i.e., her grave marker; two other sources state her birth occurring in the year 1790, i.e., the register of her burial and her obituary.

48. *Ontario, District Marriage Registers.*

49. The convention was founded in 1840. Not many of their annual reports remain extant. Washington Christian is listed as an ordained minister in the *Ninth Annual Report of the American Baptist Missionary Convention*. Subsequent to his death, he is also listed as "deceased" in some reports e.g. 1854; see Remy, "Report."

commodious place of worship, has increased their number, given them a spirit of earnest and united prayer for the prosperity of his cause. Their Sabbath School is in a flourishing state, they have raised funds for a library, yet they lament that they have done so little compared with what they might have done, they make an earnest appeal for aid in liquidating the debt on their chapel. Shall that appeal be made in vain?[50]

Most Baptist congregations in Canada West and Canada East were rather small during the 1840s, and the march toward a federal Baptist union—a work that Christian was keenly interested in—was rather stilted owing to the communion question, so it is not surprising that his appeal for funds largely fell on deaf ears. Further, having tapped New England, Christian would have to look farther afield for financial assistance. By the summer of 1842, he was on his way to Jamaica.[51]

Christian spent about a year in Jamaica canvassing the churches. The *Montreal Register* reported the results of this endeavour under the banner "The Liberality of the Jamaica Baptists":

> Most pleasing proofs are constantly given of the generous disposition of our colored brethren in the West Indies. However their former oppressors may calumniate their characters and slander their ministers, their contribution to the cause of God abundantly testify their gratitude and benevolence. In this respect, at least, their praise is in all the churches. A very gratifying expression of their kindness has recently come before our notice in the *Jamaica Baptist Herald*. Some months ago, W. CHRISTIAN, the worthy preacher of the colored church in Toronto, went to that Island to seek aid in liquidating a debt on their place of worship. He was most kindly received by the missionaries and their flocks, who sympathies were strongly excited in behalf of the colored race in Canada, who have found here a refuge from American slavery. We trust their bounty will prove of lasting benefit to the colored inhabitants of Toronto. The sum already raised by the churches is about £280, which is nearly the amount of the debt.[52]

50. *Canadian Baptist Magazine* (5.3), 68.

51. See *Montreal Register* (3.45); following the Rebellion of 1837, the British, in 1841, united the colonies of Upper and Lower Canada into the Province of Canada, and renamed the former colonies Canada West and Canada East. Washington Christian was a member of the General Committee for the Canada Baptist Union. He, along with Robert Alexander Fyfe (1816–1878), represented their Toronto churches.

52. *Montreal Register* (2.28), 141; also cited in *Northern Baptist*, 139–40.

Having succeeded in his mission, Washington Christian boarded the brig "Silenus," bound for Boston on 12 September 1843.[53] Though he arrived home to his wife and his congregation with happy news, the journey took a tremendous toll on his health.[54]

As is so often the case in the life of the Church militant, blessing in Washington Christian's church was accompanied by trial. The reports of 1843 and 1844 to the Haldimand Association reflect this combination:

> Toronto church, since the last association, have been much confused. They have at times felt very much disheartened but arise above the troubles of the way. When favored with the divine presence, they can say, "we will not fear what man can do to us." Their Sabbath School is increasing, and there is a Juvenile Temperance Society formed in it. Through the liberality of the Baptists in Jamaica, their chapel is entirely free of debt.[55]

> Toronto 1st Church—This worthy band has unitedly resisted the various evils that have in times past threatened to divide them and are at present enjoying the sweets of internal peace, though not enjoying all the communicable fulness of the love of Christ; they desire that they may enjoy more. They earnestly request the prayers of their brethren in the churches. Elder Christian remains their pastor.[56]

The early months of 1845 saw their "neat and commodious place of worship" made complete. The debt on the building and the land having been discharged, the deed was finally transferred from Peter McGill to the church:

> That by Indenture of Bargain and Sale dated the tenth day of February, in the year of our Lord, one thousand eight hundred and forty-five, made between the Honorable Peter McGill, of the city of Montreal, Esquire, of the first part, and Wm. Henderson Edwoods, of the city of Toronto, Hair Dresser, Newton Carey, of the same place, Barber, William Henry Harris, of the same place Shopkeeper, and Thomas Williams, of the same place, Tanner, of the second part, a true copy of which said Indenture is hereunto annexed, a certain lot in Toronto aforesaid was conveyed to the said William Henderson Edwoods, Newton Carey,

---

53. "Massachusetts, Boston Passenger Lists."
54. Biography in the *Amherstburg Association Minutes*.
55. Haldimand Baptist Association Minutes (1844), 7.
56. *Minutes of the Twenty-Seventh Anniversary*, 10.

William Henry Harris, and Thomas Williams, in trust, and for the purposes in the said Indenture more particularly set forth and declared.[57]

This legal transfer necessitated that Christian and the church draft a trust deed that would, among other things, outline the purposes for which the building and land were to be used. While this document has not been located, two things can be gleaned from supplemental sources. First, it contained the name of the church First Coloured Calvinistic Baptist Church. This unique name not only conveyed something of Christian's and the church's theological makeup, but also their ministerial intent, i.e., they were determined to continue ministering to the destitute of their African American brothers and sisters. Second, the trustees—Edwoods, Carey, Harris, and Williams—all of whom were African American, were appointed for life. A later historian provides the reason for such a stipulation: "It was not intended to exclude white persons, and there have been white members of the congregation from time to time, but it was feared that the whites might become dominant and alienate the property from its original intention, so the original deed contained the name First Colored Calvinistic Church, by which it became known."[58] The provisions set out in the trust deed were, without question, well intended, but they led to all manner of upset for Christian and his church.

The reports to the Haldimand Association for the years 1845 and 1846 demonstrate that the occasions of discord within the congregation had become full-blown. For 1845, there is no summary of any letter from the church but there is a report on its current membership. It is telling. From 1844 to 1845, the membership dropped from 145 members to just 49.[59] For 1846, the secretary of the Association made this succinct and sobering summary: "*First Toronto*—Mention is made of 'sore combats' and 'numerous trials' endured in the past year. 'Coldness' and 'want of love to God' are deplored. The state of the Sabbath School is spoken of in encouraging terms."[60] At the heart of the sore combats and numerous trials was church polity. Most Canadian Baptist churches of the period appointed a single elder to be responsible for the spiritual well-being

---

57. *Provincial Freeman*, 2.

58. "Twas Sixty Years."

59. *Minutes of the Twenty-Seventh Anniversary*, 4; *Minutes of the Twenty-Eighth Anniversary*, 3.

60. *Minutes of the Twenty-Ninth Anniversary*, 9.

of the congregation, and a diaconate to exercise oversight on practical matters. Christian's church was no exception. The provisions of the trust deed, however, allowed for the exercise of "arbitrary power" on the part of the trustees, opening them up to conflict with the elected officers of the church.[61] This is precisely what happened at First Coloured Calvinistic Baptist Church of Toronto—it is unknown what particular issue brought the parties into such strife. It was also a contention that was not resolved until long after Christian's death.[62] Sadly, Christian was not able to meld his congregation together. Having only the support of one of the trustees, Thomas Williams (ca. 1787–1873),[63] Christian's ministry to the church came to an abrupt end in 1847. He presided over a meeting of the American Abolition Society, of which he was the Vice-President, held at "the Baptist Chapel, Queen Street" in the early summer,[64] and he continued to officiate at the committals of his people—the last intermittent being registered on the 14th of June.[65] Sometime during the height of summer, his ministry at his beloved church came to a close. One writer sums up this period of his ministry, from 1841 to 1847, in stark terms: "Though the old man purchased the ground, and built the Meeting-house for them, by his efforts, yet that same party turned him out of his pulpit, and treated him so unkindly, that he died virtually from a broken heart."[66]

The church Christian founded would continue after his departure, but struggle marked most of its life for the nineteenth century. Christian continued to minister for the next three years, particularly in the southwest of the province, while maintaining his residence in Toronto. He preached his last sermon on June 23, 1850 in the city of Buffalo. After the service concluded he returned to his room feeling quite unwell. A time of sufficient recovery having passed, he was taken home to Toronto by his faithful friends, Thomas Williams and his wife, but he would only live another five days.[67] His death came on July 3, 1850. His good friend, Rev. James Pyper, preached his funeral sermon with the prominent Toronto Congregationalist minister, John Roaf (1801–1862), among the

---

61. Robertson, *Robertson's Landmarks of Toronto*, 471–72.

62. Bill No. 104.

63. *Provincial Freeman*, 2.

64. "Abolition Convention."

65. "Potter's Field Cemetery 1."

66. *Provincial Freeman*, 2. The same article also records Washington's wife, Ann: "His beloved widow received but little better treatment."

67. Biography in the *Amherstburg Association Minutes*.

many attendees.⁶⁸ He was buried in the Potter's Field cemetery on July 5, 1850.⁶⁹ The Haldimand Association carried this succinct and exhortative tribute in its annual report for the year 1850:

> Whereas, during the past Associational year, God has removed from our midst, by death, one of our justly venerated Pioneers in the Gospel Ministry, Elder Washington Christian, of Toronto, whose labours have been abundant and successful in various parts of our Zion, therefore, Resolved. That this Association offer their sincere sympathy to his afflicted family, and also express their high estimation of him as a man of God, and Minster of the Gospel of Christ, by seeking to imitate his example and virtuous life.⁷⁰

BIBLIOGRAPHY

Primary Sources

ARCHIVES

Allen, I. M., *The Triennial Baptist Register: No. 2—1836*. Philadelphia: Baptist General Tract Society, 1864.

Bill No. 104 (1871–1872), *Legislative Assembly of Ontario*.

"First Baptist Church: One Hundred Fifty-Fifth Anniversary, 1826–1881," Canadian Baptist Archives, McMaster University, Hamilton, ON.

Haldimand Baptist Association Minutes, 1837, 1844–1847, 1849, 1851.

Jarvis Street Baptist Church: Directory and Historical Sketch, 1897.

"Massachusetts, Boston Passenger Lists, 1820–1891." *FamilySearch*. Online: https://www.familysearch.org/en.

Minutes of the Baptist Church at York, Upper Canada (Jarvis Street Baptist Church Archives, Toronto, ON), September 4 and 11, 1831.

"Potter's Field Cemetery 1, 1826–1850" (Ontario, Toronto Trust Cemeteries, 1826–1989). *FamilySearch*. Online: https://www.familysearch.org/en.

Remy, E. de St. "Report on the Toronto Negroes for Lord Sydenham," April 5, 1841. Lieutenant Governor's Correspondence, Upper Canada, Governor General's Office, Miscellaneous Records 1835–1841, Volume 5 (Ref. RG7-G-14, R178-95-9-E; Film H-1178 Images 438–45). Library and Archives Canada.

Stewart, Alexander. "Register of Sermons Preached Chiefly at York, Upper Canada, 1827 to 1833," Louis Melzack Collection, Thomas Fisher Rare Book Library, Toronto, ON.

Tapscott, Samuel. "Journal, Ms." Canadian Baptist Archives, McMaster University, Hamilton, ON.

68. Biography in the *Amherstburg Association Minutes*.

69. "Potter's Field Cemetery 1." The death date for the burial register indicates July 2nd. Christian's body was reinterred in the Necropolis on 4 June 1862.

70. *Minutes of the Thirty-Third Anniversary*.

Monographs

Birney, James Gillespie. *Letters of James Gillespie Birney, 1831–1857: Volume 1*, edited by Dwight L. Dumond. Gloucester, MA: P. Smith, 1966.

Price, Thomas. *Slavery in America: With Notices of the Present State of Slavery and the Slave Trade Throughout the World*. London: G. Wightman, 1837.

Robertson, John Ross. *Robertson's Landmarks of Toronto: A Collection of Historical Sketches of the Old Town of York from 1792 to 1837 and of Toronto from 1834 to 1904*. 4th ed. Toronto: Evening Telegram, 1904.

Rolph, Thomas. *A Brief Account, Together with Observations, Made During a Visit in the West Indies, and a Tour through the United States of America, in Parts of the Years 1832–3: Together with a Statistical Account of Upper Canada*. Dundas, ON: G. Heyworth, 1836.

Newspapers and Magazines

"Abolition Convention." *The Globe*, July 3, 1847.

The Canadian Baptist Magazine and Missionary Register 1.8, January 1838.

The Canada Baptist Magazine and Missionary Register 2.4, September 1838.

The Canada Baptist Magazine and Missionary Register 3.7, January 1840.

The Canada Baptist Magazine and Missionary Register 3.12, June 1840.

The Canada Baptist Magazine and Missionary Register 4.12, June 1841.

The Canada Baptist Magazine and Missionary Register 5.3, September 1841.

The Canada Baptist Magazine and Missionary Register 5.4, October 1841.

"Centennial Year Marked by Church: Slave Days Recalled by Members of First Baptist; Meetings Back to 1827," *The Globe*, March 16, 1934.

"Church Founded by Slaves Marks its 145th Year," *The Toronto Star*, April 29, 1972.

"Colored Baptists' Church Has a History," *The Toronto Daily Star*, October 23, 1926.

"DIED. On the 18th Instant, at her Residence, Victoria-Street, after a Long Illness of Many Months, MRS. ANN Christian, Aged 72 Years." *The Globe*, March 20, 1862.

"Edwoods and Others Naturalization Bill." *Journal of the Legislative Council of Upper Canada: First Session of the Thirteenth Provincial Parliament* (1837).

"Founded by Slaves: Church Grows with Toronto," *The Globe and Mail*, December 21, 1957.

Frost, Karolyn Smardz, "Escaped Slaves Helped Build T.O." *Toronto Star*, Feb 11, 2007.

The Liberator (Boston, MA), December 4, 1840.

Mascoll, Philip, "Downtown Church Born of Slavery," *Toronto Star*, November 24, 1996.

The Montreal Register 2.28, July 13, 1843.

The Montreal Register 3.45, November 7, 1844.

"New Church Dedicated: Colored Baptists Open their University Avenue Home," *The Globe*, July 15, 1907.

The Northern Baptist; A Magazine Intended for the Use of the Junior Members of the Baptist Denomination 1, 1843.

The Provincial Freeman (Windsor, Toronto, Chatham, ON), 1855.

"'Twas Sixty Years since: Oldest Baptist Congregation Seeks New Home," *The Globe*, July 6, 1905.

"University Avenue Baptist Church Celebrated its Eightieth Birthday Yesterday," *The Globe*, November 2, 1914.

Winter, Jesse, "Connected by the Underground Railroad," *Toronto Star*, Jul 16, 2016.

York Commercial Directory, 1837, 1843–1844, 1846–1847.

Secondary Sources

Amherstburg Regular Missionary Baptist Association. *Pathfinders of Liberty and Truth: A Century with the Amherstburg Regular Missionary Baptist Association*. Buxton, ON: Amherstburg Regular Missionary Baptist Association, 1940.

"Christian, Washington." *Dictionary of Canadian Biography*. No pages. Online: http://www.biographi.ca/en/bio/christian_washington_7E.html.

Tomlinson, Glenn. "A Hard Beginning." In *Set for the Defense of the Gospel: A Bicentennial History of Jarvis Street Baptist Church, 1818-2018*, edited by Michael A.G. Haykin and Roy M. Paul, 11–39. Toronto: Jarvis Street Baptist Church, 2018.

———. *From Scotland to Canada: The Life of Pioneer Missionary Alexander Stewart*. n.p., 2008.

———. *Washington Christian (1776–1850) & The Dissolution of the Dividing Wall*. n.p., 2021.

10

"It Has Pleased God to Make Us of a Different Colour"

Black Baptists in Victoria, British Columbia, 1876–1881

Taylor Murray

Typically, British Columbia does not immediately spring to mind when one considers the history of Black Baptists in Canada. This is not to say, of course, that there were no Black Baptists west of the Rocky Mountains or that their stories were inconsequential. In fact, as this chapter shows, the Black experience is an inextricable piece of the history of Baptists in British Columbia. When the First Baptist Church of Victoria formally organized in 1876, it was the first Baptist church in Canada west of Winnipeg and had the unique distinction of being comprised almost equally of Black and White members. This racial dynamic continued for a time, but in 1881, the Black members withdrew from the church and a little over two years later the church dissolved.

Various historians have either mentioned or chronicled the formation of this church and the schism.[1] This chapter, therefore, has not

---

1. The events have been given robust treatment in Richards, "Baptists in British Columbia," 47–64. For other examples, see McClaurin, *Pioneering*, 244–48; Fitch, *Baptists of Canada*, 244–45; Renfree, *Heritage and Horizon*, 180–81; and Heath, Friesen, and Murray, *Baptists in Canada*, 49. Some denominational histories of the region, on the other hand, have omitted this racial dynamic altogether (see Harris, *Baptist Union*; and Thompson, *Baptist Story*).

unearthed some unknown episode. Instead, it retraces these events with the intention of documenting a different perspective: the Black Baptist experience. While the most detailed contemporary record of these events is found in the personal writings of John Clapp Baker (1828–1912), the president of the Missionary Board of the North Pacific Coast Convention, there is an equally revealing account in a letter written by Fortune Richard (b. 1807), one of the Black members of the church who was well known throughout the city. Although this latter writing has received significantly less attention, it presents valuable insight into how the Black members viewed the event and many of their coreligionists. This chapter begins by looking at the context of mid-to-late nineteenth century Victoria, before turning to the formation of the city's first Baptist church and its schism along racial lines, with special attention given to Richard's account. As the first Baptist church in Canada west of Winnipeg, the Black experience—turbulent though it was—is central to the story of Baptists in British Columbia.

CONTEXT OF MID-TO-LATE NINETEENTH-CENTURY VICTORIA

The story of Black British Columbia dates to 1858, when a "Pioneer Committee" of Black immigrants from San Francisco settled in Victoria.[2] The choice to resettle in the north came out of a feeling of hopelessness south of the border. It was only one year removed from the United States Supreme Court's Dred Scott decision, which had denied citizenship to people of African descent. In California, the situation seemed dire, as Black inhabitants faced a slew of discriminatory restrictions with few opportunities for upward mobility. Crawford Kilian sums: "the city's [San Francisco's] Black residents had poor prospects. Those who had sweated to earn money or property saw little chance of holding what they had gained. Those who had yet to succeed saw little chance of doing so . . . California was an El Dorado for White men only."[3] On April 20, 1858, the Black pioneers set sail for Victoria.[4]

---

2. The Colony of Vancouver Island and the Colony of British Columbia were separate until 1866 and were not part of Canada until 1871.

3. Kilian, *Go Do Some Great Thing*, 13.

4. The Pioneer Committee initially consisted of sixty five members, but not all were prepared to depart on the designated day, and thus that number dropped to thirty five. See Kilian, *Go Do Some Great Thing*, 16.

As these Black pioneers relocated to Victoria in search of a new life, so too did a flood of White settlers, both from the United States and elsewhere in British North America. Many years away from the completion of the railway that would eventually unite the future country "from sea to sea," most arrivals were funnelled through the northern United States. Excitement generated by reports of gold discovered in the Fraser River drew thousands to the region over the next decade. In Kilian's words, "the members of the Pioneer Committee must have felt mixed emotions. Ahead was a land that seemed to promise equality, opportunity and perhaps even great wealth. But the four hundred White men who were their fellow passengers must have looked grimly familiar."[5]

The Black settlers found mixed opportunities in Victoria. In 1864, an anonymous Black visitor to Victoria from California published an article in *The Liberator*, an east-coast anti-slavery American newspaper, documenting their experiences. The author found that while Victoria was not as hopeless as San Francisco seemed, nor was it the place of expected equality. Noting the positives, the author also observed that due to the real estate market, many Black settlers had become "comparatively wealthy."[6] Ultimately, however, the author summed, "There is as much prejudice, and nearly as much isolation, in Victoria as in San Francisco." According to the anonymous author, Blacks in Victoria were routinely denied service in bars, barbershops, and hotels; barred from basic civil functions, such as jury duty, and had limited political capital.[7]

Of each of the social structures in place, churches appear to have been among the most accommodating. The anonymous author from *The Liberator* noted that alongside schools, churches were "free from caste."[8] Indeed, many churches in Victoria were comprised of both White and Black members. This arrangement was not without its complications or caveats, however. The anonymous author had to concede that they believed the mixed congregations had been only "grudgingly and

---

5. Kilian, *Go Do Some Great Thing*, 16.

6. "The Colored Inhabitants of Vancouver Island" in *Liberator* (April 15, 1864), 32. All quotations from this article are cited from the reprinted version, as found in Foner, "Colored Inhabitants," 31–33.

7. "The Colored Inhabitants of Vancouver Island" in *Liberator* (April 15, 1864), 31–33.

8. "The Colored Inhabitants of Vancouver Island" in *Liberator* (April 15, 1864), 31–32.

unwillingly awarded."⁹ Likewise, a book entitled, *Four Years in British Columbia and Vancouver*, published in 1862, noted that on one occasion in Victoria's early history, "the whites objected to the blacks being allowed to go to the same church with them, and actually appealed to the Bishop to prevent it." Although "The Bishop was firm in his refusal to do anything of the kind," the result was that "many [White would-be attendees] stayed away from church."[10] The same book describes at least one church in the city that was "anti-black."[11]

The opportunities and challenges Black settlers encountered are well captured in the experiences of a future prominent member of the Baptist church, Fortune Richard. Born in Florida in 1807, Richard was one of the members of the Pioneer Committee who arrived in the late 1850s.[12] Two examples from Richard's early years in Victoria illustrate the anonymous author's point. First, in 1861, sixty Black men formed the Victoria Pioneer Rifle Corps with Richard in command. They created this volunteer militia, which was "the colony's lone military force for several years," because Victoria had denied Black inhabitants from serving in the city's fire brigade.[13] Second, in 1863, Richard—along with two other Black men, James Fountain and Adolphus Calamandus Richards—was restricted from entering the local theatre. The trio launched individual lawsuits against the manager of the theatre, which each came to naught.[14] While Victoria offered Black settlers more opportunities than they had south of the border, so too did it retain some of the same challenges.

ESTABLISHING FIRST BAPTIST CHURCH, VICTORIA

Among those early Black immigrants to Victoria were some of the first Baptists in the city. Fielding Spotts and Augustus Christopher—two individuals who would become founding members of the later Baptist

---

9. "The Colored Inhabitants of Vancouver Island" in *Liberator* (April 15, 1864), 31–32.

10. Mayne, *Four Years*, 351. The above quotation is from the same source.

11. Mayne, *Four Years*, 351.

12. Kilian, *Go Do Some Great Thing*, 28. Richard applied for citizenship in Victoria in 1861. See "Applications for Citizenship" in *Daily British Colonist* (December 4, 1861), 3. McDonough, *Francis Richard Family*, 80. Richard was a ship carpenter by trade.

13. Edwards, "War," 43. For letters penned by Richard as he served in this capacity, see Pilton, "Negro Settlement," 115, 230.

14. Pilton, "Negro Settlement," 198.

church—arrived in the late 1850s and applied for citizenship in 1861.[15] Historian John B. Richards has astutely observed that it appears that those individuals who would become early members of First Baptist Church were Baptists when they arrived in Victoria because, according to the local press, "No baptism by immersion was held in British Columbia until 1877."[16] It appears that those early Baptists initially had little interest in forming their own church. One possible explanation comes from a journal entry from an Anglican minister in the area, Edward Cridge, who wrote that the Black arrivals "did not intend to establish a distinct Church [sic] organization at Victoria but to join some Ch[urch] already in existence here."[17] Simply put, when the Black pioneers arrived, they did not find a Baptist church. As various historians have noted, Baptists were relative latecomers to the western region of Canada. Indeed, Baptists from other parts of the country did not formally begin mission work west of the Ontario border until 1873, when they sent their first missionary to Winnipeg.[18] As such, it appears as though Black immigrants to Victoria would have filtered into various other churches in the region.

It would not be until nearly two decades after the arrival of the Pioneers that the Baptists in Victoria assembled and formally organized a church. In March 1875, Alexander Clyde, a White arrival from Stratford, Ontario and a Baptist, published a notice in the local newspaper that read: "All the Baptists in and round [sic] Victoria are requested to meet at the house of A. Clyde . . . on Friday, April 2d at 7 p.m. for the purpose of making arrangements toward organizing a Baptist Church. Come one, come all."[19] Similar notices appeared in the newspaper over the following year.[20] By early 1876, the assembled Baptists decided to take the next step

---

15. "Applications for Citizenship" in *Daily British Colonist* (December 4, 1861), 3; and Richards, "Baptists in British Columbia," 48–49.

16. Richards, "Baptists in British Columbia," 49n29. For a report of that baptismal service, see "Baptismal Service" in *Daily British Colonist* (February 23, 1877), 3.

17. This was from the personal journal of Edward Cridge, an Anglican minister, as quoted in Kilian, *Go Do Some Great Thing*, 30. Richards ("Baptists in British Columbia," 45–46) opines that those Baptists who arrived likely joined the Congregational church, though he admits that this is conjectural.

18. Heath, Friesen, and Murray, *Baptists in Canada*, 47. For another representative example of a study that comments on the Baptists' late arrival in the west, see Renfree, *Heritage and Horizon*, 168.

19. "Notice" in *Daily British Colonist* (March 31, 1875), 2.

20. See *Daily British Colonist* (August 7, 1875), 3; *Daily British Colonist* (August 13, 1875), 3.

in formally organizing by inviting a pastor, and in March of that year they called the Rev. William Carnes from Ontario as their pastor.²¹ With a collection of interested supporters and a pastor, First Baptist Church of Victoria organized on May 3, 1876.

The list of charter members was divided almost equally down racial lines. White signatories were Alexander Clyde, Fanny Clyde, Alfred Oldershaw, Thomas Mathews, Caleb Bishop, William Carnes, and John Sluggett; while Black signatories were Fielding Spotts, Julia Spotts, Maddison F. Bailey, Mary Bailey, Thomas Pierre, Ann Pierre, Sally Page, and Augustus Christopher. Although there were more Black members than White ones, each of the earliest officers were White men: Carnes was the pastor; Bishop, Clyde, and Sluggett served as the first deacons; Oldershaw was the clerk; and Mathews was the treasurer.²² This racial and gender leadership dynamic was not necessarily unique for the era, but it nevertheless provides insight into the character and policies of this young church. Because the closest Baptist church in Canada was in Winnipeg, in September of that year the infant church in Victoria instead opted to affiliate with their coreligionists south of the border in the Puget Sound Baptist Association, which subsequently became the Baptist Association of Puget Sound and British Columbia.²³

Almost as soon as the church formally organized, they encountered difficulties. In January 1877, they completed construction on a new church building, for which they amassed a debt of $6,000 with an interest rate set at ten percent.²⁴ With help from Baptists south of the border, they succeeded in paying down about half of their debt; however, even half proved to be a princely sum for this largely self-sustaining church. Members made several other attempts to pay down this debt, including hosting community events and appealing to Baptists in central Canada for help, but each proved unsuccessful.²⁵

21. See *Daily British Colonist* (March 19, 1876), 3; *Daily British Colonist* (June 9, 1876), 3; *Daily British Colonist* (July 13, 1876), 3.

22. The membership and officer lists are from McClaurin, *Pioneering*, 244–45.

23. McClaurin, *Pioneering*, 246.

24. McClaurin, *Pioneering*, 245. For the local press' evaluation of the new building, see "Opening of the Baptist Church Edifice" in *Daily British Colonist* (January 26, 1877), 3; *Daily British Colonist* (January 23, 1877), 3.

25. For example, in late Fall 1877, they hosted a "Tea and Entertainment" event, which required a one-dollar admission fee and optional donations. They made $242 from the event (see *Daily British Colonist* (November 27, 1877), 2; and *Daily British Colonist* (December 16, 1877), 3. On their appeal to the central region, see W. S. Freed,

At the same time, the church struggled to retain a pastor for any extended period. Apparent and unspecified hostilities between Carnes and several members of the church had triggered the pastor's resignation in May 1877, a little over a year after his arrival.[26] His successors—again, all White men—each had equally brief pastorates: J. H. Teale (September 1877–December 1878); George Everton (February 1879–February 1880); and T. Spanswich (acting, June 1880–August 1880). In a letter to the *Canadian Baptist*, the author explained that the church's significant debt and the high costs of living meant that they were unable to pay a pastor's salary, which had spiralled into further problems: because they had been unable to keep a pastor, their numbers had dropped, which in turn meant that their collections had also dropped.[27] It was not until the pastorate of Joseph Beaven (May 1881–June 1883), a Baptist from California, that the church had a stable pastor for at least two years; however, his pastoral charge did not begin until after the church had suffered a split along racial lines.[28]

A CHURCH DIVIDED

March 1881 was a pivotal time for this young church. That month, John Clapp Baker, the president of the Missionary Board of the North Pacific Coast Convention, travelled to Victoria to visit the congregation. Baker had been a close friend to Baptists in British Columbia practically since the church's conception. He had visited them in early 1877 and was responsible for raising at least half of the funds needed to pay off the debt they had incurred by the construction of their building. As the church had been without a full-time pastor for over a year, the initial reason for his visit in 1881 was "to see if the condition and prospects of the church were such that I could recommend the settlement of a pastor."[29] Finding the church in its dire financial situation, he noted that "both the white and colored members of the church had borne alike the unusually large expense which the church has been obliged to meet in carrying forward

"Appeal from British Columbia" in *Canadian Baptist* (January 6, 1881), 3.

26. Letter to J. C. Baker (May 7, 1877) (published in Baker, *Baptist History*, 260).

27. W. S. Freed, "Appeal from British Columbia" in *Canadian Baptist* (January 6, 1881), 3.

28. The above list of pastors is from the church's old website, www.fbcvictoria.wordpress.com (accessed 9 March 2021).

29. J. C. Baker, Address to First Baptist Church of Victoria, 31 March 1881, as printed in Baker, *Baptist History*, 263.

its work to the present time and refocused his efforts on settling what he saw as tensions exacerbated by the multiracial composition of the church."[30]

Baker's report and address to the church, and his reflections on the matter, were published as part of a larger collection, *Baptist History of the North Pacific Coast*, which went to press the year of his death.[31] It was Baker's belief that division upon racial lines was inevitable: "the union of the two classes in one church could not exist for many years; but it was hoped and believed that it would continue until the church had grown to such numbers and ability that, when the change did come, there would be a brotherly division, and each would be ready and able to take up a separate work marked by the color line."[32] He believed that difficulties within the church were a reflection of racial tensions within Victoria in general. He summed: "the church had become divided on the color line, a division which for years had been growing not only in the church, but also in the city generally."[33]

Operating under the belief that the church had effectively "divided on the color line," Baker recommended that the church form a six-person committee consisting of three White members and three Black members, ostensibly to solve the perceived racial tensions within the church. The White members were Caleb Bishop, Alexander Clyde, and A. J. Clyde; and Black members were Thomas Pierre, Madison Bailey, and Fortune Richard. According to Baker's records, on March 31, 1881, the committee presented the following recommendation to the church:

> Your committee, appointed to recommend a plan for the more successful prosecution of the work of the First Baptist Church of Victoria, taking all the circumstances of the case into consideration, and the present embarrassment of our work, would respectfully recommend that the entire business and management of the church be given into the hands of either the colored members or the white members as the church shall decide by vote.[34]

30. J. C. Baker, Address to First Baptist Church of Victoria, 31 March 1881, as printed in Baker, *Baptist History*, 263.

31. Baker, *Baptist History*, 262–63.

32. Baker, *Baptist History*, 260.

33. Baker, *Baptist History*, 262.

34. First Baptist Church of Victoria Committee Report, 31 March 1881, as printed in Baker, *Baptist History*, 262.

After receiving this recommendation, Baker addressed the church. From his perspective, "there seemed to be little, if any, probability that you could [work harmoniously] in the future on account of race prejudice on the one hand, and race sensitiveness on the other."[35] He believed that following the committee's recommendation had several benefits, including that it would "draw to the support of the Baptist cause the entire Baptist element in the city, both white and colored."[36] The church voted ultimately to hand operations over to the White members.[37]

In addition to Baker's records, the most detailed account of these events came from the pen of one of the Black members of the six-person committee, Fortune Richard, who published his account in the local press in January 1882. In his mid-70s at the time he published his report, Richard had been a member of the Pioneer Committee and, as noted above, had been central to several high-profile episodes of racial discrimination in Victoria in the past. His desire to publish his account of what happened at the Baptist church was triggered by the publication of an article in the November 1881 edition of an American-based newspaper, the *Baptist Beacon*. While the article to which he was responding is no longer extant, contextual clues suggest that it had come from the pen of Baker, who, in addition to his work with the Missionary Board of the North Pacific Coast Convention, had also served as the editor of the *Baptist Beacon*.[38]

---

35. J. C. Baker address to First Baptist Church of Victoria, 31 March 1881, printed in Baker, *Baptist History*, 262.

36. J. C. Baker, Address to First Baptist Church of Victoria, 31 March 1881, as printed in Baker, *Baptist History of the North Pacific Coast*, 263.

37. Unfortunately, the extant documents do not outline the exact voting percentages. Richards ("Baptists in British Columbia," 57) suggests that the vote was tied between Black members and White members and that Baker offered the tiebreaker; however, I have been unable to locate evidence that this was the case. According to Baker's records (*Baptist History of the North Pacific Coast*, 264), after the committee's report, "the management [of the church] was offered to the colored people; but they were not willing to accept it, and it was finally given in charge [sic] of the white members." The report does not clarify why the Black members rejected the operation of the church. There are several possible explanations here. First, as explored in greater detail below, the Black members had a deep distrust of Baker and did not believe they would be treated fairly in this exchange. Second, the Black members were unwilling to assume the substantial debt that the church had incurred in its first few years of operation. Third, it is conceivable that the Black members objected to dividing the church in the way Baker suggested. Fortune Richard's recollection of the events, discussed below, provide some insight into each of these possibilities, though none are definitive.

38. Richards ("Baptists in British Columbia," 61) likewise agrees that it was likely Baker.

From Richard's perspective, that article had been published with the purpose of using the situation in Victoria as evidence that "white and colored races cannot harmonize in the Church." This observation, he continued sarcastically, "entitled [the author] to some suitable recognition for his new discovery."[39]

No matter the occasion that prompted Richard's article, his account suggests that the Black members had a different perspective than Baker. When the church called Baker, Richard noted, none of the members had discussed withdrawing or forming a separate church. Yet, when he arrived, Richard remembered him to have said:

> I have found things in a worse condition than when I was here last. The Church is laboring under a very heavy debt, in fact almost too heavy to carry. I find, also, prejudice inside the Church and prejudice without. *All the whites that would join are already within; we shall get no more.* I have a better opportunity of knowing public sentiment than most of you have. Now, before I could or would recommend to the Missionary Board the expenditure of any money on the church one party or the other must take the entire business management of the church.[40]

The image that Richard presents appears more like forced segregation at the hand of an American interloper. Moreover, his article reveals a deep distrust of Baker among the Black congregants. According to Richard, Baker offered the Black members a mere $300 to build a new church in the city, which they rejected because "the people knew too well what value to attach to his promises."[41]

Returning to the article published in the *Baptist Beacon*, Richard expressed his outrage over the fact that the author had apparently used the events in Victoria as a case study to discourage other multiracial churches. By holding up this "ungodly course" of racial divisions, noted Richard, the author was "endeavoring to make others believe that the

---

39. Fortune Richard, "The Colored Question in the Baptist Church, Victoria" in *Daily British Colonist* (January 28, 1882), 2. The article itself was actually a paid advertisement. It is unclear why this was the case. Historian John B. Richards cites this article briefly in passing, though he does not engage with its contents (see Richards, "Baptists in British Columbia," 61).

40. As quoted in Fortune Richard, "Colored Question in the Baptist Church, Victoria" in *Daily British Colonist* (January 28, 1882), 2 (emphasis mine).

41. Fortune Richard, "Colored Question in the Baptist Church, Victoria" in *Daily British Colonist* (January 28, 1882), 2.

two races cannot harmonize."[42] As he approached the conclusion of his article, Richard posed rhetorically: "what crime have the colored people committed to merit this unprovoked attack? Their only fault is that it has pleased God to make us of a different colour."[43]

Richard identified Baker's proposal to divide the church along racial lines as an "absurd idea" because "there are a number of Churches in Victoria, and in almost all of them . . . colored members are treated kindly; in none are they regarded as a hindrance to persons joining."[44] That, obviously, had not fully been Richard's experience in the Baptist church. Contrasting the other churches in the city with his own, he explained: "In some they are on the official board, and in others they hold various positions . . . the Baptist Church in Victoria is the only church tolerating proscription on account of race." Finally, he concluded,

> from an early date in the establishment of this Church there have been and are yet a few of its members afflicted with the disease known as 'negrophobia.' It generally attacks the poor and ignorant, who have nothing but the colour of their skin to boast of; and it is almost always fatal to weak minds; but on the well-balanced minds of the truly great it has no effect.[45]

Richard's assessment suggests that he believed racial harmony was possible, as demonstrated in the many churches in Victoria, but that some of the Baptists had fallen prey to racism's pernicious sting—a tension that Baker saw and acted on. As noted above, Richard had personally experienced discrimination in Victoria due to the colour of his skin—and, in the end, although the churches were relatively "free from caste,"[46] it obviously did not mean that they were free from all racism.

---

42. Fortune Richard, "Colored Question in the Baptist Church, Victoria" in *Daily British Colonist* (January 28, 1882), 2.

43. Fortune Richard, "Colored Question in the Baptist Church, Victoria" in *Daily British Colonist* (January 28, 1882), 2. The two different spellings for "colour/color" appear here as they do in the original.

44. Fortune Richard, "Colored Question in the Baptist Church, Victoria" in *Daily British Colonist* (January 28, 1882), 2.

45. Fortune Richard, "Colored Question in the Baptist Church, Victoria" in *Daily British Colonist* (January 28, 1882), 2.

46. "The Colored Inhabitants of Vancouver Island" in *Liberator* (April 15, 1864), 31–32.

AFTERMATH

Following the decision of the church vote, the White members took over operations and the Black members left. Upon losing half of its membership, unsurprisingly, the church's finances did not significantly improve. In January 1883, they were forced to sell their building.[47] After meeting in community halls for several months, the church dissolved on Sunday, June 3, 1883. Yet, that was not the end of the story. Only a few days later, on Tuesday, June 5, 1883, many of the former members who had been involved in the life of the first Baptist church gathered and organized a new congregation, which they named Calvary Baptist Church.[48] On the fiftieth anniversary of the beginning of Baptist work in British Columbia, they wrote that this new church "arose Pheonix-like from the ashes" of the original church.[49]

Calvary Baptist Church was not an exact copy of the previous iteration. Learning from the past, the newly reorganized church added a statement against racial discrimination into their covenant: "We express our willingness to unite in forming a Baptist church with the understanding that no distinction shall ever be made in respect to race, color or class."[50] It is unclear how many of the Black former members joined the new church. One such member was Fielding Spotts, a member of the Pioneer Committee and a charter member of the First Baptist Church. Historian John B. Richards notes that Spotts' decision to remain in the Baptist fold "illustrated the triumph of religious conviction over social pressure," before adding that many former Black members "drifted from Baptist affiliations" or "gave up church-going altogether."[51]

CONCLUSION

In discussing the historiography of Black Baptists in North America, James M. Washington once identified an issue he called "the burden of Baptist historians." In sum, he noted that historians must discern between what is "merely interesting" and what is "vital." Yet, more often than not, continued Washington, they have determined that the Black experience

---

47. "Sale of the Baptist Church" in *Daily British Colonist* (January 13, 1883), 3.

48. This church has since changed its name back to "First Baptist Church."

49. "History of Baptist Church Reviewed at Convention," *Victoria Daily Times*, 24 June 1926, 16.

50. As quoted in McClaurin, *Pioneering*, 248.

51. Richards, "Baptists in British Columbia," 59.

is not vital to the story.⁵² Intentional or not, overlooking these important stories results in gaps within the literature, a sanitized narrative, or an incomplete picture. To that end, this chapter is a preliminary attempt at locating and identifying the Black experience in the early history of Baptists in British Columbia. As Black settlers sought to escape racial discrimination in the United States, they found that it followed them to their new home—and, as Baptists soon learned, even into their pews. To be sure, this was not a specifically *Baptist* problem. In fact, the available evidence suggests that churches (Baptist included) were more open to racial diversity than society at large; yet, even so, the experience within the First Baptist Church of Victoria suggests that churches faced many of the same issues.

There is significant space to expand this narrative. One wonders, for example, what each of those Black members did after withdrawing from the church. Some, such as Fielding Spotts, eventually returned to the Baptist community; however, many others, such as Fortune Richard, have all but disappeared from the narrative. While historians are at the mercy of the available sources, it is important that we do not overlook these events and people as *merely interesting* details and characters. Stories like the schism at the First Baptist Church of Victoria are indeed *vital*, even if they are uncomfortable.

BIBLIOGRAPHY

Primary Sources

Monographs

Baker, J. C. *Baptist History of the North Pacific Coast with Special Reference to Western Washington, British Columbia, and Alaska.* Philadelphia: American Baptist Publication Society, 1912.

Mayne, R. C. *Four Years in British Columbia and Vancouver Island: An Account of their Forests, Rivers, Coasts, Gold Fields, and Resources for Colonisation.* London: John Murray, 1862.

Newspapers and Magazines

Canadian Baptist (Toronto, ON), 1881.
Daily British Colonist (Victoria, BC), 1861, 1875–1877, 1882.
The Liberator (Boston, MA), 1864.

---

52. Washington, "Baptist Amnesia," 53. The preceding quotes are from the same source.

Secondary Sources

Edwards, Malcolm. "The War of Complexional Distinction: Blacks in Gold Rush California and British Columbia." *California Historical Quarterly* 56 (1977) 34–45.

Fitch, E. R. *The Baptists of Canada: A History of their Progress and Achievements.* Toronto: Baptist Young People's Union of Ontario and Quebec, 1911.

Foner, Philip S. "Colored Inhabitants of Vancouver Island," *BC Studies* 8 (1970–1971) 29–33.

Harris, J. E. *The Baptist Union of Western Canada: A Centennial History, 1873–1973.* Saint John, NB: Lingley, n.d.

Heath, Gordon L., Dallas Friesen, and Taylor Murray. *Baptists in Canada: Their History and Polity.* McMaster Ministry Studies Series 5. Eugene, OR: Pickwick, 2020.

Kilian, Crawford. *Go Do Some Great Thing: The Black Pioneers of British Columbia.* Madeira Park, BC: Harbour, 2016.

McClaurin, C. C. *Pioneering in Western Canada: A Story of the Baptists.* Calgary, AB: C. C. McLaurin, 1939.

McDonough, Mark A. *The Francis Richard Family: From French Nobility to Florida Pioneers, 1300–1900.* n.p., 2010.

Pilton, James William. "Negro Settlement in British Columbia, 1858–1871." MA thesis, University of British Columbia, 1951.

Richards, John Byron. "Baptists in British Columbia: A Struggle to Maintain 'Sectarianism.'" MA thesis, University of British Columbia, 1964.

Renfree, Harry A. *Heritage and Horizon: The Baptist Story in Canada.* Eugene, OR: Wipf and Stock, 2007.

Thompson, Margaret E. *The Baptist Story in Western Canada.* Calgary, AB: Baptist Union of Western Canada, 1974.

Washington, James M. "Baptist Amnesia: Why is There no Tombstone for the Black Baptist Tradition?" *American Baptist Quarterly* 26 (2007) 44–62.

11

AUBA Mothering and Maternal Activism in Education

KÉSA MUNROE-ANDERSON

ANY ACKNOWLEDGEMENT OF NOVA Scotia as the birthplace of African presence in Canada is incomplete without recognizing the organization that has served as the flagship, the backbone, and the very heartbeat of historic African Nova Scotian (ANS) communities: the African United Baptist Association of Nova Scotia (AUBA).[1] With its first church planted on April 14, 1832, by ex-enslaved Rev. Richard Preston, prior to the British Slavery Abolition Act of 1833 and before Emancipation Day of August 1, 1834, the legacy of the AUBA is a remarkable testament of the resistance, survival, and resilience of ANS people. Despite being born into and forced to develop within a pervasive climate of anti-Black systemic and institutionalized racism, this organization is, arguably, the most influential ANS organization in history. Fundamental to the establishment of the AUBA as an association of churches in 1854 is the tenacity and audacity of African people described as "unlettered, unprepared to enter a free society and without resources," but whose faith in God, self-determined identity, and fervent spirituality fostered an institutional spiritual centre of community support, development, and growth.[2]

---

1. The AUBA was first named the African Baptist Association (ABA) at the point of its establishment in 1854 and later became the African United Baptist Association (AUBA)

2. Oliver, *Brief History of the Colored Baptists*, 15.

Defiantly, up from the great afflictions of slavery, the AUBA's churches emerged as beacons of hope, opportunity, advancement, resources, and agency necessary for the knitting together of strong communities. The Association's legacy as the mother voice, hands and feet of activism, the nurturing body, and the moral, protective, and innovative intellect of its people is reflected in the instrumental way the institution organized and supported formal and informal education and learning opportunities for ANS communities. Therefore, the AUBA's efforts towards educational advancement for ANSs must be heralded as central to the development of ANS communities both historically and contemporarily, with attention turned towards the influence and impact of its women and their collaborative role with the organization's men in supporting these efforts.

Not unlike other church associations of the time, the AUBA has a tradition of predominantly male formal leadership beginning with its founder Father Richard Preston and forerunners including David George and continuing to the present day. However, this legacy of male leadership should not preclude the significant leadership roles played by its oft under-sung female leaders. Women like Dr. Pearline Oliver served valiantly with the AUBA's men as church and community builders and civil rights activists fighting for equality in education and employment opportunities for ANSs. Sylvia Hamilton[3] highlights the invisibility of women like Violet King and Phillis George, the wives of esteemed ministers Boston King and David George, whose lives history has obliterated. Likewise, we too should question the silence on the life of Rev. Preston's wife Mary, who is hardly mentioned in the history books that speak of her husband. It is important that we *write in* those ANS women whose names, contributions, and voices have been *written out* of history.

In the representation of pastors serving the pastorate of its member churches, however, the AUBA's all male leadership trend ended on November 23, 1996, when Rev. Tracey Rebecca Grosse of Cherry Brook became the first woman minister to be ordained in the AUBA. Though a historic first, the dates of Rev. Tracey Grosse's ordination and that of Dr. Pearline Oliver's induction as the first female Moderator of the AUBA twenty years earlier are by no means indicative of the AUBA women's leadership capacity. AUBA women, though not given the opportunity to serve as pastors, moderators and in many other roles as AUBA leaders prior to this time, "numerically and financially"—particularly through

---

3. Hamilton, "Our Mothers Grand and Great," 87.

the Ladies Auxiliary—were seen as "the strength and backbone of the Association."[4] Recognizing the significance of Black women's contributions to Black churches, as well as the supportive role played by the Black church in the lives and families of Black women, ANS human rights activist and journalist Dr. Carrie Best declares: "Long before there was a Women's Liberation Movement as such, the Black female was involved in a death struggle for physical and mental survival both for herself and her family. Her strength has been the Black church, and the strength of the Black church has always been the Black woman."[5] The relationship between the AUBA and ANS women was a symbiotic one with women benefitting mutually from the respect and dignity offered them through the AUBA and its churches, an acknowledgement not received beyond their communities.[6]

Arguably, the AUBA would have failed had it not been for the leadership of ANS women. This is ironic since the Association was thirty-seven years old before the names of women appeared as delegates. Rather, it was "the cooperative efforts of *women and men*" that "made the ultimate progress possible" for this body.[7] In 1913, the Association passed a motion asking each church to form a Women's Missionary Society. Then, in 1916, the AUBA asked all churches to send a minimum of one woman to the 1917 Association, the year the Ladies Auxiliary was founded. Praised as "perhaps the brightest gem in the work of the Association," the Ladies Auxiliary was seen as responsible for exemplary support of their churches, elevating the "prestige" of ANSs and, therefore, as "worthy of emulation."[8] Such developments demonstrate the AUBA leaders' recognition of and value for the strong leadership contributions ANS women offered their communities and this organization.

Throughout the AUBA's history, the vital leadership of women to orchestrating and supporting educational advancement in numerically female-dominated congregations by promoting it as central to community development cannot be overstated. This chapter examines the Association's history through the Afrocentric, Black Feminist perspective of mothering through female-male leadership as critical to the educational

---

4. Pachai, *Nova Scotia Black Experience*, 188.
5. Best, *That Lonesome Road*, 172.
6. Hamilton, "Women at the Well," 194.
7. Pachai, *Nova Scotia Black Experience*, 188 (emphasis mine).
8. 68th Annual Meeting Minutes (1921).

development and success of ANS communities from the time of its inception to the present day. It argues that the strength of the AUBA as an organization, particularly in attaining its educational development goals, is dependent upon its mothering of ANS communities and exemplary maternal activism demonstrated by its women leaders. Without these leadership efforts, the AUBA, and by extension ANS communities, would not have survived.

THE AUBA AS "MOTHER"

As an organization, the AUBA has consistently exemplified and embodied the role of "African mother" in ANS communities, nurturing the community's leadership and legacy in education by passing on knowledge, advocacy for and access to education from one generation to the next. So intrinsic was the centrality of mothers and motherhood to the fabric of the AUBA that the organization voted in 1854 to name Cornwallis Street Baptist—Father Preston's first church—the "Mother Church" of the AUBA.[9] Prior to this, Father Preston underscored the significant role of mothers to families, particularly in African and African diasporic cultures, as he travelled to Nova Scotia from Virginia in search of his mother whom he was told had also fled to Nova Scotia. Father Preston found his mother at the first door at which he knocked in the Preston Township. When his mother opened the door, she recognized him because of the birthmark on his face.

The redemptive story of Father Preston's reunion with his mother demonstrates that the interconnectedness between African children and their mothers, in this case a male child and his mother, was indestructible. Attempts to destroy and defy the value of motherhood through slave masters separating and selling children of African women to other slave owners, and the double punishment of these slave owners having sons whip their mothers during slavery, though traumatic and physically, psychologically, and emotionally horrific, were not successful. Though "forced to reproduce the Western empire," their bodies ravaged and raped, and children stolen, these African women managed to embody the resilience of Africa, their "material and metaphoric mother" and the "ground from which Black women emerge."[10] The AUBA is a testament that even such vicious acts could not diminish the centrality of mothers

9. Pachai, *Nova Scotia Black Experience*, 120; Oliver, *Brief History*, 24.
10. Davis, "Embodying," 154.

and motherhood to ANS life, organizations, and communities. The significance of *mother* to the AUBA's nurturing of leadership and legacy in education for the ANS community is crucial to its ability to resist the oppression of anti-Black racism and for ANS women, the interlocking violence of sexism, misogyny, and anti-Black racism.

Unlike Eurocentric feminisms, African feminism emphasizes the "centrality of motherhood in African households and family organizations and the agency and power of mothers as the source of solidarity."[11] Interrelationships, interconnectedness, and interdependence are promoted and valued between women, men, and children as well as between the living and nonliving within these African communities. Similarly, African American and African Nova Scotian feminist understandings of othermothering and Black motherhood are reflected in the resistance and collective Black women's consciousness of the AUBA, as those assuming the mother-role were seen as responsible for providing education, social, political awareness to their biological children, and the children of the entire ANS community.[12] Bernard's articulation of Black motherhood as a contradictory possibility of being either a "site of oppression, or an opportunity for creativity, empowerment, and social action" was pronounced throughout the AUBA's work and history.[13] Through the efforts of both ANS men and women in dire conditions, this organization's self-determination, and work towards liberation via the path of survival provided critical results. They developed knowledge responsive to their need to build relationships, to heal themselves and their communities from the traumas of enslavement and racist oppressions, and to foster transformative change through education.[14] Exemplifying what Paris defines as "survival theology," the AUBA as mother-figure made the "maintenance, preservation, and enhancement of meaningful life" for ANSs its primary concern. The AUBA was focused on survival: "Making a way out of no way," "keeping body and soul together," "Being alive and kicking," and "remaining on this side of the grave" which were all folk sayings proving their daily "defeat of suffering and social injustice, the end of which is death."[15] According to Black feminism, "those who live in

---

11. Chilisa, *Indigenous Research Methodologies*, 261.
12. Collins, *Black Feminist Thought*; Bernard et al., "'She Who Learns Teaches,'" 68.
13. Bernard and Bernard, "Passing the Torch," 47.
14. Chilisa, *Indigenous Research Methodologies*, 276.
15. Paris, *Moral, Political and Religious Significance of the Black Church*, 21.

a particular situation are best situated to speak, educate, and transform that situation."[16] The women and men of the AUBA proved this first voice way to be most appropriate and effective in providing education to their communities, especially since such opportunities and basic rights would have been ignored otherwise due to anti-Black racism.

As the umbilical cord and lifeline of ANS communities, it would make sense that the AUBA's influence in every aspect of community life would be significant. According to Pachai and Bishop, throughout ANS history, "no other institution has had the pervading influence of the black Baptist church."[17] However, little has been written about the crucial role these churches, their leadership, and membership have played in championing formal and informal education for ANS communities in the face of egregious systemic, anti-Black racism. As the oldest ANS organization, and the precursor for numerous other ANS organizations since its inception, the AUBA has demonstrated stalwart advocacy, provision of academic and leadership development, opportunities, and programming, and other tangible means of educational support filling gaps in services to community. This support was granted to ANSs without partiality whether they were baptized members of an AUBA church or not because "the church belonged to the community," was "the embodiment of the community" and, therefore, this organization and ANS communities were inseparable and indistinguishable.[18] The AUBA was a unifying force for these communities, serving as the "institutional centre" for cultural identity with which everyone in the community could identify, emphasizing the significance of Black leadership, "black identity, black freedom, and black independence" as critical qualities for ANSs success.[19] These four core components formed the foundation for the AUBA's value and advocacy for better educational opportunities for ANS people.

THE AUBA AS EDUCATION ADVOCATE

That education was a priority for the AUBA was cemented into this organization's foundation early on. Peter E. MacKerrow, who wrote the only

16. Brigham and Parris, "Black Women's Africentric and Feminist Leadership Voices," 75.

17. Pachai and Bishop, *Historic Black Nova Scotia*, 19.

18. Paris, *Moral, Political and Religious Significance of the Black Church*, 16; Pachai and Bishop, *Historic Black Nova Scotia*.

19. Paris, *Moral, Political and Religious Significance of the Black Church*, 16; Abucar, *Struggle for Development*, 46; Pachai and Bishop, *Historic Black Nova Scotia*, 26.

existing history of the first 100 years of the AUBA, and who served as its clerk and secretary-treasurer (1876–1906), indicated that it was the aim of the AUBA's founders that it "result in great spiritual benefit *and educational improvement*" for ANS communities.[20] Paris too supports this view that the Association's first course of action towards helping their people survive was through the educational and economic development of ANS communities.[21] Association leaders raised the matter of illiteracy as a major concern during the quarter period of 1879–1904, describing it as a time when the "evil" of illiteracy was "valiantly fought" by the Association.[22] The writer expounds: "It was to be expected that a people so recently delivered from slavery where laws prohibited them acquiring an education, would be handicapped for years. They were passing through an age when the theme song was 'If you educate an [sic] Negro, you unfit him for a slave.'"[23] MacKerrow too reminds his readers that many of the former enslaved African people who fled the United States from enslavement to Nova Scotia could not read because learning to read "was considered a great crime by the slave-holder."[24] Those who converted to the Baptist faith, could only do so by talking to God themselves in the plantation fields, as they would not have been permitted to read the Bible even if they had secretly learned to read.[25]

MacKerrow compares Richard Preston to African American abolitionist Frederick Douglas, as he, like Douglas, determined to learn to read and write despite the threat of harm he risked experiencing for breaking the law. Preston saw education as a pathway to "Go Forward" as was his motto, clearly demonstrating how the values of the Association's founding Father were aligned with and influenced this organization's goals from its inception.[26] Preston took this motto further when Father John Burton and the congregation of the First African Church encouraged him to attain a formal education to improve his skills as a minister and to seek ordination in England. Preston pursued both in 1831 and returned to Nova Scotia more equipped to lead the African Baptist Church

---

20. Oliver, *Brief History of the Colored Baptists*, 36 (emphasis mine).
21. Oliver, *Brief History of the Colored Baptists*, 36.
22. Oliver, *Brief History of the Colored Baptists*, 34.
23. Oliver, *Brief History of the Colored Baptists*, 34.
24. MacKerrow, *Brief History*, 18.
25. MacKerrow, *Brief History*, 18.
26. MacKerrow, *Brief History*, 19.

located on Cornwallis Street in Halifax, and the community of churches across Nova Scotia that would eventually become the AUBA.

The value of formal education was upheld by the AUBA's Education Committee established to oversee matters regarding the education of ANS communities and, by default the Association itself. Committed to sustaining this legacy, the Education Committee sought to have the value of education and its significance exemplified by its ministers for their membership. This committee encouraged all its ministers in the early days to gain formal education and training to complement their talents: "The education committee struck first at our pulpits, for while the early ministers were gifted, their lack of training handicapped their leadership."[27] Simultaneously, the AUBA's Education Committee advocated for ANS access to schools in their community and to proper education in these schools: "The education committee struck also at the communities and wherever schools remained closed or were improperly run they attacked with the spoken and written word."[28] Hamilton also notes the influence of AUBA leaders on efforts to improve education for ANSs in groups external to the Association: "Church leaders were also community leaders who championed the struggle for equality for the entire community. The African Education Committee (ca.1880), which petitioned the provincial legislature to eliminate racially segregated schools, had key African Baptist church officials at its core.[29]

"Throughout the Association's history, education has always been front and centre on its agenda. In 1953, Rev. William Pearly Oliver, clerk and compiler of the AUBA, in his "Centennial Message" to the Association admonished his fellow members that "greater advantage must be taken of the available forms of education and training" to improve the earning power within ANS communities, and therefore the Association.[30] Oliver underscores the vital connection between education and economic survival, as education was seen as the key to economic thriving not only for some ANSs but for entire communities. Hence, consistently throughout the Association's work various committees emphasized the significance of all membership, and hence all ANS communities, doing their part to take advantage of educational opportunities; and preached accountability

27. Oliver, *Brief History of the Colored Baptist*, 34.
28. Oliver, *Brief History of the Colored Baptist*, 34.
29. Hamilton, "Women at the Well," 194.
30. Oliver, *Brief History of the Colored Baptist*, 14–15.

to government to provide equal opportunities for ANS children to gain a public-school education. Evidence of this is seen throughout Association Minutes with the *Ways and Means Committee* and *Education Committee* reporting and calling often for the AUBA's continued advocacy to secure better education for their children throughout the province. Specifically, a 1917 Report on Education urged parents to send their children to the public school and "if there is a School in your community to see that a competent teacher be obtained and kept for an indefinite time."[31] Noting the systemic racial discrimination evident in the detestable neglect in education for ANS children particularly in rural Nova Scotia, the Ways and Means Committee stated:

> [W]e believe that there is a serious lack of interest in this important matter. The Laws of the Province make it obligatory that every child of school age be compelled to attend Public School ten months in the year, until he or she passes the seventh grade. If this were done there would be a noticeable improvement in the intellectual life of our people. The fault in many instances seems to be with the various school sections, which do not put sufficient stress upon the value of education to make the necessary provisions for this most important work.[32]

Evident during this time, with a strong connection to the legacy of slavery, was the low societal and teacher expectations of ANS learners an ideology that doomed them to maintain their "place" in society as lower class, supporting the status quo. A constant refrain of Association meetings was their activism and encouragement of their members to join in the fight for adequate school buildings with qualified and fairly paid teachers.[33]

The struggle for education was always a church and community affair. As early as 1820, ANSs who came as members of the Freed Blacks from the War of 1812 and settled in the Preston Township between 1812 and 1825 "petitioned the government to establish a school and place of worship."[34] Community members housed the teacher for the community's school in their home. However, since the government placed the responsibility of supplying a school on each ANS community's shoulders,

---

31. 64th Annual Meeting Minutes (1918), 29.
32. 64th Annual Meeting Minutes (1918), 16.
33. 64th Annual Meeting Minutes (1918); 65th Annual Meeting Minutes (1919).
34. Abucar, *Struggle for Development*, 10.

the AUBA churches played a major role in supporting the education of its members. As ANSs were afforded few opportunities to earn an adequate living and obtain formal education, and many of them lived in poverty or on humble means, to place this burden of providing their own education was clearly a tactic of withholding education from them. Nevertheless, the AUBA found a way around these tactics. For example, the Association "forged a link between the church and school" in the Preston Township, and the leadership of the church oversaw education in the Prestons (also known as the Preston Township including East Preston, North Preston, and Cherry Brook/Lake Loon communities) for more than three generations.[35] Additionally, in Beechville, the community's one-room school became dilapidated and was eventually replaced by a brand-new school in 1949 through the efforts of Dr. W. P. Oliver, then pastor of Beechville United Baptist Church, and others of the church and community.[36] In fact, the land on which the new school was constructed was donated by that AUBA church. The same was the case in Upper Hammonds Plains where the one room schoolhouse was built on property belonging to Emmanuel Baptist Church. Stories of delipidated and unfit school-building structures were common for ANS communities, and another example of the lack of care and concern provided to their learners by government officials.

WOMEN OF THE AUBA AND EDUCATION LEADERSHIP THROUGH MATERNAL ACTIVISM

The AUBA's women played an instrumental role of *maternal activism* in education development work through the Association and for the wider ANS communities. Although their leadership contributions to education have been clouded by historical omissions giving the impression that this work was solely led by the AUBA's men, such a consideration could not be farthest from the truth. As Mahon explains:

> Black women were often excluded from traditional public spheres of activism like civil rights leadership organizing as well as the documentation of those movements. Circumventing these gendered restrictions to the public sphere of activism, Black women took to organizing in private spaces. Refusing the historical erasure of Black women's civil rights activism in Nova

---

35. Abucar, *Struggle for Development*, 11.
36. Evans and Tynes, *Telling the Truth*, 21.

Scotia involves understanding women's activist roles as a maternalistic form of nonviolent direct action.[37]

Mahon refers to the limiting effects of this exclusion of ANS women's activism as the "historical amnesia silencing women's contributions to ... civil rights struggles."[38] Although this author may have been referring exclusively to more recent exclusion of AUBA women, the same can be said of their historic invisibility. It is important to note that even in the institution of the Black church where Black women were said to have received dignity and respect, ANS women had to carve out their own spaces for activism. Their fight for educational opportunities for ANS communities was a critical part of this struggle. Before AUBA women formally organized in 1917, they were making their presence known as leaders in education within the Association. The first women delegates documented as attending the Association was in 1891, but prior to this date women were contributing to education in their churches by serving as Sabbath School teachers and as day-school teachers in their communities. After their first participation in the Association, Oliver notes that AUBA women began to speak out on various issues including education, Temperance, and missions work.[39] In 1909—the Bright Light Mission Band women's missionary group of Upper Hammonds Plains donated five dollars to Acadia University—evidence of ANS women's active support of education even for institutions where they had been historically alienated.

It was in the 1900s when the AUBA turned its attention to the education of Black children, particularly those who were orphaned, that the exceptional leadership of the women leaders in collaboration with the male leaders emerged. When the desperate need to provide care and training for the children became apparent, the Association rose to the occasion with the males providing strategic planning for this Institute and the women providing initial and continuous leadership through financial support.[40] The esteemed James Robinson Johnston (LLB), graduate of the Faculty of Law, Dalhousie University and the first African Nova Scotian to earn a degree from this institution, developed for the Association a

---

37. Mahon, "Mothers."
38. Mahon, "Mothers."
39. Oliver, *Brief History*, 39.
40. Oliver, *Brief History of the Colored Baptists*, 38–40; Pachai and Bishop, *Historic Black Nova Scotia*, 61–63.

plan to formally organize education efforts for Black children through the establishment of a Normal and Industrial Institute. This institute would be akin to that of Hampton Institute, an all-Black educational institution founded in 1868 in Virginia, United States. Also, Rev. Moses B. Puryear, originally of the United States and pastor of Cornwallis Street Baptist Church rallied the support of both church and civic leaders for this vision in 1914. The AUBA wholeheartedly supported this venture through a resolution based on a "duty of the Race to produce its own leaders" to "be architects to carve our place in this Western civilization" and pledged to "endorse by moral and financial aid the proposed Institute to be known as the Industrial School of Nova Scotia for Colored Children."[41]

Rev. Puryear led the school's incorporation, the appointment of a board, and secured Miss Jackson, a "highly qualified woman" from Philadelphia to be its matron.[42] Further, the Association had acquired a small home to house this institute. However, misfortune struck and during the week the institute was scheduled to open, the Halifax Explosion destroyed this building. Instead, in 1921, under the leadership of James A. R. Kinney and through the investment of a 211-acre farm by the government, the AUBA opened the Nova Scotia Home for Coloured Children.

One of the AUBA women's most remarkable gestures in support of educational endeavours in their early years of the Association was their legacy of patronage to the Nova Scotia Home for Coloured Children. It is noteworthy that in 1908, while plans were still underway to build and establish the Normal and Industrial Institute, plans that appear to have been male-led, two women—Louisa Bailey of Halifax and Martha E. Jones of Truro—each gave twenty dollars to this cause. These two women were also *the first* to contribute to this Institute. In the years to follow the establishment of the Ladies Auxiliary, 1919 to 1920, the women raised one thousand and one hundred dollars for the Home for Colored Children and the Association.[43]

AUBA women's continued support of this institution, which included a school and residence for ANS children rejected by other orphanages, was an unwavering example of how women's behind-the-scenes work, through financial support and fundraising efforts, represents *maternal activism*. Margaret Upshaw, for example, hired by the Association to

---

41. 61st Annual Meeting Minutes (1915).
42. Oliver, *Brief History of the Colored Baptists*, 39.
43. Hamilton, "Women at the Well," 196.

organize and promote women's work in its churches for thirty dollars a month, was recorded as having collected hundreds of dollars for the Colored Home, along with other funds for AUBA allotments and other work between 1919 and 1922 when she passed away suddenly.[44] AUBA records show that the male leaders often called upon the fundraising expertise of the Ladies Auxiliary to assist when the Association could not meet its financial pledges, which in part supported education in ANS communities. In the aftermath of the Depression, which left ANS communities suffering and many experiencing starvation, the Association implored the assistance of the Ladies Auxiliary to help the organization through a time of financial crises. This crisis impacted the AUBA's ability to fulfil its courageous five-year financial plan of faith launched by James A. R. Kinney and his executive, which aimed to raise two thousand and five hundred dollars per year for the work of the churches, schools, and community.[45] Between 1935 and 1949, the Ladies Auxiliary assumed this responsibility by hosting Pew Rallies at Victoria Road, Dartmouth; Cornwallis Street Baptist, Halifax; and Second Baptist Church in New Glasgow, raising as much as two hundred and fifteen dollars during one rally.

Through the Ladies Auxiliary and Women's Institute (the AUBA's formal governing body formed in 1956 to provide oversight for all women's work), AUBA women continue to provide annual financial contributions to the Home for Colored Children, now known as the Akoma Family Centre. Further to financial support, however, the Women's Institute as a body of advocacy and maternal protection was one of the first groups to demand an investigation into allegations of abuse impacting former residents of the Nova Scotia Home for Colored Children due to systemic and institutionalized anti-Black racism.[46] Their social justice activism along with the voices of former residents resulted in an apology from the provincial government in 2014 and a government funded Nova Scotia Home for Colored Children Restorative Inquiry process announced in 2015 and completed in 2019.

Central to the AUBA women's leadership in education was a maternal activism of "political mobilization and biological and social motherhood" that opposed social injustices for the betterment of younger

---

44. Oliver, *Brief History of the Colored Baptists*, 40.

45. Oliver, *Brief History*, 45.

46. Restorative Inquiry, "Journey to Light: A Different Way Forward."

generations.⁴⁷ This form of maternal activism was particularly exemplified through the Black Schoolhouses, the segregated schools located in ANS communities. The separation of White and Black students in schooling was legislated and enacted in Nova Scotia by 1865, reflecting the ideologies of White supremacy at work through both the adamance of White parents to keep their children separate from Black children and the reinforcement of this desire through the justice system.⁴⁸ Despite education being upheld as a fundamental right according to the Universal Declaration of Human Rights (1948) and Black communities' belief that education was the pathway to their children having a better life, systemic anti-Black racism was deeply entrenched in the Nova Scotian education system. This reality was proof of historian James W. St. G. Walker's stance that "the most important manifestation of colour prejudice in Canadian history is in education."⁴⁹ The last segregated school in Nova Scotia did not close until 1986 in Guysborough County.

AUBA women's hands-on, personal, and direct provision of education to ANS youth in these one-room schoolhouses give testimony of their commitment to education in collaboration with the wider advocacy of their male leadership and other supporters. Moreau honours "Black Nova Scotian women (and men)" whom she says, "established the first Black educational system" through the church:⁵⁰

> The literature reveals that, until the 1950s, formal education for Blacks in Nova Scotia was not a legal or civic right (Moreau 1996; Pachai 1987; Boyd 1976; Oliver 1970). As a result, in many parts of the province, Blacks were bluntly refused formal education with Whites. Black women (and men) through their church established "little Black schools" taught mostly by women who saw it as their religious calling to educate community members as best they could.⁵¹

The AUBA's female-male collaboration towards the improvement of education for ANSs is also evident in their advocacy for better school building conditions. Notwithstanding the unacceptable physical conditions of these school buildings, the inadequate school supplies and

47. Mahon, "Mothers."
48. Hamilton, "Stories," 93–95.
49. Walker, *History of Blacks in Canada*, 107.
50. Moreau, "Feminization."
51. Moreau, "Feminization."

learning resources, the nurture and high expectations provided ANS students by their ANS teachers could be deemed a precursor to that of Africentric Schools. While Association minutes record a strategic plan for the membership to raise money each year to support priorities, including the improvement of educational facilities in the rural areas and better care of schoolteachers,[52] another pressing matter emphasized was representation of teachers from their communities: ANS teachers. It is here that we see the direct impact of AUBA women on the trajectory of ANS youth: "We are pleased to note that more of the young coloured men and women of Nova Scotia are equipping themselves for positions as teachers in our schools. We hope that in the near future all our schools may be supplied with efficient teachers of our race."[53]

What these minutes fail to specify and what would have been impossible to predict in 1921 is that the majority of these teachers were women and members of the AUBA's Ladies Auxiliary or church. One such teacher was Alfaretta Berry Anderson, the wife of AUBA minister Rev. Martin L. Anderson, who taught in segregated schools for forty years. Alfaretta Anderson is celebrated for re-opening the Greenville School in the 1930s after it had been without a teacher and closed for many years, serving three generations of families in the community of Greenville.[54] Other teachers of segregated schools include Margaret Upshaw, Marie Hamilton, Portia White, Hattie Daye-Ashe, Ada Clayton, Gertrude Tynes, Isabel Shepherd Jones, Donna Sealy, Edith Mitchell Cromwell, and Marion Skinner. Therefore, when the AUBA petitioned government for more respectable wages for ANS teachers, they were advocating for these women and others like them to come who were connected to the Association and their communities.

It is important to note that although the AUBA's contributions toward the educational development of ANS communities were admirable up to 1917, it was through the establishment of the Association's Ladies Auxiliary during the body's annual assembly that year that education work blossomed. In August of 1917, the women of the Association organized around a well on the premises of the East Preston Baptist Church, a gathering known as the historic *Women at the Well*. The admirable contributions to the AUBA and ANS communities these women would

---

52. 76th Annual Meeting Minutes (1929).
53. 68th Annual Meeting Minutes (1921).
54. Evans and Tynes, *Telling the Truth*, 33–34.

make from this time forward are examples of Black women's tradition of self-reliance and self-help through education in action. Further, in 1956, the Ladies Auxiliary groups decided another development was required to sustain the work of AUBA women across its member churches. During their October meeting, they birthed the Women's Institute as a governing body to guide all women's work within the Association. To the present day, the Women's Institute continues to meet annually during the third weekend of October.

Sylvia Hamilton describes the work of the Ladies Auxiliary and Women's Institute of AUBA churches as "central to the educational and social development of African Nova Scotians."[55] In addition to their generous financial giving and fundraising, these women proved through their programming and steadfast advocacy that they deeply valued educational advancement. One of their most outstanding endeavours was to organize and host the first Convention of Coloured Women in Canada on May 27, 1920, less than three years after the Ladies Auxiliary formed officially, where they educated women on numerous topics including *Education*, led by F. A. Pelley. Amongst the women who organized this auspicious occasion were Maude Sparks, Maggie Upshaw, Muriel States, and Bessie Wyse.

The magnitude of the Ladies Auxiliary's accomplishment through this conference, and all the endeavours of AUBA women prior to and following 1920, must be placed in perspective of the historical significance of women's rights during this time. As Hamilton points out, the ANS women of the AUBA organized this Canada-wide conference for Black women nine years before the Person's Case. The audacity of these women to lead such a bold charge as to call Black women together to address their educational, spiritual, and community issues, before women of any colour were considered people by Canadian law, and during a time when their humanity as people of African descent was still in question, was courageous indeed.[56] Fifty women attended this gathering in Halifax, and in 1921 the Ladies Auxiliary hosted another successful convention.

Even to the present day, the Ladies Auxiliary of each member church and the umbrella Women's Institute continue to uphold this legacy of financially supporting the educational growth and development of African Nova Scotians. Annually, the Women's Institute contributes towards

55. Hamilton, "Our Mothers Grand and Great," 89.
56. Hamilton, "Women at the Well," 190–91.

the Nova Scotia Home for Colored Children/Akoma Family Centre, the AUBA Scholarship, Acadia Divinity College, Canadian Baptist Missions, the Black Cultural Centre of Nova Scotia, Atlantic Baptist College (currently Crandall University), and the Donald and Evelina Skeir Memorial Scholarship Fund.[57] Additionally, the Institute continues to annually award the Gertrude E. Smith Memorial scholarship—named in honour of one of the leaders of the Women's Institute and established in 1981 by Dr. Pearleen Oliver. This scholarship supports ANS students pursuing post-secondary education. Historically, the Women's Institute encouraged its member groups to hold Education Services in the spring to raise funds for the AUBA Scholarship Fund. Moreover, during their annual sessions held on the third weekend of October each year, the Institute honours the academic achievements of AUBA women through public recognition and a tangible token of their acknowledgement.

The Women's Institute's focus on programing also brought information on important subject matters related to family, health, development, and well-being to their members. It supported essay writing, public speaking and leadership skill development for youth and arranged a Radio Apprentice Program for indigenous Black students of Nova Scotia in collaboration with a broadcast agency. This opportunity offered the students post-secondary tuition, bursaries, a summer job while in school and employment at the completion of their tertiary education.[58] The Institute played a valuable role in organizing programs that raised awareness on domestic violence and community violence in general. In 2007, they organized a forum to discuss the church's response to violence in communities. During the forum on community violence, workshops were organized on the themes, "Working towards healthy communities," "Health and Healthy Relationships," "Violence and how it affects us," "Youth: What is your role?" and "Seniors: What is your role?" The Women's Institute conducted extensive work to educate on domestic violence through the "Journey to Light" project that was funded by the Nova Scotia Status of Women. Additionally, the women developed the "No More Secrets" video documentary to provide awareness on domestic violence against women in ANS communities. The Institute also enlisted the services of a daughter of the Association, Sylvia Hamilton, as filmmaker and facilitator of videos complete with a discussion guide, and a

---

57. "Our History," 4.
58. "Our History," 4.

copy of this package was provided to each AUBA church. The Institute facilitated Table Talks in ANS communities as well as workshops for frontline workers within the provincial government's Victim Services, police victim services, Student Support Workers, women's centres, sexual health centre executives, and men's treatment programs. In 2013, the Women's Institute also led workshops on Elder Abuse and Mental Health and Wellness. Through additional Nova Scotia Advisory Council on the Status of Women funding, they received a grant to educate on Bullying and Elder Abuse.[59]

AUBA WOMEN PIONEERS IN EDUCATION

AUBA women's traditions of maternal activism and othermothering have also been remarkably illustrated in the lifework of specific women over the course of the Association's history. One outstanding example is AUBA pastor, Ladies Auxiliary and Women's Institute member and former president, Dr. Joyce Ross, founder of the East Preston Day Care. When she established the Daycare in 1974, Dr. Ross was responding to an academic need she uncovered in East Preston's school-aged children: many of them required auxiliary and remedial help.[60] Dr. Ross stated that the goal of the Daycare was to provide ANS learners with exposure to the "outside surroundings as well as teach them the basic skills they'd need to succeed in the public schools."[61] Additionally, the Daycare provided parents reliable and consistent childcare while they completed their own schooling. Dr. Ross states that the ANS children educated at the East Preston Daycare Centre performed so well academically when they entered public school that Department of Education personnel "asked us to pull back a little": "[T]hey said that our children were too far advanced as compared to the other children. I told them, 'Advance our children a grade, if they are too advanced, that's not my problem, that's your problem. You told us that they were so far in the hole, so, so far down. Now you want us to pull us back? I'm not doing that."[62]

The success of the East Preston Daycare Centre and by extension, ANS learners, is due to the resolute activism and dedication of community educator and champion Dr. Ross who fought provincial government

---

59. "Our History," 16.
60. Steem and Steem, "Interview."
61. Steem and Steem, "Interview."
62. Steem and Steem, "Interview."

for funding to open the Daycare. Dr. Ross served as Executive Director for this establishment for thirty-four years. The Centre did not only provide a source of educational enrichment for ANS children in the East Preston community and beyond, but it also became an umbrella for healthcare as a family health resource centre and pre-and-postnatal program for single mothers, a family education centre and reading program for children needing additional support, a seniors' program, and a computer literacy program.[63]

Another AUBA champion of education exemplifies maternal activism as the protector of the history of the AUBA, social justice defender of ANS people in general, and ANS women's advocate specifically. That person is Dr. Pearleen Oliver. No discussion about the AUBA's role in education, and specifically one that highlights the contributions of the Association's women, could be complete without recognizing this activist whose work in social justice for ANSs broke all gender and racial barriers of her time. Not only did Dr. Pearleen Oliver serve as the first woman Moderator of the AUBA, and inaugural president of the Women's Institute, but she has written more historical books on the AUBA than any other person.[64] Dr. Pearline Oliver authored *A Brief History of the Colored Baptist of Nova Scotia: 1782–1953* (1953), *Song of the Spirit—An Historical Narrative on the history of the Beechville Baptist Church* (1994), *A Root and a Name* (1977), and *From Generation to Generation* (1985). Known for her determination to address and remove barriers impacting ANSs from accessing employment and education, particularly during the 1940s and 1950s, she was also co-founder of the Nova Scotia Association for the Advancement of Coloured People (NSAACP). In 1947, Dr. Oliver won the fight for the admission of African Canadian women into nursing schools in Canada.[65] Dr. Oliver also advocated through the Halifax Coloured Citizens Improvement League to have racially offensive curriculum—such as depictions of caricatures like *Little Black Sambo*—removed from public school texts and ANS and African Canadian history, heritage, and knowledge contributions to Canadian society included. This church and community educator also initiated and supported the Adult Learning Education Programs in Beechville in the 1950s.[66] Known

---

63. Williams, *Black Women*, 71.
64. Pachai and Bishop, *Historic Black Nova Scotia*, 28.
65. Williams, *Black Women*, 71.
66. Steem and Steem, *Mothers of the Civil Rights Movement*.

as one who actively made space for ANSs to learn, Dr. Oliver supported advocacy of Beechville community leaders like Bernice Hamilton in the 1950s and 1960s who demanded that the municipal councilor re-open the community's former segregated schoolhouse as a community centre for Beechville members. Not only were they successful, but the renovated Beechville Centre, which opened as a recreation and education space in 1961, remains open today as the Lakeside Community Centre.[67] Dr. Oliver was instrumental in organizing nightly study opportunities for the community's children and youth at this centre, managed the schedule for the centre's recreational and educational programs, and also assisted with a campaign to renovate the centre. Additionally, in 1963, this leader, her husband and family were among the founding organizers of the Beechville Education and Community Development Association.[68]

Dr. Oliver also made invaluable contributions to education by mentoring girls towards career pathways, organizing youth training groups, and securing continuing education and music classes for specific communities. As the spouse of AUBA pastor Rev. Dr. William Pearly Oliver, also a staunch advocate for education and racial justice for ANSs, Dr. Oliver is remembered for her determination to address racial and gender injustices impacting ANS communities, with the cause of education being one to which she devoted much attention. A pioneer in the work of maternal activism, Dr. Oliver's exemplary leadership has dynamic implications: "Her activism represents broader trends of Black female leadership in Nova Scotia that connects the symbol of motherhood with social justice initiatives. Black women's roles in the church, school, and youth advocacy were essential to the advancement of civil rights."[69]

Within the last two decades of the AUBA's leadership, its member churches have continued to explore new ways to provide informal education to its youth and adults through various programs. Some churches, including the Victoria Road United Baptist Church, have partnered with the Black Educators Association (BEA) to house the Cultural and Academic Enrichment Program (CAEP) for school-aged youth. Other program examples include the *Save Our Sons, Save Our Sisters Rites of Passage Program* involving the East Preston United Baptist Church, Cornwallis Street Baptist Church (renamed New Horizons Baptist Church),

---

67. Steem and Steem, *Mothers of the Civil Rights Movement*.
68. Steem and Steem, *Mothers of the Civil Rights Movement*.
69. Steem and Steem, *Mothers of the Civil Rights Movement*.

Emmanuel Baptist Church, and a member of the Halifax Association—New Beginnings Ministries. Additionally, the East Preston Baptist Church's development of the East Preston Empowerment Academy[70] in 2014 has provided an Adult Learning Program, a Graduate Equivalency Diploma (GED) preparatory program, a Trade Apprenticeship Program, and more recently a youth academic enrichment program servicing ANS learners. In partnership with government and community partners alike, this academy offers ANS adult and youth pathways to success in a culturally responsive learning environment that would be otherwise inaccessible. The Academy offers transformative learning that continues to enrich the lives of ANS adults and youth in a manner that upholds the AUBA's educational values and legacy.

CONCLUSION

Since its inception to the present day, the AUBA has demonstrated resolute devotion to building, supporting, and sustaining the educational development of ANS people and their communities. The umbrella organization of ANS communities, and for many years the only ANS organization, the AUBA has served the role of *mother* in its female-male leadership response to these communities' educational needs that otherwise would neither have been valued nor met. As the struggle to attain equitable formal education for ANS learners continues, and as "Achievement Gap" labels implicitly cast deficit biases on these learners, it is more important than ever to recognize the significant historic AUBA collaborative leadership efforts towards the development and protection of equitable educational opportunities for ANSs. This history provides the road map for how government agencies and ANS community organizations can work together towards an actualization of ANS learner success that moves beyond survival to thriving, from an ANS perspective. Crucial to this success is the acknowledgement of the need for an inclusive memory that recalls the contributions of both the AUBA's men *and* women who led, influenced, upheld, and supported the education of ANS people and continue to do so both directly and behind the scenes. The high value the AUBA's leaders collectively placed on education in the face of systemic and institutional anti-Black racism, sexism, and misogynoir over its 168 years of existence reflects their journey of exceptional faith enacted through collective work and responsibility. May these

70. Now called the Africadian Empowerment Academy

legacies and contributions inspire equitable change and development in education and serve as sacred stones in the collective memories of ANS people and all others across Canada for years to come.

BIBLIOGRAPHY

Primary Sources

Archives

"Our History" (African United Baptist Association of Nova Scotia Women's Institute), n.d.
61st Annual Meeting Minutes of African United Baptist Association, 1915.
63rd Annual Meeting Minutes of African United Baptist Association, 1917.
64th Annual Meeting Minutes of African United Baptist Association, 1918.
65th Annual Meeting Minutes of African United Baptist Association, 1919.
68th Annual Meeting Minutes of African United Baptist Association, 1921.
76th Annual Meeting Minutes of African United Baptist Association, 1929.
77th Annual Meeting Minutes of African United Baptist Association, 1930.

Monographs

MacKerrow, P. E. *A Brief History of the Coloured Baptists of Nova Scotia and their First Organization as Churches A. D. 1832*. Halifax, NS: Nova Scotia Printing Company, 1895.

Secondary Sources

Abucar, Mohamed. *Struggle for Development: The Black Communities of North and East Preston and Cherry Brook, Nova Scotia 1784-1987*. Halifax, NS: McCurdy, 1988.
Bernard, C., et al. "'She Who Learns Teaches': Othermothering in the Academy: A Dialogue among African Canadian and African Caribbean Students and Faculty." *Journal of the Association for Research on Mothering* 2 (2000) 66–84.
Bernard, Wanda Thomas, and C. Bernard. "Passing the Torch: A Mother and Daughter Reflection on their Experiences across Generations." *Canadian Woman Studies* 18 (1998) 46–55.
Best, Carrie. *That Lonesome Road*. New Glasgow, NS: Clarion, 1977.
Brigham, S., and S. Parris. "Black Women's Africentric and Feminist Leadership Voices from Nova Scotia." In *Women, Adult Education, and Leadership in Canada*, edited by Darlene E. Clover et al., 73–83. Toronto: Thompson, 2016.
Chilisa, Bagele. *Indigenous Research Methodologies*. Los Angeles: Sage, 2012.
Davis, Amira, M. "Embodying Dillard's Endarkened Feminist Epistemology." In *Black Feminism in Education Black Women Speak Back, Up, and Out*, edited by Venus E. Evans and Bettina L. Love, 153–60. New York: Lang, 2015.
Evans, D., and G. Tynes. *Telling the Truth—Reflections: Segregated Schools in Nova Scotia*. Hantsport, NS: Lancelot, 1995.

Hamilton, Sylvia. "Our Mothers Grand and Great: Black Women of Nova Scotia." In *Fire on the Water: An Anthology of Black Nova Scotian Writing*, edited by George Elliott Clarke, 2:85–92. Lawrencetown Beach, NS: Pottersfield, 1995.

———. "Stories from *The Little Black School House*." In *Cultivating Canada: Reconciliation through the Lens of Cultural Diversity*, edited by Ashok Mathur et al., 93–112 Ottawa: Aboriginal Healing Network, 2011.

———. "The Women at the Well: African Baptist Women Organize." In *And Still We Rise: Feminist Political Mobilizing in Contemporary Canada*, edited by Linda Carty, 189–203. Toronto: Women's, 1993.

Oliver, Pearleen. *A Brief History of the Colored Baptists of Nova Scotia:1782–1953*. Halifax: McCurdy, 1953.

Mahon, Danielle. "Mothers of the Civil Rights Movement: African Nova Scotia Women Leadership in Civil Rights Organizing, 1953–1974." *Mothers of the Civil Rights Movement* (April 13, 2021). No pages. Online: https://storymaps.arcgis.com/stories/5d64684e728b4b6d876138029920d387.

Moreau, Bernice. "The Feminization of the Black Baptist Church in Nova Scotia." In *Feminist Success Stories*, edited by Karen Blackford, Marie-Luce Garceau, and Sandra Kirby, 251–60. Ottawa: University of Ottawa Press, 1999.

Pachai, Bridglal. *The Nova Scotia Black Experience through the Centuries*. Halifax, NS: Nimbus, 2007.

Pachai, Bridglal, and H. Bishop. *Historic Black Nova Scotia*. Halifax, NS: Nimbus.2006.

Paris, Peter J. *The Moral, Political and Religious Significance of the Black Church in Nova Scotia*. Dartmouth, NS: Black Cultural Centre for Nova Scotia, 1989.

Walker, James W. St. G. *A History of Blacks in Canada: A Study Guide for Teachers and Students*. Ottawa: Minister of State for Multiculturalism, 1980.

Williams, Dolly. *Black Women Who Made a Difference in Nova Scotia*. Dartmouth, NS: Halcraft. 2007.

Steem, Joy, and Matthew Steem. "An Interview with Dr. Joyce Ross." *Radix* (December 19, 2020). No pages. Online: https://www.radixmagazine.com/2020/12/19/an-interview-with-dr-joyce-ross.

12

Revisiting the Reverend Jennie Johnson (1868–1967)

Women's Ordination and Intellectual History in the Black Baptist Tradition

NINA REID-MARONEY

October 26th, 1909, I was ordained at Goblesville, Michigan. Due to convention regulations of that day, it was necessary that I be ordained in Michigan in the Free Baptist Convention. When I returned from my Ordination, I found a certain amount of prejudice against ordination of women, and this, coupled with other difficulties that arose, made it impossible for me to carry on there in the church that had largely been built by my own efforts. No crime had I committed against the laws of God, rather I had encountered the coldness of man-made rules and regulations.[1]

WHEN THE REVEREND JENNIE Johnson wrote this brief description of her ordination, she was 84 years old, reflecting on a long life of Christian service in an age that sought to silence her call to ordained ministry. In a biography of Johnson published in 2013, I sought to recover Johnson's story, situating her life within a feminist reading of scholarship on North American Black history, religion, and the history of

---

1. Johnson, *My Life*, 5.

women's activism.² Since that time, more recent scholarship has offered new approaches to the rich but sometimes fragmentary record of Black women's intellectual history in Canada. Attending to textual sources, visual culture, community memory, and Black Baptist history, this chapter revisits Jennie Johnson in light of emerging historiography, and argues that Johnson's self-reflexive meditation on her life as an ordained woman in the Baptist tradition offers fresh insight on African Canadian intellectual history in the nineteenth and twentieth centuries.

Johnson's life spanned a century, from Reconstruction in the 1860s to the modern civil rights movement in the 1960s. Recounting the events of that life risks falling into the dangers of what historian Barrington Walker describes as the act of "simple story-telling" at the expense of a more critical and revelatory historiography. There is a dangerous fallacy, too, as Walker notes, in Black Canadian histories that mine the record to present the lives of "exceptional" figures, as though one person's struggle can suddenly render the entangled constraints of White supremacy and patriarchy an artefact of the past.³ The study of Jennie Johnson offers a counterweight, focusing on an exceptional figure whose experience nonetheless complicates rather than simplifies our understanding of Black Canadian history.

While Johnson's place as the first ordained woman to minister in her own church in Canada speaks to one aspect of her life's story, even that designation points to the limitations of trying to define her significance using liberal concepts of linear progress. Indeed a discussion of *firsts* in the ordination of women in Canada—do we mean Ella Hadassah Kinney Sanders, the first woman ordained by a Canadian denomination (1901) but not the first ordained woman to serve in Canadian ministry (she was ordained the night before she sailed from New Brunswick for South Africa); Lydia Gruchy, widely cited as the first woman ordained in Canada by a mainline denomination (1936); Addie Aylestock, the first Black woman ordained in Canada who served in a Canadian congregation (1951); or Jennie Johnson, ordained in Michigan but the first ordained woman settled in her own church in Canada (1909), reveals not a timeline of progress but the *persistence* of opposition to women's ordination across racial

---

2. Reid-Maroney, *Reverend Jennie Johnson*.

3. Walker, "Future," 37–39. As part of his discussion of the problem of focusing on "firsts" in Black Canadian history, Walker urges historians to embrace the insights of Paul Gilroy's *Black Atlantic*, including its complicating of "modernist chronotypes" in historical narratives that remain tied to liberal constructions of agency and progress.

and denominational lines.⁴ The experience of one woman (or even four) did not mean that barriers of racial prejudice or gendered oppression had been broken in some permanent sense; rather, the lack of progress highlights the radicalism of Johnson's claim to spiritual authority. To her calling she ascribed a divine power to disrupt "man-made regulations," and in her reflections on time, place, and history, Johnson challenged mythologies of easy racial progress in the "promised land" of Canada.

In situating Jennie Johnson and Black Baptist theology in Canada within the conceptual framework of the Black Atlantic, this chapter also addresses Walker's call for Canadian historians to attend to Paul Gilroy's contention that the Black Atlantic "constitutes the dark side of the Enlightenment—a 'counterculture of modernity'—that long anticipated the conditions of modernity that we now call 'postmodern.'"⁵ In important ways that have yet to be fully examined, women such as Johnson found in Baptist theology a point of engagement with modernity that called its sufficiency into question while supplying an appeal to divine sovereignty. Johnson's seeking of ordination in the Black Baptist church drew primarily not on the language of advancement or respectability or racial uplift, but on a transcendent sense of time and purpose that cut across the grain and unpinned the structures of the very institutions she sought to lead. Moving as she did between the churches of the Amherstburg Association in Canada and those of the Free Will Baptist Association in Michigan, Johnson balanced complex ideas of history, continuity, and the fleeting and broken promise of progress. Through the lens of layered theological tradition, she saw a world fallen short, and a world shaped by acts of redemption that drew on the divine, rather than the human, capacity for hope. In the wider context of African Canadian historiography, the study of Johnson and the relationship between religion and resistance exposes the tension between theological and practical iterations of the language of a *promised land*. The analysis offered in this chapter is predicated on the idea that Black Canadian churches should be understood as part of the rich and complex intellectual history that linked African Canadian communities to the ideological currents of the Black Atlantic.⁶

---

4. Heath, Friesen, and Murray, *Baptists in Canada*, 72; Wotton, *With Love, Lydia*; "Addie Aylestock."

5. Walker, "Future," 40. For an introduction to postmodernity and the African American context, see Evans, "African-American Christianity."

6. Reid-Maroney, "Possibilities."

To situate Johnson in the context of Black Baptist culture, it is useful to start with an ending. Jennie Johnson passed away in the city of Detroit on a mild December morning in 1967, her long life dissolved in what the papers called a *gentle end*. Six of Johnson's colleagues in ordained ministry, all of them men, spoke at her funeral service. The long procession of mourners then made its way from Prince Albert Baptist Church in Chatham Township to the cemetery in the town of Dresden; there, the Reverend Johnson was buried next to her mother, and not far from the grave of the Reverend Thomas Hughes, the English cleric who had baptised her as an infant almost a century before.[7] They marked the passing of this remarkable woman and the end of one hundred years of life—from the era of Reconstruction to the modern civil rights movement—and the accomplishments of her religious leadership on both sides of the border. But the weight of that occasion within the Black community in Southwestern Ontario was felt by those in her immediate acquaintance, who knew her as an ordained minister, and who understood that her life of resistance over the span of a century was grounded in her life as a preacher and founder of churches.

Johnson was born in 1868 on a farm on the 10th concession of Chatham Township, the daughter of Isaiah Johnson and Charlotte Butler Johnson. Her father's family came to Canada out of enslavement in New Jersey, a state that had a long slow history of gradual emancipation. The emancipation law passed in the state in 1804 did not free those born into servitude before that date—it came too late for Jacob and Margaret Johnson, Jennie's grandparents. We do not know when or how Margaret Johnson or her daughter Margaret came to Canada; Jacob and three sons endured a harrowing journey during which one son was recaptured and died. Reunited in Canada, the family settled in Chatham Township, sometime before 1840. Johnson's mother's family came from Knox County, Indiana—part of the Old Northwest that was free under the terms of the Articles of Confederation that established the United States after the revolution. Even there, freedom on paper did not always play out as freedom in practice. Virginia had laid claim to much of this territory in the late eighteenth-century, and Virginian, along with French traders in the region, brought slaves into the Indiana Territory with them. Johnson's grandfather, Joseph Butler, had been born into slavery, but purchased his own freedom and that of his wife, Julia Jenkins. Joseph, Julia, and

---

7. Ladd, "Recollections"; "Rev Jennie Johnson Dies."

their children, including Charlotte, who would become Jennie Johnson's mother, left for Canada sometime between the fall of 1840 and the spring of 1841. Charlotte Butler and Isaiah Johnson were married in the early 1840s and settled along the 10th concession.[8]

The community Johnson's grandparents helped to establish stood at the ideological crossroads of Black activism in the nineteenth-century Atlantic world. In the autobiographical pamphlet that she published in 1951, Johnson traced her sense of calling to her early life, and to the Black abolitionist community in which that call to ordination was framed and answered. In her ministry as a Black woman moving in and through Christian institutions structured around racialized and gendered assumptions about religious authority, Johnson drew on early experiences to construct a spiritual narrative that undergirded her sense of call to ordination despite the prohibitions and strictures that made her way difficult. Her writing of her life's story boldly underscored moments in which feminist and antiracist theologies opened the way for her. The first paragraphs related the story of her birth, and the action of her mother in both giving and saving her life. Charlotte Johnson, who was an experienced midwife, feared that her child was stillborn and massaged her heart to restart it in the moments after the birth. The sense of being sought and rescued by the confluence of divine love and mother love stayed with Johnson for the rest of her life. As Johnson wrote, "from that moment on" her life had been "devoted to the work of her Redeemer. I am proud to make that statement and to add that my faith has never once been shaken during my eighty-three years."[9] By her own assessment, her mother's intervention in "bringing life to that stilled little heart" acted as a means of grace, in which birth and spiritual rebirth, compressed in the same moment, depended on the action of a woman.[10] In a subsequent passage that emphasized the spiritual continuities of her life of faith, Johnson noted that at the age of seven, she first became aware of a clear call to Christian ministry during her morning prayers at her mother's knee. Both early experiences that Johnson linked to her spiritual life as a child centred her mother as the channel of grace and offered intimations of Johnson's later insistence that Christian ministry was women's work.

8. Johnson, *My Life*, 3; Dungy, *Planted by the Waters*, 37; Reid-Maroney, *Reverend Jennie Johnson*, ch. 1.

9. Johnson, *My Life*, 3.

10. Johnson, *My Life*, 2.

In addition to locating the models for a practical feminist theology in Johnson's framing of her early experience, we can also note the influence of Black abolitionist culture on her religious life and her concept of divine call and human response. As an infant, Johnson and her siblings were baptised in the Church of England by Reverend Thomas Hughes. Sent to the village of Dresden by the Bishop of Huron in 1859, Hughes opened a racially integrated church and school, and held additional services outside the village, including at the small frame schoolhouse in Chatham Township, close to the Johnson family farm. Hughes' antislavery work among the Black abolitionists communities of the district, and his reputation as a man who "knew no complexional distinctions" in his work as priest and teacher provided important context for Johnson's understanding of the possibilities for interracial activism and for shared theological traditions as a foundation for building racial equality.[11] Black Anglicans transformed Hughes's work from a "Mission to Fugitive Slaves in Canada," as characterized by the London office of the Colonial Church and School Society, to a vibrant activist community linked to Black abolitionist centres in Philadelphia, Oberlin, Cleveland, Detroit, and across the lower Great Lakes. Two of the teachers at the Anglican school that Hughes established—Alfred Whipper and Aaron Highgate—infused the Anglican mission station with the hope and power of Black abolitionist ideologies constructed in the American republic and applied in the small Canadian village of Dresden. Hughes was also involved in the life of the school Johnson attended on the 11th concession of Chatham Township. When Johnson returned to the Anglican church for anniversary services in the 1960s, she celebrated her personal historical connection to the antislavery commitments of the Church of England, and to the first communion into which she had been baptised.[12]

While the thread of interracial commitment to justice and the common ground of evangelical belief remained an important component of Johnson's theological and intellectual world, Black churches—both Baptist and Methodist—provided emancipatory theologies that transformed Johnson's spiritual life and practice. To understand this dynamic, it is important to recall the background of the Black abolitionist community

---

11. The assessment of Hughes comes from a member of his congregation, Parker T. Smith to Jacob C. White Jr. November 1861. MS letter, Jacob C. White Papers, Moorland-Spingarn Library, Howard University, Washington DC.

12. Reid-Maroney, *Reverend Jennie Johnson*, 131; "Daughter of Refugee Slave," *North Kent Leader*, 7 June 1967.

in which she had been raised. The Johnsons lived in Chatham Township, just a mile from the site of the British American Institute and the Dawn settlement established by Josiah Henson and Hiram Wilson in the 1840s.[13] Johnson and other members of her family sometimes attended the Methodist church in which the charismatic Henson ministered. As Johnson described him, Henson had been a "slave of man but a freeman of God."[14] At the centre of the community of Black abolitionists in the district, Henson and the church drew support from families who had been attracted to Dresden and the rural communities surrounding it by Henson's practical activism. By the time Johnson knew Josiah Henson, he had become clearly associated in international literary and public landscape with the fictional character of Uncle Tom; yet his place in the Black community derived not from his links to Stowe's antislavery novel, but from his leadership as someone who had emancipated himself from enslavement, had returned to the United States to guide members of his family and others to freedom using the practical network of the underground railroad, and had the vision to establish a school and settlement that would offer a way to more fully realize the promise of freedom in Canada West. Even critics who disagreed with aspects of Henson's management and fundraising, or were discomfited by Henson's association with the fictional character of Uncle Tom understood the power of his public persona, his activism on behalf of freedom seekers, and his enduring symbolic importance among his neighbours.[15] In this sense, turning to the Methodist Episcopal church, Johnson argued, was "not a revolt against the Anglican communion, but a banding together of people the same color, the same background, and with common problems, and an eagerness to prosper and earn for themselves complete freedom in their adopted land."[16] In identifying the role of the Methodist Church in helping to solidify and support those seeking *complete freedom* Johnson suggested something of her own trajectory toward religious traditions rooted in shared struggle and shared aspiration. She also exemplified the fluidity of denominational life, moving between but remaining connected

---

13. On Josiah Henson and the British American Institute, see Reid-Maroney, *Reverend Jennie Johnson*, 21–29.

14. Johnson, *My Life*, 2.

15. For an early example of Henson's charismatic leadership overriding the judgement of his critics, see Douglass, "First of August Celebration."

16. Johnson, *My Life*, 2.

to Anglican, Methodist, and Baptist congregations that shared the geographic and theological space of Black abolitionist Dresden.

Like the Methodists, Black Baptists in Dresden were connected to the political world of abolition and Black organizing through denominational networks that grew and strengthened under the pressures of the turbulent decade of the 1850s. Baptist activists—William Newman and Samuel Davis among them—had established Dresden's Baptist congregations, tying what might at first appear to be a remote community in Canada West into the centre of Black political life organizing through the Colored Convention movement, through vigilance committees, through the Black press, and through the Amherstburg Baptist Association.[17] Antislavery news from centres like Philadelphia, Detroit, Cincinnati, Cleveland, Buffalo, and Pittsburgh circulated in print and in person through the congregations of small Canadian churches and the politically engaged preachers who led them. In this sense, Black Baptist churches worked, as historian Steven Hahn has written of free Black communities in the US, to build "circuits of communication and experience, interconnected processes of negotiation and agitation, [and] much deeper wells of aspiration and practice" than is generally acknowledged.[18] Churches served as "important political meeting grounds and as sites for the construction of new black politics" agitating for the end of racial slavery and mounting everyday resistance against the anti-Black racism that eroded civil rights and the prospect of full freedom.[19]

Against the backdrop of changes within both the British Methodist Episcopal denomination and the churches of the Amherstburg Association, Jennie Johnson's denominational life turned toward the Baptists. Josiah Henson died in 1883—Johnson attended his funeral, and in the years that followed, as the controversy over a possible reunion with the African Methodist Episcopal Church roiled Henson's congregation, Johnson began attending revival services led by the Reverend Samuel Lynn.[20] Lynn served in the First Baptist congregation with Samuel Davis

---

17. On the Reverend Samuel Davis, see Ripley et al., eds., *Black Abolitionist Papers: Volume II*, 494–54; Shreve, Shreve, *AfriCanadian Church*, 56–57; Richardson, "Life and Times." On William Newman, see Ripley et al., eds., *Black Abolitionist Papers: Volume II*.

18. Hahn, *Political Worlds*, 23.

19. Hahn, *Political Worlds*, 23.

20. Johnson, *My Life*, 3. On the debate over the British Methodist Episcopal reunion with the African Methodist Episcopal Church, and the opposition in Dresden and

and took over Davis's role when the latter answered a call to teach and preach in southern churches during Reconstruction.[21] In the early 1880s, the Baptist churches of Dresden, Chatham, and the rural communities surrounding them still constituted a vital extended community in which the gospel carried its edge of social justice and its emancipatory power. At the same time, new controversies broke through to the surface of denominational life. As the Reverend D. D. Buck noted in his account of the matter, Lynn differed from Davis and most of the churches in the Amherstburg Association over the question of open communion: "No doubt but that he was a loyal member of the Baptist Church and was a minister of that body that made himself felt. But he believed the Lord's Supper was for all Christians, from the teachings of St. Paul 1 Corinthians 11:28."[22] Turning to space in which he could practice what he preached of the open table, Lynn resigned his pastorate at the First Baptist church and began a series of evening services on the outskirts of town, in the same schoolhouse in which the Johnsons met Thomas Hughes in the 1860s. Jennie Johnson attended Lynn's meetings, and experienced a conversion that she described in her autobiography: "In 1885, February 1st, at the age of 16, I was called directly to the ministry. I went to a church meeting in School House No. 18, Chatham Township. It was then that I came to know the Lord Jesus Christ as my Saviour and Friend, and my heart was filled with a burning desire to spread His Blessed Word among the people of my community."[23]

The compressed timeline of Johnson's Baptist conversion at Lynn's revival and her immediate taking up of the call to ministry makes it worth considering how the open communion doctrine informed her emerging theology of ordination. Her interpretation of Lynn's practice as inclusion, and as the breaking of old barriers to full participation in the transformative power of the faith opened new vistas of ministry to her; she began preaching alongside Lynn at the schoolhouse revivals. She had just turned sixteen the summer before her conversion. Within a few months, Lynn's revivals turned to a call for a new church. "Cornerstone was laid on June 10th, 1886," Johnson wrote, "Mr. Lynn and I assumed

Chatham churches, see Edwards, *From Slavery to Bishopric*, 151–61.

21. Dungy, *Planted by the Waters*, 37; *Chatham Daily Planet*, 12 July 1915.

22. Buck, *Progression*, 211–12. On the closed communion stance of the Amherstburg Association, see Article 13 of the "Articles of Faith and Practice," printed in Amherstburg Regular Missionary Baptist Association, *Pathfinders*.

23. Johnson, *My Life*, 3–4.

pastoral duties."[24] By the time the building of the new church—Union Baptist, Chatham Township—rose from the clearing on the small parcel of land Lynn had purchased across the road from the schoolhouse, Jennie Johnson worked in a fulsome partnership of preaching alongside Lynn. To this Lynn offered no objection, and Johnson, immersed in the work, found the space to envision ordination, and the education she would need to pursue it.

As part of her emerging feminist consciousness in ministry, Johnson turned to the example of other Black Baptist women in her circle of experience. Her autobiography draws attention to women who had taken on leadership in churches. She acknowledged the example of Elizabeth Shadd Shreve, Mary Ann Shadd's sister, who preached across Amherstburg Association churches in the rural communities surrounding Chatham, and who did so in ways that challenged expectations of female quietude and respectability. While Shreve served as President of the AMA Women's Missionary Association—a role that was both powerful and constrained by gendered expectations of female respectability—she also broke with the expectations. In 1881, she was the first woman to formally address the Amherstburg Baptist Association. She travelled on her preaching circuit on horseback through remote areas and in all weather, actions which Johnson and others rendered in heroic terms, drawing out the gendered tensions in Shreve's modes of activism.[25] Jennie Johnson also included reference in her life story to Mary Branton Tule, a young woman raised in Dover Township near Chatham, who attended Spelman College and travelled to South Africa as a missionary and teacher. By including both women in her autobiography, Johnson placed her own life in the context of a larger movement of women's activism within the Amherstburg Association, and placed herself in the company of particular women whose work in the church tested the limits of the Amherstburg Association's Article 17 on the role of women in the church.[26] Johnson's relationship to other women in leadership roles highlights not exceptionalism but continuities within a faith tradition and church polity born of resistance against oppression, and still possessed of some latitude

24. Johnson, *My Life*, 4.

25. Elizabeth Alexander, "Biography of Madam E.W. Shreve" in *Pathfinders of Liberty and Truth*, 65–66.

26. On Mary Branton, see *Pathfinders of Liberty and Truth*, 66; Shreve, *AfriCanadian Church*, 100–102; Amherstburg Baptist Association "Articles and Practice of Faith," printed in *Pathfinders*, 9.

for women inclined to heed their sense of call, whether or not it stayed within the lines of denominational discipline.

Johnson's choice to attend the AME Church's Wilberforce University brought her experience at Union Baptist Church into sharper focus. In the year before she began her studies at Wilberforce, Johnson moved to Flint, living with her brother James Henry Johnson, and working in domestic service to save money to pay for her college fees. When she arrived in Xenia, Ohio, and first approached the hilltop campus in the fall of 1892, it was just after the University's separate theological seminary opened with a ceremony featuring speeches from President McKinley and Frederick Douglass. She left just before the arrival of W. E. B. Dubois, who taught classics there while he finished his Harvard dissertation. Wilberforce was an extraordinary experience, and opened rich avenues of scholarship to its students, but while the school was proud of its ecumenical appeal, it was also firmly set in the AME doctrinal tradition. Johnson faced the disappointing reality of the lack of opportunity for female missionaries in the AME Church—and the retrenchment of the AME position on the ordination of women. The AME Church and Wilberforce were both radical challenges to the tenets of White supremacy, but part of that challenge was purchased at the cost of women's power and place.[27] In attending Wilberforce, Jennie Johnson thus entered a contested space where the place of women had yet to be decided. Female students at Wilberforce (particularly those interested in theology) remained caught between the gender ideology espoused by traditional figures such as Payne and the call for greater opportunity for women sounded in the 1880s by the more progressive AME bishop, Henry McNeal Turner.[28]

Returning to Canada, Johnson resumed her duties assisting Samuel Lynn. She also began preaching in another Baptist congregation a few miles to the west, known then as the Second Union Baptist Church and organized by Lynn in 1894 during a fresh season of revival. In this congregation she found herself in the company of women's spiritual authority and prophetic leadership, in sharp contrast to the AME and to her home congregation of Union Baptist. The acceptance of Johnson's call to ministry depended deeply on local circumstance and contingent relationships. When Lynn retired, Union Baptist congregants signalled their resistance to Johnson's stepping in to replace the man she had worked alongside for

---

27. McGinnis, *History*; Payne, *Treatise*, 171; Dodson, "Nineteenth-Century AME Preaching Women."

28. Angell, *Bishop Henry McNeal Turner*; Angell, "Controversy."

two decades; at Second Union Baptist, however, a few miles marked a great difference in response. Here, congregants welcomed Johnson and the idea of an ordained woman leading the church. "Good friends there assured me of their faith in my ministry," Johnson wrote, "and urged me to come among them and carry out my work."[29]

Johnson also had friends in the Michigan Association of Freewill Baptists (MAFB) where she appears in the records of Association meetings, beginning in the year following Lynn's retirement. The Michigan Association ordained her in October 1909. Connecting to a cross border Baptist association and developing close ties to Michigan Baptist congregations was in keeping with long traditions going back to the origins of the Amherstburg Association, but Johnson's work extended that network in new directions. Although there is no record of how she came to meet Freewill Baptists in Michigan—a predominantly White denomination—there are clear theological affinities linked to the historical Freewill Baptist antislavery stance and its practice dating from the 1850s of ordaining women as ministers. Perhaps Jennie Johnson had met Mattie Greene, an ordained minister at the Xenia Freewill Baptist church during the period in which Johnson lived in Xenia as a student at Wilberforce. Johnson may also have met Freewill Baptists during the years she spent working in Flint before she attended Wilberforce. What is clear is that by 1909 Johnson moved confidently through the FWB network, and when she came home to Canada, she led Second Union Baptist into the Michigan Free Baptist Association.[30]

The recounting of her fluid denominational history raises fascinating questions about the relationship between the sweeping and vibrant abolitionist culture in which Johnson was raised and her approach to transcending the barriers against the ordination of women. In seeking theological pathways that emphasized openness, freedom, inclusion, and community, Johnson managed to find and emphasize the most liberating possibilities embedded within the nineteenth-century Anglican, Methodist, and Baptist traditions that surrounded her. Her own work was influenced by the expansive moral vision and in the pursuit of social justice that flowed through the small congregations in which she had worshipped as a child, complete with their connections to the language and power of Black emancipatory theologies circulating across the Atlantic

29. Johnson, *My Life*, 8.

30. On Freewill Baptists in Michigan, see Baxter, *History*; Gilbert, *Historic Hillsdale College*; Dennett, "Free Will Baptist Women."

world. In seeking out Free Will Baptists for ordination in 1909, Johnson tapped into a fresh wellspring of doctrine that affirmed her call to ministry. She also forged relationships in the denomination across racial lines at a moment in Free Will Baptist history that was especially propitious. The people among whom she found welcome, and who were in turn welcomed in the life of Prince Albert Baptist Church, championed racial justice, not just in their links to the abolitionist movement, but in their contemporary moment.[31]

During the years between her ordination in 1909 and her move to Flint in 1925, Johnson's stipend as the ordained minister of Prince Albert Baptist Church was supplemented by the income from the small farm that she owned in Chatham Township, providing Johnson with a measure of economic independence. Writing of Black women teachers in twentieth-century Canada, historian Funké Aladejebi points to the importance of economic security as well as networks and friendships that defined their professional lives.[32] In some ways, Johnson's career paralleled that of women making their way in the professions of teaching and nursing. Her specialised education and call enlarged her sense of the world and the ways she might engage with other people; but in the absence of ordained women role models within the Baptist Church in Canada, Johnson's professional network consisted of ordained ministers, most of them men, and many of them White. This network included the Civil War veteran and FWB minister Abraham Whitaker who came to celebrate the opening of the new building for Prince Albert in 1915, and the Reverend George Vercoe, who helped Johnson open her Colored Christian Centre—part settlement house, part mission church, part school—in Flint in 1928. Throughout her working life, Johnson countered the lack of models for her own call to professional life by mentoring others, both in the formal support that the Colored Christian Centre gave to girls seeking to enter medical and teaching professions, and in her informal mentorship and ministry to young women in her churches, such as Hilda Carter, active in the first chapters of the Canadian League for the Advancement of Coloured People, and later, one of the teachers who helped challenge racial segregation in Essex County schools. It is difficult to measure the full impact of Johnson's ordination on the young women of her community—what did it mean to have a woman leading not only in the intellectual and

31. For examples of twentieth-century activism among Johnson's friends and colleagues in the MFBA, see Roberts, *History*, 44–46.

32. Aladejebi, *Schooling the System*.

activist spaces of the Women's Missionary Circle but leading in the intellectual and activist spaces of pulpit and communion table? Presiding at marriages and administering the ordinances of communion and baptism highlighted the radicalism of Johnson's challenge to the constraints on women's claim to authority and power.

Yet, beyond the spaces of the Prince Albert Baptist Church tucked away on a quiet concession in Chatham Township, how was Johnson known or understood in her own time? Because Prince Albert Baptist Church under her leadership remained in the Free Will Baptist tradition and outside the Amherstburg Association, and because she moved to Michigan in 1928, Johnson's work operated on the periphery of the larger network of Black Baptist Churches in Canada. Johnson remained in contact with her home community and followed closely the work of the National Unity Association in Dresden and Chatham, supporting her neighbours and members of her extended family as they challenged racial segregation and worked toward passage of Ontario's Fair Accommodation Practices Act. But with her own activism on behalf of her race moving in and beyond the borders of race, denomination, and nation, few outside the network of churches in Chatham, Buxton, and Amherstburg took note.

I have argued elsewhere that Johnson's tendency to highlight community and downplay personal accomplishment made it more difficult to trace evidence of Johnson herself in the historical record.[33] In the past decade, new scholarship and methodologies have begun to address this question in ways that reframe Johnson's place in Black Canadian women's history. Part of this work involves recognition and inclusion of Johnson in historical scholarship, from a forthcoming entry on Johnson in the *Dictionary of Canadian Biography* to Taylor Murray's evocatively titled article, "Against 'Historical Amnesia': A Bibliography of Baptists in Canada, 1990–2019," in which Johnson is included.[34] Writing of women in the

---

33. Reid-Maroney, *Reverend Jennie Johnson*, 134. The work concluded with this observation and challenge: "Johnson lived Christianity as the transcending of racial and gender categories, an act made even more powerful because those categories were wound around her in a long and tangled snare of history. If the edge of the theology she used to transcend centuries-old categories was so sharp as to cut through the snare, it remains for us to consider how and why the story of Canada's first ordained woman remained quietly tucked away in the rural churches she had served, protected even by her own admonition ('God forbid that I should glory, save in the cross of Jesus Christ') while the rest of the twentieth century slipped by."

34. Murray, "Against 'Historical Amnesia.'"

Black Baptist tradition in Canada, Wendy Porter places Jennie Johnson in the company of Elizabeth Shadd Shreve, Mary Branton Tule, and Hattie Rhue Hatchett, arguing that all four women reshaped churches and the world around them in "ways that are still poignant and relevant one hundred years later."[35] The scholarly recognition of her place in the history of the churches and communities she loved would have been welcome to Johnson, who understood the connection between historical consciousness and movements for social reform.

In 1962, Johnson addressed her place in the history of Baptists communities in an exchange of letters with the Reverend L. A. Gregory, Secretary of the Baptist Convention of Ontario and Quebec. Gregory, who met Johnson at the Convention gathering in Windsor, wrote to ask for additional information about her experience.[36] Johnson sent materials relating to her life, and an accompanying letter: "I shall be most pleased to have you place any books and papers of my ministry in the McMaster Divinity College. As we older harvesters drop out there remains no authentic history of the earlier struggles. It is a cheering thought that interested younger students will always have a ready source of reference in the McMaster Divinity College library."[37] Johnson's correspondence with Gregory and her interest in providing the materials of an *authentic history* raises the question of historical sources, and points to her own efforts to archive the materials of her ministry.

Johnson's style of extemporaneous preaching meant that she did not leave behind extensive volumes of sermons or files of correspondence. As she had noted in a letter to Gregory, "in moving about during the last years, some of my records have been lost."[38] Between Chatham Township, Flint, Xenia, and Detroit, Johnson's cross-border life of service in various churches and denominations did not lend itself to the safekeeping of papers in a single repository or home base. At the same time, however, Johnson countered this problem by taking particular care to publish two autobiographical pamphlets. She produced the first one in 1928 just after the opening of her Colored Christian Centre in Flint, recording the history of the Centre's founding, celebrating the people who had helped her, and providing an account of the opening services as well as information

35. Porter, "Quartet," 90.
36. "L. A. Gregory."
37. "Jennie Johnson."
38. "Johnson to Gregory."

about her own family history, her community in Ontario, and influential people she had come to know. The second pamphlet Johnson wrote and published in 1951. She titled it *My Life* and divided it into brief sections that covered the history of her family, her religious upbringing, her conversion, ministry, education, ordination, and the life of the churches she had founded. Both of these brief narratives have elements of scrapbooks about them; they evoke the editorial and authorial practices of resistance described in Ellen Gruber's *Writing with Scissors*. They included narrative sections, photographs, historical references, material from church services, excerpts from newspapers and letters, and a fictional short story based on Johnson's life written by one of her friends. In gathering these materials in the form of a published pamphlet, Johnson created an alternative history of herself and her community that resisted the stereotypical portrayals of Black life in the White press.[39] All around her she felt history disappearing. Shortly before publishing her second pamphlet, *My Life*, Johnson had led efforts to gain the support of the town council in Dresden for a museum dedicated to Henson and to the public memory of the abolitionist period that Henson represented.[40] In taking on the council and the problem of representation of the Black abolitionist past, Johnson drew out the activist possibilities of historical consciousness. While her published pamphlets are slim, each works as a small but carefully curated archive that opens outward and maps the way to further research.

Writing of Black women's intellectual history in the United States, Mia Bay, Farah J. Griffin, Martha S. Jones, and Barbara D. Savage note that Black women often went about their intellectual work without the institutional supports of educational institutions and libraries that would have ordinarily generated textual material for the historical record. Instead, for Black women activists and community leaders, "the oral expression of ideas often mixed with the material demands of communities."[41] Even in the textual material she produced, Johnson gestured toward community context and invited a broader reading of her life experience by including a heading for "People I Have Known."[42] This practice constituted an historical method that highlighted Johnson's own valuing of connection

---

39. Johnson's voice in the Dresden newspaper articles celebrating her birthdays or visits to town was often rendered in something approaching plantation dialect (see, for example, "Daughter of Refugee Slave").

40. "Uncle Tom's Cabin Back."

41. Bay et al., *Toward an Intellectual History*, 5.

42. Johnson, *Colored Christian Centre*, 8.

and relationship. Applying this method to manuscript materials, such as church meeting minutes in which Johnson's participation is briefly noted, the otherwise laconic entries can be read as part of a more fulsome historical record of community that would otherwise have disappeared.

Beyond her home congregations, the record of Johnson's participation in wider church bodies offers a glimpse of her life in the broader context of twentieth century Protestantism. The October meetings of the Michigan Free Will Baptist Association in the year Johnson was ordained illustrate the point. The afternoon session of the meeting was opened by songs and prayer led by "Sister Johnson of Canada," while the morning session had been devoted to an address on higher criticism by the University of Michigan scholar of ancient Hebrew, Leroy Waterman. Waterman's biblical scholarship informed his work on the Revised Standard Version of the Bible; he summed up his approach to biblical criticism and faith as bringing "the Bible into direct contact with life today as a living part of its reality."[43] Johnson, too, sought to bring the Bible into direct contact with her experience—her identification of "certain scriptures" used against her, and her reinterpretation of those scriptures to support her ordination constituted a lived and embodied version of biblical criticism, with radical implications both in and beyond the racialized and gendered religious spaces transformed by Johnson's presence.

Seeking to expand the range of historical sources that trace Johnson's influence, we can also consider the evidence of Johnson's life recorded in the built environment of the places in which she ministered. The brick structure of Prince Albert Baptist Church, renovated and financed through Johnson's influence and connection to the Michigan Free Will Baptist Association does not include her name on the cornerstone.[44] In the commemorative text of the stone, which gave recognition to Johnson's male protégé, the Reverend J. C. Browning, but not to Johnson, we have to read what is not there, and, in the absence, find traces of history's weight, the exclusion and the violence Johnson struggled against as she sought to live out her calling.

Such absences serve to open interpretive space in which to consider what we know of her life and work in the moments when she chose to represent herself to the world. In the two formal photographic portraits of Johnson that survive, we see the careful self-fashioning presented in the

43. Minutes of the Twentieth Session (1909).

44. Johnson's role in the financing of the new building is recorded in Minutes (1913).

language of visual culture. In the first portrait Johnson stands in formal studio pose, dressed in a fashionable travelling costume, her hand resting on the back of a decorative chair. Published by the Reverend Daniel Dana Buck in his 1907 documentary project in Black life in the United States and Canada *Progression of the Race,* the portrait, is a powerful image. Choosing to stand rather than to sit for the portrait and wearing clothes suitable for a young woman on the move, Johnson looks prepared for a journey. The timing of the image suggests that it may have been a photograph taken in Flint before Johnson set out for Wilberforce. The second portrait is of an older Johnson. Here Johnson's stance is as confident and forthright as in the earlier portrait. One hand rests on a decorated cross while the other holds a large and well-worn Bible. The American flag draped in the background, piano stool, and flowers all suggest that it was taken at the Coloured Christian Centre in Flint, possibly on the day the Centre opened. Most strikingly, Johnson wears her white clerical robes. Her gaze holds the camera. The image appropriates the masculine tradition of episcopal portraiture, as Johnson, surrounded by the symbols of her faith, claims her authority as an ordained minister.[45] In each image, Johnson presents herself as a woman entirely self-possessed. She has, to borrow Brittney Cooper's phrase, moved "beyond respectability" and its constraints on Black womanhood within the Christian tradition.[46] Yet as Cooper argues, even in historiographies that notice and include Black women's contribution to the intellectual lives of their communities, "many Black women thinkers labor under the exigencies of historical triage. Their names exist almost like family photos relegated to a wall we rarely touch."[47] This chapter is part of a broader effort to engage with the implications of Johnson's life and thought in ways that resonate with the emerging field of African Canadian intellectual history. We can start by liberating the historical portrait of Jennie Johnson from the static site of a wall that no one sees, and by situating her once more at the centre of a dynamic discourse on race, redemption, and the transformative possibilities carried within her emancipatory theology of women's ordination.

---

45. For a detailed analysis of Johnson's photographs, see Reid-Maroney, "Possibilities."

46. Cooper, *Beyond Respectability,* 2.

47. Cooper, *Beyond Respectability,* 2.

BIBLIOGRAPHY

Primary Sources

ARCHIVES

"Jennie Johnson to L.A. Gregory, 26 January 1962." MS. Johnson files, Canadian Baptist Archives, McMaster Divinity College, Hamilton, ON.
"Johnson to Gregory, 31 January 1962." MS. Johnson files, Canadian Baptist Archives, McMaster Divinity College, Hamilton, ON.
"L. A. Gregory to Jennie Johnson, 12 February 1962." MS. Johnson files, Canadian Baptist Archives, McMaster Divinity College, Hamilton, ON.
Minutes of Prince Albert Free Baptist Church, June 30, 1913.
Minutes of the Twentieth Session, Michigan Association of Free Will Baptists, October 29, 1909 (Michigan Association of Free Will Baptist Records, Bentley Historical Library, University of Michigan, Ann Arbor. Leroy Waterman, "Higher Criticism" typescript, Box 3, Leroy Waterman Papers).

MONOGRAPHS

Buck, Daniel Dana. *The Progression of the Race in the United States and Canada, Treating of the Great Advancement of the Colored Race*. Chicago: Atwell, 1907.
Edwards, S. J. Celestine. *From Slavery to Bishopric: The Life of Bishop Walter Hawkins of the Methodist Episcopal Church in Canada*. London: John Kensit, 1891.
Johnson, Jennie. *My Life*. Dresden, ON, 1951.
Payne, Daniel A. *A Treatise on Domestic Education*. Cincinnati, OH: Cranston and Stowe, 1889.

NEWSPAPERS AND MAGAZINES

"Daughter of Refugee Slave Attends Dresden Anniversary." *North Kent Leader*, June 7, 1967.
Douglass, Frederick. "First of August Celebration at Dawn Settlement, Canada West." *Frederick Douglass' Paper*, August 11, 1854.
"Rev Jennie Johnson Dies in Detroit Nursing Home." *Dresden News*, December 14, 1967.
"Uncle Tom's Cabin Back in the Limelight." *Dresden Times*, November 4, 1948.

OTHER

Ladd, Glen. "Recollections of Rev. Miss Jennie Johnson." *CBC Radio*. July 2, 1967.

Secondary Sources

"Addie Aylestock." *The Canadian Encyclopedia*. No pages. Online: https://www.thecanadianencyclopedia.ca/en/article/addie-aylestock.
Amherstburg Regular Missionary Baptist Association. *Pathfinders of Liberty and Truth: A Century with the Amherstburg Regular Missionary BaptistAssociation*. Buxton, ON: Amherstburg Regular Missionary Baptist Association, 1940.

Angell, Stephen Ward. *Bishop Henry McNeal Turner and African American Religion in the South*. Knoxville: University of Tennessee Press, 1992.

———. "The Controversy over Women's Ministry in the African Methodist Episcopal Church during the 1880s: The Case Study of Sarah Ann Hughes." In *This Far by Faith: Readings in African American Women's Religious Biography*, edited by Judith Weisenfeld and Richard Newman, 94–109. New York: Routledge, 1996.

Aladejebi, Funké. *Schooling the System: A History of Black Women Teachers*. Montreal: McGill-Queen's University Press, 2021.

Baxter, Norman Allan. *History of the Free Will Baptists: A Study in New England Separatism*. Rochester, NY: American Baptist Historical Society, 1957.

Bay, Mia E., et al. *Toward an Intellectual History of Black Women*. Chapel Hill: University of North Carolina Press, 2015.

Cooper, Brittney C. *Beyond Respectability: The Intellectual Thought of Race Women*. Champaign: University of Illinois Press, 2017.

Dennett, Lena Fenner. "Free Will Baptist Women." *American Baptist Quarterly* 13 (1994) 391–94.

Dodson, J. "Nineteenth-Century AME Preaching Women." In *Women in New Worlds: Historical Perspectives on the Wesleyan Tradition*, edited by Rosemary Skinner Kyler and Hyler Thomas, 276–89. Nashville: Abingdon, 1981.

Dungy, Hilda. *Planted by the Waters: A Family History of the Jones-Carter Families*. Wallaceburg, ON: Standard, 1977.

Evans, James H., Jr. "African-American Christianity and the Postmodern Condition." *Journal of the American Academy of Religion* 58 (1990) 207–22.

Gilbert, Arlan K. *Historic Hillsdale College: Pioneer in Higher Education*. Hillsdale, MI: Hillsdale College Press, 1991.

Gilroy, Paul. *The Black Atlantic*. Cambridge, MA: Harvard University Press, 1993.

Hahn, Steven. *The Political Worlds of Slavery and Freedom*. Cambridge, MA: Harvard University Press, 2009.

Heath, Gordon L., Dallas Friesen, and Taylor Murray. *Baptists in Canada: Their History and Polity*. McMaster Ministry Studies Series 5. Eugene, OR: Pickwick, 2020.

McGinnis, Frederick. *A History and Interpretation of Wilberforce University*, Blanchester, OH: Brown, 1941.

Murray, Taylor. "Against 'Historical Amnesia': A Bibliography of Baptists in Canada, 1990–2017," *The Journal of Baptist Studies* 9 (2018) 77–82.

Reid-Maroney, Nina. "Possibilities for African Canadian Intellectual History: The Case of 19th-Century Upper Canada/Canada West." *History Compass* 15 (2017) 1–9, DOI: 10.1111/hic3.12432.

———. *The Reverend Jennie Johnson and African Canadian History, 1868–1967*. Rochester, NY: University of Rochester Press, 2013.

Walker, Barrington. "The Future Has a Past: Canadian History and Black Modernity." In *Unsettling the Great White North: Black Canadian History*, edited by Michele A. Johnson and Funké Aladejebi, 31–50. Toronto: University of Toronto Press, 2022.

Wotton, Patricia. *With Love, Lydia*. Winnipeg: Patricia Wotton, 2012.

Porter, Wendy. "A Quartet and an Anonymous Choir: The Remarkable Lives and Ministries of Four Black Baptist Women in Late Nineteenth-Century Ontario." In *Canadian Baptist Women*, edited by Sharon M. Bowler, 89–112. McMaster General Studies Series 8. Canadian Baptist Historical Society Series 3. Eugene: Pickwick, 2016.

Richardson, William. "The Life and Times of Samuel H. Davis: An Anti-Slavery Activist." *Afro-Americans in New York Life and History* 33 (2009) 47–89.

Ripley, C. Peter, et al., eds. *The Black Abolitionist Papers: Volume II. Canada, 1830–1865.* Chapel Hill: University of North Carolina Press, 2015.

Roberts, Winsor Hall. *A History of the College Baptist Church, 1855-1955.* Hillsdale, MI, 1955.

Shreve, Dorothy S. *The AfriCanadian Church: A Stabilizer.* Jordan Station, ON: Paideia, 1983.

13

Revisiting Accounts of the Life of Mr. David George

Hannah Lane

THE 1953 CENTENNIAL OF the African United Baptist Association inspired reflections on its origins and achievements. From spending time with the Association's congregations over the years, the annual representative from the United Baptist Convention began his tribute with the names of key founders, starting with David George. Lay leader and activist Pearleen Oliver stated, "David George's credit and glory was that through hardship and persecution he started an inter-racial work in Nova Scotia."[1] Oliver and her predecessor in denominational history Peter McKerrow synthesized nineteenth-century sources[2] which relied on David Benedict's 1813 broad survey,[3] and David George's memoir which, like that of his contemporary Methodist Boston King, was mediated by co-religionists.[4]

Academic studies drawing on a wider range of sources began to appear in the 1960s and the archival research done by James W. St. G. Walker, Ellen G. Wilson, and Grant Gordon has remained foundational

---

1. Oliver, *A Brief History*, 11, 21; Clarke, *Directions Home*, 46–57.

2. McKerrow et al., *Brief History*; Fingard, "McKerrow"; Bill, *Fifty Years*, ch. 2.

3. Benedict, *General History*, 279.

4. Rippon, "Account"; Troxler, "Re-Enslavement," 70; Brooks and Saillant, "Note," 36–39.

to subsequent discussions of George's life, including this chapter.[5] By the 1990s, the Atlantic world (rather than the modern nation-state) oriented scholarship on colonial North America. Paul Gilroy adapted the concept of a "Black Atlantic" from art history, showing how individuals such as George could be "simultaneously more Euro-American and more African," but without incorporating essentialist notions of "pan-Africanism" or a mythical "racially flexible Atlantic world."[6] Studies influenced by these new approaches have provided clarifications and deeper context to the life of David George.[7]

George was born ca. 1743[8] in Virginia to West African parents and lived with brothers and sisters, whose fate is never mentioned again in his memoir, on a tobacco property with a vicious owner. Around age nineteen, he escaped and fled into the Carolinas and southern indigenous lands. There he became an unfree labourer in various Euro-American and indigenous households, both among the nearby Muskogee Creek and among those Natchez who had joined the Carolina Creek earlier in the century. Finally, his first owner in Virginia and his most recent indigenous owner came to terms that sold George to George Galphin, a trader already known to him. Galphin's home and commercial base was known as Silver Bluff, South Carolina, roughly fourteen miles upriver from Savannah, then the seat of government for Georgia. Galphin "balanced violence with paternalism" in various ways that may explain the somewhat positive portrait in George's memoir.[9]

George married Phillis in about 1770 and we can only imagine her life as a spouse, parent, co-farmer, and partner in ministry.[10] He later wrote in his memoir that "my wife had a brother, who was half an Indian by his mother's side and half a Negro," and from this, some scholars have assumed that Phillis could also have been of partly indigenous origin, perhaps Muskogee Creek. Given that southeastern indigenous kinship groups were matrilineal, it is surprising that George did not say "their"

5. Walker, *Black Loyalists*; Whitfield, "African Diaspora," 220–23; Walker, "Critical Histories," 34–36; Wilson, *Loyal Blacks*; Gordon, *From Slavery to Freedom*. See also Grant, "Black Immigrants."

6. Saillant, "First Black Atlantic," 19.

7. Whitfield, "African Diaspora," 228–29; Clifford, *From Slavery to Freetown*; Brown, "Black Loyalists."

8. David George was listed as around 40 years old in "Muster Book."

9. Rippon, "Account," 474; Rindfleisch, *George Galphin's Intimate Empire*, 11.

10. Hamilton, "Naming Names."

rather than "his,"[11] so it is possible that he was referring to his wife's stepbrother.

After the birth of their first child, George began his spiritual journey within the eighteenth-century trans-Atlantic movement of Protestant religious renewal, described by North American writers as a Great Awakening. George recalled that he had occasionally attended Church of England services in Virginia, but while at Silver Bluff he met a man "of my own color, named Cyrus" from Charleston, whose conversation encouraged in George to a period of melancholy, conviction of sin, introspection, and prayer. These stages followed the psychological and literary conventions of evangelical discourse: "Soon after I saw that I could not be saved by any of my own doings, but that it must be by God's mercy ... the Lord took away my distress ... I had such pleasure and joy in my soul, that no man could give me."[12]

Soon after, George heard the preaching of a George Liele, who was younger than George and whom David George had known "ever since he was a boy." Liele originally worked in the household of Henry Sharp, a Baptist deacon, who had moved to a nearby settlement whose founding Galphin had partly sponsored. Unprecedentedly, Liele while enslaved had been licensed as a probationer by a Baptist church led by Sharp's brother-in-law. George's response to Lieles's sermon confirmed the authenticity and fullness of the conversion, and in 1773, Galphin allowed them both to begin using part of one of his sawmills for a Baptist church.[13]

The Silver Bluff congregation and a small congregation near Savannah became the two oldest Afro-Baptist churches in the thirteen colonies. The controversy as to precise chronology and precedent relates in part to definitions of continuous, to whether at early points congregations may have included listeners who were not considered Black.[14] Another aspect of the controversy concerns these churches' origins in the practice of itinerant ministers preaching to gathered congregations in places not yet formally organized as a church or not yet within a building

11. Rippon, "Account," 477; Pybus, *Epic Journeys*, 47; Rindfleisch, *George Galphin's Intimate Empire*, 8.

12. Rippon, "Account," 475.

13. Rippon, "Account," 475–76; "Account of Several Baptist Churches," 332–37; Rindfleisch, *George Galphin's Intimate Empire*, 79; Frey, *Water*, 37–39.

14. Many studies have explored how constructs and vocabulary in European and other languages concerning social identity/ies related to skin colour or ancestry have varied over time and space. See, for example, Turda and Quine.

designated as a church. For example, on November 18, 1772, a few years before George's conversion, the German Calvinist minister at the Presbyterian church in Savannah noted that he "preachd [sic] at Mr Galphin's ... place." That he also "enlarged on Infant Baptisms" suggests that he was preaching to a congregation that included families with unbaptized children and perhaps also to listeners influenced by theology favouring believers' baptism.[15]

The communities along the lower Savannah river, already influenced earlier by Whitefield and the Wesleys, became, in the 1770s, a small but ultimately flourishing hotbed of Black or Black and White congregations listening to itinerating or local preachers.[16] According to George, "Brother Palmer . . . pastor at some distance from Silver Bluff" had baptized George, his wife, and others, formed them "into a church, and gave us the Lord's supper"; "Then I began to exhort in the church, and learned to sing" Isaac Watts's *Psalms and Hymns*. George was recognized as a preacher, "received instruction from Brother Palmer how to conduct myself," and learned to read from children in the community school, but covertly, as this was forbidden to enslaved people by the laws of Carolina and Georgia.[17]

Early African-American church historian Walter H. Brooks reasoned that since a Connecticut Baptist minister at the time (Wait Palmer) was a family friend of itinerant Baptist missionaries known to have served on both sides of the Savannah River in this period, Wait Palmer could have done the same and "best fits the case . . . until we can find another Elder Palmer, whose claim is absolutely certain."[18] Some historians have accepted this without paying attention to Brooks's original cautionary note.[19] The first surviving records of the Charleston Baptist Association, however, listed a Rev. Joshua Palmer among their ministers in 1785: his descendants and other historians have shown that this English immigrant Palmer had obtained land in South Carolina much earlier, and was probably the preacher mentioned by George.[20]

15. Zubly, *Journal*, 20; Rindfleisch, *George Galphin's Intimate Empire*, 213.
16. Sidbury, *Becoming African in America*, 70; Frey and Wood, *Come Shouting to Zion*, 88–117.
17. Rippon, "Account," 476.
18. Brooks, *Silver Bluff Church*, 45; Kellison, *Forging a Christian Order*, 41.
19. Gordon, *From Slavery to Freedom*, 24–25.
20. Townsend, *South Carolina Baptists*, 27; Frey, *Water*, 38; Meszaros, "Reverend Joshua Palmer."

Palmer continued to work intermittently with George "till the American war was coming on, when the Ministers were not allowed to come amongst us lest they should furnish us with too much knowledge." As early as fall 1774, some British commentators had publicly or privately considered the advantages of arming slaves against Patriot supporters.[21] News of the beginning of armed conflict in Massachusetts in April 1775 and of the intention of Virginia's governor to arm and set free such slaves as "should assist me if I was attacked" led to the prohibition of itinerant preachers among enslaved communities.[22] A reminder that George and Liele were part of a wider movement occurred in Savannah in May, where David Margate, a Black preacher from the Huntingdonians, an Evangelical movement within the Church of England, was preaching.[23] To an audience of Blacks and Whites in Savannah, Margate spoke of "God's Deliverance to the Negroes, from the power of their Masters, as he freed the Children of Israel from Egyptian Bondage," a longstanding theme of Afro-Christianity. This convinced slave owners that Margate meant to incite rebellion, and a local merchant and patron of the institution which had sponsored him arranged for Margate to escape by sea.[24] Only a few Baptist churches in the Upper South were intermittently anti-slavery in the 1780s and 1790s, and studies suggest that about 40 percent of Baptist preachers in South Carolina in this period owned slaves.[25]

In 1775, the provincial Congress in Charleston, formed from nearly all the members of the last royal provincial assembly, had become the de facto colonial government. It sent a small group, including a leading Baptist minister, to the inland settlements perceived as more neutral or Loyalist than the coastal region, to persuade them to support the Patriot side or at least not to support the British. The church that had licensed George Liele was among the mainly Loyalist churches: its minister was expelled from the colony and deacon Henry Sharpe became an officer in a new Loyalist regiment.[26] Lord Dunmore's proclamation in November 1775 technically only offered freedom to male slaves and indentured servants belonging to "Rebels" and willing to serve in British forces, but was

21. Morgan and O'Shaughnessy, "Arming Slaves," 188–89.
22. Frey, *Water*, 38; Morris, ed., *Yes, Lord, I Know the Road*, 218.
23. Whytock, "Huntingdonian Mission."
24. Frey, *Water*, 38; Sidbury, *Becoming African in America*, 69–70.
25. Najar, "Meddling with Emancipation," 162; Kidd and Hankins, *Baptists in America*, 99–100.
26. Smith and Kidd, *Order and Ardor*, 23–24; Davis, "Loyalism," 250–53.

rhetorically broadened in statements by other key British officers in 1776 and formally in 1779.[27] The implications for the Silver Bluff community of enslaved persons were clear.

After the British took Savannah in late 1778, Galphin and some of his household left Silver Bluff. David George later remembered that his family and "fifty or more slaves" went to the British forces in Ebenezer, where he was imprisoned for roughly a month because White Loyalists "had reported that I was planning to carry the Black people back again to their slavery." This statement has confused some scholars,[28] but the source of this rumour is evident from the initial British relationship with Galphin. Marching to Augusta in January 1779, Archibald Campbell's British regiment met "90 of Golphins [sic] Negroes" who had "deserted his Plantation and joined the Troops." But Campbell used the slaves as a "bargaining chip with Galphin to dissuade him from influencing the Creeks to remain neutral in the war" and "three days later Campbell received a 'penitential Letter from Golphin.'" Campbell then sent David George's group to Savannah "'to be preserved for Mr. Golphin, in Case he continued to act in the same friendly part toward us.'"[29] Although initially equivocal, Galphin eventually became the new Commissioner of Indian Affairs in the southeast for the Continental Congress.[30] Because George had previously worked for Galphin in his trade and communications with the Creek who were being courted by both Patriot and British leaders, it is not surprising that someone had rumoured that George knew of this possibility.

The risk faced by the Silver Bluff former slaves was not exceptional during the war in the south. British officials "forced runaways to return to Loyalist masters . . . sent troops to suppress slave strikes on Loyalist-owned plantations" and "sold blacks taken as plunder from Patriot plantations."[31] Thus, the British strategy along the lower Savannah river in 1779 anticipated the betrayal and re-enslavement of Black Loyalists[32]

---

27. Wilson, *Loyal Blacks*, 29.

28. Rippon, "Account," 476–77; Gordon, *From Slavery to Freedom*, 31; Piecuch, *Three Peoples*, 161.

29. Paulett, *Empire*, 111; Pybus, *Epic Journeys*, 39.

30. Rindfleisch, *George Galphin's Intimate Empire*, 170–75.

31. Taylor, *American Revolutions*, 228; Troxler, "Re-Enslavement," 73.

32. Although the usage of "Black Loyalist" has been debated (see Whitfield, "African Diaspora," 227–29), the phrase in its broadest sense has remained useful and prevalent.

in Nova Scotia, one of the key forces that drove many to leave, a little over a decade later, for Sierra Leone.

Loyalist officer Colonel Thomas Brown, a relatively recent English immigrant who had lived not far from Silver Bluff[33] released David George, who rejoined George Liele. Both then engaged in preaching and farming in the Savannah area. Henry Sharpe had emancipated Liele, and, by December 1777, Liele and others, including George, had organized a Baptist church in Savannah.[34] Like Liele and other Black refugees in Savannah, George relied on the "patron-client relationships"[35] between Black Loyalists and British officers. George was so weakened by smallpox that the household depended wholly for a while on the income his wife earned doing laundry for General Clinton, until George could work as a butcher and rent a house and field.[36]

After the formal ending of hostilities in North America in early 1782, the British began leaving Savannah for Charleston. The remaining senior British officer and the Patriot governor of South Carolina agreed that many but not all Blacks "claiming freedom as loyalists" would be allowed to leave after investigation and approval by a committee. Among an estimated 1,500 Loyalists evacuated from Charleston, George and his family left Charlestown in November and arrived in Halifax after 22 days.[37]

In Nova Scotia, leading Loyalists had proposed the mouth of a south shore river, known to Mikmaq as L/Sogumkeagum and as Port Razoir/Roseway to Europeans, as the site for a new community because of its strategic location for seafaring, despite its unsuitability to farming.[38] By spring 1783, George "got leave to go to Shelburne because no way was open for me to preach to my own colour in Halifax." In Shelburne, George found "Numbers of my own colour": free or recently freed Black Loyalists, indentured servants, and "several hundred slaves." He began holding meetings in the nearby "woods, at a camp," attracting listeners by the singing of hymns on weeknights, followed by Sunday services by

33. Jasanoff, *Liberty's Exiles*, 21–23.

34. Rippon, "Account," 477; "Account of Several Baptist Churches," 334–36; Little, "George Liele," 188–92.

35. Byrd, *Captives and Voyagers*, 160.

36. "David George's Lease and Passports."

37. Rippon, "Account," 477; Jasanoff, *Liberty's Exiles*, 75–76; Wilson, *Loyal Blacks*, 45–47.

38. MacKinnon, *This Unfriendly Soil*, 5.

the river, "to which a great number of White and Black people came." After George had held almost continuous evening services, "The White people, the justices, and all, were in an uproar." They tried to force him back into the woods, but George was able to both live and gather people for services in an improvised structure on land allotted to a White Loyalist. Within a few weeks, George's wife arrived with their three young adult sons and two daughters, and by this time George had acquired a small town lot with a stream "convenient for baptizing at any time."[39]

By the winter of 1783, the community was ready to form a church: either as partners in ministry or as the first two members, George and his wife heard the testimony of four Black converts, and by the summer of 1784 the church had "about fifty members,"[40] within a larger congregation. They included Sampson Colbert who became a lay preacher in Saint John, who later died on the voyage to Sierra Leone, and a White couple who remained in Shelburne. George remembered William and Mrs. Taylor as having come from England to Shelburne, and Benedict went even further and thought that they had come from the same London church as the editor of George's memoir. Twentieth-century genealogists and archivists have suggested, however, that the William Taylor of Shelburne who died in 1810 may have come from Massachusetts.[41]

David George faced considerable and at times life-threatening opposition as an evangelical, as a Baptist, as a preacher, and as a Black man. A Methodist itinerant had experienced physical threats while preaching in Shelburne shortly before George's arrival. An incident in George's first months in Shelburne illustrates both the racism George encountered and recurring themes of early evangelical texts: the struggle of an individual seeker against the opposition of family members, and the ways in which outdoor baptisms functioned as spectacle for sympathizers, critics, or observers.[42] When a White couple, William and Elizabeth Holmes,

---

39. Rippon, "Account," 478; Walker, *Black Loyalists*, 40; Gordon, *From Slavery to Freedom*, 52–53, 63.

40. Gordon, *From Slavery to Freedom*, 54–55. George later "baptized about twenty" in Birchtown, and Liele recalled the membership of George's church at around 60 at the time of his last letter from George before the departure to Sierra Leone (see Rippon, "Account of Several Baptist Churches," 336).

41. Rippon, "Account," 478–79; Benedict, *General History*, 295; Gordon, *From Slavery to Freedom*, 56–57, 298–99; Elliott and Public Archives of Nova Scotia, eds., *Legislative Assembly*, 213.

42. Morgan, *Public Men and Virtuous Women*, 114; Goodwin, *Into Deep Waters*, 32–33.

sought to join David George's church, their "relations, who lived in the town, were very angry, raised a mob, and endeavoured to hinder their being baptized." The local justices of the peace intervened on behalf of the couple, but soon "after this the persecution increased," peaking and converging with the Shelburne riots in July 1784. Contemporaries and historians have explained the riots over several days as the intersection of racism[43] and a segregated job market in which Blacks paid significantly less than Whites were able to obtain more unskilled employment than some soldiers, and former soldiers' grievances with the government over land promised to them. "Forty or fifty disbanded soldiers" tore down George's house along with others and attempted to burn the meeting house.[44]

During the riots, George was assaulted and forced out of the meeting house. He later heard that his meeting house had been used as a tavern by a man who claimed, "The old Negro wanted to make a heaven of this place, but I'll make a hell of it." George preached from Birchtown for the rest of the year, but, as he obliquely noted, "my own colour persecuted me there."[45] This passage could reflect the fact that the Birchtown Loyalists included adherents of the Church of England, some of whom had become Huntingdonians[46] who might have regarded believer's baptism by immersion as a challenge to their religious practice and Methodists, who in this period sometimes accepted both infant baptism and believers' baptism by immersion. Other lay leaders may also have seen David George as a rival undermining their own status in their congregations.[47] Yet other Black evangelicals also experienced opposition from their own communities. As Violet King "was the first person at BurchTown that experienced deliverance from evil tempers, and exhorted and urged others to seek and enjoy the same blessing, she was not a little opposed by some of our Black brethren."[48] Both David George's and Boston King's recollections were for their own denominational press, which may explain why neither mentioned the other by name, even though they were both in

---

43. See also Walker, *Black Loyalists*, 55, 62, and Huskins, "New Hope," 119.
44. Rippon, "Account," 479–80; Marston, "Benjamin Marston's Diary."
45. Rippon, "Account," 480.
46. Walker, "Marrant, John."
47. Walker, *Black Loyalists*, 75; Wilson, *Loyal Blacks*, 122.
48. King et al., *Life*, 22.

the Shelburne area before King moved to Preston and then migrated to Sierra Leone.

George's memoir recalled summer 1785 as "notable for a considerable revival of religion," and he began to travel further away from Shelburne in subsequent years. He preached to congregations in other Nova Scotian communities, including Liverpool and the Halifax area, as well as what today is the Wolfville area on the Fundy shore. Precisely when David George first went to New Brunswick is unclear owing to a typographical error in the reproduction by Rippon of his license from Governor Sir Thomas Carleton. George recorded in his memoir that his second trip to Fredericton and Saint John occurred when the river in between was still navigable, perhaps late in 1790, and was followed by a mission to Preston, Nova Scotia. While returning from that mission, he suffered severe frostbite, from which he recovered only partially in spring 1791.[49]

For parts of 1790 and 1791 the New Light preacher Harris Harding visited Shelburne, with more success "among the coloured population" than among the rest of the community.[50] Perhaps one of these visits occurred while David George was elsewhere, but Harding also attended some of George's services and provided a vivid description of one: "Singing Hosannahs to the Son of David, Several of them frequently was obliged to Stop and rejoice, soon after David Began Prayer." George was "overcome with Joy" and "turned to me with many Tears like Brooks Running down his Cheeks desiring me to Call upon that worthy Name ... My Soul was upon Mount Zion."[51]

Harding's letters from Shelburne also invoked the preaching and writings of Henry Alline, and historians have considered the extent to which David George's ministry may have actively benefited from or simply converged with the New Light movement. Alline's memoir noted that he had a few Black and White converts in Falmouth, and in another entry that "I have often seen in the compass of my travels, poor servants and slaves shouting forth the Redeemer's praise; while their masters stood in open rebellion, and rejected the simplicity of the Gospel."[52] This could be literal, but Alline could also have been invoking the rhetoric of biblical

---

49. Rippon, "Account," 480–82; See diaries of June 18, 1786, and January 11, 1790, in Perkins, *Diary*; Gordon, *From Slavery to Freedom*, 63–68.

50. Davis, *Life and Times*, 34; Harding to Dimock, 1 Sept 1791, in *New Light Letters*, 155; Goodwin, *Into Deep Waters*, 43–46.

51. Harding to Lavina D' Wolf, 20 Aug 1791, in *New Light Letters*, 131.

52. Walker, *Black Loyalists*, 74; Alline, *Life and Journal*, 18, 90.

passages concerning servants and slaves. George Rawlyk's claim, however, that "the Black Methodist and Baptists in Sierra Leone shared a New Light heritage that probably owed more to Henry Alline and Freeborn Garrettson and their New Brunswick and Nova Scotia disciples than it did to their American slave experiences" exceeded the evidence and defies logic concerning influence and causation. Rawlyk followed others in incorrectly identifying "Brother Palmer" as a New Englander, but also downplayed the significance of the Afro-Christianities which existed before the American Revolution. He was on stronger ground in concluding that David George's preaching would have resonated with audiences that had heard Henry Alline and other New Light preachers.[53] More significantly, unlike other Black evangelical groups who operated within Wesleyan Methodism or the Church of England, after the initial donation of the meeting house lot, David George's Baptists were entirely independent of "white agency."[54]

Whether individual migrants such as the George family or groups such as the Birchtown inhabitants, the Black Loyalists received far less and worse land and provisions than White refugees. They were paid significantly less, confined to certain kinds of occupations, and often forced to re-indenture themselves or their children sometimes for lifetime terms. Moreover, a significant number were abducted and re-enslaved, some forcibly removed from the colony.[55] During the 1780s and early 1790s, Shelburne magistrates heard various court cases about White efforts to control Blacks, including the re-enslavement of Black Loyalists. The Shelburne Black population lived in such poverty that more than half of those who would leave for Sierra Leone lacked even the most basic items of clothing.[56]

One of the key leaders of various Black communities was a former sergeant in the Black Pioneers, Thomas Peters, who had led one group to the Digby area and later moved to New Brunswick. In 1790, Peters collected petitions from 100 families in New Brunswick and 102 in Annapolis County authorizing him to travel to London and to demand that the original land grants be honoured either in Nova Scotia or elsewhere.

53. Rawlyk, *Canada Fire*, 40–41.
54. Walker, *Black Loyalists*, 74.
55. Walker, *Black Loyalists*, ch. 3; Wilson, *Loyal Blacks*, 86–96, 100–108. See also Whitfield, *North to Bondage*.
56. Troxler, "Re-Enslavement," 79, 84; Clarkson and Fergusson, *Clarkson's Mission to America*, 101, 107.

Petitions also addressed other issues, including the continued existence of slavery in Nova Scotia. In the same years, the new state of Massachusetts, which then included the District of Maine, had begun its judicial abolition of slavery. Peters knew that British abolitionists had established a company for the purposes of founding a free Black settlement on the coast of West Africa. He met with the directors and agreed to lead a group of Black settlers from New Brunswick or Nova Scotia to Sierra Leone. Ironically, the committee planning the project had earlier considered and rejected New Brunswick as one possible location for the colony.[57]

The British government agreed to pay the cost of transport, and The Sierra Leone Company sent former naval officer turned abolitionist John Clarkson to present the project and recruit participants. His *Journal*, commissioned by his more famous abolitionist brother and part of the genre of evangelical and philanthropic confessional writings intended to be shared publicly,[58] has remained a key source for late eighteenth-century Nova Scotia and New Brunswick Black history, as well as the life of David George. After two weeks in Halifax in October 1791, Clarkson sailed to Shelburne where he met George. As in other communities, Clarkson and George encountered significant opposition to the Sierra Leone project, and even threats to George's life and to those who attended Clarkson's meetings, because of the project's potential effect on the supply of cheap labour.[59]

Historians have estimated that the 1196 who ultimately embarked were no more than one third or less of the free Black population. The unhealthy, disabled, infirm elderly, and elderly single women were excluded from emigrating, unless they had a family member who would include them within his household. Apprentices, bound tenants, indentured servants, and individuals with unresolvable debts were not allowed to leave unless they could be released or release themselves from these obligations.[60]

Most of the Black Loyalists who went to Sierra Leone were Methodists, with smaller groups of Huntingdonians, other adherents of the

57. Walker, *Black Loyalists*, 94–96; Walker, "Peters, Thomas"; Land and Schocket, "New Approaches."

58. Scanlan, *Freedom's Debtors*, 28–29.

59. Clarkson and Fergusson, *Clarkson's Mission to America*, 51–53, 50; Walker, *Black Loyalists*, 118–23; Wilson, *Loyal Blacks*, 199–213.

60. Clarkson and Fergusson, *Clarkson's Mission to America*, 72; Walker, *Black Loyalists*, 128.

Church of England,[61] and Baptists. Almost all Shelburne Baptists agreed to migrate, except for some who had more personal ties to North America, for example, "a few of the sisters whose husbands were inclined to go back to New York; and sister Lizze, a Quebec Indian, and brother Lewis, her husband, who was half Indian." Another Baptist contingent came from the Halifax area, chiefly from a congregation based in Preston.[62]

David George's family appeared first on the list of Birchtown/Shelburne emigrants in November 1791; his occupations were listed as preacher, sawyer and former soldier, and, before leaving, George was able to sell some of the land and buildings he had acquired.[63] Reading Clarkson's *Journal* through the lens of the new 'animal history' adds to the picture of David George's household: Clarkson rationed the number of dogs that would be allowed on the embarking vessels to one for every six families, except for David George and three others to whom Clarkson had already promised "their dogs". Dogs' value as protectors was evident in Clarkson's note that not long after arrival in Sierra Leone, the George's Newfoundland dog was attacked by a leopard, but alerted the settlers early enough that they were able to drive the leopard away.[64]

While they gathered and waited in Halifax, Clarkson named David George, Thomas Peters, and Methodist preacher John Ball as representatives for the passengers in dealings with Clarkson. Along with other preachers, David George continued to lead services in the barracks where the embarkees waited. He also "preached from house to house" in Halifax and gave his "farewell sermon" in the Methodist Meeting House.[65]

The vessels embarked in January, and when the last arrived in Sierra Leone on March 9, the Nova Scotian preachers led in singing, "worship", and "thanksgiving."[66] On the first Sunday, the Church of

61. Walker, *Black Loyalists*, 68–69. Clarkson and Fergusson, *Clarkson's Mission to America*, 94. In 1796, the governor of Sierra Leone estimated Nova Scotian household heads as 270 Wesleyans, 70 Huntingdonians, and 60 Baptists (see Sidbury, *Becoming African in America*, 231).

62. Rippon, "Account," 481, 483; Clarkson and Fergusson, *Clarkson's Mission to America*, 95.

63. This may refer to George's assistance with the fortifications of Savannah; see Walker, "Dictionary of Canadian Biography."

64. Clarkson and Fergusson, *Clarkson's Mission to America*, 72; Clarke's Journal, 24 May 1792 cited in Gordon, *From Slavery to Freedom*, 116.

65. Rippon, "Account," 483; Clarkson and Fergusson, *Clarkson's Mission to America*, 104–5, 108; Sutherland, "Marchinton, Philip."

66. The recollections of Anthony Elliot are cited in Wilson, *Loyal Blacks*, 233.

England chaplain led the morning "Divine Service," and David George also preached, although whether within the same service or separately is not clear.[67] Clarkson later wrote: "the Nova Scotians sang the appropriate Hymn, The Year of Jubilee is come [Return ye ransomed sinners home] creating such sensations as I have not power to describe."[68]

The Sierra Leone Company had bought land from Temne leaders for the "Old Settlers" (formerly enslaved persons who had migrated from England in 1787), for the Nova Scotians, and for a few British families. The precise limits of these lands were debated by the Temne, who thought the Company and its settlers asked for too much. In the initial months especially, the Nova Scotians struggled to survive during food shortages, disease, and the shock of encounter with a radically different habitat. The identities and political or economic interests of the three groups of settlers were also intermittently at odds: David George was among those who represented Clarkson and negotiated better relations with the "Old Settlers" in August 1792.[69]

Over the long run, the key issues that David George and the other Nova Scotians faced over the next decade involved their livelihoods, land, leadership, governance, and "church and state." The surveys and division of the land that the Company had bought for the Nova Scotians were not completed until the following year. The Temne wanted to retain more water access; the Company directors wanted to block the Nova Scotians from river or shore lots, from which, as David George and others protested, they had also been excluded in Nova Scotia.[70] The compromise was a lottery to determine which settlers would have river lots. Clarkson and the Company had promised more land to each male settler and household than they had actually bought from the Temne. Although David George and Thomas Peters received nine acres and Moses Wilkinson seven, most households did not receive more than one or two acres.[71]

This delay and the shortages of provisions made it necessary for the Nova Scotians to engage in other economic activities. Yet Clarkson and the Company hindered this pursuit of what Rommel-Ruiz has called a

---

67. Clarkson and Fergusson, *Clarkson's Mission to America*, 171.

68. Clarkson cited in Wilson, *Loyal Blacks*, 234; Walker, *Black Loyalists*, 383.

69. Wilson, *Loyal Blacks*, 268.

70. Walker, *Black Loyalists*, 153; Wilson, *Loyal Blacks*, 262–63; Schwarz, "Land and Settlement."

71. Fyfe, *History*, 47; Jasanoff, *Liberty's Exiles*, 296.

"communitarian idea of competency."[72] Access to the various occupations within the company and settlement was clearly racialized, and those Nova Scotians who did obtain positions were paid in credit for company supplies whose prices were not competitive. When the Nova Scotians insisted on wages in coin, Clarkson visited the Nova Scotian congregations, including that of David George, to try to persuade them that payment in coin would lead to greater alcohol consumption and drunkenness. Similarly, Clarkson tried to discourage the Nova Scotians from small scale trading with incoming vessels, which he saw as a corrupting influence, directly or indirectly connected to the slave trade.[73]

The most significant controversy over land concerned the terms on which it had been offered to the Nova Scotians. Historians debate whether Clarkson was engaging in self-delusion, wishful thinking, or outright deceit in promising the Nova Scotians that they would own freehold land subject only to local property taxes, such as existed in all British jurisdictions. In fact, the Company offer assumed an additional annual quitrent as a means of what they saw as recovering the costs of the project.[74] Resistance to the quitrent persisted throughout the decade. When Clarkson's successor as governor of the colony finally began attempting to collect it in 1797, David George's Baptists agreed to comply, the Huntingdonians "left it to the individual conscience, but the leaders said they did not intend to pay. The far more numerous Methodists said anyone who paid the rent would be expelled."[75]

As the quitrent debate illustrates, the land issue intersected with debates over leadership and governance among the Nova Scotians from their earliest weeks in Sierra Leone. Of the three intermediaries appointed by Clarkson, Thomas Peters—whose travel to and lobbying in London had initiated the project—seemed a natural and popular leader. In early 1792, David George had been among those who had signed a petition stating the Nova Scotians' grievances and presented by Peters to Clarkson.[76] Tensions between Peters and Clarkson increased until Clarkson believed that Peters and his supporters were leading an uprising and attempting to take over the government of the colony. According to Clarkson, David George

72. Rommel-Ruiz, "Colonizing the Black Atlantic," 361.

73. Walker, *Black Loyalists*, 153–54, 174–75; Clifford, *From Slavery to Freetown*, 147.

74. Wilson, *Loyal Blacks*, 206; Fyfe, *History*, 34.

75. Wilson, *Loyal Blacks*, 329.

76. Wilson, *Loyal Blacks*, 250.

at this point had preached against Thomas Peters's conduct despite being threatened with assassination, Clarkson had received warning of this from unnamed Preston letter writers, and historians have debated the extent to which this was also a conflict between Methodists and Baptists,[77] rather than just between Peters and Clarkson.

Subsequently, Peters came into conflict with other Nova Scotians over his handling of property inherited by a widow with two children. A rival claimant to part of the estate accused Peters of theft, while Peters claimed he was only collecting a debt owed by the deceased. An all-Nova Scotian jury required Peters to return the property and pay the costs of the trial. Historians have interpreted this incident as either manufactured or influenced by the Company including Clarkson against Peters or, alternatively, reflecting Peters's sense of entitlement arising from what he had done for the community.[78] But a third view that could reconcile disparate testimonies is that Peters was telling the truth about the debt, but that according to the Nova Scotian jury, in the moral economy of eighteenth-century evangelicalism, he should have forgiven the debt, rather than claim it from the widow and orphan. Shortly afterwards, Peters died of one of the local fevers. As the originator of the emigration project and a key figure in Freetown's early history, his public memory has for some commentators exceeded that of the other Methodist leaders and of David George.[79]

Of the governors, Clarkson was the least unpopular, and when Clarkson returned to England in late 1792 to marry, the Nova Scotians, including George, petitioned him to return. They were not successful, and the company replaced him with another council member in April 1793.[80] With several letters of recommendation from various Evangelical Church of England clergy, George traveled to England with Clarkson and stayed first with Rev. John Newton, another Evangelical minister, today most remembered as the author of the popular hymn *Amazing Grace*.[81] George attended Baptist Association meetings and also preached, though

---

77. Walker, *Black Loyalists*, 149–50; Clifford, *From Slavery to Freetown*, 125–27; Sidbury, *Becoming African in America*, 102; Gilbert, *Black Patriots*, 233.

78. Walker, *Black Loyalists*, 151; Wilson, *Loyal Blacks*, 251–55; Gilbert, *Black Patriots*, 234.

79. Blyden, "This Na [sic] True Story," 362.

80. Fyfe and Jones, eds., *Our Children Free and Happy*, 30–31.

81. "Amazing Grace." https://www.themorgan.org/exhibitions/online/TheDiary/John-Newton

precisely where is not clear. During this visit, George provided his life recollections to Baptist laymen who published the text in the Baptist *Annual Register* and also collected donations for his congregation and a future chapel.[82]

The various usages of 'friend' in late eighteenth- and early nineteenth-century prose, ranging from supporter of a cause to a spouse, have made it challenging to determine the nature of Clarkson's and George's friendship. Clarkson attended George's services and even private prayer meetings, and made frequent references to George in his journal. When Clarkson left Freetown in late December 1792, he noted separately among the general gifts those he received from Phillis George.[83] Another Nova Scotia writing later to Clarkson, however, claimed that: "We have not had any satisfaction of the Companys [sic] good will toward us, & Mr. George has spoken very much against you since he came back from London." Some have suggested that in Clarkson's ongoing conflict with the Company over various issues, George sided publicly with the Company because he had been so well treated in London.[84] It is also possible that George had expressed disappointment that Clarkson's promises had not been fulfilled, or alternatively that the letter writer wanted, for some unknown reason, to diminish George's status with Clarkson and the Company.

The governing council of the colony and other officials constituted a "white governing class" that was administratively incompetent, self-aggrandizing, and internecine in its relations with each other and with governors and the directors of the company in England.[85] Initially, the only officials elected by the Nova Scotians were ten constables, but beginning in 1793, every ten households elected men who would then choose another man for a group whom the company conceived as intermediaries between them and the Nova Scotians or adjudicators of causes of less importance. Both men and women until 1797 voted in the elections, and as historians have noted, the Nova Scotians increasingly regarded this system as a form of representative government, whose conflicts concerning

---

82. Gordon, *From Slavery to Freedom*, 123–25.

83. Jasanoff, *Liberty's Exiles*, 299, 411.

84. Fyfe and Jones, eds., *Our Children Free and Happy*, 34, 72; Schama, *Rough Crossings*, 385.

85. Walker, *Black Loyalists*, 147–49, 151; Clarkson and Fergusson, *Clarkson's Mission to America*, 60, 173.

the relative authority of the representatives and the council were not unlike those which had occurred in thirteen colonies.[86]

Other issues for the Nova Scotians both during their first year with Clarkson and in later years involved the council's inability to control the behaviour of company employees or crew on arriving vessels towards the Nova Scotians, an issue which intersected with the West African and European slave trade. The company maintained diplomatic relations with West African kingdoms engaged in the slave trade and relied on vessels from the European slave trade which brought supplies or mail. Clarkson had supported those Nova Scotians who had aided escaped slaves, but at times some of his successors considered themselves obliged to return them to other West Africans or to European vessels.[87]

The Nova Scotians were at risk of being re-enslaved if they left the colony, and of becoming entangled in the local slave trade, in part because according to Temne law a "runaway slave" became the property of the household in which the individual had found "refuge".[88] One of the Nova Scotians whom George had appointed as a Baptist preacher and elder for the Preston community, Hector Peters, became estranged from his family and community for a few years, probably for this reason. The 1802 census described him as having left his wife and living outside the colony, and the colony's only newspaper reported him as engaged in the slave trade. Peters returned after the abolition of the trans-Atlantic slave trade, when amnesty was also given to West African based slave traders.[89]

In June 1794, violence between visiting slave trade vessel crew members and Nova Scotian employees of the Sierra Leone Company had converged with other grievances. These escalated into what Clarkson's successor Zachary Macaulay perceived as an uprising against his government. Macaulay was relatively young at the time, and his personality and actions would be criticized not just by the Nova Scotians and their historians, but also by some of Macaulay's British contemporaries.[90] Another conflict occurred over the disposition of supplies and property the colonists had salvaged during the brief French occupation in 1794. By

86. Brown, "Black Loyalists," 111–12; Sidbury, *Becoming African in America*, 105.

87. Fyfe, *History*, 40, 54; Scanlan, *Freedom's Debtors*; Lowther, *African American Odyssey*, 134–35.

88. Walker, *Black Loyalists*, 171–74; Lowther, *African American Odyssey*, 155–56.

89. Gordon, *From Slavery to Freedom*, 344; Fyfe, *History*, 100–101.

90. Wilson, *Loyal Blacks*, 313–15; Pybus, *Epic Journeys*, 189; Jasanoff, *Liberty's Exiles*, 299.

late 1797, after the peak of anti-quitrent agitation, Macaulay's opponents had formed a quasi-shadow government connected with a by now separate community outside Freetown.[91]

In these flashpoints, David George and the Baptists functioned either as mediators with or as supporters of the governor, often in contrast with the Methodists. Some have explained this as a legacy of George's relationship with Clarkson or the product of an Afro-Baptist political culture of cooperation or at least pragmatism concerning powerful authorities. Possibly in return for greater loyalty, Baptists were overrepresented among contracts, licences, or jobs provided by the company.[92] In May 1796, an English Methodist lay preacher complained that George was "Macaulay's tool."[93]

In the 1796 conflicts over relations between church and state, George clearly sided with the other Black preachers. Macaulay had introduced a new requirement that "future marriages would be valid only if performed by the Chaplain, or some person designated by the Governor, after having the banns called in the Church." Macauley wrote that he had deliberately "avoided any definition of who were persons in holy orders," but that "No sooner had the notice met David George's eye than he began to exclaim most outrageously against it, talked loudly of the violation of their religious rights, and of the call there was to resist such acts even to blood."[94]

Macaulay was responding to what he saw as the immoral informality of the Nova Scotians' marriage practices, including easy divorce. Some scholars have interpreted this debate solely as a conflict between African American cultural customs, shaped also by the prohibition of marriages among enslaved persons in many English colonies, and a European view represented by Macaulay. Wallace Brown noted "echoes here of the unpopular New Brunswick Marriage Act of 1791, which limited marriage ceremonies to Anglican clergy."[95] Revisiting this topic within the history of the family suggests that this issue was part of a wider change.

---

91. Wilson, *Loyal Blacks*, 329–32; Sidbury, *Becoming African in America*, 116–17; Schama, *Rough Crossings*, 386.

92. Walker, *Black Loyalists*, 199–200; Wilson, *Loyal Blacks*, 314; Clifford, *From Slavery to Freetown*, 141, 172; Sidbury, *Becoming African in America*, 108–9; Gilbert, *Black Patriots*, 239–40.

93. Cited in Gordon, *From Slavery to Freedom*, 338.

94. Fyfe, *History*, 71; Macaulay, *Life and Letters*, 140.

95. Clifford, *From Slavery to Freetown*, 180–81; Brown, "Black Loyalists," 112.

England's first statutory marriage law was only a little over forty years old and contrasted with the older tradition of free verbal consent in front of witnesses, which persisted in Scotland. When Macaulay reproached George for having allowed a son and daughter in law to become a couple within his household after only one public declaration,[96] Macaulay was not representing a homogenous Euro-American point of view. Scholars of New England have shown that sexual relations before marriage was not a scandal in some eighteenth-century communities provided the couple actually married, but that attitudes changed in the nineteenth century.[97]

The marriage issue was particularly charged for David George because it occurred within a longer conflict involving British missionaries present in the colony at this time, as well as within theological debate between George and Macaulay. John Garvin, the lay Methodist preacher who had complained about George, and Jacob Grigg, an English Baptist minister with Radical political inclinations, were particularly critical of Macaulay and the Company. Together with Rev. John Clarke, a Scottish Presbyterian, the company's chaplain at the time, they served as visiting preachers for Nova Scotian congregations, while repeating accusations or information about each other to Macaulay or George and others, in the course of various controversies. According to Macaulay, despite initially welcoming Clarke's preaching, David George had come to believe the accusations that Clarke had subsequently abused all the Black preachers and called them blasphemers, and that this along with the new marriage law was part of a wider campaign to close the Nova Scotian chapels. Later, Macaulay persuaded George that these accusations were false, and that George had misunderstood the meaning of the new regulation. George also later complained to the Baptist Missionary Association about Grigg.[98]

The sources on the marriage regulation are also about debate between George and the governor over other religious issues. We have relatively few glimpses of David George's religious beliefs beyond the call to a conversion such as he experienced himself, believers' baptism, and a commitment to regular worship. The membership of the church in Savannah, which David George had joined, created a covenant which combined belief, preferred religious practices, and pragmatic survivalist

96. Wilson, *Loyal Blacks*, 353.
97. Ulrich, *Good Wives*, 122–23.
98. Macaulay, *Life and Letters*, 123, 137–38, 145; Walker, *Black Loyalists*, 201–2; Pybus, *Epic Journeys*, 186.

statements about hierarchy, power, and slavery.[99] The covenant stated that "We hold to be Baptised in a river, or in a place where there is much water, in the name of the Father, and of the Son, and of the Holy Ghost," but appears to have not assumed that believers baptism required an adult level of psychological maturity: "We hold to receive and admit young children into the Church according to the Word of God." Like the official or unofficial practices of a few Baptist or hybrid New Light churches in the English colonies, the covenant said nothing about open as opposed to closed communion (where participation in the communion ritual required not just conversion, but also previous baptism by immersion).[100] This is not surprising, as this debate was not relevant to churches formed of the newly Christianized or newly evangelical.

The covenant avowed pacifism, which again would have been politically safer for a church of enslaved persons, but one could speculate that this might also have referred back to older Anabaptist tradition or possible exposure to the Moravian missionaries who had visited Savannah. Before the French attack on Freetown in 1794, David George expressed concern over British engagement in the Revolutionary and Napoleonic wars, as the First Republic had abolished slavery.[101] The Savannah covenant also committed to food practices that some have argued reflected eighteenth-century Afro-Christians' wish to distance themselves from West African or Caribbean cultural traditions but could also have reflected Islamic influences on West Africa.[102]

Surviving sources from the Sierra Leone period only document instances in which Macaulay or the company's chaplains reacted critically and patronizingly to David George, rather than more descriptive or positive statements about his overall theology or religious practices. Like critics of New Light enthusiasm in British North America, Macaulay "ridiculed" the dreams, visions, and emotional language that the Nova Scotian preachers used to describe their religious experiences. Macaulay stated that David George had occasionally been driven to tears or silence in their conversations, which Macaulay interpreted as his triumph in debate rather than George's frustration.[103] Macaulay "denounced George's

99. Lawson, "Pioneer George Liele," 121.

100. Sobel, *Trabelin' On*, 150–52.

101. Macaulay, *Life and Letters*, 133; restored by Napoleon in 1802, slavery was finally abolished in 1848.

102. Sobel, *Trabelin' On*, 152.

103. Wilson, *Loyal Blacks*, 354; Sidbury, *Becoming African in America*, 235.

claims from the pulpit that prayer and instruction cant [sic] convey grace," and endeavoured to persuade George that only "the written word" must "constitute the 'rule of our faith,'" rather than "mischievous effects of ... dependence on inexplicable mental impressions and bodily feelings."[104] For Macaulay, George's views constituted antinomianism, which Clarke had also charged the Methodist preachers with.[105] Antinomian or antinomianism were words used negatively in discussing whether the act of and genuine experience of divine grace and conversion could be followed by declension and reconversion, or whether divine grace and conversion could prevent an individual from subsequently committing an immoral act, or even remove obligations to follow ritual practices or moral laws. Yet even in Macaulay's characterization, George was arguing a more nuanced version of the perennial grace versus works debate: "George held tenaciously to his 'favourite proposition,' by insisting that 'those who are once' saved 'can never be deprived of their interest in him [Christ] by the greatest crimes.'"[106]

Moreover, Macaulay and modern historians occasionally conflated and confused the community of Nova Scotians, a congregation of regular churchgoers, and actual converted church members, as opposed to the "worldly blacks," the phrase George had used to refer to the unconverted in Shelburne. David George wrote in June 1795 that since his return from England in August 1793, he had baptized three Nova Scotian men, seven women, and one West African.[107] Even allowing for the relatively small size of the Baptist community, this was not a church membership growth rate suggesting easy conversion or unexamined lives.

David George was a Calvinist Baptist believing that although converts could not know this in advance only a portion of humanity could be saved, for reasons which varied within the Calvinist traditions. According to Macaulay, during the introduction of a chaplain who preceded Clarke,

---

Macaulay also criticized what he saw as either Calvinist dogmatism or irrational religious enthusiasm in his Scottish and English religious circles, while claiming that he himself was not a "controversialist" (see Whyte, *Zachary Macaulay*, 63–64, 74).

104. Sidbury, *Becoming African in America*, 115, using both the published Macaulay extracts (1900), as well as unpublished versions of Macaulay's journal and other documents.

105. Wilson, *Loyal Blacks*, 348; Sidbury, *Becoming African in America*, 117; Pybus, *Epic Journeys*, 186.

106. Sidbury, *Becoming African in America*, 115.

107. Rippon, "Account," 479; Gordon, *From Slavery to Freedom*, 207.

"An unfortunate expression of his roused David George's attention, and I was apprehensive that they would be involved in a dispute about general and particular redemption."[108] David George, however, was not an anti-mission Baptist. He wrote that he and another Nova Scotian Baptist (born in Africa), had intended to travel as missionaries to surrounding peoples but were turned back by war.[109] An excerpt from an anonymous sermon that has been attributed to David George, published in 1796, had an expansive view: "See what God is till doing for our nation, putting into de hearts of his people, to come from far distant nation, to come over de mighty waters, and great deep, to bring de salvation of God to dis nation, to Africans."[110]

The greatest conflict between the Nova Scotians and the council occurred at the end of the century, over the recurring issues of governance and taxation. After the British Parliament ended the colony's founding constitutional documents, including the quasi-representative political institutions and elections, a portion of the Nova Scotians attempted to set up an alternative government. Leaders of the uprising by late summer 1800 included David George's deacon, John Cuthbert. The role of another key Baptist lay leader, John Kizell, in the protest is unclear and based on later testimony he gave later in 1826.[111] Ironically, with the aid of newly arrived Jamaican Maroons, the colony's new governor suppressed the rebellion, and reorganized the colony under direct rule of the council.

Some historians have assumed that since David George was not among the critics of the council or rebels named at this time, he must have supported the government.[112] But the council's own records suggest that, when it came to armed conflict, many Nova Scotians chose to either keep their opinions to themselves or remain neutral. The roughly one sixth of the household heads who followed the rebels were mainly from outside Freetown, which "remained peaceful", as "most stayed at home. Many who had opposed government constitutionally declined to

---

108. Macaulay, *Life and Letters*, 54; Walker, *Black Loyalists*, 201. Walker mistakenly assumed that the Methodist preacher would have been equally critical.

109. Fyfe, *History*, 55–56; Gordon, *From Slavery to Freedom*, 131; Lowther, *African American Odyssey*, 138–39.

110. Cited in Wilson, *Loyal Blacks*, 341.

111. Gordon, *From Slavery to Freedom*, 128, 215; Lowther, *African American Odyssey*, 150–52.

112. Clifford, *From Slavery to Freetown*, 194–95; Gilbert, *Black Patriots*, 241; Egerton, *Death or Liberty*, 219.

take up arms." None of the Methodist lay leaders joined. The governor claimed to have thirty Nova Scotians, fourteen Europeans, and about fifty West Africans to defend him: "the remainder he could not hope would be more than neutral." Influenced by the debate over the impact of New Light revivalism on Nova Scotia during the American Revolution, Wallace Brown argued that in Sierra Leone, while "religious organization gave the Nova Scotians the means to mount political opposition, at the same time it injected a conservatism fatal to revolution."[113]

Only a few glimpses of David George's final decade appear in surviving documents. A lay leader wrote in 1807 to the English Baptists criticizing David George for allegedly having charged another member of the church with self-aggrandizement and mismanagement of supplies sent from England. This letter may explain why George Rawlyk concluded that George must have become "worn down by the harsh realities of his environment and by his own inner spiritual struggles and the weakening influence of the divine impressions." In the absence of other sources, Rawlyk may have assumed that the declension narrative that shaped his interpretations of other late eighteenth and early nineteenth-century evangelical preachers also applied to David George.[114] Frail enough by August 1809 to write a will, George probably died in the following year. He was succeeded by Hector Peters, who had returned to the church.[115]

As an evangelical press developed only sporadically in the Maritime colonies beginning in the late 1820s, tracking the influence and cultural memory of David George for this period is linked to the history of the churches he founded. According to one account, "the additions of white people" to the first Halifax church "have always been small; but the labours of Mr. Burton, and others, among the blacks in Halifax, and the adjacent settlements of Preston and Hammonds Plains, have been very successful." The writer euphemized the conflict over the influx of Evangelicals from the Church of England, changing cultural expectations of some Halifax Baptists, especially those influenced by racism and middle-class aspirations, and the resulting new churches.[116] This brief history of Baptist churches in Nova Scotia did not mention Shelburne

113. Fyfe, *History*, 84–85; Brown, "Black Loyalists," 115.

114. Gordon, *From Slavery to Freedom*, 157–58, 345–47; Rawlyk, *Canada Fire*, 43; Goodwin, *Into Deep Waters*, 9.

115. Gordon, *From Slavery to Freedom*, 158.

116. *Baptist Missionary Magazine* (April 1829), 1, 10; Boyd, "Preston, Richard"; Allwood, "Joseph Howe," 75–80. See also Griffin-Allwood, "Reason to Be."

itself, but included the nearby Ragged Island settlements, today the area around Lockeport. Mrs. Elizabeth Locke's obituary noted that she had been baptized by "that successful minister of the Gospel, the Rev. David George."[117] A later report noted that three women had acquired a deed for a future meeting house site in Shelburne, where David George "had first laboured . . . amidst trials of no ordinary character."[118]

This chapter's tour of the life and historiography of David George reflects some of the issues identified in current scholarship on the Black Atlantic or Black History in Canada. Especially where primary sources are so few and so indirect, archivism—preoccupation with and writing organized around sources[119]—very much defines narratives of George's life. David George escaped from enslavement by Galpin and other Euro-American or indigenous households in the southern English colonies. Yet his congregations in the Maritimes and in Sierra Leone experienced varying forms of unfreedom, and their freedom was still limited by economic and ideological constraints, whether racialized, or also about notions concerning gender and family. A perennial theoretical debate for biographers is whether individual agency is a timeless force in history, or merely a conceptual "product" of an "Enlightenment project" that excluded people like George, or an intermittent force depending on context. The regional West African slave trade and the impact of the Nova Scotians on the Tembe are other examples of uncomfortable topics in more critical history that moves beyond inspirational "storytelling".[120]

Yet for critical history to have any impact, it must still be combined with making "local black history . . . accessible to people outside of the academy."[121] To return to the theme with which this chapter began, David George has "remained a rallying point for the Black Baptists of Nova Scotia."[122] Yet until recently, outside the world of historians of evangelicalism or of the Maritime colonies of British North America, David George was "virtually unknown in Canada."[123] Recent attention to David George owes much to transcripts of his "Life" now available online, to

---

117. *Christian Messenger* (December 27, 1844).
118. *Christian Messenger* (December 10, 1847); Jacklin et al., *Churches*, 58–60.
119. Walker, "Exhuming."
120. Walker, "Critical Histories," 50, 31.
121. Whitfield, "African Diaspora," 224.
122. Pachai, *Nova Scotia Black Experience*, 52.
123. Nickerson, "Why Didn't They Teach That?" 16.

the work of institutions such as the virtual exhibition of the Nova Scotia Archives cited earlier and the Black Loyalist Heritage Centre, as well as to the archivist/historian Ruth H. Whitehead.[124] Stephen Davidson's 1975 Honour's Thesis at Acadia launched his many works for a broad readership.[125] Because public history is most often generated within modern nation states, the United States, Canada, or Sierra Leone, preserving the transnational Black Atlantic component can require more effort and resources.[126] Social media and digital history have also expanded access to literature inspired by David George and others, as well as studies that are theologically informed or from within denominational history,[127] or about activism today.[128] However brief and fragmentary, his *Account* now has a life of its own, enduring historical significance, and, for many, spiritual power, and a wider and more diverse readership than ever before.

BIBLIOGRAPHY

Primary Sources

ARCHIVES

Clarkson, J., and Charles Bruce Fergusson. *Clarkson's Mission to America, 1791–1792*. Nova Scotia. Public Archives 11. Halifax, NS, 1971.

"David George's Lease and Passports, 1779–1781." *Nova Scotia Archives* (1782 or 1783). Online: https://archives.novascotia.ca/africanns/archives/?ID=19.

Marston, Benjamin. "Benjamin Marston's Diary, 26 July 1784." Winslow Family Papers, MG H2, Vol. 20–22. University of New Brunswick Archives.

"Muster Book of the Free Black Settlement of Birchtown." Library and Archives Canada, MG9 B9-14 (Item 1292), 1784.

MONOGRAPHS

Alline, Henry. *The Life and Journal of the Rev. Mr. Henry Alline*. Boston: Gilbert and Dean, 1806.

Benedict, David. *General History of the Baptist Denomination in America: Sabin Americana, 1500–1926*. Boston: Manning and Loring, 1813.

Bill, I. E. *Fifty Years with the Baptist Ministers and Churches of the Maritime Provinces of Canada*. Saint John, NB: Barnes, 1880.

---

124. Rippon, "Account"; see also Black Loyalist Heritage Centre (blackloyalist.novascotia.ca) and Whitehead, *Black Loyalists*.

125. Davidson, "Leaders"; *Birchtown*; *Black Loyalists*.

126. Johnson, "Black Loyalist Descendants."

127. See, for example, Clarke, *Saltwater Spirituals*; Sanneh, *Abolitionists Abroad*; Erskine, *Plantation Church*; Mutale, "Remembering Rev. David George."

128. White, "One Month."

Davis, John. *Life and Times of the Late Rev. Harris Harding*. Yarmouth: Printed for the Compiler, 1866.

Macaulay, Zachary. *Life and Letters of Zachary Macaulay, by his Granddaughter Viscountess Knutsford*. London: Edward Arnold, 1900.

Zubly, John J. *The Journal of the Reverend John Joachim Zubly A.M., D.D. March 5, 1770 through June 22, 1781*. Savannah: Georgia Historical Society, 1989.

NEWSPAPERS AND MAGAZINES

Baptist Missionary Magazine of Nova-Scotia and New- Brunswick, 1829.
Christian Messenger, 1844, 1847.

OTHER

Rippon, John. "An Account of the Life of Mr. David George, from Sierra Leone in Africa; Given by Himself in a Conversation with Brother Rippon of London, and Brother Pearce of Birmingham." *Baptist Annual Register* 1 (1790–1793) 473–84.

———. "An Account of Several Baptist Churches, Consisting Chiefly of Negro Slaves: Particularly of One at Kingston, in Jamaica; and Another at Savannah in Georgia." *Baptist Annual Register* 1 (1790–1793).

Secondary Sources

Allwood, Philip G. A. "Joseph Howe Is their Devil: Controversies among Regular Baptists in Halifax, 1827–1868." In *Repent and Believe: The Baptist Experience in Maritime Canada*, edited by Barry Moody, 75–87. Hantsport, NS: Lancelot, 1980.

Blyden, Nemata. "This Na [sic] True Story of Our History: South Carolina in Sierra Leone's Historical Memory." *Atlantic Studies* 12 (2015) 355–70.

Boyd, Frank S., Jr. "Preston, Richard." *Dictionary of Canadian Biography*. No pages. Online: http://www.biographi.ca/en/bio/preston_richard_8E.html.

Brooks, Joanna, and John Saillant. "A Note on the Texts." In *"Face Zion Forward": First Writers of the Black Atlantic, 1785–1798*, edited by Joanna Brooks and John Saillant, 35–46. Boston: Northeastern University Press, 2002.

Brooks, Walter H. *The Silver Bluff Church: A History of Negro Baptist Churches in America*. Washington, DC: R. L. Pendleton, 1910.

Brown Wallace. "The Black Loyalists in Sierra Leone." In *Moving on: Black Loyalists in the Afro-Atlantic World*, edited by John Pulis, 103–34. New York: Garland, 1999.

Byrd, Alexander X. *Captives and Voyagers: Black Migrants across the Eighteenth-Century British Atlantic World*. Baton Rouge: Louisiana State University Press, 2008.

Clarke, George Elliott. *Directions Home: Approaches to African-Canadian Literature*. Toronto: University of Toronto Press, 2012.

———. *Saltwater Spirituals and Deeper Blues*. Porters Lake, NS: Pottersfield Press, 1983.

Clifford, Mary Louise. *From Slavery to Freetown: Black Loyalists After the American Revolution*. Jefferson, NC: McFarland, 2005.

Davidson, Stephen E. *Birchtown and the Black Loyalist Experience: From 1775 to the Present*. Halifax, NS: Formac, 2019.

———. *Black Loyalists in New Brunswick: The Lives of Eight African Americans in Colonial New Brunswick 1783–1834*. Halifax, NS: Formac, 2020.

———. "Leaders of the Black Baptists of Nova Scotia, 1782–1832." BA thesis, Acadia University, 1975.

Davis, Robert Scott. "Loyalism and Patriotism at Askance: Community, Conspiracy, and Conflict on the Southern Frontier." In *Tory Insurgents: The Loyalist Perception and Other Essays*, edited by Robert M. Calhoon et al., 229–83, Rev. and exp. ed. Columbia: University of South Carolina Press, 2010.

Egerton, Douglas R. *Death or Liberty: African Americans and Revolutionary America*. Oxford: Oxford University Press, 2009.

Elliott, Shirley B., and Public Archives of Nova Scotia, eds. *The Legislative Assembly of Nova Scotia, 1758–1983: A Biographical Directory*. Halifax, NS: Province of Nova Scotia, 1984.

Erskine, Noel Leo. *Plantation Church: How African American Religion Was Born in Caribbean Slavery*. Oxford: Oxford University Press, 2014.

Fingard, Judith. "McKerrow, Peter Evander." *Dictionary of Canadian Biography*. No pages. Online: http://www.biographi.ca/en/bio/mckerrow_peter_evander_13E.html.

Frey, Sylvia R. *Water from the Rock: Black Resistance in a Revolutionary Age*. Princeton, NJ: Princeton University Press, 1993.

Frey, Sylvia R., and Betty Wood. *Come Shouting to Zion: African American Protestantism in the American South and British Caribbean to 1830*. Chapel Hill: University of North Carolina Press, 1998.

Fyfe, Christopher. *A History of Sierra Leone*. 3rd corr. impression ed. London: Oxford University Press, 1968.

Fyfe, Christopher, and Charles Jones, eds. *Our Children Free and Happy: Letters from Black Settlers in Africa in the 1790s*. Early Black Writers. Edinburgh: Edinburgh University Press, 1991.

Gilbert, Alan. *Black Patriots and Loyalists: Fighting for Emancipation in the War for Independence*. Chicago: University of Chicago Press, 2013.

Goodwin, Daniel C. *Into Deep Waters: Evangelical Spirituality and Maritime Calvinistic Baptist Ministers, 1790–1855*. McGill-Queen's Studies in the History of Religion 2.54. Montreal: McGill-Queen's University Press, 2010.

Gordon, Grant. *From Slavery to Freedom: The Life of David George, Pioneer Black Baptist Minister*. Hantsport, NS: Lancelot, 1992.

Grant, John N. "Black Immigrants into Nova Scotia, 1776–1815." *The Journal of Negro History* 58 (1973) 253–70.

Griffin-Allwood, Philip G. A. "Reason to Be: The African Baptist Association as a Response to Systemic Racism." *Canadian Baptists of Atlantic Canada* (August 10, 2007). Online: https://baptist-atlantic.ca/wp-content/uploads/2012/02/RWG-reason-to-be.pdf.

Hamilton, Sylvia. "Naming Names, Naming Ourselves: A Survey of Early Black Women in Nova Scotia." In *We're Rooted Here and They Can't Pull Us Up: Essays in African Canadian Woman's History* edited by Peggy Bristow, 13–40. Toronto: University of Toronto Press, 1994.

Huskins, Bonnie. "New Hope in Shelburne, Nova Scotia: Loyalist Dreams in the Journal of British Engineer William Booth, 1780s–90s." In *The Consequences of Loyalism: Essays in Honor of Robert M. Calhoon*, edited by Rebecca Brannon and Joseph S. Moore, 104–21. Columbia: University of South Carolina Press, 2019.

Jacklin, Darren, et al. *The Churches of Shelburne County, 1765–1950*. Shelburne, NS: Shelburne Genealogical Society, 2006.

Jasanoff, Maya. *Liberty's Exiles: American Loyalists in the Revolutionary World*. New York: Alfred A. Knopf, 2011.

Johnson, Kathy. "Black Loyalist Descendants from Sierra Leone Return to their Birchtown Roots." *Saltwire* (September 3, 2019). No pages. Online: https://www.saltwire.com/nova-scotia/lifestyles/black-loyalist-descendants-from-sierra-leone-return-to-their-birchtown-roots-347880.

Kellison, Kimberly R. *Forging a Christian Order: South Carolina Baptists, Race, and Slavery, 1696–1860*. Knoxville: University of Tennessee Press, 2023.

Kidd, Thomas S., and Barry Hankins. *Baptists in America: A History*. Oxford: Oxford University Press, 2019.

King, Boston, et al. *The Life of Boston King*. Halifax, NS: Nimbus and Nova Scotia Museum, 2003.

Land, Isaac and Andrew M. Schocket. "New Approaches to the Founding of the Sierra Leone Colony, 1786–1808." *Journal of Colonialism and Colonial History* 9 (2008). No pages. Online: https://muse.jhu.edu/article/255263.

Lawson, Winston A. "Pioneer George Liele in Jamaica, the British Colony." In *George Liele's Life and Legacy: An Unsung Hero*, edited by David T. Shannon et al., 115–28. Macon, GA: Mercer University Press, 2013.

Little, Thomas J. "George Liele and the Rise of Independent Black Baptist Churches in the Lower South and Jamaica." *Slavery and Abolition* 16 (1995) 188–204.

Lowther, Kevin. *The African American Odyssey of John Kizell: A South Carolina Slave Returns to Fight the Slave Trade in His African Homeland*. Columbia: University of South Carolina Press, 2012.

MacKinnon, Neil. *This Unfriendly Soil the Loyalist Experience in Nova Scotia, 1783–1791*. Montreal: McGill-Queen's University Press, 2008.

Meszaros, Donna. "Reverend Joshua Palmer of South Carolina and Union County, South Carolina." *Palmer Family History*. No pages. Online: https://palmerfamilyhistory.weebly.com/reverend-joshua-palmer.html.

Morgan, Cecilia. *Public Men and Virtuous Women: The Gendered Languages of Religion and Politics in Upper Canada, 1791–1850*. Toronto: University of Toronto Press, 1996.

Morgan, Philip D., and Andrew Jackson O'Shaughnessy. "Arming Slaves in the American Revolution." In *Arming Slaves: From Classical Times to the Modern Age*, edited by Philip D. Brown and Christopher Leslie Brown, 180–207. New Haven: Yale University Press, 2006.

Morris, J. Brent, ed. *Yes, Lord, I Know the Road: A Documentary History of African Americans in South Carolina, 1526–2008*. Columbia: University of South Carolina Press, 2017.

Mutale, Elias. "Remembering Rev. David George." *Canadian Baptists of Atlantic Canada* (2021). Online: https://vimeo.com//518172517.

Najar, Monica. "Meddling with Emancipation: Baptists, Authority, and the Rift over Slavery in the Upper South." *Journal of the Early Republic* 25 (2005) 157–86.

Nickerson, Graham A. J. "Why Didn't They Teach That? The Untold Black History of New Brunswick." *Journal of New Brunswick Studies* 12 (2020) 15–23.

Oliver, Pearleen. *A Brief History of the Colored Baptists of Nova Scotia:1782–1953*. Halifax: McCurdy, 1953.

Pachai, Bridglal. *The Nova Scotia Black Experience through the Centuries.* Halifax, NS: Nimbus, 2007.

Paulett, Robert. *An Empire of Small Places: Mapping the Southeastern Anglo-Indian Trade, 1732–1795.* Early American Places. Athens: University of Georgia Press, 2012.

Perkins, Simeon. *The Diary of Simeon Perkins,* edited by Charles B. Fergusson. New York: Greenwood Press, 1969.

Piecuch, Jim. *Three Peoples, One King: Loyalists, Indians, and Slaves in the Revolutionary South, 1775–1782.* Columbia: University of South Carolina Press, 2013.

Pybus, Cassandra. *Epic Journeys of Freedom: Runaway Slaves of the American Revolution and their Global Quest for Liberty.* Boston: Beacon, 2006.

Rawlyk, George A. *The Canada Fire: Radical Evangelicalism in British North America, 1775–1812.* Montreal/Kingston: McGill Queen's University Press, 1994.

Rindfleisch, Bryan C. *George Galphin's Intimate Empire: The Creek Indians, Family, and Colonialism in Early America.* Indians and Southern History Series. Tuscaloosa: University of Alabama Press, 2019.

Rommel-Ruiz, Bryan W. "Colonizing the Black Atlantic: The African Colonization Movements in Postwar Rhode Island and Nova Scotia." *Slavery & Abolition* 27 (2006) 349–65.

Saillant, John. "The First Black Atlantic: The Archive and Print Culture of the Transatlantic Slave Trade and Slavery." In *A Companion to American Literature,* edited by Susan Belasco et al., 322–39. Hoboken, NJ: Wiley, 2020.

Sanneh, Lamin O. *Abolitionists Abroad: American Blacks and the Making of Modern West Africa.* Cambridge, MA: Harvard University Press, 2001.

Scanlan, Padraic X. *Freedom's Debtors: British Antislavery in Sierra Leone in the Age of Revolution.* The Lewis Walpole Series in Eighteenth-Century Culture and History. New Haven: Yale University Press, 2017.

Schama, Simon. *Rough Crossings: Britain, the Slaves, and the American Revolution.* New York: Ecco, 2006.

Schwarz, Suzanne. "Land and Settlement: Temne Responses to British Abolitionist Intervention in Sierra Leone in the Late Eighteenth and Early Nineteenth Centuries." *African Economic History* 49 (2021) 222–48.

Sidbury, James. *Becoming African in America: Race and Nation in the Early Black Atlantic.* Oxford: Oxford University Press, 2009.

Smith, Eric C., and Thomas S. Kidd. *Order and Ardor: The Revival Spirituality of Oliver Hart and the Regular Baptists in Eighteenth-Century South Carolina.* Columbia: University of South Carolina Press, 2018.

Sobel, Mechal. *Trabelin' On: The Slave Journey to an Afro-Baptist Faith.* Princeton, NJ: Princeton University Press, 1988.

Sutherland, D. A. "Marchinton, Philip." *Dictionary of Canadian Biography.* No pages. Online: http://www.biographi.ca/en/bio/marchinton_philip_5E.html.

Taylor, Alan. *American Revolutions: A Continental History, 1750–1804.* New York: W. W. Norton, 2016.

Townsend, Leah. *South Carolina Baptists, 1670–1805.* Baltimore, MD: Genealogical, 1974.

Troxler, Carole W. "Re-Enslavement of Black Loyalists: Mary Postell in South Carolina, East Florida, and Nova Scotia." *Acadiensis* 37 (2008) 70–85.

Ulrich, Laurel Thatcher. *Good Wives: Image and Reality in the Lives of Women in Northern New England, 1650–1750*. New York: Vintage, 1991.

Walker, Barrington. "Critical Histories of Blackness in Canada." In *Unsettling the Great White North: Black Canadian History*, edited by Michele A. Johnson and Funké Aladejebi, 31–49. Toronto: University of Toronto Press, 2022.

———. "Exhuming the Archive: Black Slavery and Freedom in the Maritimes and Beyond." *Acadiensis* 46 (2017) 196–204.

Walker, James W. St. G. "Marrant, John." *Dictionary of Canadian Biography*. No pages. Online: http://www.biographi.ca/en/bio/marrant_john_4E.html.

———. "Peters, Thomas." *Dictionary of Canadian Biography*. No pages. Online: http://www.biographi.ca/en/bio/peters_thomas_4E.html.

Walker, James W. St. G. *The Black Loyalists: The Search for a Promised Land in Nova Scotia and Sierra Leone 1783–1870*. Toronto: University of Toronto Press, 1992.

White, Evelyn C. "One Month after George Floyd's Murder, 'Woke' White People in Nova Scotia Should Look at their Own Repeating History." *Halifax Examiner*, June 25, 2020. No pages. Online: https://www.halifaxexaminer.ca/commentary/one-month-after-george-floyds-murder-woke-white-people-in-nova-scotia-should-look-at-their-own-repeating-history.

Whitehead, Ruth Holmes. *Black Loyalists: Southern Settlers of Nova Scotia's First Free Black Communities*. Halifax, NS: Nimbus, 2013.

Whitfield, Harvey Amani. "The African Diaspora in Atlantic Canada: History, Historians, and Historiography." *Acadiensis* 46 (2017) 213–32.

———. *North to Bondage: Loyalist Slavery in the Maritimes*. Vancouver, BC: UBC Press, 2016.

Whyte, Iain Alexander. *Zachary Macaulay 1768–1838: The Steadfast Scot in the British Anti-Slavery Movement*. Liverpool Studies in International Slavery 5. Liverpool, UK: Liverpool University Press, 2011.

Whytock, Jack C. "The Huntingdonian Mission to Nova Scotia, 1782–1791: A Study in Calvinistic Methodism." *Canadian Society of Church History Historical Papers* (2003) 149–70.

Wilson, Ellen Gibson. *The Loyal Blacks: The Definitive Account of the First American Blacks Emancipated in the Revolution, their Return to Africa and their Creation of a New Society There*. New York: Capricorn, 1976.

Appendix

Photos of First Baptist Church, Amherstburg, Ontario
(Chapter 8: Architecture and Experience at the First Baptist Church,
Amherstburg | *Jennifer Cousineau*)

FIGURE 1

First Baptist Church, Amherstburg, Ontario, front elevation, 1848–1849
(Jennifer Cousineau, Parks Canada, 2010)

FIGURE 2

First Baptist Church, Amherstburg, Ontario, south elevation, 1848–1849
(Jennifer Cousineau, Parks Canada, 2010)

FIGURE 3

The rear addition to the First Baptist Church was made in 1958
(Jennifer Cousineau, Parks Canada, 2010)

APPENDIX 299

FIGURE 4

The rear addition to the First Baptist Church was made in 1958
(Jennifer Cousineau, Parks Canada, 2010)

FIGURE 5

Interior looking toward the west end of the First Baptist Church
(Jennifer Cousineau, Parks Canada, 2010)

Figure 6

Interior looking toward exit doors at the back of the
First Baptist Church (Jennifer Cousineau, Parks Canada, 2010)

Figure 7

The pulpit and communion table, the First Baptist Church
(Jennifer Cousineau, Parks Canada, 2010)

APPENDIX 301

FIGURE 8

Baptismal pool beneath the floor behind the pulpit, added in 1907 (Jennifer Cousineau, Parks Canada, 2010)

FIGURE 9

Baptismal pool added in 1907 (Jennifer Cousineau, Parks Canada, 2010)

302 APPENDIX

FIGURE 10

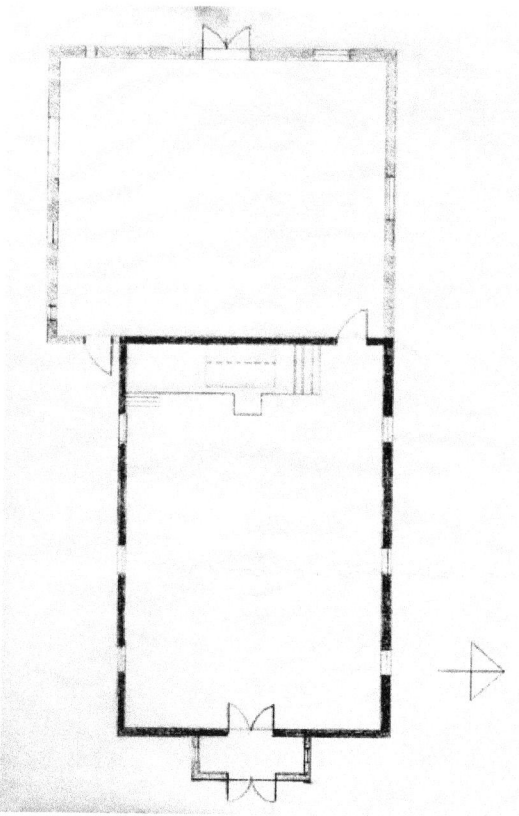

Plan, First Baptist Church. Original structure (1848–1849) in bold, additions (front vestibule: 1883; church hall: 1958) in hatching (Jennifer Cousineau, Parks Canada, 2011)

Index of Persons

Abucar, Mohamed, 227, 231
Aladejebi, Funké, 4, 6, 257
Alexander, Elizabeth, 254
Alexander, Ken, 24, 25, 27, 36, 37
Allen, Richard, 103, 173, 193
Anderson, Alfaretta, 236
Anderson, Benedict, 122
Anderson, Martin, 236
Angell, Stephen Ward, 254
Arenson, Adam, 4
Armstrong, John G., 121, 126
Aylestock, Addie, 246

Bailey, Alexander, 153
Bailey, Jenna, 6, 7
Bailey, Louisa, 233
Bailey, Madison, 213, 215
Bailey, Mary, 213
Bakan, Abigail B., 58
Baker, John Clapp, 209, 214–18
Ball, John, 277
Barker, Anthony, 168
Barrett, William, 127, 151
Barss, Gordon P., 68
Baskerville, Peter A., 76
Bates Neary, Hilary, 4
Bates, Niya, 163, 164
Baxter, Norman Allan, 254
Bay, Mil E., 260
Bauman, Chad M., 9
Beaver, Joseph, 214
Bebbington, David, 120
Bell, D. C., 32
Benchetrit, Jenna, 22
Benedict, David, 266, 273
Berger, Carl, 118

Berger, Peter, 118, 123
Bernard, C., 226
Bernard, Wanda Thomas, 226
Bertley, Leo W., 124
Best, Carrie, 224
Bibb, Henry, 57, 67, 70, 104–7
Bibb, Mary, 105–7
Bigsby, John J., 168
Billings, Hamont, 109
Binga, Anthony, 56, 61, 162, 170, 174, 178
Birney, James Gillespie, 191, 192
Bishop, Caleb, 213, 215, 227, 240
Blackett, Richard J., 85, 87
Bliss, Michael, 76
Blyden, Nemata, 281
Bonner, Claudine, 105
Boome, William, 153
Bordewich, Fergus, 50, 53
Boyd, Frank, S., 63, 120
Brand, Dionne, 24
Brown, John, 60
Brown, Thomas, 272
Brown, Wallace, 283
Brown-Kubish, Linda, 78, 82
Browning, J., 261
Brigham, S., 227
Bristow, Peggy, 23
Brackney, William, 169, 170, 172, 173, 176, 177, 179, 190
Brugan, A. W., 178
Brooks, Walter, 269
Brown, Dudley, 13, 49, 137
Brown, John, 111
Brown, Wallace, 28–34, 282, 284, 289

Brown-Kubisch, Linda, 6, 82
Boyd, Frank, 148–52
Bradford, Sarah H., 177
Britton, Rhonda, 159, 262
Buck, D. D., 253
Buckner, Phillip, 118
Bunch, Adam, 166
Burton, John, 147, 148, 289
Byrd, Alexander X., 272

Cahill, Barry, 155
Calarco, Tom, 55
Campbell, Mavis S., 35
Carey, Lott, 135
Carey, Newton, 202
Carleton, Thomas, 275
Carnes, William, 213
Carter, Hilda, 257
Cary, Mary Ann Shadd, 4, 81
Chilisa, Bagele, 226
Chioneso, N. A., 8
Christensen, Carole Pigler, 25
Christopher, Augustus, 211, 213
Clarke, George Elliott, 3, 8
Clarke, Septimus, 150
Clarkson, J., 275–77, 279, 280, 282, 285, 287
Clayton, Ada, 236
Clifford, Mary Louise, 51, 63, 267, 280, 281, 284, 288
Clyde, Alexander, 212, 213, 215
Clyde, Fanny, 213
Coffin, Levi, 53, 55, 167, 170
Colbert, Sampson, 273
Cole, Douglas, 118
Collins, Patricia H., 226
Cone, James H., 9, 43, 50
Cook, Terry, 119
Cooper, Afua, 23, 26, 75, 93, 105
Cooper, Brittany C., 262
Cornwallis, Edward, 143
Cousineau, Jennifer, 11, 14, 56, 57
Creese, Gillian, 4
Cridge, Edward, 212
Cromwell, Edith Mitchell, 236
Collamer, Jacob, 111
Cuthbert, John, 287

Davidson, Stephen E., 51, 63, 291
Davis, Samuel, 101–3, 194, 226, 252
Day, William Howard, 91, 104, 108, 110
Daye-Ashe, Hattie, 236
Delany, Martin, 60, 112
Delgado, Richard, 9
Dennert, Lena Fenner, 256
Desmond, Viola, 12
Dett, Nathaniel, 163, 164
Dinius, Marcy, 107
Dodson, J., 254
Donovan, Kenneth, 3
Douglas(s), Frederick, 66, 89, 227, 251, 255
Drew, Benjamin, 4, 54, 58, 60, 111, 179
Dubois, W. E. B., 254
Duncan, Carol B., 11, 22, 55
Dungy, Hilda, 249, 253
Dutton, Stephen, 194, 198, 199

Edwards, Malcolm, 211
Edwoods, William Henderson, 69, 71, 195, 202, 203, 206
Egerton, Douglas R., 288
Ernest, John, 106
Este, David C., 5–7
Evan, Ephraim, 195
Evans, Curtis J., 23
Evans, D., 231, 236
Everton, George, 214

Fabius, Chanee D., 8
Fairfax, Donald, 159
Fels, Agnes, 199
Fels, John, 189
Fergusson, Charles Bruce, 275–77, 279, 282
Fingard, Judith, 120, 145
Finkelman, Paul, 171
Fitch, E. R., 208
Floyd-Thomas, Stacey, 22
Foner, Eric, 51–53, 57, 66, 70
Foss, Andrew, 109
Fosty, Darril, 63, 68
Fosty, George, 63, 68
Fountain, Daniel L., 2

INDEX OF PERSONS 305

Fountain, James, 211
Foyn, Sean Flynn, 121
Francis, Daniel, 122
Franklin, John Hope, 171
Freed, W. S., 213–15
French, George, 174
Frey, Sylvia R., 268–70
Friesen, Dallas, 5, 76, 77, 177, 208, 212, 246
Frost, Karolyn Smardz, 6, 76, 93, 165–67, 171, 196
Fuentes, Marisa, 102
Fyfe, Robert A., 79, 279, 281, 283, 284, 288, 289

Gaines, Kevin K., 75, 120, 134
Galphin, George, 267
Gara, Larry, 52, 53, 64, 165
Gardner, Eric, 101, 103, 104
Garrett, Thomas, 53
Garrin, John, 285
Garrison, William Lloyd, 102
Garvey, Ellen Gruber, 112
Gatewood, William B., 128
George, David, 51, 63, 147, 148, 223, 266–91
Gerbner, Katharine, 2
Gibbs, Jacob R., 53
Gibbons, Marianna, 64
Gilbert, Alan, 281, 284, 288
Gilbert, Arlan K., 256
Gillard, Denise, 12, 51
Gilroy, Paul, 246, 267
Ginsburg, Ellis, 165, 171
Ginsburg, Rebecca, 165, 175
Glaze, Avis, 24, 25, 27, 36, 37
Glenn, N. D., 51
Goddu, Teresa, 101,
Goodheart, Adam, 50, 64–66
Goodwin, Daniel C., 273
Gordon, Grant, 5, 33, 36, 147, 266, 267, 270, 273, 275, 282–84, 288, 289
Gradert, Kenyon, 102
Gregory, L. A., 259
Green, Earnest, 126
Green Jeffrey, 76, 94
Grigg, Jacob, 285

Griffin, Farah, 260
Griffith-Allwood, Philip, 177, 289
Griffiths-Croft, Julia, 89, 112
Grindal, Peter, 127
Grosse, Tracey R., 223
Gruber, Ellen, 260

Hahn, Steven, 252
Hamilton, Bernice, 241
Hamilton, Marie, 236
Hamilton, Sylvia, 223, 224, 227, 235, 237, 238, 267
Hamilton, Thomas, 112
Hankins, Barry, 270
Harding, Harris, 275
Harris, J. E., 208
Harris, William Henry, 202, 203
Hatchett, Hattie Rhue, 259
Hawkins, Horace H., 82, 174
Heath, Gordon L., 5, 12, 13, 76, 77, 120–22, 125, 129, 177, 208, 212, 246
Hemans, Felicia, 103
Henson, Josiah, 231
Hepburn, Roger, 51, 64
Hicks, Beecher H., 50
Higginbotham, Evelyn Brooks, 120
Highgate, Aaron, 250
Hill, Daniel G., 3, 24, 27–29, 36–39, 40, 42, 55, 82, 83, 85, 87, 168, 178
Hochschild, Adam, 136
Holmes, Elizabeth, 273
Holmes, William, 273
Howe, S. G., 178
Hughes, Thomas, 248, 250, 253
Hughes-Smith, Barbara, 85
Huskins, Bonnie, 274

Jackson, John Henry, 49
Jackson, Leon, 101
Jasanoff, Maya, 272, 279, 282
Johnson, Charlotte Butler, 248, 249
Johnson, Henry, 153
Johnson, Isaiah, 248, 249
Johnson, Jacob, 248
Johnson, Jennie, 245–65
Johnson, Margaret, 248

INDEX OF PERSONS

Johnson, Michele A., 4, 6
Johnston, James, 154, 155, 158, 232
Jones, Charles, 281
Jones, Isabel Shepherd, 236
Jones, Martha, 233, 260
Joost, Mathias, 121

Kay, Roy, 131
Kellison, Kimberly R., 269
Kidd, Thomas, 270
Kilian, Crawford, 6, 209–12
Killingray, David, 138
King, Boston, 266, 274
King, Violet, 279
King, William, 60
Kinney, James A. R., 155, 156, 233
Kirkland, E., 61
Kizell, John, 287
Kling, David W., 118

La Roche, Cheryl Janifer, 57, 64
Ladd, Glen, 248
Landon, Fred, 56, 169
Lane, Hannah, 16
Lang, Mathew, 200
Lawes, Marvia E., 135
Lawson, Winston A., 286
Lennie, Tom, 85
Leonard, Joseph, 146
Lewis, James K., 54–56, 58, 60, 61, 67, 168, 169, 172, 174, 176, 177
Liberty, John, 172
Liele, George, 268, 270, 272, 273
Lightfoot, Madison J., 174
Little, Thomas J., 272
Locke, Elizabeth, 290
Lodoen, Shannon, 23
Loguen, J. W., 168
Lootens, Tricia, 103
Love-Joy, Vivian, 63
Lowther, Kevin, 283, 288
Lynn, Samuel, 252

Macaulay, Zachary, 282–88
MacKerrow, P. E., 5, 12, 34, 51, 63, 121, 124–29, 133, 152, 153, 158, 229, 266

MacKinnon, Neil, 272
Mahon, Danielle, 232, 235
Mailloux, Steven, 102
Malaspina, Ann, 66
Mamiya, Lawrence H., 21
Mann, Adve, 49
Margate, David, 270
Martin, J. Sella, 94, 95
Marwick, Alice E., 120
Mascoll, Philip, 190
Mason, John Murray, 111
Matthews, Edward, 109
Matthews, Thomas, 213
Mayne, R. C. 211
McBeth, H. Leon, 177
McCalla, Douglas, 76
McCaskill, Barbara, 101
McClaurin, C. C., 208, 213
McCormick, Ronald K., 32
McCoy, Beth, 110
McGann, Jerome, 113
McGill, Peter, 198, 199, 202
McGinnis, Frederick, 254
Meszaros, Donna, 269
Mitchell, Eliza, 93
Mitchell, William M., 58–60, 75, 100, 103, 104, 107, 110–13
Miles, Tiya, 165
Miller, Carmen, 123
Millman, T. R., 40
Montgomery, William E., 50, 51
More, Hannah, 100
Morgan Cecilia, 273
Morgan, Jo-Ann, 109
Morgan, Philip D., 270
Moody, Barry, 5
Moore, Samuel, 109
Moore-Davis, Irene, 78, 83
Morris, E. C., 104
Morris, J. Brent, 270
Moreau, Bernice, 235
Mothe, Gordon de La, 21
Munroe-Anderson, Késa, 15
Murphy, Terence, 33, 38, 40, 41,
Murray, Taylor, 5, 15, 76, 77, 177, 208, 212, 246, 258
Mursell, Arthur, 113

INDEX OF PERSONS

Najar, Monica, 270
Nelson, Louis, 163, 164
Nettles, Henry, 175
Newfield, Gareth, 126
Newman, Nathaniel, 101
Newman, William P., 78, 80, 102, 252
Newton, John, 281
Nickerson, Graham, A., 290
Niles, Lyndrey A., 125
Niven, Laird, 29
Nutter, David, 148, 149

O'Connor, June, 9
O'Shaughnessy, Andrew Jackson, 270
Oldershaw, Alfred, 213
Oliver, A. Pearlean, 5, 124, 144, 145, 157, 222, 223, 227, 231–34, 240, 241, 266
Olsavsky, Jesse, 114
Quarles, Benjamin, 166

Pachai, Bridglal, 35, 36, 150, 153–55, 157, 159, 224, 226, 227, 240, 290
Page, Robert, 118, 123
Page, Sally, 213
Pakenham, Thomas, 135
Palmer, Joshua, 269, 270
Palmer, Wait, 269
Paris, Peter J., 5, 12, 226, 227
Parris, S., 227
Paulett, Robert, 270
Payne, Daniel, 103, 254
Pease, Jane H., 62
Pease, William H., 62
Pelly, F. A., 237
Penlington, Norman, 118
Perlin, Roberto, 33, 38, 40, 41
Perry, Charlotte Brontë, 87
Peters, Thomas, 277, 279, 281
Piecuch, Jim, 270
Pierre, Ann, 213
Pierre, Thomas, 213, 215
Pilton, James William, 211
Pitcan, Mikeala, 120
Plummer, Kevin, 50

Porter, Wendy, 6, 259
Preston, Mary, 223
Preston, Richard, 124, 127, 149–52, 158, 222, 223, 225, 227
Price, Thomas, 195
Purvis, Robert, 64
Puryear, Moses, 154–56, 233
Pybus, Cassandra, 283, 285
Pyper, James, 204

Randolph, Ann, 200
Randolph, John, 198, 199
Rankin, John, 53, 276
Rawlyk, George A., 5, 289
Reid-Maroney, Nina, 13, 16, 106
Renfree, Harry A., 5, 63, 177, 208, 212
Rhodes, Jane, 68–70
Richard, Fortune, 209, 211, 215–18, 220
Richards, Adolphus Calamandus, 211
Richards, John Byron, 208, 212, 216, 217, 219
Richardson, William, 252
Rice, Isaac, 82, 169
Ricketts, Shannon, 165
Riley, Jennifer, 5, 14, 78, 134
Rindfleisch, Bryan C., 267–70
Ripley, C. Peter, 71, 76, 80, 81, 93–95, 252
Rippon, John, 266–68, 270, 272–75, 277, 287
Roberts, Winsor Hall, 257
Robertson, John Ross, 190, 192, 200, 204
Robinson, Julie Marie, 54
Rolph, Thomas, 191
Rommel-Ruiz, Bryan W., 280
Ross, Joyce, 239
Roy, Michael, 101
Ruck, Calvin, 121, 126
Russell, Hilary, 167

Sadlier, Rosemary, 49, 50
Saint Augustine, 118
Saunders, Charles B., 154

INDEX OF PERSONS

Saunders, Ella Hadassah Kinney, 246
Savage, Barbara, 260
Sawallisch, Nele, 11, 123
Scanlan, Padraic X., 276
Schama, Simon, 282, 284
Schwarz, Suzanne, 279
Schweniger, Loren, 171
Sealy, Donna, 236
Sidbury, James, 281, 284
Siebert, Wilbur H., 68
Simcoe, John Graves, 165, 165
Sellick, Lester B., 31
Senior, Hereward, 28–32, 34
Serafini, Sedonia, 101
Setran, David, 8
Shadd, Adrienne, 93
Shadd, Mary Ann, 54, 55, 57, 70, 78, 80, 81, 254
Sharp, Henry, 268, 270, 272
Shaw, Mellisa, 138
Shelton, Wallace, 108
Shepard, R. Bruce, 4
Shreve, Dorothy S., 5, 38, 39, 40–42, 55, 56, 60, 62, 76, 80, 171, 175–77
Shreve, Elizabeth Shadd, 254, 259
Sidbury, 269, 277, 284, 286, 287
Siemerling, Winfried, 2, 120
Simcoe, John Graves, 69
Simpson, Donald, 3, 67, 76, 79–81, 85, 167, 168
Skier, Donald, 159
Skinner, Marion, 236
Sluggett, James, 213
Smallwood, Stephanie, 102
Smedley, Robert Clemens, 51, 52, 64
Smith, Addison, 62
Smith, Eric C., 270
Smith, Parker T., 250
Smith, Timothy L., 2
Sobel, Mechal, 170, 177, 286
Spanswhich, T., 214
Sparks, Maude, 237
Spears, L. G., 170
Spencer, Elaine A. Brown, 11
Spires, Derrick, 101, 101
Sport, Prince William, 150

Spotts, Fielding, 211, 213, 219, 220
Spotts, John, 213
Stanford, Peter, 101
Stanley, Brian, 135
States, Muriel, 237
Steem, Joy, 239, 241
Steem, Mathew, 239, 241
Stefancic, Jean, 9
Steward, Austin, 62
Stewart, Alexander, 188
Still, William, 4, 53, 111
Stouffer, Allen P., 122, 166
Stowe, Harriet Beecher, 55, 64, 109, 167, 251
Stuart, Charles, 168

Tapscott, Samuel, 192
Taylor, Alan, 1, 270
Taylor, Graham G., 76
Teale, J. H., 214
Teelucksingh, Jerome, 6
Thomas, James, 152
Thompson, Eugene M., 41
Thomson, Colin, 23, 27
Tobin, Jacqueline L., 81
Tomlinson, Glenn, 15, 187, 190
Torbet, Robert G., 177
Townsend, Leah, 269
Troxler, Carole W., 270, 275
Troy, William, 75, 100, 101, 103, 104, 107–13, 179
Tucker, Veta Smith, 6, 76, 164, 165
Tule, Mary Brandon, 254, 259
Tulloch, Headley, 35, 126
Turner, Henry McNeal, 254
Tynes, Gertrude, 236

Ulrich, Laurel Thatcher, 285
Upshaw, Margaret, 233, 236, 237

Vachon, André, 26
Vinci, Alexandra, 68
Volf, Miroslav, 8

Walker, Barrington, 3, 9, 10, 165, 246, 246
Walker, David, 107

Walker, James W. St. G, 3, 51, 69, 121, 235, 266, 267, 273–77, 280–85, 288, 290
Walters, Kerry S., 51–53, 57, 58, 63–65, 67, 70, 132, 145, 146, 149, 173
Ward, Samuel Ringgold, 112
Watkins, Paul, 4
Washington, Booker T., 133, 154
Washington, Christian, 187–208
Washington, James M., 219
Waterman, Leroy, 261
Weinfeld, Morton, 25
Wells, J. E., 79
Wetmore, Donald, 31
Whipper, Alfred, 250
Whitaker, Abraham, 257
White, Jacob C., 250
White, Portia, 158, 236
White, William Jr., 12, 120, 155
Whitehead, Ruth H., 291
Whitfield, Harvey Amani, 3, 63, 102, 112, 121, 147, 267, 271, 290
Whytock, Jack C., 270
Williams, Thomas, 202–4, 240

Wilson, Ellen, 266, 270, 272, 277, 279
Wilson, Hiram, 251
Wiffen, Jeremiah Holmes, 114
Wilberforce, William, 100
Wilks, William, 54
Williams, Dolly, 240
Williams, Savanah E., 5, 240
Wilson, Ellen Gibson, 31–33, 35, 146, 267, 280, 284–87
Wilson, Ivy, 112
Wilson, Paul, 13, 79
Winks, Robin W., 3, 23, 25–27, 35, 36, 41, 69, 78, 80–83, 124, 168
Winter, Jesse, 190
Wotton, Patricia, 247
Wyes, Bessie, 237
Wylie, William, 166

Yelin, Louise, 121

Zaami, Mariama, 10
Zeman, J. K., 177
Zubly, John, 269

Index of Subjects

Abolish/Abolitionist, 13, 16, 36, 37, 46, 52, 53, 56, 57, 60, 64–66, 89, 94, 95, 101, 103–7, 109, 111–13, 150, 153, 165, 168, 175, 176, 178, 191, 228, 250
Abandoned, 60
Acadia, 16, 27
Acadia Divinity College, 238
Acadia University in Wolfville, 124, 156, 157, 232
Act of 1793, The Act to Prevent the Further Introduction of Slaves and to Limit the Term of Contracts for Servitude within This Province, 36, 37, 166
Activism, Black, 249
Adult Baptism, 177 (see Baptism of Believers)
Adult Learning Education Programs in Beechville, 240
African Abolition Society, 124
African American, x, 1, 13, 51, 53, 69, 83, 106, 112, 163, 187, 195–96, 203, 226, 228
African Canadian, Africadians, AfroCanuncks, Africcanadians, 1–4, 8, 16, 53, 106, 240
African Baptist, x
African Baptist Association of Nova Scotia (ABA), x, 118, 124, 132, 150, 151, 154, 156, 266 (see African United Baptist Association of Nova Scotia [AUBA, AUBANS])

African Baptist Chapel, 160 (see Cornwallis Baptist, Cornwallis Street United Baptist Church)
African Baptist Church of Halifax, African Chapel, 150, 229 (see Cornwallis Baptist, Cornwallis Street United Baptist Church)
African Baptist Church of New York, 189
African Baptists of Nova Scotia, 151, 158
African Baptist Church of St. Thomas, 60
African Diasporic, 225
African Education Committee, 229
African Feminism, 226
African Methodist Episcopal (Zion) Church (AME), 40, 103, 173
African Nova Scotians (ANS), 16, 143–52, 154, 158, 222–43
African Nova Scotian Feminist, 226
African Prince, 129
African United Baptist Association of Nova Scotia (AUBA, AUBANS), x, xi, 5, 6, 11, 14, 16, 44, 59, 124, 127, 137, 138, 152, 153, 157–59, 222–42
Africville, xi, 12
Afrocentric, Afri-centric, 224, 236
Afrocentric/Afrocentrist Christian Awakening, x, 5, 42, 47
Albany, 52
Aliens, 66

310

INDEX OF SUBJECTS

America(s), American(s), 21–23, 25, 27, 28, 37, 41–46, 49–51, 54, 66, 68, 87–90, 96, 121, 129, 144, 210, 216, 217
American Abolition Society, 204
American Baptist Missionary Convention, 200
American Baptist Free Mission Society (ABFMS), 61, 79, 83, 84, 176
American Blacks, 1, 67
American Black Baptist(s), 12
American Civil War, 1, 3, 61, 69, 166, 178 (see Civil War)
American Colonies, 27, 28
American Missionary Association, 105
American Patriots, 189
American Quaker, 166
American Revolution(ary) War, 1, 33, 63 (see Revolutionary War and War of Independence)
American Slaves/Slavery/Slaveholders, 3, 120, 127, 139, 149, 171, 175, 201 (see Slaveholder[s] and Slave Master[s]/Owner)
American South, 2
Amherstburg, 13, 14, 39, 41, 42, 54, 56, 59, 60, 82, 108, 162, 163, 165–72, 174, 175, 179, 180, 182, 183
Amherstburg (Anti-Slavery) Regular (Missionary) Baptist Association (ABA, AARBA, ARMBA), 41, 42, 53, 55, 57, 61–63, 77, 82, 83, 85, 105, 107, 124, 162, 171, 173–76, 180, 182, 247, 252, 254, 256
Amherstburg Association Conference, 181
Amherstburg Association in Ontario (AAO), 11
Amherstburg First Baptist Church, 14, 56, 106, 175, 181, 182 (see First Baptist Church of Amherstburg)

AMA Women's Missionary Association, 254
Angel, 114, 135
Anglican, Anglican Church, 28, 31, 34, 36, 40, 51, 129, 133, 145, 146, 149, 152, 212 (see Church of England)
Anglican Missionary, 147 (see Mission[s], Missionary)
Anglo African Magazine, 112
Anglo-French, 119
Anglo-Saxon, 119, 120, 130
Anglophile, 14
Annapolis, 30, 33
Anti-Black Violence, 102
Anti-Slavery, 2, 84, 100, 106, 109, 110, 112, 114, 127, 166, 175, 176, 195 (see White Abolitionists)
Anti-Slavery Baptist Association, 79
Anti-Slavery Society of Canada, 81
Antinomian, 287
Antislavery Gospel, 105
Antislavery Newspapers, 101
Antislavery Print, 105
Apocalyptic, ix
Apostle, x
Appalachian Mountains, 53
Architecture(al), 14, 15, 162, 164, 171, 178, 181
Architectural History, 164
Archives, Archivist(s), 15, 16
Argyll Congregational Chapel, 100
Articles of Capitulation, 27
Articles of Fatih, 42
Asia, 135
Assimilation, 120
Asylum, 45
Attorney General, 37
Atlantic, 107, 267
Atlantic Baptist College/Crandall University, 238
Atlantic Canada, 3
Atrocities, 44
Auditory Church, 179, 181, 182
Augustinian, 118
AUBA Scholarship, 238

AUBA's Ladies Auxiliary, 236 (see Ladies Auxiliary)
Aural Cultures, 103
Avon River, 100

Baltimore, 40
Baptism of Believers, 177, 181
Baptismal pool, x
Baptist Archives, Wolfville, Nova Scotia, 10, 16
Baptist Abolitionists, 150
Baptist Association for Coloured People, 171
Baptist Association of Puget Sound and British Columbia, 213
Baptist Church at York, 189
Baptist Churches, 41, 42, 54, 105–7, 126, 150, 174, 188, 192
Baptist Convention of Ontario and Quebec, 259
Baptist History of the North Pacific Coast, 215
Baptist Missionaries, 135
Baptist Youth Provincial Union, 154
Bath, 100
Bay Street, 196
Beech Hill, 150
Beechville Community Leaders, 241
Beechville Education and Community Development Association, 241
Beechville United Baptist Church, 231
Bedford Basin, xi
Begging, 75, 80–83, 87, 89, 90, 94; "Begging Society," 82
Belfast, 85
Belgium, 136
Benevolence/Benevolent, 27, 77, 152, 201
Berlin Conference, 135
Berry Street Church in Ulster, 87
Bethlehem, xi
Bible, Biblical ix, 8, 32, 42–45, 77, 102, 103, 105, 114, 118, 128, 130, 146, 169, 175, 228; "Bibles for the Slave", 105
Biography, 16

Birchtown, 29, 30, 32, 34, 274, 276, 278
Birmingham, 95, 107
Bishop(s), ix, 211
Black Abolitionist, 16, 89, 96, 100–102, 104, 106, 110–12, 114
Black Activist, 103, 110
Black African, 129
Black American Pastor, 94
Black Amherstburg Regular Baptist Missionary Association, 77
Black Atlantic, 2
Black Baptist History, 103
Black Baptist Print Culture, 101, 105–7
Black Baptist Spirituality, 123
Black Baptist Writers and Editors, 101
Black Canadian, 2, 4, 7, 8, 22, 104, 178
Black Canadian Baptist, 12
Black Canadian Experience, 8, 9, 10, 22, 23, 132
Black Canadian Methodist, 12
Black Christianity, 12, 131
Black Church(es), 1, 44, 50, 57, 63, 71, 134, 156, 163, 169, 176, 178, 183, 224, 232
Black Community/Communities/Settlement/Settlers, 1, 4, 5, 7, 10, 50, 52, 55, 58–60, 63, 81, 82, 111, 119–21, 124, 125, 127–30, 132–39, 145–49, 151–53, 156, 164, 167, 169, 173, 178, 210, 235, 276
Black Codes, 54, 68, 69
Black Congregants, xi, 38, 145, 149, 174, 217
Black Cultural Centre of Nova Scotia, 238
Black Diaspora, 23, 24
Black Educators Association (BEA), 241
Black Evangelical, 11
Black Feminist/Feminism, 224, 226
Black History, 8, 10, 23
Black Immigrants, 4, 7
Black Lay Leaders, 146

INDEX OF SUBJECTS   313

Black Liberation Theology, 9
Black Literary Tradition, 112
Black Loyalist Heritage Centre, 291
Black Loyalist(s), 4, 5, 30–32, 34, 36, 124, 125 (see Canadian Loyalists)
Black Methodist, 59
Black Motherhood, 226
Black Nationalist, 5
Black Nova Scotian Baptist, xi
Black Nova Scotia(ns), x, 5, 6, 179
Black Pastor, 147 (see Pastor[s], Pastorate)
Black Press/Newspapers, 13, 57, 101, 103, 105
Black Refugees, 3, 5, 38, 46, 144, 147, 165, 169
Black Regular Baptists, 13, 75, 76, 81, 83 (see Coloured Regular Baptist Church)
Black Soldiers/Militia, 69, 126
Black United Front of Nova Scotia, 157
Black Uplift, Black Social Uplift, 75, 96
Black Women's Civil Rights Activism, 231
Blacks Slave(s), 3, 25, 27
Blasphemy, 45
BME Church in Niagara Falls, 163
BME Church in St. Catharine, 163 (see Salem Chapel)
Body of Christ, x
Boers, 128–30
Boer War, Anglo-Boer War, Second Anglo-Boer War, 129
Bois Blanc Island, 167, 181
Bond Street Baptist Church, 79, 93
Book of Revelation, 114
Botanic Gardens, 86
Brethren, 199, 202
Bright Light Mission Band Women's Missionary Group of Upper Hammonds Plains, 232
Brindley Town, 29
Bristol, 86–88
British, British Regime, Britain, ix, 8, 11–15, 22, 26–29, 32, 34–38, 41, 51, 54, 62, 69, 70, 81, 83–85, 89, 90, 92, 93, 96, 108, 110, 119–21, 125, 127–30, 144, 153, 166, 168, 196, 201, 219 (see Briton)
British Abolitionists, 89, 94
British Colonial Law, 69
British Columbia, 15, 208, 212, 214, 220
British Crown, 62
British Imperial Expansion, 128
British North America, 165, 166, 210
British Press, 109
British Slavery Abolition Act of 1833, 222
British Wesleyan Methodists, 32
Briton, 149
Brothers, Brotherhood, 15, 136, 162, 196, 203
Brothers of Charity at Lewisburg, 25
Buffalo, 103, 204
Bullying and Elder Abuse, 239
Burial, 26
Buxton Mission, 39
Buxton Settlement, 89

California, 209, 214
Calvary Baptist Church, 219
Calvinist, 287
Carolina, 45
Catechism, 26
Catholic Church, 3, 25, 162 (see Roman Catholic[ism])
Canaan, 177
Canada Baptist Magazine and Missionary Register, 194, 196
Canada Baptist Missionary Society, 195
Canada Baptist Union, 201
Canada East, 201
Canada West, 13, 15, 22, 36, 38, 41, 45, 55, 56, 75–77, 83, 84, 86–89, 96, 100–102, 104–7, 111, 162, 170, 173, 174, 177, 178, 180, 201, 208 (see Upper Canada)

314 INDEX OF SUBJECTS

Canadian Abolitionist Communities, 109
Canadian Africans, 23
Canadian Anti-Slavery Baptist Association (CASBA), 61, 62, 176
Canadian Baptist Archives at McMaster Divinity College, 10, 16
Canadian Baptist Churches, 203
Canadian Baptist Missions, 238
Canadian Baptist Trans-Congregational Polity, 41
Canadian Black Baptist, 12, 123
Canadian Exceptionalism, 132
Canadian Imperialism, 129
Canadian League for the Advancement of Coloured People, 257
Canadian Loyalists, 189 (see Loyalists)
Canadian Military, 156
Canadian Protestant, 129
Canadian Racial State, 3
Canadian Regular Baptists, 79, 96
Canterbury, 94
Cardiff, 95
Caribbean, 1, 7, 28, 54
Carolina Creek, 267
Carolinas, 267
Cayuga, 60
Celestial, 42
Central Canadian Regular Baptists, 75
CFL, 49
Chapel, 34, 62, 85–87, 92, 202
Chattel, 25
Chatham, 39, 40, 59, 60, 62, 78, 82, 84, 110, 250-54, 257-9
Charleston, 32, 272
Charybdis, 9
Chedabucto, 29
Christ, Christ-Borne, x, 21, 77, 89, 136, 189, 202
Church, Church Polity, 103, 123–25, 134, 136, 145–52, 156, 158, 159, 163, 164, 168–70, 172, 173–78, 192, 195, 198, 200–204, 209–19, 222–24, 229, 232, 234, 238
Church Clerk, 154, 174
Church of England, 176, 252, 278, 279, 287
Church on March Street, 188
Cincinnati, 83, 108, 110
Cincinnati Vigilance Committee, 108
Circular Letter (of 1851), 77, 82, 125, 128
Citizenship, Citizen(s), 14, 69, 118–20, 125, 126, 131, 132, 138, 144, 212
Civil Disobedience, 50
Civil Rights, 2, 248
Civil War, 53, 58, 64, 69, 85, 92, 93, 100, 103, 111, 170, 176, 257
Clandestine/Clandestinity, 65, 66
Classism, 12
Clergy, ix, 12, 125, 146
Cleveland, 105
Code Noire, 25
Code of 1685 (1728), 25
Colchester Baptist Church, 61
Colchester County, 36, 41, 54
Colonial Settlement at Wilberforce, 63 (see Wilberforce Settlement/Settlers)
Colonization, Colonialism, Colony, Colonies, Colonize, Colonial, 3, 14, 24–26, 28, 34, 36, 38, 54, 56, 62, 69, 70, 119, 144, 188, 196, 201
Colored Christian Centre, 257, 259, 262
Colour, Coloured, 91, 113, 132, 134, 143, 148, 153, 154, 170, 171, 189–93, 201, 214–18, 235
Coloured Baptist, 104, 199
Coloured Baptist Church in Toronto, 87, 92
Coloured Community of Western Canada, 89
Coloured Minister, 86 (see Ministries, Minister[s][ed], Ministerial,)
Colored race, 130

Coloured Regular Baptist Church, 84
Community/Communities, 2, 51, 53, 57, 58, 69, 70, 77, 81, 82, 94, 102, 105, 109–11, 118, 134, 144–47, 150, 152, 154, 159, 163, 167, 171, 224–32, 234, 236–38, 242
Communion, 25, 176
Conductor(s), 57, 84
Confederation, Articles of, 248
Congo, 136
Congregationalists, 105, 112, 204
Consecrate, 78
Conservative, 28
Consiel Superieur, 26
Constitution, 42
Constitution for The Association for the Education and Elevation of the Coloured People of Canada, 84
Continental Congress, 271
The Contribution of the African United Baptist Association to Public Education, 1854–1940, 5
Convention of Coloured Women in Canada, 237
Cornwallis Baptist, Cornwallis Street United Baptist Church, ix, 14, 126, 143, 147, 151–55, 225, 229, 233, 234, 241 (New Horizons United Baptist Church)
Cork Ladies' Association, For the Religious and Moral Improvement of the Fugitive Slaves and Coloured Races in Canada, 91
Cotton Gin, Mills, 69, 109
Counter-Culture of Modernity, 3
Covenant, 42
COVID-19, 16
Critical Histories of Blackness, 10
Critical Race Theory (CRT), 9
Crown, 119
Crown of Glory, 131

Cultural, Culture, 14, 16, 21, 42, 54, 70, 102, 128, 164, 168, 180, 225, 227
Cultural and Academic Enrichment Program (CAEP), 241
Cultural Insurgency, 13
Cultural Narrative, 119 (see Narrative[s])

Dalhousie University School of Law, 154, 232
Dance, 23
Dartmouth, 29
Dawn Settlement in Dresden, Dawn, 12, 62, 63, 78, 102
Deacon(s), 39, 162, 197, 213
Delaware, 53
Deliverance, 127, 177
Democracy, 51
Denomination, Nondenominational, Multi-denominational, 2, 57, 94, 103–6, 122, 125, 169, 181
Department of Education, 239
Dependency, 28
Depression, 76, 234
Descendents, 54
Detroit, 27, 39, 41, 58–60, 62, 69, 84, 109, 163, 173, 181, 259
Detroit River Borderland/Region, 165–68, 181
Detroit Second Baptist, 175
Detroit-Windsor Corridor, 167
Diaspora, 35, 45, 46, 106, 113
Diasporic Communities, 112
Digby, 29
Diocese of Quebec, 25
Diplomatic Racism, 4
Dissidents, ix
Divine, Divine Spirit, 133, 137, 192
Diving Lord, xi
Doctrine, Doctrinal, 126, 169, 171
Dominicans, 25
Dominion, 130, 132
Donald and Evelina Skeir Memorial Scholarship Fund, 238
Dover Township, 254

316   INDEX OF SUBJECTS

East Preston Daycare Centre, 239, 240
East Preston Empowerment Academy, 242
East Preston United Baptist Church, 241, 242
Ecclesiastical, Ecclesiastical Council, 39, 179
Economic/Economy, 25, 51, 57, 65, 75, 87, 124, 228
Edinburgh, 107
Edmonton, 7
Education, Educational, 16, 50 54, ,62, 75, 84, 85, 87, 113, 124, 130, 132, 134, 143, 153, 155, 158, 225–39, 241–43
Education Committee, 229
Edwoods and Others Naturalization Bill, 69, 195, 196
Egalitarianism, 12
Egypt, 43, 44, 131, 169, 177
Elder(s), xi, 54, 84, 162
Elder Abuse and Mental Health and Wellness, 239
Elgin Settlement at Buxton, Elgin, Elgin Association 39, 62, 63
Emancipation, Emancipatory, 44, 70, 105, 114, 187, 222
Emancipation Act of 1793, 69 (see Act of 1793, The Act to Prevent the Further Introduction of Slaves and to Limit the Term of Contracts for Servitude within This Province)
Emancipatory Theology, 105, 114
Emigration, 91, 105
Emmanuel Baptist Church, 242
Empire(s), 23, 37, 44, 69, 118, 120, 123, 128–30, 166 (see Imperial, Imperialism)
Empowerment, 21, 43, 44, 47, 70, 164
English, England 14, 22, 25, 32, 34, 38, 85, 87, 90, 91, 108, 109, 125–29, 144, 150, 179, 189, 228

English Architect, 179 (see Architecture[al])
Enlightenment, 247
Enslavement, Enslaver, Enslaved, 24–26, 35, 37, 44, 46, 105, 109, 112, 162, 165, 169, 222
Ephemera, 13
Epistemologies of Erasure, 102
Eschatology, 131
Essex County, 60, 257
Esther Clarke Wright Archives/ Atlantic Baptist Archives at Acadia University, 10
Ethiopia, 44, 45, 129, 131
Ethnicity, 14
Euro-American, 267
Europe, European, 8, 21, 24, 35, 44, 45, 114, 118
European Colonization, 123
Eunuch, 45
Evangelical, Evangelistic 38, 40, 122, 134, 139, 152, 177, 190, 195, 274, 289
Execution, 26
Exodus, 45, 46, 177

Family, Families, 28, 128, 136, 238
Feminism, 226, 245, 250, 254
Final Judgment, 131
First African Baptist Church, 40, 228
First Baptist Church, 14, 15
First Baptist Church of Amherstburg, 11, 55–57, 83, 162–64, 166, 168–72, 176, 178–80, 182, 183
First Baptist Church of Chatham, 58, 182
First Baptist Church of North Cayuga, 61
First Baptist Church of Puce River, 62, 182
First Baptist Church of Sandwich, 50, 172, 182
First Baptist Church of Toronto, First Baptist Toronto, 2, 55, 190, 193, 195, 200

First Baptist Church of Victoria, 15, 208, 212, 213, 215, 220
First Baptist Church of Windsor, 58, 59, 87, 182
First Baptist Congregation of Chatham, 59
First Coloured Calvinistic Church, 15, 187, 203, 204
First Peoples (Panis), 3
First Regular Baptist Church in Dresden, 182
First World War, 126, 138 (see Great War)
Flint, 259
Fort Malden, 37, 56
France, French, French Regime, 12, 22, 25–27, 129, 167, 168, 178
Franciscans, 25
Fraser River, 210
Fraudster, 94
Fredrickton, 33
Free Baptist Mission in Haiti, 109
Free Christian Church, 94
Free Mission Society, 89
Free State, 58
Free Will Baptist Association, 247
Free/Unfree, Freedom, 16, 26 ,41, 46, 50, 51, 53, 54, 58, 62, 64–69, 87, 93, 100, 105, 108, 113, 114, 127, 131, 145, 163–67, 169–72, 176, 267
Freemen, 56
Freetown, 35, 281, 282, 284, 286, 288
Friendships, 28
Fugitive, Fugitive Slave, Fugitive Slave Act(s) of 1850, of 1793, 1, 13, 37, 39, 50, 53–61, 63–69, 76, 81, 82, 84, 86, 87, 90, 91, 93, 108, 111, 158, 165, 166, 169, 170, 175
Fugitive Slave Movement, 167

Gender, 26
General Convention for the Improvement of the Colored Inhabitants of Canada, 106
Georgia, 49, 267

Georgian, 100
Gertrude E. Smith Memorial Scholarship, 238
Glasgow, 85, 86
God, ix, 33, 40, 45, 77, 110, 118, 123, 127–29, 131, 133, 136, 148, 157, 171, 175, 177, 178, 181, 182, 190, 193, 194, 197, 199, 201, 205, 218, 222, 228
Gosfield Baptist Church, 60
Gospel, 31, 33, 39, 89, 108, 137, 189, 194, 195, 205
Gospel Ministry, 205
Gothic, 179
Government Authority, 126
Governor, 24, 148
Governor of Quebec, 27
Grace, 136
Grand River, 61
Grants, 28
Granville Mountain, x
Great Awakening, 32, 51, 177
Great Britain, x, 45
Great Celestial Cause, 173
Great Exodus, 69
Great Fire of London 166, 180
Great Lakes, 105, 110
Great Pulteney Street, 100
Great War, 121, 138, 139 (see First World War)
Greenville School, 236
Grosse Ile, 167
Guildford County, 83
Guysborough County, 235

Haiti, 62
Haldiman Association, 78, 84, 87, 93, 193, 196, 198, 202, 203, 205
Halifax, x, 29, 127, 143, 147–49, 151, 153, 157, 233, 237, 272–78, 281, 289
Halifax and Dartmouth Ministerial Association, 156
Halifax Board of Trade, 155
Halifax Coloured Citizens Improvement League, 240
Halifax Explosion of 1917, 156, 233

318 INDEX OF SUBJECTS

Halifax Harbour, xi
Haligonian ix, 155
Hamilton, 10, 54, 55, 78
Hammat Billing's illustration, 109
Hammonds Plains, 147, 150, 289
Hampton Institute, 233
Heaven, 118, 131
Heavenly Father, 199 (see God)
Hebrew Bible, 177 (see Bible, Biblical)
Hebrews, 44, 175, 190
"Heroic Age", 176
Higher Criticism, 261
Historic Sites and Monuments Board of Canada, 167
Hogan's Alley Remixed, 4
Holland, 129
Holy Bible, xi, 129 (see Bible, Biblical)
Holy Spirit, 2
Home Mission Board of the Convention, 156
Honorary Captain, 156
Horton Street, 61
Hospital General, 25
Hull, 91
Humiliation, 26
Huntingdonians, 274, 277, 278, 280
Huron Line Road, 58

Illinois, 53
Immigrants, Immigration, 37, 54, 56, 67, 68, 144, 196, 209, 212 (see Migration)
Immorality, 23
Imperial, Imperialism, 14, 21, 119–21, 123, 127, 129, 130
India, ix, 135
Indian, 24, 267
Indiana, 53, 248
Indigenous, 24, 25, 35, 167, 267
Indentured Servants, 30, 83
Independence, 27, 51, 79
Industrial School of Nova Scotia for Colored Children, 233
Institutions, Institutionalize, 75–77, 92, 96
Insurrection, 65

Integrationist, 5
Intellectual Activism, 112
Intellectual History, 260, 262
Intelligentsia, 12
Intendant, 24
Intermarriage, 25
Internet, 53
Invisible Institution, 2, 50, 58
Ireland, Irish, 38, 85
Israel, Israelites, ix, 177

Jamaica, 201, 202
Jamaican Immigrants, 145
Jarvis Street Church, 192
Jesuits, 25
Jesus, ix, xi, 152, 178
Jim Crow, 1
Jingoism, 129, 130
Jordan River, ix, xi
Journal of the House of Assembly, 69, 196
Justice, Injustice, 12, 14, 34, 45, 88, 120, 123, 130, 138, 144, 145, 195, 235, 241
Juvenile Temperance Society, 202

Kentucky, 191
Kettle Creek, 60
Kingston, 40
Kingsville, 60

Labourers, 25, 30
Ladies Auxiliary, 224, 234, 237, 239
Lake Erie, 61, 62, 104
Lake Ontario, 196
Lakeside Community Centre, 241
Land of Milk and Honey, 46
Lear, xi
Legacy, 68
Legend, 63, 64, 70
Legislative Assembly and Legislative Council, 166
Legislative Council of Upper Canada, 40
Lexicon of Print, 114
Liberality, 201, 202

Liberation, Liberty, Liberated, 43, 50, 65, 66, 87, 108, 113, 129, 137, 166, 167, 177
Liberia, 62
Licentiates, 151
Lieutenant Governor, 36, 165
Literary, 101, 104, 109, 113, 171, 228
Literary Scholar, 112
Little Black Sambo, 240
Little River Baptist Church, 62, 63
Little Tracadie, 29
Liverpool, 30
Lord, Lord Jesus Christ, x, 34, 35, 126, 170, 198, 202 (see Jesus)
London, 34, 35, 60, 61, 94, 95, 107, 112, 276
Long Point Baptist Association of Canada West, 42, 174
Louisiana, 25, 113
Lower Canada, 37, 41, 63
Lower Great Lakes, 29
Loyalist Migration, 124
Loyalists, 27–30, 33, 54, 144, 272 (see United Empire Loyalists)
Lucknow Rebellion, ix,

Madagascar, 24
Madison Lightfoot, 59, 174
Malden, 167
Manchester, 85, 107
Manchester Independent Chapel, 88
Manservant, 66
Manumission, 65
March Street Baptist Church, 188, 189, 190–93
Marginalized, 14, 122, 144, 163, 164
Maritime Baptist Convention, 149, 156
Maritimes, 1, 3, 7, 28, 36, 63, 124, 135
Market Lane, 188
Maroons, 144, 145
Marriage, 26, 28
Martyrs, ix
Masonic Lodge, 188
Masquerade, 66
McMaster Divinity College, 259

Methodist, 31, 36, 41, 51, 105, 129, 133, 134, 195, 250–52, 255, 273, 276, 278, 280
Methodist Episcopal Meeting, 198
Mexico, 129
Michigan, 106, 167, 174
Michigan Association of Freewill Baptists, 256
Michigan Freewill Baptist Association, 261
Middle Passage, 21
Migration, 1, 56–59, 62, 69, 133, 167, 168
Mikmaq, 272
Military Chaplain, 6
Militia, Military, 211
Minister for African Nova Scotian Affairs, 159
Ministries, Minister(s)(ed), Ministerial, 25–27, 39, 41, 56, 63, 82, 84, 101, 102, 110, 126, 134, 137, 151, 152, 156, 168, 169, 175, 176, 188, 191, 192, 195, 201, 203, 204, 212, 236, 267
Minority, Minority community, 120
The Minutes and Proceedings of the General Convention for the Improvement of the Coloured, Inhabitants of Canada, 45
Mission(s), Missionary, 2, 56, 79, 82, 85, 109, 122, 123, 134–36, 145, 152, 168, 169, 170, 171, 193, 201, 212, 285
Missionary Board of the North Pacific Coast Convention, 209, 214, 216, 217
Missionary Society, 193
Mississippi, 53
Missouri, 53
Moderator, 42, 223, 240
Montreal, 24–26, 29, 202
Mossley, 86
Mother Church, 156, 157, 171, 190, 225
Motherhood, 241
Motherland, 44

Mount Pleasant, 60, 61

Napoleonic War, 286
Narrative(s), 107, 112–14 (see Slave Narratives)
Natchez, 267
Nation(s), 120, 121, 133
National Baptist Convention, 104
National Convention of the Colored Citizens, 103
National Historic Site/Event, 14, 163, 167
National Identity, 50, 119, 120, 125, 127
National Register of Historic Places in the United States, 173
National Unity Association, 258
Native American(s), 24, 25, 83
Naturalized, Naturalization, 69, 196
Nazrey AME Church in Amherstburg, 163, 170
Negrophobia, 218
Neumatological, 51
New Brunswick, 34, 63, 124, 147, 273, 276, 279
New Brunswick Marriage Act, 284
New Canaan, 60, 61
New Canaan Baptist Church, 61
New England, 27, 28, 198, 201
New France, 3, 24–27, 29, 44
New Horizons United Baptist Church, ix, x, 2, 14, 143–45, 158, 159, 160
New Imperialism, 121
New Jersey, 28
New Jerusalem, 128
New Light, 32, 275, 286
New Orleans, 65
New York, 28, 29
New York State Vigilance committee, 66
New York Times, x, 52
New World, 34
Newspaper, 13, 52, 64–66, 79, 86, 89, 101–3, 114, 157, 210, 212, 216
NFL, 49

Niagara, Niagara Falls, 15, 40, 41, 56, 194
Niagara Baptist Association, 61
Nicodemus, 135
Normal and Industrial Institute, 233
North, Northern, Northern States, 50, 55, 57, 62, 64–69, 165, 175, 176
North America(n), 25, 27, 50, 52, 53, 60, 68, 70, 90, 95, 165, 183, 219, 267 (see America[s], American[s])
North Carolina, 83, 179
North Preston, xi
Nova Scotia(n)(s) ix, x, 3–5, 10, 13–15, 27, 29–36, 42, 44–46, 62, 63, 118, 119, 124, 125, 127, 131, 132, 137, 138, 143–45, 147–53, 155, 159, 222, 225, 228–31, 235, 238, 241, 266–91
Nova Scotia Advisory Council, 239
Nova Scotia Association for the Advancement of Colored People (NSAACP), 157, 240
Nova Scotia Home for Colored Children/Akoma Family Centre, 154, 155, 159, 233, 234
Nova Scotia Home for Colored Children Restorative Inquiry, 234
Nova Scotia Status of Women, 238, 239
North Star (Myth), 58, 69, 132

Oberlin, 110
Obscure, 60
Odysseys Home, 2
Ohio, 53, 84, 92, 106
Old King Street Baptist School Room, 88
Old Testament, 119, 131
Oliver LeJeune, 24
Ontario, 6, 10, 29, 40, 59, 70, 82, 84, 164, 168, 176, 179, 182, 212
Ontario's Fair Accommodation Practices Act, 258

INDEX OF SUBJECTS 321

Oppressor, Oppressed, x, 21, 30, 44–46, 78, 103, 164
Order of Canada, 158
Order of Good Cheer, 24
Ordination, 54, 56, 228, 245–65
Origins, 51–53, 58, 60, 177
Orion, 130
Orphanage, 154

Pamphlet Literature, 102, 113
Pan-Africanism, 267
Pandemic, 16
Panis, 24–26
Pastor(s), Pastorate, x, 31, 61, 62, 75, 79, 92, 146, 148, 151–54, 156–59, 162, 179, 190, 195, 197, 200, 213, 214, 223
Paternalism, Paternalistic, 42, 267
Patriotism, 119
Penmark, 95
People of Colour, 88
Peter, ix
Peterborough, 79
Petition, Petitioners 153
Pharaoh, ix, 44
Philadelphia, 53, 65, 66, 233
Philanthropists, Philanthropic, 39, 40, 57
Pike Road, 60
Pioneer Committee, 210, 211, 219
Pioneers, 34
"Pious Fraudster", 92
Plantation, 25, 49, 228
"Plausibility Structure," 123
Plymouth, 95
Poet Laureate, 8
Politicians, Political, 54, 33, 75, 102, 110, 123, 125, 137, 147, 153, 226
"Politics of Respectability," 120
Port Royal, 24
Potter's Field Cemetery, 205
Power, 26
Prairies, 12
Prayer, 58, 123, 130, 175, 197, 201, 202
Preacher, Preach(ed), Preaching, 31, 33, 34, 40, 46, 56, 62, 108, 146, 147, 151, 152, 159, 170, 174, 179, 180, 189, 194, 202, 204, 229
Presbyterians, 39, 56, 82, 129, 169
Preston Township, 230, 231, 289
Priest(s), 25, 26
Prince Albert Baptist Church, 248, 257, 258, 261
Prince Edward Island, 124
Principles of Intersectionality, 3
Print Culture, 102, 105, 113
Printers, 13
Pro-Slavery, 108
Professional Athletes, 49
Prohibition, 134
Promised land, 15, 30, 45, 46, 177, 187, 247
Prophets, Prophecy, ix, 44, 111, 131
Proslavery Journalists, 64
Protestant, Protestantism, 38, 40, 51, 101, 102, 119, 133, 134, 164, 178
Province of Freedom, 34
Provincial Baptist Youth Fellowship (BYF), 155
Provincial Legislative Assembly, 195, 229
Prussia, 129
Psalms, Psalmist, 114, 131
Public History, 16
Publishers, Printers, 13, 107
Puget Sound Baptist Association, 213
Pulpiteers ix,
Puritan, 177

Quebec, 27, 28, 135
Queen and Victoria Streets, 198, 199, 204
Queen of Sheba, 44
Queen Victoria, 87, 129
Queens Bush, 78

Radicalism, 102
Radio Apprentice Program, 238
Ragged Island, 290
Railroad, Railroad Agents/Workers, 52, 57, 58, 61, 62, 64–70, 71

322 INDEX OF SUBJECTS

(see Underground Railway/
   Road[Workers])
Ramsgate, 95
Readers, 13
Reading, 95
Rebellion, 27
Reciprocity, 163
Reconstruction, 9, 104, 246, 248
Redeemer, Redemption,
   Redemptive, x, 51, 114, 131,
   196
Reformation, 180
Reformer, 6, 76
Refuge, 46, 62, 66–68
Refugee, 37, 45, 124, 166, 170, 175,
   176, 178
Refugee Home Society (RHS), 81,
   82
Regular Baptist Church, 79
Relocation, 76
Reparations, 43
Resistance, 76
Retheorization, 9
Retrieval, 9
Reuban, 113
Revised Statutes of Luisiana, 113
Revisionism, 64
Revolt, 25
Revolutionary War, 32, 36, 124, 286
   (see War of Independence)
Richard Preston Centre for
   Excellence, 159, 160
Richmond, 66, 169
Richmond Street, 190, 191, 196
Riot of 1784, 34
Revivalism, 32, 34
Rocky Mountains, 208
The Role of the African United
   Baptist Association in the
   Development of Indigenous
   Afro-Canadians in Nova
   Scotian, 1782 to 1978, 5
Roman Catholic(ism), 25–27, 44,
   135, 177, 178
Routes, 64, 66
Royal Navy, 127
Rubicon ix,

Runaways, 66 (see Fugitive, Fugitive
   Slave, Fugitive Slave Act[s]
   of 1850, of 1793)
Rural, 69

Sabbath, 171, 193, 201, 202, 232
Sacraments, 25, 26
"Sacred Canopy", 119
Sacrificial, 78
Safe House(s), 52
Saint John, New Brunswick, 29,
   30, 34
Saint Thomas United Baptist
   Church, xi
Sainthood, xi
Saints ix,
Salem Chapel, 40, 163
Salvation, 41
Salvific, 45
San Francisco, 209, 210
Sanctuary, 164
Sandwich East Township, 62
Sandwich, Sandwich First Baptist
   Church, 59, 105, 163, 175
Sanitization, 23
Sanitized Narrative, 220
Savanah, 267, 272
Saviour, x, 114
Scandalize, 76
Schism, 15, 208
Scholarship, Scholarly, 64, 75
School(s), 68, 85, 86, 123, 146, 147,
   153, 155, 170, 171, 201, 210,
   229–32, 234–36, 239, 241
School Superintendent, 154
Scots (Lowland/Highland),
   Scotsman, Scotland, 38, 85,
   90, 129, 188, 189, 198
Scripture(s), Scriptural 33, 102, 177,
   197
Scylla, 9
Second Baptist Church, 41
Second Baptist Church New
   Glasgow, 156, 234
Second Baptist Church of Detroit,
   83, 171, 173
Second Baptist Church of London,
   61

INDEX OF SUBJECTS 323

Second Union Baptist Church, 255
Secular, 12, 23, 25, 31, 153–55, 173
Secular Community, 156
Segregation, Segregated, 1, 31, 38, 46, 62, 153, 229, 235, 236, 241
Sermons, 86, 87, 108, 123, 125, 204
Settlers, (Re)Settlement(s), 27, 29, 31–33, 35, 37, 55, 62, 69, 70, 76, 89, 104, 122, 132, 164, 167–72, 176
Seven Years War, 27
Sexism, 12, 226, 242
Sharecropping, 30
Sheba, ix
Sheffield Nottingham, 90
Shelbourne, 29, 30
Shelburne, 272, 273
Shiloh Baptist Church, 6, 7
Shrewsbury Baptist Church, 62, 182
Siege of Magdala, 128
Sierra Leone, 272, 275, 276, 280, 286
Sierra Leone (Company), 3, 16, 33–36, 46, 135, 144, 147, 277, 279, 283
Sieur de Monts, 24
Silver Bluff, South Carolina, 33, 267, 271
Slave Catcher, 53, 58, 171
Slaveholder(s), ix, 2, 26, 40, 127, 165, 166, 175, 176, 191, 228
Slave Master(s)/Owner, ix, 26, 65, 83
Slave Narratives, 110
Slave Patrols, 59
Slave States, 52
Slave Trade (West Africa), 283, 290
Social Justice, Social Injustice, 122, 143, 147, 151, 154, 157–59, 177, 234
Social Reform, 122, 133, 136
Social Uplift, 92
Socialization, Social, 2, 14, 15, 21, 42, 51, 62, 68, 75, 119, 120, 123, 124, 128, 134, 137, 139, 147, 164, 169, 171, 219, 226
Sojourner, 118, 126, 133
Solomon, ix
Soul Food, 99

South, Southern, 50, 65, 66, 68, 87, 175, 189, 190
South Africa, 130
South African War, 129
South Americans, 23
Southern Ontario, 163, 164 (see Ontario)
Spain, 129
Spirit, Spiritual, Spirituality, 21, 41, 50, 118, 124, 143, 145, 146, 164, 177, 178, 182, 193, 201, 222, 237
Spiritual Awakening, 181, 182
St. Catharines, 15, 40, 54, 55, 194
St. George's Methodist Church in Philadelphia, 173
St. John, 33
St. Mark's Anglican Church, 40
St. Paul's Church, 51
Stamp Act of 1765–1756, the Act, 8, 27, 28
Station, Stationmaster(s), 57, 64, 68
Steamboats, 60
Steam Powered Locomotive, 52
Student Support Workers, 239
Sub-Saharan Africa, 1, 7
Sunday School, 42
Supreme Court's Dred Scott Decision, 209
Switzerland, 129
Syracuse, 65

Tax Reforms, 27
Tea Act of 1773, 28
Temna, 279, 283
Temperance, 42, 134, 232
Terauley (Bay Street), 84
Terminus, Termini, 53, 54, 55, 58, 59, 63, 166
Thames River, 59, 62
Theology, Black Baptist, 247
Theology, Theological, Theologians, xi, 13, 102, 104–7, 111, 203
Theology of Print, 102
Theology of the Press, 102
Toronto, 13, 15, 41, 49, 50, 54–56, 69, 75, 79, 80, 84, 89, 90, 92, 95, 96, 100, 187, 188, 190,

324 INDEX OF SUBJECTS

191, 193, 195, 196, 198–200, 202, 204
Toronto Argonauts, 49
Toronto Baptist Church, 60
Torture, 26
Typographic, 107
Transatlantic Antislavery Movement, 100, 114
Transatlantic Slave Trade, 13, 44, 102
Transnational Evangelicalism, 12, 125
Treasurer, 42, 213
Treaty of Utrecht, 27
Trial, 26
True Band Society, 78, 81, 96
Truro, 233
Tuskegee Institute in Alabama, 154

Uncivilized, 23
Uncle Tom, 251
Underground Railway/Road(Workers), x, 2, 4, 13, 14, 38, 39, 49, 50–55, 57–60, 63–67, 70, 84, 86, 90, 107, 109–11, 114, 164, 166, 167, 171, 175, 183, 189, 190, 251
Union Army, 69
Union Baptist Church in Chatham, 182
Union Border Mission, 82
United Baptist Convention, 266
United Empire Loyalists, 28, 167
United Presbyterian, 191
United States, US, 22, 29, 38, 40, 46, 49, 50, 52, 54, 57, 60, 67–70, 79, 88, 92, 100, 114, 125, 127, 131, 132, 134, 147, 148, 154, 156, 162, 165, 169, 171, 176, 190, 209, 210 , 220 , 228, 233
United States Senate, 111
Universal Declaration of Human Rights, 235
Upper and Lower Canada, 201
Upper Canada, 1, 3, 4, 7, 14, 15, 22, 29, 36–38, 40, 41, 50, 51, 54, 55, 57, 62, 67–70, 102, 165, 167–69, 176, 177, 189, 194, 196, 199 (see Upper Province)
Upper Canada Anti-Slavery Society, 195
Upper Canada Baptist Missionary Society, 192
Upper Canadian Legislature, 69
Upper Hammonds Plains, 231
Upper Province, 192
Upper St. Lawerence, 29
Urban, 28, 69
Ursulines, 25

Victim Services, 239
Victoria, 209–14, 216–20
Victoria Pioneer Rifle Corps, 211
Victoria Road (Dartmouth), 234
Victoria Road United Baptist Church, 241
Victorian Canada, 75, 123
Vigilance Committee, 81, 96, 114
Violence, 30, 108, 114, 132, 143, 238
Virginia, x, 33, 54, 83, 108, 113, 127, 169, 187, 191, 225, 233

"The Walking Peacher", 162
Wales, 85, 95
War of 1812, 1, 37, 62, 165, 167, 230
War of Independence, 28
Washington, 51
Ways and Means Committee, 132, 138, 230
Wellington Street, 61
Welsh Calvinistic Methodists, 32
Welsh, Welshman, xi, 38, 103, 189
West Africa, 283, 291
West Indian/Indies, 25, 54, 201
Western Association, 60
Western Civilization, 35, 233
Western District/Region, 174, 212
Western States, 45
Weymouth Falls, xi
Whitby Association, 194
White Abolitionists, 57, 60, 102, 110, 111
White Allies, 110

White American Baptist Free Mission Society (ABFMS), 78
White Antislavery Missions, 109
White Baptist, 12, 78, 79, 103, 124, 130, 132, 133, 134, 170, 171, 173, 177
White Community, 4, 156
White Co-Religionist, 126
White First Baptist Church, 169
White Leadership, 149
White Loyalists, 28, 29, 31, 54, 271
White Missionary, 109
White Protestant, 38, 40, 128
White Revivalist Preachers, 180
White Supremacist, 2, 10, 21, 43, 235
Wilberforce Settlement/Settlers, 102, 210
Wilberforce University, 255
Windsor, 13, 56, 58, 59, 70, 75, 85–88, 90, 92, 96, 100, 108, 167, 172, 181, 182

Winnipeg, 15, 208, 209, 212, 212
Wisdom, 45
Wolfville, 10, 15, 124
Women's Activism, 246
Women's Institute, 237, 239, 240
Women's Liberation Movement, 224
Women's Missionary Circle, 258
Women's Missionary Society, 224
Word, 102, 105
"The Word", 180
World War I, 156 (see First World War)
Worship, 51, 54–56, 58, 113, 145, 169, 181, 191, 199, 201

Xenia, 259
Xenia Freewill Baptist Church, 256

Yankee, 79
Yonge Street Church, 195, 198
York, 15, 190, 193

Zion Baptist Church, 55, 108